C000072161

NO POLITICS BUT CLASS POLITICS

Walter Benn Michaels & Adolph Reed, Jr.

**Edited and with a Foreword
by Anton Jäger & Daniel Zamora**

ERIS

ERIS

57 Berkeley Square
London W1J 6ER

ISBN 978-1912475-57-5

eris.press

Printed and bound by CPI Group (UK) Ltd, Croydon CR0 4YY

Contents

For Ken Warren

ANTON JÄGER & DANIEL ZAMORA

Foreword

In April 2021, as the world economy slowly began to crawl out of its corona crater, the American magazine *Forbes* published its annual ranking of world billionaires. Although part of an annual tradition, 2021's ranking was also singular: the pandemic had thrown millions out of jobs, devastated labor markets, and left more than four million dead. The magazine had more prosaic news to announce: its global register had grown by 493 units, adding $5 trillion in wealth to the planet's upper percentile. Over the course of the pandemic year, the new economy had spawned a new billionaire every seventeen hours. Such numbers, *Forbes* editor Randall Lane noted, "will engender endless amounts of consternation". Capitalism was still "the greatest system ever for generating prosperity", but it was now clearly having a hard time "lifting all boats"[1].

Despite the pandemic's deleterious effects, Lane had also "rarely felt so optimistic".[2] And there were understandable reasons for this optimism. When analyzed more closely, the results of the *Forbes* survey announced net-positive changes for the future. "The newly super-rich", he argued "have never felt more different, looked more different or acted more different." The murder of George Floyd had "triggered a reckoning concerning race and social justice", opening opportunities for those left behind and, in turn, changing "what a billionaire looks like". While Lane conceded that the highest percentiles remained "disproportionately white"[3], the overall share of women and minorities in the ranking had grown significantly, with the top increasingly looking "like the world around them"[4]. In the upcoming post-pandemic economy, Lane noted, people of color would make up most of the new billionaires worldwide and, more importantly, most would now be self-made. Here was a class of meritocratic and dynamic billionaires who embodied "economic dynamism, not bloodline dynasties".[5]

The list compiled by *Forbes* joins a now familiar genre of class apologism crossed with celebration of increasing upper-class diversification. The staggering rise in inequality following the 2008 crisis went hand in hand with an increasing focus on and concern for what the economist Paul Krugman has called "horizontal inequality", mainly applied to disparities of race and gender. Like many of his ad-hoc analyses, Krugman's push for an anti-discrimination revolution was not of his own coinage. "It's almost like a mathematical theorem"[6], the literary critic Walter Benn Michaels argued nearly a decade and a half ago in *The Trouble with Diversity: How We Learned to Love Identity and Ignore Inequality*, that, "as economic inequality rises, so does the enthusiasm for addressing every other, *non*-economic kind of inequality."[7] Far from being a political paradox or a patent example of corporate hypocrisy, the triumph of anti-discrimination as a global model of social justice has slowly mutated into one of the pillars of the meritocratic justification of inequality. In a society where forty per cent of Americans are unable to cover a $400 emergency bill but where Jeff Bezos can buy a half-a-billion yacht, equality of opportunity can still offer a convenient substitute for any socialist alternative. As long as the occasional glass ceiling can be broken and workers undertake training to become 'less white', the conversation about unions at Amazon warehouses can be evaded.

In the United States alone, estimates for corporate spending on 'awakening sessions', 'racial sensitivity trainings', or 'self-reflexive workshops'—facilitated by a veritable army of consultants, coaches, and trainers—now run close to $8 billion[8]. Either hired in-house by companies like Google or Facebook or as contractors by public agencies and schools, these 'diversity officers' or 'awareness leaders' have been relentlessly shaping the therapeutic culture that inflects our

understanding of social issues. In 2019, for instance, almost half of the
S&P Top 500 companies employed diversity professionals, and the vast
majority had organized mandatory training courses for their personnel
in the previous three years. "For capitalism to continue to thrive", as
Forbes noted in one of its editorials, "equality of opportunity is paramount."[9] As any economist would concede, the commitment to competitive markets (or, in other words, *meritocratic markets*), while it naturally
diminishes Krugman's "horizontal inequality", logically intensifies economic inequality. In that sense, as Michaels and Adolph Reed, Jr. have
been arguing for several decades, it would be a mistake to understand
a politics of identity and a politics of class as involved in a type of trade
off. In fact, the focus on anti-discrimination as a model of social justice was, to Reed, *already a class politics*; a program to the benefit of
those at the top of the ladder regardless of their gender or race. "You
definitely know you're in a world that loves neoliberalism", Michaels
noted, "when the fact that some people of color are rich and powerful is
regarded as a victory for all the people of color who aren't".[10]

The essays assembled in this volume constitute one of the most sustained and coherent critiques of contemporary anti-racism advanced
from the left. Spanning more than a quarter century of writing on topics
as diverse as photography, the history of the civil rights movement, and
the class function of higher education, they offer a precious alternative
to the identitarian approaches that have become increasingly prevalent
on the political left. Such a perspective has become especially relevant
in a context where the criticism of identity has largely been monopo-
lized by a right which is dedicated only to promoting its own version of
identitarianism. Often caught up in competing versions of identity politics, or in the empty opposition of 'woke vs. anti-woke', the left needs
now more than ever an alternative account of what a class politics could
mean today. Reed and Michaels's point has never been that racism is
not a problem or that it is undeserving of total eradication. Their claim,
rather, is that its solution has little to do with the problem of capitalist
inequality. In making this claim, the arguments assembled in this volume offer the most articulate alternative yet offered to what they call
a right *and* left neoliberalism. *No Politics but Class Politics* offers an

extensive overview of Reed and Michaels's arguments concerning the question of identity, the rise of anti-racism, diversity programs, and the relation of each of these components to a specifically 'neoliberal aesthetic'.

The political realignment now steadily spreading beyond the United States did not take place overnight. It implies not only the constitution of race and identity as the main interpretative framework for understanding inequality in America (and, increasingly, beyond), but also the slow disarticulation of the agenda of the civil rights movement from any commitment to reshaping the economic relations that produce inequality in the first place. Fully grasping such a turn requires a careful study of how race was rebranded as a cultural identity by the early twentieth century, and of how what Touré Reed has termed a "conservative 'racial democratic' vision of civil rights"[11] — committed to anti-discrimination while accepting class stratification — triumphed in the post-segregation era. By the late 1960s, while black power militancy and liberals were both retreating from popular mobilization and coalition politics, the embrace of a cultural politics and of "symbolic payoffs" had been officialized[12]. Reed and Michaels's writings took shape against both a general retreat of the post-war civil rights vision and the consolidation of the neoliberal counterrevolution.

Their collaboration, begun in the early 2000s, had little in the way of biographical destiny to it. Michaels, one of the most influential Americanists of his generation, had specialized in late nineteenth- and early twentieth-century American literature and literary theory. Trained at the University of California, Santa Barbara and captivated by the works of Beckett and Borges, and then by the literary critic Hugh Kenner, he oriented his philosophical interests towards literary theory and authors such as Paul de Man and Jacques Derrida. Kenner, who was Michaels's teacher at Santa Barbara and later his colleague at John Hopkins, had become a scholar renowned for his original readings of Modernist writers. Extremely prudent about the internal workings of a text and about the reasons why it was organized in a certain way, he offered a model of taking texts seriously — of understanding, as Michaels noted, "what its own theory of itself was".

At first Michaels's work engaged with questions concerning the ontology of texts, with points of contact with philosophers and legal scholars alike. His seminal essay "Against Theory" (1982)[13], co-authored with literary scholar Steven Knapp, argued that the meaning of a text was nothing other than what its author intended it to mean. The act of interpretation required no connections between authorial intentions and meaning, as both were, in fact, the very same thing. More precisely, to recognize something as language (in other words, as meaningful) already implied the presence of an author. Words could only be words (as opposed to just *resembling* words) if they were intended to be so. In literature departments taken with Derrida's deconstructionism and law institutes captivated by Antonin Scalia's textualist originalism, Michaels's theory was unlikely to find many friends. The argument that the work — be it the American Constitution or a poem by Emily Dickinson — meant what its author intended, rather than what the 'text itself' supposedly said or what it might mean to 'us', was controversial both among those who hoped theory could offer an interpretive method and those who, like the philosopher Richard Rorty, thought the fact that it could *not* made for open and 'pluralist' accounts of reading.

While these discussions seem at first quite disconnected from the arguments assembled in this volume, they took on a surprising resonance with the increasing centrality of identity politics. In particular, the pluralism that privileged the subject's experience of the text — and thus replaced disagreement over competing interpretations with either tolerance for or celebration of different experiences — provided a model for the emergence of an identitarian liberalism. Pluralism turns differences of opinion (about a text or about the kind of politics we want) into differences of identity (what we need or think depends on who we are). And in a world of *differences* rather than political *disagreements*, it is, as Michaels noted, "identities that matter; the relevant thing about you is not what you believe but who you are, who you were and who you want to be".[14] Identity, as he would later come to argue in both *Our America* (1995) and *The Shape of the Signifier* (2004), was mutating into the dominant explanation of the meaning of our actions. Furthermore, cultural identity was picking up where racial identity had left off in

15

serving as the ground of our beliefs and practices. Indeed, the reinvention of 'race' as a marker of cultural identity after the demise of biologism played a crucial role in turning debates about how to organize the political economy into discussions about proportionality: which group was affected by existing arrangements?

While Michaels's early work carried little political valence, it was always concerned with literary works as somehow more than literature. Part of what would later be called 'New Historicism' was precisely meant to think about literary works in relation to social and economic structures. It marked, as Michaels argued, "an effort to think about what literature was trying to do in terms that were not confined to the ones produced by the texts themselves".[15] This offered a way to establish a whole range of new relationships between the texts and their context, offering what Fredric Jameson called an elegant route out of the established base-superstructure *cul de sac* and toward homologies that didn't require complex casual accounts.[16] If two arguments looked alike, there was no need to establish a strong causal connection between them; if Faulkner's argument on racial difference was the same as Lothrop Stoddard's, one could engage in comparisons. While not overtly political, Michaels's close readings of texts were strongly pitted against the culturalist turn. Almost like Foucauldian *dispositives*, works of art were dissected as translations of economic and political structures. From the reinvention of 'race' in the bibliographies of Hemingway, Fitzgerald, and Cather discussed in *Our America* to the move to performativity, identity, and affect in *The Shape of the Signifier*, Michaels's style was consistently non-liberal. It was only later, however, notably with *The Beauty of a Social Problem* (2015), that he would engage more directly with the contradictions of capitalist society, thinking out his own notion of what he called a 'class aesthetic'.

Born in 1948 in New York, Michaels was never a 'red-diaper baby' as Reed, Jr. was. While his great-grandfather was a union activist and his grandfather a union lawyer, this labor legacy left hardly a trace on his professional life or his politics as a student or young scholar. His upbringing in a union family could, however, explain his early dislike for the genre of moral activism that became prevalent in academia starting in the late 1960s. Being trained by people like Hugh Kenner, who was strongly conservative and a contributor to *National Review*, probably reinforced his conviction that we can't judge the value of an argument or a text by its author's politics alone. While teaching at Berkeley (from 1977 to 1986) he soon developed a lasting irritation with the "moralism that the academy was committed to"[17]. It was far from the bottom-up coalition building to which union activists engaged themselves.[18] While he hardly articulated a coherent left politics at the time, it was clear to him that there was nothing anti-capitalist about either liberal pluralism or academic activism. But it was only by the mid-2000s, when he grew increasingly appalled by ideas like Huntington's 'clash of civilizations' and by the degree to which '90s multiculturalism had moved out of the classroom and into the workplace as the corporate world's way of managing demands for equality, that Michaels's work took a more sharply political turn. While the *Trouble With Diversity* (2006) came directly from the argument made earlier in *Our America*, it articulated more clearly the significance of the persistence and use of race after it had become obvious that there is no such thing as race. The book was neither a pamphlet nor a political statement. In a distinctively modernist style of criticism, his writing has always been about making his argument as clear as possible rather than "persuading anybody of anything"[19]. Like a philosopher, each of his texts offers a sharp understanding of its conceptual outlines. For any of us who read *The Trouble with Diversity* (and especially for the authors of this preface) it is hard to forget how it radically clarified a whole set of debates that were (and still are) dominant on the political scene, both on the right and on the left. More exciting perhaps was Michaels's characteristic refusal to adopt an attitude of persuasion towards his readers—their feelings being wholly irrelevant to his argument. "He makes $175,000 a year", an unconcerned Michaels wrote to his audience, "but he wants more . . . one of his motives for writing this book was the cash advance offered him by his publishers."[20] Whether we personally liked him or not was irrelevant to the arguments put forward in the book. This is an essential feature that, in terms of how they conceive their work, Michaels and Reed share. It is also one of the strengths of the essays collected in this volume: whether the reader agrees or disagrees, they help clarify the terms of the discussion.

On his side, Reed had a more classical education in political science, moving out of late 1960s black radicalism into labor militancy in the 1970s and 1980s. He taught successively at Yale, the New School, and the University of Pennsylvania. Reed was a 'red-diaper' baby; his father, Adolph Reed, moved in the communist orbit politically. Reed's Southern youth unfolded under the abiding shadow of Jim Crow. As he noted in a recent 'non-memoir', "my age cohort is basically the last, black or white, for which the Jim Crow regime is a living memory — for good and ill." The realities of racial domination in a Southern city formed a constant in Reed's early life, from bars to schools to his first neighborhood interactions. Yet Reed — partly through his father, partly through his education — was also keenly aware of how the South's specific system of racial apartheid concealed even more hideous class realities. Jim Crow, he saw, was built on the ruins of the Reconstruction and Populist period of the late nineteenth century, when a short-lived coalition of white and black farmers mounted a final assault on the power of the planter class. "While the Jim Crow order was explicitly and definitively about race", Reed later noted, "at the same time it was fundamentally not really about race at all." [21] (The argument was a recurrent one in the family: in a 1992 interview, for instance, reminiscing on Jim Crow and his early socialist militancy, Reed's father postulated that "most of the problems within a society [could] be traced to . . . the mal-distribution of the wealth and the related perverted priorities in economic and politics" [22].) For a man who grew up in Jim Crow Arkansas, the statement was a testament to life-long labor radicalism.

Like his father before him, Reed's initial writings tried to take stock of a double defeat and victory. On the one hand, the Civil Rights revolution had clearly buried the old Jim Crow order. At the same time, the broader program that underlay the labor wings of the Civil Rights bloc — exemplified by figures such as Bayard Rustin and A. Philip Randolph, and by their 1966 *Freedom Budget* — had clearly lost out by the close of the 1960s. Supply-side economics, upward redistribution, and tax optimization (read: tax cuts) were the laws of the land. Although still contested during the Reagan era, they began to solidify into a cross-partisan consensus in the 1990s. Rustin and Randolph's promise of biracial full employment and welfare rights was receding. With them the promise that the United States would get its own welfare state, already thwarted by the 1947 Taft-Hartley law and the lifting of wartime price controls, was disappearing into the distance. Reed came of age in this new world amidst the ruins. During and after his undergraduate education at the University of North Carolina, Chapel Hill he ran through radical circles, pondering the transition from America's Old and New Left. After several years of work as an organizer in North Carolina, he pursued doctoral studies in political science at Atlanta University, coincident with the triumphalist period of the city's transition from white to black-led local government. He worked for several years also in the administration of Maynard H. Jackson, Atlanta's first black mayor, himself a testimony to the manifold victories of the Civil Rights movement.

In his 1979 piece "Black Particularity Reconsidered", Reed tried to make sense of this paradoxical black integration into a new capitalist America.[23] The 1970s had ended legally sanctioned exclusion, but inclusion in the new capitalist order hardly brought full emancipation. Black Southerners two generations earlier had begun a migration out of the South into Northern factories, getting jobs in defense industries or urban service sectors. By the middle of the 1970s, global overcapacity was already hitting the core of the US economy. Since blacks entered the labor market under the credo 'last hired, first fired', the weight of the post-industrial transition fell on their shoulders. Unemployment skyrocketed, urban decline accelerated, crime rates went up. The constituents of new black mayors in the South and North began to demand the "locking up of their own", as the researcher James Forman termed it, stopping the crime wave with carceral rather than social policy.[24] The civil rights coalition had achieved victory in defeat and defeat in victory, while the New Left's "social amnesia" misunderstood the "decline of political opposition" to an insurgent right in the 1980s.[25]

Reed never denied the real achievements of 1960s radicalism in all its diversity. "The premise that activism failed", he noted coolly in 1986, "should not be read as belittling either the heroic sacrifices made by individuals or the actual successes of their movements", from "the destruction of racial segregation as a social system" to "the opening of pluralist politics to clienteles that previously had been excluded, and the articulation of feminist voices".[26] Yet to Reed, most analysts of the post-segregation era appeared curiously ill-equipped to deal with the paradoxical situation of defeat-in-victory. While radicals "fantasized about a 'new man' in the abstract", he noted in the late 1970s, "capital was in the process of concretely putting the finishing touches on its new individual".[27] "Beneath the current black-female-student-chicano-homosexual-old-young-handicapped . . . struggles", he concluded, "lies a simple truth: there is no coherent opposition to the present administrative apparatus."[28] An "examination of black radicalism in the wake of its integration" offered "a microcosmic view of the plight of the left as a whole", including the "reconstitution of domination" which reoccurred in the 1970s.[29] The idea that blacks were a particularly oppressed minority whose culture of community could provide a holdout against capitalist commodification seemed increasingly far-fetched to Reed. Symbolic invocations of an ecumenical 'black interest' would do little to comprehend the real material divisions within the progressive camp, or the new dynamics of inequality that succeeded the Keynesian growth regime. Part of the US's black population delivered mayors and senators and was ascending into the higher ranks of the business class. Behind the fact of integration stood the persistent and stubborn fact of *class*, with deindustrialization, automation, and capital flight threatening black Americans above all.

Reed extended this diagnosis to Jesse L. Jackson's 1984 primary campaign. In the throes of the Reagan revolution, Jackson tried to extend Fred Hampton's early 1970s rainbow coalition into the arena of electoral politics. To Reed, the shifting terrain of post-Civil Rights black politics meant not only that Jackson was now beholden to a conservative Democratic establishment, but also that he had to engage with an increasingly changed media terrain. "The central fact of the Jackson phenomenon", Reed noted, "has gone unnoticed: that it was a ritualistic event — a media-conveyed politics of symbolism, essentially tangential to the critical debate over reorganization of American capitalism's governing consensus." [30] With its preference for image over policy, and its keener interest in protest than in politics, the Jackson campaign signaled the exhaustion and domestication of the black radical tradition, not its vindication. 'Race' played a curious role in this realignment, creating a sense of a unitary constituency based on skin color. But Reed claimed this interest obscured the increasing *divergence* within that black constituency, with one section profiting from the post-Civil Rights achievements — the opening of employment opportunities and affirmative action programs — and another section increasingly subject to a managed marginalization in despoiled inner cities.

The 'dialectic of defeat' which had ailed left-wing America since Nixon only strengthened during the Reaganite ice age. [31] "The key fact", Reed noted in the mid-1990s, "is that we do not have the popularly based, institutionalized, mass political movement that we need to realize any meaningful progressive agenda in the United States." [32] The movement could not "be convoked magically overnight or by proxy", nor could it "be galvanized through proclamations, press conferences, symbolic big events, resolutions or quixotic electoral candidacies". [33] Twenty years later, shortly before Bernie Sanders's first presidential campaign, Reed drew up a similarly morose diagnosis after the Occupy protests: the creation of a left-wing constituency, he noted, "cannot occur via MSNBC or blog posts or the *New York Times*". [34]

By 2012 the stakes of this intellectual debate reached far beyond party politics. The political retreat of the civil rights movement meant that racial inequalities and tensions would continue to fester, and liberalism's explanatory mechanisms had meanwhile become severely antiquated. 'Race' had been one of the most cunning inventions of early capitalism. It offered a way of justifying slavery in an age in which status- or caste-based differences between humans were becoming increasingly difficult to justify — an age in which the ownership of men (the primary means by which the Southern cotton economy could make its labor coercion work) now had to be fashioned on a new legal basis. Systems of racial hierarchy were subsequently fatally weakened by the mid-century Civil Rights drive and by global decolonization. Yet while legal segregation systems collapsed, the idea of race as a primary explainer of how American society worked, survived. Charles Murray's biological fatalism spoke to a deeper mood. On the centrist left, writers such as William Julius Wilson were reinventing the 'culture of poverty' thesis and the underclass for the 1990s, essentializing the sources of inner-city poverty.[35] As Reed noted in a reflection on the 'underclass thesis' in 2016, the ideology of "the urban underclass" sought to "naturalize hierarchy by attributing it to a population defined by durable cultural and behavioral defects, which make it impervious to social intervention". To Reed, this paradigm had sanctioned a "retreat from social provision and underwritten a punitive turn in social policy".[36] Reed's hometown of New Orleans offered the perfect microcosm for this transition, in which black self-help literature and neoliberal governance had engineered a perfect storm. Reed's race revival was hardly confined to the hard right; on the left, too, new racial readings of the American past seemed to be making headway, reading the entirety of American political development through the lens of 'race'.

It is surprisingly easy to find avatars for all the tendencies in the contemporary debate on 'race' in the United States—from Ta-Nehisi Coates to Mark Lilla. With respect to Michaels's and Reed's own arguments, the journal *nonsite* has been at the center of their intellectual and political project over the last decade. Conceived as an anti-neoliberal instrument—whether in its account of the ontology of the work of art or in its relation to identity—it became a natural space for the expression of their converging intellectual interests. The arguments that emerged from their collaboration mark out Reed and Michaels not only as two of the sharpest commentators on the contemporary class-race discussion on the American scene, but also as writers with a potentially international reach. In his introduction to the first edition of *Capital*, Karl Marx warned German readers with a phrase from Tacitus—*de te fabula narratur* ('stories are being told about you')—indicating that Germany would soon approximate British industrial conditions. The essays in this collection speak to an attempt to get to grips with a peculiarly American predicament, but in many ways this predicament is no longer exclusively American. In continental Europe too, anti-discrimination turned into the programmatic center of a left which believed, as

Tony Blair put it in 1999, that the "class war was over". In the face of the narrow right-wing definition of meritocracy which ignored the blatant inequalities prevalent under capitalism, a new 'third way left' was shaped in order to create an 'inclusive' 'cosmopolitan global society'. This "new politics", Anthony Giddens wrote, "defines equality as *inclusion* and inequality as *exclusion*".[37] Rather than a redistributive welfare state or an attempt to limit the market, we needed investment in social capital to enhance individuals' abilities in the economic game and eventually to offer them proper tools to be efficient entrepreneurs in the neoliberal 'high-risk economy'. "Rather than giving people goods", Giddens argued, "we should give them capabilities and responsibilities."[38] In Europe as in the US, the notion of 'class' was slowly abandoned as an analytic category, and concerns over corporate power, union rights and the distribution of wealth were increasingly left aside among the modernized social-democratic parties.

While figures such as Bernie Sanders and increasing struggles to unionize workers in places like Amazon leave space for some optimism, the corporate diversity project is far from receding. In 2020, surrounded by a troupe of friends, co-workers, and employees, the CEO of JPMorgan Chase & Co. Jamie Dimon took the knee in front of one of his bank's vaults, the blue circle logo of his corporation displayed on its walls. A picture of the scene was posted to Dimon's Twitter account, with the CEO clarifying that he was "committed to fighting against racism and discrimination wherever and however it exists". The same bank which had helped to tank black wealth during the Great Recession was now proclaiming fealty to the global anti-racist uprising. Dimon's corporation was eminently ready for intersectionality and denunciations of structural racism, which offered finance execs like Dimon a way to treat racial disparities as a problem of identity rather than capitalism. Yet, as Michaels noted, "if a hundred years of Jim Crow taught us that racism cannot solve the problem of class deprivation, the last thirty years of diversity should have taught us that anti-racism can't do the job either."[39]

ADOLPH REED, JR.

Marx, Race, and Neoliberalism

A Marxist perspective can be most helpful for understanding race and racism insofar as it perceives capitalism dialectically, as a social totality that includes modes of production, relations of production, *and* the pragmatically evolving ensemble of institutions and ideologies that lubricate and propel its reproduction. From this perspective, Marxism's most important contribution to making sense of race and racism in the United States may be demystification. A historical materialist perspective should stress that 'race'—which includes 'racism', as one is unthinkable without the other—is a historically specific ideology that emerged, took shape, and has evolved as a constitutive element within a definite set of social relations anchored to a particular system of production.

Race is a taxonomy of ascriptive difference, that is, an ideology that constructs populations as groups and sorts them into hierarchies of capacity, civic worth, and desert based on 'natural' or essential characteristics attributed to them. Ideologies of ascriptive difference help to stabilize a social order by legitimizing its hierarchies of wealth, power, and privilege, including its social division of labor, as the natural order of things.[1] Ascriptive ideologies are just-so stories with the potential to become self-fulfilling prophecies. They emerge from self-interested common sense as folk knowledge: they are 'known' to be true unreflectively because they seem to comport with the evidence of quotidian experience. They are likely to become generally assumed as self-evident truth, and imposed as such by law and custom, when they converge with and reinforce the interests of powerful strata in the society.

Race and gender are the most familiar ascriptive hierarchies in the contemporary United States. Ironically, that is so in part because egalitarian forces have been successful in the last half-century in challenging them and their legal and material foundations. Inequalities based directly on claims of race and gender difference are now negatively sanctioned as discrimination by law and prevailing cultural norms. Of course, patterns of inequality persist in which disadvantage is distributed asymmetrically along racial and gender lines, but practically no one—even among apologists for those patterned inequalities— openly admits to espousing racism or sexism. It is telling in this regard that Glenn Beck stretches to appropriate Martin Luther King, Jr., and denounces Barack Obama as racist, and that Elisabeth Hasselbeck and Ann Coulter accuse Democrats of sexism. Indeed, just as race has been and continues to be unthinkable without racism, today it is also unthinkable without anti-racism.

Crucially, the significance of race and gender, and their content as ideologies of essential difference, have changed markedly over time in relation to changing political and economic conditions. Regarding race in particular, classificatory schemes have varied substantially, as have the narratives elaborating them. That is, which populations count as races, the criteria determining them, and the stakes attached to counting as one, or as one or another at any given time, have been much more fluid matters than our discussions of the notion would suggest. And that is as it must be because race, like all ideologies of ascriptive hierarchy, is fundamentally pragmatic. After all, these belief systems emerge as legitimations of concrete patterns of social relations in particular contexts.

Race emerged historically along with the institution of slavery in the New World. A rich scholarship examines its emergence, perhaps most signally with respect to North America in Edmund Morgan's *American Slavery, American Freedom* and Kathleen Brown's *Good Wives, Nasty Wenches, and Anxious Patriarchs*. Both focus on the simultaneous sharpening of distinctions between slavery and indentured servitude, and the institutional establishment of black and white, or African and English, as distinct, mutually exclusive status categories over the course of the seventeenth century in colonial Virginia.[2] Race and racism took shape as an ideology and material reality during the following century, initially in the context of the contest between free- and slave-labor systems and the related class struggle that eventually produced the modern notion of free labor as the absolute control of a worker over her or his person.[3] After defeat of the Confederate insurrection led to slavery's abolition, race as white supremacy evolved in the South as an element in the struggle over what freedom was to mean and how it would be harmonized with the plantocracy's desired labor system and the social order required to maintain it. That struggle culminated in the planter-dominated ruling class's victory, which was consolidated in racialized disfranchisement and imposition of the codified white supremacist regime of racial segregation.

In the latter half of the nineteenth century, the West Coast fights over importation of Chinese labor and Japanese immigration also condensed around racialist ideologies. Railroad operators and other importers of Chinese labor imagined that Chinese workers' distinctive racial characteristics made them more tractable and capable of living on less than white Americans; opponents argued that those very racial characteristics would degrade American labor and that Chinese were racially 'unassimilable'. Postbellum Southern planters imported Chinese to the Mississippi Delta to compete with black sharecroppers out of the same racialist presumptions of greater tractability, as did later importers of Sicilian labor to the sugar-cane and cotton fields.

Large-scale industrial production in the late-nineteenth and early-twentieth centuries, of course, depended on mass labor immigration mainly from the eastern and southern fringes of Europe. The innovations of race science—that is, of racialist folk ideology transformed into an academic profession—promised to assist employers' needs for rational labor force management and were present in the foundation of the fields of industrial relations and industrial psychology. Hugo Münsterberg, a founding luminary of industrial psychology, included 'race psychological diagnosis' as an element in assessment of employees' capabilities, although he stressed that racial or national temperaments are averages and that there is considerable individual variation within groups. He argued that assessment, therefore, should be leavened with consideration of individuals' characteristics and that the influence of 'group psychology' would be significant

> only if the employment not of a single person, but of a large number, is in
> question, as it is most probable that the average character will show itself
> in a sufficient degree as soon as many members of the group are involved. [4]

As scholarship on race science and its kissing cousin, eugenics, has shown, research that sets out to find evidence of racial difference will find it, whether or not it exists. Thus, race science produced increasingly refined taxonomies of racial groups—up to as many as sixty-three 'basic' races. The apparent specificity of race theorists' just-so stories about differential racial capacities provided rationales for immigration restriction, sterilization, segregation, and other regimes of inequality. It also held out the promise of assisting employers in assigning workers to jobs for which they were racially suited. John Bodnar and his co-authors reproduce a Racial Adaptability Chart used by a Pittsburgh company in the 1920s that maps thirty-six different racial groups' capacities for twenty-two distinct jobs, eight different atmospheric conditions, jobs requiring speed or precision, and day or night shift work. For example, Letts were supposedly fair with pick and shovel, and concrete and wheelbarrow, bad as hod carriers, cleaners and caretakers, and boilermaker's helpers; good as coal passers and blacksmiths as well as at jobs requiring speed or precision; and good in cool and dry, smoky or dusty conditions; fair in oily or dirty processes; and good on both day and night shifts. [5]

Of course, all this was bogus, nothing more than narrow upper-class prejudices parading about as science. It was convincing only if one shared the folk narratives of essential hierarchy that the research assumed from the outset. But the race theories did not have to be true to be effective. They had only to be used as if they were true to produce the material effects that gave the ideology an authenticating verisimilitude. Poles became steel workers in Pittsburgh, Baltimore, Buffalo, Chicago, and Gary not for any natural aptitude or affinity but because employers and labor recruiters sorted them into work in steel mills.

Even the New Deal embedded premises of racial and gender hierarchy in its most fundamental policy initiatives. The longer-term implications of the two-tiered system of social benefits thus created persist to the present day. This extensive history illustrates that, as Marxist theorist Harry Chang observed in the 1970s, racial formation has always been an aspect of class formation, as a "social condition of production". Race has been a constitutive element in a capitalist social dynamic in which "social types (instead of persons) figure as basic units of economic and political management".[6] Chang perceptively analogized race to what Marx described as the fetish character of money. Marx, he noted, described money as "the officiating object (or a subject *as* an object) in the reification of a relation called value" and as a "function-turned-into-an-object". Race is similarly a function—a relation of hierarchy rooted in the capitalist division of labor—turned into an object.[7] "Money seeks gold to objectify itself—gold does not cry out to be money." Similarly, "the cutting edge of racial determinations of persons is a social 'imposition' on nature", which on its own yields no such categories.[8]

Although discussing race specifically, Chang also puts his finger on the central characteristic of ideologies of ascriptive hierarchy in general:

> In practice, the political economic raison d'etre of racial categories lies in the iron-clad social validity which is possible if relations are objectified as the intrinsic quality of 'racial features'. . . . Blacks as the absence of the minimum guarantee of bourgeois rights (against enslavement and bondage) presupposes White as a guarantee of immunity from such social degradation.[9]

This formulation applies equally to populations stigmatized as feebleminded, natural-born criminals, 'white trash', poverty cultures, the underclass, crack babies, superpredators, and other narratives of

ascriptive hierarchy. Each such narrative is a species of the genus of ideologies that legitimize capitalist social relations by naturalizing them.
The characteristic linking the species of this genus of ascriptive ideologies is that they are populations living, if not exactly outside "the minimum guarantee of bourgeois rights", at least beneath the customary
floor of social worth and regard. In practice, the latter devolves toward
the former.

Chang's perspective may help us see more clearly how ascriptive
ideologies function. It certainly is no surprise that dominant classes
operate among themselves within a common sense that understands
their dominance unproblematically, as decreed by the nature of things.
At moments when their dominance faces challenges, those narratives
may be articulated more assertively and for broader dissemination.
This logic, for example, underlay the antebellum shift, in the face of
mounting anti-slavery agitation, from pragmatic defenses of slavery
as a necessary evil—a stance that presumed a ruling class speaking
among itself alone—to essentialist arguments, putatively transcending
class interests, namely, that slavery was a positive good. It also may be
seen in the explosion of racialist ideology in its various forms, including eugenics, in justifying imperialist expansionism and consolidating
the defeat of populism and working-class insurgency in the years overlapping the turn of the twentieth century. That same dynamic was at
work displacing the language of class and political economy by culture
and culturology in the post-war liberalism that consolidated the defeat
of CIO radicalism. Later, racial essentialism helped reify the struggles
against Southern segregation, racial discrimination, inequality, and
poverty during the 1960s by separating discussions of injustice from
capitalism's logic of reproduction. Poverty was reinvented as a cultural
dilemma, and 'white racism' singled out as the root of racial inequality.

In this way, Chang's perspective can be helpful in sorting out several
important limitations in discussions of race and class characteristic of
today's left. It can also help to make sense of the striking convergence
between the relative success of identitarian understandings of social
justice and the steady, intensifying advance of neoliberalism. It suggests a kinship where many on the left assume an enmity. The rise of

neoliberalism in particular suggests a serious problem with arguments that represent race and class as dichotomous or alternative frameworks of political critique and action, as well as those arguments that posit the dichotomy while attempting to reconcile its elements with formalistic gestures—for example, the common 'race and class' construction.

This sort of historical materialist perspective throws into relief a fundamental limitation of the 'whiteness' notion that has been fashionable within the academic left for roughly two decades: it reifies whiteness as a transhistorical social category. In effect, it treats 'whiteness'— and therefore 'race'—as existing prior to and above social context. [10] Both who qualifies as white and the significance of being white have altered over time. Moreover, whiteness discourse functions as a kind of moralistic exposé rather than a basis for strategic politics; this is clear in that the program signally articulated in its name has been simply to raise a demand to 'abolish whiteness', that is, to call on whites to renounce their racial privilege. In fact, its fixation on demonstrating the depth of whites' embrace of what was known to an earlier generation's version of this argument as 'white skin privilege' and the inclination to slide into teleological accounts in which groups or individuals 'approach' or 'pursue' whiteness erases the real historical dynamics and contradictions of American racial history.

The whiteness discourse overlaps other arguments that presume racism to be a *sui generis* form of injustice. Despite seeming provocative, these arguments do not go beyond the premises of the racial liberalism from which they commonly purport to dissent. They differ only in rhetorical flourish, not content. Formulations that invoke metaphors of disease or original sin reify racism by disconnecting it from the discrete historical circumstances and social structures in which it is embedded, and treating it as an autonomous force. Disconnection from political economy is also a crucial feature of post-war liberalism's construction of racial inequality as prejudice or intolerance. Racism becomes an independent variable in a moralistic argument that is idealist intellectually and ultimately defeatist politically.

This tendency to see racism as *sui generis* also generates a resistance to precision in analysis. It is fueled by a tendency to inflate the language of racism to the edge of its reasonable conceptual limits, if not beyond. Ideological commitment to shoehorning into the rubric of racism all manner of inequalities that may appear statistically as racial disparities has yielded two related interpretive pathologies. One is a

> constantly expanding panoply of neologisms—'institutional racism', 'systemic racism', 'structural racism', 'color-blind racism', 'post-racial racism', etc.—intended to graft more complex social dynamics onto a simplistic and frequently psychologistic racism/anti-racism political ontology. Indeed, these efforts bring to mind [Thomas S.] Kuhn's account of attempts to accommodate mounting anomalies to salvage an interpretive paradigm in danger of crumbling under a crisis of authority. [11]

A second essentialist sleight-of-hand advances claims for the primacy of race/racism as an explanation of inequalities in the present by invoking analogies to regimes of explicitly racial subordination in the past. In these arguments, analogy stands in for evidence and explanation of the contemporary centrality of racism. Michelle Alexander's widely read and cited book, *The New Jim Crow*, is only the most prominent expression of this tendency; even she has to acknowledge that the analogy fails because the historical circumstances are so radically different. [12]

From the historical materialist standpoint, the view of racial inequality as a *sui generis* injustice and dichotomous formulations of the relation of race and class as systems of hierarchy in the United States are not only miscast but also fundamentally counterproductive. It is particularly important at this moment to recognize that the familiar taxonomy of racial difference is but one historically specific instance of a genus of ideologies of ascriptive hierarchy that stabilize capitalist social reproduction. I have argued previously that entirely new race-like taxonomies could come to displace the familiar ones. For instance, the 'underclass' could become even more race-like as a distinctive, essentialized population

> by our current folk norms, multiracial in composition, albeit most likely including in perceptibly greater frequencies people who would be

classified as black and Latino 'racially', though as small enough pluralities to preclude assimilating the group ideologically as a simple proxy for nonwhite inferiors. [13]

This possibility looms larger now. Struggles for racial and gender equality have largely divested race and gender of their common sense verisimilitude as bases for essential difference. Moreover, versions of racial and gender equality are now also incorporated into the normative and programmatic structure of 'left' neoliberalism. Rigorous pursuit of equality of opportunity exclusively within the terms of given patterns of capitalist class relations—which is after all the ideal of racial liberalism—has been fully legitimized within the rubric of 'diversity'. That ideal is realized through gaining rough parity in distribution of social goods and bads among designated population categories. As Walter Benn Michaels has argued powerfully, according to that ideal, the society would be just if one per cent of the population controlled ninety per cent of the resources, provided that blacks and other non-whites, women, and lesbian, gay, bisexual, and transgender (LGBT) people were represented among the one per cent in roughly similar proportion as their incidence in the general population. [14]

Given the triumph of racial liberalism, it is entirely possible that new discourses of ascriptive difference might take shape that fit the folk common sense of our time and its cultural norms and sensibilities. Indeed, the explosive resurgence in recent years of academically legitimated determinist discourses—all of which simply rehearse the standard idealist tropes and circular garbage in/garbage out faux scientific narratives—reinforces that concern.

The undergirding premises of intellectual programs like evolutionary psychology, behavioral economics, genes and politics, and neurocriminology are strikingly like straight-line extrapolations from Victorian race science—although for the most part, though not entirely, scholars operating in those areas are scrupulous, or at least fastidious, in not implicating the familiar racial taxonomies in their deterministic sophistries. Some scholars imagine that 'epigenetics'—a view that focuses on the interplay of genes and environment in producing organisms and genotypes—avoids determinism by providing causal explanations that are not purely biological. Recent research purporting to find epigenetic explanations for socioeconomic inequality already foreshadows a possible framework for determinist 'underclass' narratives that avoid the taints associated with biological justifications of inequality and references to currently recognized racial categories. [15] Ironically, some enthusiasts for this epigenetic patter expressly liken it to Lamarckian evolutionary theory, which stressed the heritability of characteristics acquired after birth, as though this were insulation against determinism. As historian of anthropology George Stocking, Jr. and others have shown, Lamarckian race theory was no less determinist than its Darwinian alternative, which posited strictly biological determinism. As Stocking notes, Lamarckians' dependence on a "vague sociobiological indeterminism" made it all the more difficult to challenge their circular race theories. [16] In any event, narrow approaches that reduce ascriptive ideology to reified notions of race/racism are not at all up to the challenge posed by this new determinist turn.

Finally, the adamant commitment to a race-first perspective on inequalities that show up as statistical disparities has a material foundation. The victories of the Civil Rights movement carried with them a more benign and unavoidable political imperative. Legal remedies can be sought for injustices understood as discrimination on the basis of race, gender, or other familiar categories of invidious ascription; no such recourse exists for injustices generated through capitalism's logic of production and reproduction without mediation through one of those ascriptive categories. As I have argued elsewhere,

> this makes identifying 'racism' a technical requirement for pursuing certain grievances, not the basis of an overall strategy for pursuit of racial justice, or, as I believe is a clearer left formulation, racial equality as an essential component of a program of social justice. [17]

Yet, for those who insist that racial reductionism is more than a pragmatic accommodation to the necessities of pursuing legal or administrative grievances, something more is at play. A historical materialist

34

perspective can be helpful for identifying the glue that binds that commitment to a race-first political discourse and practice.

All politics in capitalist society is class, or at least a class-inflected,
politics. That is also true of the political perspective that condenses
in programs such as reparations, anti-racism, and insistence on the
sui generis character of racial injustice. I submit that those tendencies
come together around a politics that is "entirely consistent with the neoliberal redefinition of equality and democracy" along disparitarian
lines. That politics

> reflects the social position of those positioned to benefit from the view that
> the market is a just, effective, or even acceptable system for rewarding tal-
> ent and virtue and punishing their opposites and that, therefore, removal
> of 'artificial' impediments to its functioning like race and gender will make
> it even more efficient and just. [18]

This is the politics of actual or would-be race relations administrators, and it is completely embedded within American capitalism and its
structures of elite brokerage. It is fundamentally antagonistic to working-class politics, notwithstanding left identitarians' gestural claims to
the contrary.

WALTER BENN MICHAELS

What Matters

In the US, there is (or was) an organization called Love Makes a Family. It was founded in 1999 to support the right of gay couples to adopt children and it played a central role in supporting civil unions. A few months ago, its director, Anne Stanback, announced that, having "achieved its goals", Love Makes a Family would be ceasing operations at the end of this year, and that she would be stepping down to spend more time with her wife, Charlotte. Our "core purpose", she said, has been "accomplished".

It's possible of course that this declaration of mission accomplished will prove to be as ill-advised as some others have been in the last decade. Gay marriage is legal in Connecticut, where Love Makes a Family is based, but it's certainly not legal everywhere in the US. No one, however, would deny that the fight for gay rights has made extraordinary strides in the forty years since Stonewall. And progress in combating homophobia has been accompanied by comparable progress in combating racism and sexism. Although the occasional claim that the election of President Obama has ushered us into a post-racial society is obviously wrong, it's fairly clear that the country that's just elected a black president (and that produced so many votes for the presidential candidacy of a woman) is a lot less racist and sexist than it used to be.

But it would be a mistake to think that because the US is a less racist, sexist and homophobic society, it is a more equal society. In fact, in certain crucial ways it is more unequal than it was forty years ago. No group dedicated to ending economic inequality would be thinking today about declaring victory and going home. In 1969, the top quintile of American wage-earners made 43 per cent of all the money earned in the US; the bottom quintile made 4.1 per cent. In 2007, the top quintile made 49.7 per cent; the bottom quintile 3.4. And while this inequality is both raced and gendered, it's less so than you might think. White people, for example, make up about seventy per cent of the US population, and sixty-two per cent of those in the bottom quintile. Progress in fighting racism hasn't done them any good; it hasn't even been designed to do them any good. More generally, even if we succeeded completely in eliminating the effects of racism and sexism, we would not thereby have made any progress towards economic equality. A society in which white people were proportionately represented in the bottom quintile (and black people proportionately represented in the top quintile) would not be more equal; it would be exactly as unequal. It would not be more just; it would be proportionately unjust.

An obvious question, then, is how we are to understand the fact that we've made so much progress in some areas while going backwards in others. And an almost equally obvious answer is that the areas in which we've made progress have been those which are in fundamental accord with the deepest values of neoliberalism, and the one where we haven't isn't. We can put the point more directly by observing that increasing tolerance of economic inequality and increasing intolerance of racism, sexism and homophobia—of discrimination as such—are fundamental characteristics of neoliberalism. Hence the extraordinary advances in the battle against discrimination, and hence also its limits as a contribution to any left-wing politics. The increased inequalities of neoliberalism were not caused by racism and sexism and won't be cured by—they aren't even addressed by—anti-racism or anti-sexism.

My point is not that anti-racism and anti-sexism are not good things. It is rather that they currently have nothing to do with left-wing politics, and that, insofar as they function as a substitute for it, can be a bad thing. American universities are exemplary here: they are less racist and sexist than they were forty years ago and at the same time more elitist. The one serves as an alibi for the other: when you ask them for more equality, what they give you is more diversity. The neoliberal heart leaps up at the sound of glass ceilings shattering and at the sight of doctors, lawyers and professors of color taking their place in the upper middle class. Whence the many corporations which pursue diversity almost as enthusiastically as they pursue profits, and proclaim over and over again not only that the two are compatible but that they have a causal connection—that diversity is good for business. But a diversified elite is not made any the less elite by its diversity and, as a response to the demand for equality, far from being left-wing politics, it is right-wing politics.

The recent furore over the arrest for 'disorderly conduct' of Henry Louis Gates helps make this clear. Gates, as one of his Harvard colleagues said, is "a famous, wealthy and important black man", a point Gates himself tried to make to the arresting officer—the way he put it was: "You don't know who you're messing with." But, despite the helpful hint, the cop failed to recognize an essential truth about neoliberal America: it's no longer enough to kowtow to rich white people; now you have to kowtow to rich black people too. The problem, as a sympathetic writer in *The Guardian* put it, is that "Gates's race snuffed out his class status", or, as Gates said to the *New York Times*, "I can't wear my Harvard gown everywhere". In the bad old days this situation almost never came up—cops could confidently treat all black people, indeed, all people of color, the way they traditionally treated poor white people. But now that we've made some real progress towards integrating our elites, you need to step back and take the time to figure out "who you're messing with". You need to make sure that nobody's class status is snuffed out by his race.

In the wake of Gates's arrest, among the hundreds of people protesting the injustice of racial profiling, a white cardiologist married to a black man put the point best when she lamented that even in the 'diverse area' where she lives (Hyde Park, Obama's old neighborhood) she'll hear people nervously say, "Look at those black guys coming towards us", to which she replies: "Yes, but they're wearing lacrosse shorts and Calvin Klein jeans. They're probably the kids of the professor down the street." "You have to be able to discern differences between people", she went on to say. "It's very frustrating." The differences she means, of course, are between rich kids and poor kids, and the frustration she feels is with people who don't understand that class is supposed to trump race. But while it's easy to sympathize with that frustration—rich black kids are infinitely less likely to mug you than poor black kids or, for that matter, poor white kids—it's a lot harder to see it as the expression of a progressive politics.

Nevertheless, that seems to be the way we do see it. The neoliberal ideal is a world where rich people of all races and sexes can happily enjoy their wealth, and where the injustices produced not by discrimination but by exploitation—there are fewer poor people (seven per cent) than black people (nine per cent) at Harvard, and Harvard's not the worst—are discreetly sent around to the back door. Thus everyone's outraged that a black professor living on prosperous Ware St. (and renting a summer vacation 'manse' on Martha's Vineyard that he 'jokingly' calls 'Tara') can be treated with disrespect; no one's all that outraged by the social system that created the gap between Ware St. or 'Tara' and the places where most Americans live. Everyone's outraged by the fact that Gates can be treated so badly; nobody by the fact that he and the rest of the top ten per cent of American wage-earners have been doing so well. Actually, it's just the opposite. Liberals—especially white liberals—are thrilled by Gates's success, since it testifies to the legitimacy of their own: racism didn't make us all this money, we earned it!

Thus the primacy of anti-discrimination not only performs the economic function of making markets more efficient, it also performs the therapeutic function of making those of us who have benefited from those markets sleep better at night. And, perhaps more important, it has, "for a long time", as Wendy Bottero says in her contribution to the recent Runnymede Trust collection *Who Cares about the White Working Class?*[1], also performed the intellectual function of focusing social analysis on what she calls "questions of racial or sexual identity" and on "cultural differences" instead of on "the way in which capitalist economies create large numbers of low-wage, low-skill jobs with poor job security". The message of *Who Cares about the White Working Class?*, however, is that class has re-emerged: "What we learn here", according to the collection's editor, Kjartan Páll Sveinsson, is that "life chances for today's children are overwhelmingly linked to parental income, occupations and educational qualifications—in other words, class."

This assertion, unremarkable as it may seem, represents a substantial advance over multiculturalist anti-racism, since the logic of anti-racism requires only the correction of disparities within classes rather than between them. If about 1.5 per cent of your population is of Pakistani descent, then if 1.5 per cent of every income quintile is Pakistani, your job is done. The fact that the top quintile is four times better off than the bottom quintile—the advantage the children of rich Pakistanis would have over the children of poor ones—is not your problem. Which is why, in a society like Britain, whose GINI coeffcient—the standard measure of income inequality—is the highest in the EU, the ambition to eliminate racial disparities rather than income inequality itself functions as a form of legitimation rather than as a critique. Which is also why, when an organization like the Runnymede Trust, which has for years been devoted to promoting "a successful multi-ethnic Britain by addressing issues of racial equality and discrimination against minority communities", starts addressing itself to class, it's undergone a real change. Racial equality requires respect for racial difference; class equality requires the elimination of class difference.

In the event, however, what *Who Cares about the White Working Class?* actually provides is less an alternative to neoliberal multiculturalism than an extension and ingenious refinement of it. Those writing in this collection understand the 're-emergence of class' not as a function of the increasing injustice of class (when Thatcher took office, the GINI score was 0.25; now it's 0.36, the highest the UK has ever recorded) but as a function of the increasing injustice of 'classism'. What outrages them, in other words, is not the fact of class difference but the 'scorn' and 'contempt' with which the lower class is treated.

You get a perfect sense of how this works from Beverley Skeggs's analysis of a story told by one of her working-class research subjects about a trip she and her friends took to Kendals in Manchester: "You know, where the really posh food is, and we were laughing about all the chocolates, and how many we could eat—if we could afford them—and this woman she just looked at us. *If looks could kill. . . .* It was like it was her place, and we didn't belong there." The point Skeggs makes is that "the gaze that embodies the symbolic reading of the women makes them feel 'out of place', thereby generating a sense of where their 'place' should be", while her more general point is that "the middle class" should be "held accountable for the levels of symbolic violence they enact in daily encounters" with the lower classes.

The focus of her outrage (indeed, insofar as we can tell from the story, the focus of the women's own outrage) is not the fact that some people can afford the chocolates and others can't, but that the ones who can are mean to the ones who can't. And this represents something of an innovation in left politics. While everyone has always disapproved of adding insult to injury, it's traditionally been the right that's sought to treat the insult as if it were the injury.

It's thus a relevant fact about *Who Cares about the White Working Class?* that Ferdinand Mount, who once advised Thatcher, is twice cited and praised here for condemning the middle class's bad behavior in displaying its open contempt for 'working-class cultures'. He represents an improvement over those who seek to blame the poor for their poverty and who regard the culture of poverty rather than the structure of capitalism as the problem. That is the view of what we might call right-wing neoliberalism and, from the standpoint of what we might call left-wing neoliberalism, it's nothing but the expression of class prejudice. What left neoliberals want is to offer some "positive affirmation for the working classes". They want us to go beyond race to class, but to do so by treating class as if it were race and to start treating the white working class with the same respect we would, say, the Somalis—giving "positive value and meaning to both 'workingclassness' and ethnic diversity". Where right neoliberals want us to condemn the culture of the poor, left neoliberals want us to appreciate it.

The great virtue of this debate is that on both sides inequality gets turned into a stigma. That is, once you start redefining the problem of class difference as the problem of class prejudice—once you complete the transformation of race, gender and class into racism, sexism and classism—you no longer have to worry about the redistribution of wealth. You can just fight over whether poor people should be treated with contempt or respect. And while, in human terms, respect seems the right way to go, politically it's just as empty as contempt.

This is pretty obvious when it comes to class. Kjartan Páll Sveinsson declares that "the white working classes are discriminated against on a range of different fronts, including their accent, their style, the food they eat, the clothes they wear"—and it's no doubt true. But the elimination of such discrimination would not alter the nature of the system that generates "the large numbers of low-wage, low-skill jobs with poor job security" described by Bottero. It would just alter the technologies used for deciding who had to take them. And it's hard to see how even the most widespread social enthusiasm for tracksuits and gold chains could make up for the disadvantages produced by those jobs.

Race, on the other hand, has been a more successful technology of mystification. In the US, one of the great uses of racism was (and is) to induce poor white people to feel a crucial and entirely specious fellowship with rich white people; one of the great uses of anti-racism is to make poor black people feel a crucial and equally specious fellowship with rich black people. Furthermore, in the form of the celebration of 'identity' and 'ethnic diversity', it seeks to create a bond between poor black people and rich white ones. So the African-American woman who cleans my office is supposed to feel not so bad about the fact that I make almost ten times as much money as she does because she can be confident that I'm not racist or sexist and that I respect her culture. And she's also supposed to feel pride because the dean of our college, who makes much more than ten times what she does, is African-American, like her. And since the chancellor of our university, who makes more than fifteen times what she does, is not only African-American but a woman too (the fruits of both anti-racism and anti-sexism!), she can feel doubly good about her. But, and I acknowledge that this is the thinnest of anecdotal evidence, I somehow doubt she does. If the downside of the politics of anti-discrimination is that it now functions to legitimate the increasing disparities not produced by racism or sexism, the upside is the degree to which it makes visible the fact that the increase in those disparities does indeed have nothing to do with racism or sexism. A social analyst as clear-eyed as a University of Illinois cleaning woman would start from there.

ADOLPH REED, JR.

The Limits of Anti-Racism

Anti-racism is a favorite concept on the American left these days. Of course, all good sorts want to be against racism, but what does the word mean exactly?

The contemporary discourse of 'anti-racism' is focused much more on taxonomy than politics. It emphasizes the name by which we should call some strains of inequality—whether they should be broadly recognized as evidence of 'racism'—over specifying the mechanisms that produce them or even the steps that can be taken to combat them. And, no, neither 'overcoming racism' nor 'rejecting whiteness' qualifies as such a step any more than does waiting for the 'revolution' or urging God's heavenly intervention. If organizing a rally against racism seems at present to be a more substantive political act than attending a prayer vigil for world peace, that's only because contemporary anti-racist activists understand themselves to be employing the same tactics and pursuing the same ends as their predecessors in the period of high insurgency in the struggle against racial segregation.

This view, however, is mistaken. The post-war activism that reached its crescendo in the South as the 'Civil Rights movement' wasn't a movement against a generic 'racism'; it was specifically and explicitly directed toward full citizenship rights for black Americans and against the system of racial segregation that defined a specific regime of explicitly

45

racial subordination in the South. The 1940s March on Washington Movement was also directed against specific targets, like employment discrimination in defense production. Black Power era and post-Black Power era struggles similarly focused on combating specific inequalities and pursuing specific goals like the effective exercise of voting rights and specific programs of redistribution.

Clarity Lost

Whether or not one considers those goals correct or appropriate, they were clear and strategic in a way that 'anti-racism' simply is not. Sure, those earlier struggles relied on a discourse of racial justice, but their targets were concrete and strategic. It is only in a period of political demobilization that the historical specificities of those struggles have become smoothed out of sight in a romantic idealism that homogenizes them into timeless abstractions like 'the black liberation movement'—an entity that, like Brigadoon, sporadically appears and returns, impelled by its own logic.

Ironically, as the basis for a politics, anti-racism seems to reflect, several generations downstream, the victory of the post-war psychologists in depoliticizing the critique of racial injustice by shifting its focus from the social structures that generate and reproduce racial inequality to an ultimately individual, and ahistorical, domain of 'prejudice' or 'intolerance'. (No doubt this shift was partly aided by political imperatives associated with the Cold War and domestic anti-communism.) Beryl Satter's recent book on the racialized political economy of 'contract buying' in Chicago in the 1950s and 1960s, *Family Properties: Race, Real Estate, and the Exploitation of Black Urban America*[1], is a good illustration of how these processes worked; Robert Self's book on Oakland since the 1930s, *American Babylon*[2], is another. Both make abundantly clear the role of the real estate industry in creating and recreating housing segregation and ghettoization.

Tasty Bunny

All too often, 'racism' is the subject of sentences that imply intentional activity or is characterized as an autonomous 'force'. In this kind of formulation, 'racism', a conceptual abstraction, is imagined as a material entity. Abstractions can be useful, but they shouldn't be given independent life.

I can appreciate such formulations as transient political rhetoric; hyperbolic claims made in order to draw attention and galvanize opinion against some particular injustice. But as the basis for social interpretation, and particularly interpretation directed toward strategic political action, they are useless. Their principal function is to feel good and tastily righteous in the mouths of those who propound them. People do things that reproduce patterns of racialized inequality, sometimes with self-consciously bigoted motives, sometimes not. Properly speaking, however, 'racism' itself doesn't do anything more than the Easter Bunny does.

Yes, racism exists as a conceptual condensation of practices and ideas that reproduce, or seek to reproduce, hierarchy along lines defined by race. Apostles of anti-racism frequently can't hear this sort of statement, because in their exceedingly simplistic version of the nexus of race and injustice there can be only the Manichean dichotomy of those who admit racism's existence and those who deny it. There can be only Todd Gitlin (the sociologist and former SDS leader who has become, both fairly and as caricature, the symbol of a 'class-first' line) and their own heroic, truth-telling selves, and whoever is not the latter must be the former. Thus the logic of straining to assign guilt by association substitutes for argument.

My position is—and I can't count the number of times I've said this bluntly, yet to no avail, in response to those in blissful thrall of the comforting Manicheanism—that of course racism persists, in all the disparate, often unrelated kinds of social relations and 'attitudes' that are characteristically lumped together under that rubric, but from the standpoint of trying to figure out how to combat even what most of us would agree is racial inequality and injustice, that acknowledgement and $2.25 will get me a ride on the subway. It doesn't lend itself to any particular action except more taxonomic argument about what counts as racism.

Do What Now?

And here's a practical catch-22. In the logic of anti-racism, exposure of the racial element of an instance of wrongdoing will lead to recognition of injustice, which in turn will lead to remedial action—though not much attention seems ever given to how this part is supposed to work. I suspect this is because the exposure part, which feels so righteously yet undemandingly good, is the real focus. But this exposure convinces only those who are already disposed to recognize.

Those who aren't so disposed have multiple layers of obfuscating ideology, mainly forms of victim-blaming, through which to deny that a given disparity stems from racism or for that matter is even unjust. The Simi Valley jury's reaction to the Rodney King tape, which saw King as perp and the cops as victims, is a classic illustration. So is 'underclass' discourse. Victimization by subprime mortgage scams can be, and frequently is, dismissed as the fault of irresponsible poor folks aspiring beyond their means. And there is no shortage of black people in the public eye—Bill Cosby and Oprah Winfrey are two prime examples, as is Barack Obama—who embrace and recycle those narratives of poor black Americans' wayward behavior and self-destructive habits.

And how does a simple narrative of 'racism' account for the fact that so many black institutions, including churches and some racial advocacy organizations, and many, many black individuals actively promoted those risky mortgages as making the 'American Dream of home ownership' possible for 'us'? Sure, there are analogies available—black slave traders, slave snitches, 'Uncle Toms' and various race traitors—but those analogies are moral judgments, not explanations. And to mention them only opens up another second-order debate about racial authenticity—about who 'really' represents the black community. Even Clarence Thomas sees himself as a proud black man representing the race's best interests.

My point is that it's more effective politically to challenge the inequality and injustice directly and bypass the debate over whether it should be called 'racism'.

I do recognize that, partly because of the terms on which the Civil Rights movement's victories have been achieved, there is a strong practical imperative for stressing the racially invidious aspects of injustices: they have legal remedies. Race is one of the legal classes protected by anti-discrimination law; poverty, for instance, is not. But this makes identifying 'racism' a technical requirement for pursuing certain grievances, not the basis of an overall political strategy for pursuit of racial justice, or, as I believe is a clearer left formulation, racial equality as an essential component of a program of social justice.

Anti-Marx

I've been struck by the level of visceral and vitriolic anti-Marxism I've seen from this strain of defenders of anti-racism as a politics. It's not clear to me what drives it because it takes the form of snide dismissals rather than direct arguments. Moreover, the dismissals typically include empty acknowledgment that 'of course we should oppose capitalism', whatever that might mean. In any event, the tenor of this anti-Marxism is reminiscent of those right-wing discourses, many of which masqueraded as liberal, in which only invoking the word 'Marxism' was sufficient to dismiss an opposing argument or position.

This anti-Marxism has some curious effects. Leading professional anti-racist Tim Wise came to the defense of Obama's purged green jobs czar Van Jones by dismissing Jones's "brief stint with a pseudo-Maoist group", and pointing instead to "his more recent break with such groups and philosophies, in favor of a commitment to eco-friendly, sustainable capitalism". In fact, Jones was a core member of a revolutionary organization, STORM, that took itself very seriously, almost comically so.

And are we to applaud his break with radical politics in favor of a style of capitalism that few actual capitalists embrace? This is the substance of Wise's defense.

This sort of thing only deepens my suspicions about anti-racism's status within the comfort zone of neoliberalism's discourses of 'reform'. More to the point, I suspect as well that this vitriol toward radicalism is rooted partly in the conviction that a left politics based on class analysis and one focused on racial injustice are Manichean alternatives.

Devolutions

This is also a notion of fairly recent provenance, in part as well another artifact of the terms on which the Civil Rights victories were consolidated, including the emergence of a fully incorporated black political class in the 1970s and its subsequent evolution. By contrast, examining, for example, the contributions to historian and civil rights activist Rayford Logan's 1944 volume *What the Negro Wants*[3], one sees quite a different picture. Nearly all the contributors—including nominal conservatives—to this collection of analyses from a broad cross section of black scholars and activists asserted in very concrete terms that the struggle for racial justice and the general struggle for social and industrial democracy were more than inseparable, that the victory of the former largely depended on the success of the latter. This was, at the time, barely even a matter for debate: rather, it was the frame of reference for any black mass politics and protest activity.

As I suggest above, various pressures of the post-war period—including carrots of success and sticks of intimidation and witch-hunting, as well as the articulation of class tensions within the Civil Rights movement itself—drove an evolution away from this perspective and toward reformulation of the movement's goals along lines more consonant with post-war, post-New Deal, Cold War liberalism. Thus what the political scientist Preston Smith calls 'racial democracy'[4] came gradually to replace social democracy as a political goal—the redress of grievances that could be construed as specifically racial took precedence over the redistribution of wealth, and an individualized psychology replaced notions of reworking the material sphere. This dynamic intensified with the combination of popular demobilization in black politics and emergence of the post-segregation black political class in the 1970s and 1980s.

We live under a regime now that is capable simultaneously of including black people and Latinos, even celebrating that inclusion as a fulfillment of democracy, and excluding poor people without a whimper of opposition. Of course, those most visible in the excluded class are disproportionately black and Latino, and that fact gives the lie to the celebration. Or does it really? From the standpoint of a neoliberal ideal of equality, in which classification by race, gender, sexual orientation or any other recognized ascriptive status (that is, status based on what one allegedly is rather than what one does) does not impose explicit, intrinsic or necessary limitations on one's participation and aspirations in the society, this celebration of inclusion of blacks, Latinos and others is warranted.

We'll Be Back!

But this notion of democracy is inadequate, since it doesn't begin to address the deep and deepening patterns of inequality and injustice embedded in the ostensibly 'neutral' dynamics of American capitalism. What A. Philip Randolph and others—even anti-communists like Roy Wilkins—understood in the 1940s is that what racism meant was that, so long as such dynamics persisted without challenge, black people and other similarly stigmatized populations would be clustered on the bad side of the distribution of costs and benefits. To extrapolate anachronistically to the present, they would have understood that the struggle against racial health disparities, for example, has no real chance of success apart from a struggle to eliminate for-profit health care.

These seem really transparent points to me, but maybe that's just me. I remain curious why the 'debate' over anti-racism as a politics takes such indirect and evasive forms—like the analogizing and guilt by association, moralistic bombast in lieu of concrete argument—and why it persists in establishing, even often while denying the move, the terms of debate as race vs. class. I'm increasingly convinced that a likely reason is that the race line is itself a class line, one that is entirely consistent with the neoliberal redefinition of equality and democracy. It reflects the social position of those positioned to benefit from the view that the market is a just, effective, or even acceptable system for rewarding talent and virtue and punishing their opposites and that, therefore, removal of 'artificial' impediments to its functioning like race and gender will make it even more efficient and just.

From this perspective even the 'left' anti-racist line that we must fight both economic inequality and racial inequality, which seems always in practice to give priority to 'fighting racism' (often theorized as a necessary precondition for doing anything else), looks suspiciously like only another version of the evasive 'we'll come back for you' (after we do all the business-friendly stuff) politics that the Democrats have so successfully employed to avoid addressing economic injustice.

ADOLPH REED, JR.

From Black Power to Black Establishment: The Curious Legacy of a Radical Slogan

16 June 1966 isn't on the commemorative calendar in black American politics, but it probably should be. On that date, Willie Ricks, a Student Nonviolent Coordinating Committee (SNCC) field secretary, and Stokely Carmichael, SNCC's new national chair, electrified[1] the crowd in Greenwood, Mississippi, on the March Against Fear from Memphis to Jackson, Mississippi, when they began chanting "Black Power! Black Power!" The chant—and Carmichael's speech before the gathering—sent shock waves through the news cycle. I remember that galvanizing moment very clearly; I was then a nineteen-year-old college student and felt a powerful rush from two snippets of the chant I heard in the press coverage of the moment when Black Power was born, as both a slogan and a movement. It seemed to offer, or augur, an exciting new brand of radicalism, and revolutionary confrontation, in the movement's next phase.

For all that initial excitement, however, Black Power was always a concept in search of its object. It condensed a variety of frustrations and aspirations, both evanescent and concrete, and suggested, in adumbrated form, a path toward addressing them. So the following year, when Carmichael and political scientist Charles V. Hamilton published the nascent movement's much-anticipated manifesto, *Black Power: The Politics of Liberation in America*[2], the effort to tease out an agenda for Black Power was likely to disappoint nearly every interested party. But the book was also underwhelming in a way that might have been instructive. Even though it was sprinkled with radical-sounding references to domestic colonialism and militant pronouncements purporting to expose the depth and overwhelming extent of American racism, the book alighted on a surprisingly conventional position. At bottom, it advanced, under a radical nameplate, the familiar pursuit of ethnic interest-group politics, of the sort that had shaped pluralist debate over a supposed politics of assimilation since Horace Kallen[3] invented cultural pluralism in the early twentieth century.

"Black Power . . . is a call for black people in this country to unite, to recognize their heritage, to build a sense of community", the authors averred.[4] "It is a call for black people to begin to define their own goals, to lead their own organizations and to support those organizations." But when they laid out the political strategy that followed from this declaration, it was little more than an affirmation of basic ethnic pluralism—"Traditionally, each new ethnic group in this society has found the route to social and political viability through the organization of its own institutions with which to represent its needs within the larger society. . . . Italians vote for Rubino over O'Brien; Irish for Murphy over Goldberg, etc."—jazzed up with a race-reductionist account of the history and sources of black inequality. And their brief against American racism centered mostly on the psychological damage that they maintained it perpetrated on black people.

In other words, Carmichael and Hamilton based their purportedly revolutionary Black Power program on the two most problematic—historically inaccurate, racialist, and fundamentally conservative—frameworks that post-war American scholars and policymakers had adopted for interpreting inequality: ethnic succession theory and, with respect to blacks in particular, historian Daryl Michael Scott's 'damage thesis'[5]. Both frameworks eschewed discussion of the role of political economy in favor of airy, group-based claims about culture as the basis for economic mobility and inequality in American life. The outlook conveyed in the particulars of the Black Power program stems in no small part from the political conditions that first gave rise to the movement. Black Power emerged at the moment when the great Civil Rights victories had been won and the institutional spine of the white supremacist regime had been broken. At that juncture, the broad movement for social justice launched a crucial debate over how best to build upon these foundational victories. In early 1965, longtime labor and civil rights activist Bayard Rustin laid out[6] one vision. He questioned whether it made sense to continue describing the struggle for black equality as "the civil rights movement" in light of its recent landmark achievements. What had to happen after the successful battle for formal equality under the law, Rustin argued, was a move "beyond race relations to economic relations". Progress toward substantive quality couldn't happen, he insisted, "in the absence of radical programs for full employment, abolition of slums, the reconstruction of our educational system, new definitions of work and leisure. Adding up the cost of such programs, we can only conclude that we are talking about a refashioning of our political economy."

Just three months after the movement launched, Rustin directly criticized[7] the priorities of Black Power. He flatly debunked the ethnic group succession narrative as a just-so story that had no bearing on black experience or, for that matter, any other in the United States. He also stressed that the union movement and New Deal redistributive policies had been the main engines of upward mobility for all Americans, black as well as white. He invoked the $100 billion program that A. Philip Randolph[8] was about to publish in *A Freedom Budget for All Americans*. This approach would be "aimed at the reconstruction of American society in the interests of greater social justice", Rustin argued—and then charged that "the advocates of 'black power' have no such programs in mind; what they are in fact arguing for (perhaps unconsciously) is the creation of a *new black establishment*."

Rustin's class-based critique of Black Power went generally unnoticed and unrebutted at the time. As political scientists Cedric Johnson[9] and Dean E. Robinson[10] have shown, the Black Power sensibility grew partly from a left-inflected racial populist strain in insurgent black political discourse in the 1950s and early 1960s. The populist tendency's internationalist, anti-colonial flourishes contributed to Black Power's radical aura, proffering at least some emotional and symbolic connection to the revolutionary insurgencies occurring across what was then called the Third World. This radical aura made it easy to overlook or dismiss Rustin's remark on the movement's class composition.

Yet astute left voices in the Black Power camp had begun to sound alarm bells. Robert L. Allen's *Black Awakening in Capitalist America*[11] exposed highly suspect corporate connections and class dynamics within Black Power politics that subverted racial communitarian ideals of control by the 'black community'. A politics resting on idealized goals like racial empowerment or community control could mean anything to anyone—until, that is, the agenda in question had to be specified as concrete policies, programs, and institutional arrangements.

As such critical details came to light over time, they served mostly to underscore the wisdom of Rustin's pioneering class critique. The Black Power sensibility didn't only appeal to college students and activists; it resonated also with the self-image and aspirations of an emergent stratum of black professional and managerial functionaries, administrators, and officials. By the middle 1970s, Rustin's admonition had become fact, and the Black Power realignment of Civil Rights protest in the direction of sharply class-skewed[12] ethnic politics remains the generally recognized baseline[13] of black politics today.

Harold Cruse, the ex-Communist writer and black nationalist, was one of the movement's few supporters to chastise the exuberant young militants for their failure to recognize their conservative nationalist ideological progenitors, such as the great apostle of black self-help Booker T. Washington[14]. Cruse interpreted both Black Power and Bookerism as variations of the same basic theme in black politics, leading from racial uplift to community empowerment. Cruse, like Carmichael and Hamilton, had embraced a group-driven and ethnic-succession model of American political history, but insisted that the likely legacy of Black Power, like Bookerism before it, was to advance the blinkered and ultimately conservative goal of race advancement.

Bookerism arose at a moment when avenues for popular black political participation were brutally closed off via disfranchisement and imposition of a white supremacist order in the South. In that context, with support from Southern and Northern ruling-class interests, a stratum of educated and cultivated black men and women asserted themselves

as spokespersons [15] for a civically mute black population. They proceeded from that foundation to organize themselves as a class to seek what
Kenneth W. Warren calls "managerial authority over the nation's Negro
problem" within limits set by the white ruling class.

By contrast, Black Power emerged at the moment when the victories
of the mid-'60s raised questions concerning the centrality of a race-first
orientation for black Americans' political activity. Notwithstanding the
movement's militant posturing and denunciatory style, Black Power remained committed at its core to asserting the necessity of a race-reductionist, black ethnic politics. And this posture, in turn, worked to shore
up the black professional-managerial class's claim to managerial authority over an anti-politics of race relations rather than to the advancement
of any substantive policy agenda. That remains the movement's greatest
legacy today.

ADOLPH REED, JR.

Beyond the Great Awokening:
Reassessing the Legacies of Past Black Organizing

This year marks the seventy-fifth anniversary of publication of *Black Metropolis*[1], St. Clair Drake and Horace R. Cayton's landmark study of Chicago. *Black Metropolis* appeared as World War II neared its end, with US political leaders fiercely debating the best ways to bring about civilian reconversion and reconstruction. Drake and Cayton recognized that the outcomes of those debates would be critical for their fellow black Americans in the post-war decades. A pair of other influential studies published around the same time, *An American Dilemma: The Negro Problem and Modern Democracy*[2] by Swedish sociologist Gunnar Myrdal, and *What the Negro Wants*[3], an anthology edited by Rayford W. Logan, likewise affirmed the central challenges of racial equality in the post-war world, stressing continued expansion of New Deal social-wage policy and the steady growth of industrial unionism as keys to black advancement.

Against this backdrop of social-democratic policy debate, Drake and Cayton laid out a rich account of changes in Chicago's black population between the 1840s and the early 1940s. They focused especially on the evolving patterns of employment and housing, and the overlapping dynamics of racial discrimination, political incorporation, and structured opportunity—what they describe as the Job Ceiling—in the 1930s and 1940s. Their description of the city's racial hierarchy was grounded in their account of material social relations—showing that, for example, competition for employment underwrote racial discrimination in labor markets, and that housing market dynamics established white exclusivity as a basis of real estate value. They assumed, that is, that 'racism' and even 'prejudice' did not constitute in themselves adequate explanations for patterned racial inequalities: "The intimate tie-up between strong folk-prejudices, economic interest, and social status is so intricate that it is difficult to unravel the threads." And, they insisted, "Race conflict in northern urban areas arises when competition is particularly keen—for jobs, houses, political power, or prestige—and when Negroes are regarded (with or without foundation) as a threat to those who already have those things or who are competing for them."

Drake and Cayton did not assume that racism is an unchanging, monolithic force eternally suppressing black people, because they knew better. Most of the book is an account of how black Americans' circumstances as individuals and as a group had altered over the previous half-century, pointing out the large and small improvements and victories that black advocates won for equality in employment opportunities, civil rights, and material security. They also stressed how blacks had made the most of the greater freedom and economic and political opportunity afforded them in Chicago and other Northern cities, in contrast to the Jim Crow regime of the South.

The book concludes with a brief speculation on the future of American politics and how black political agendas might take shape in the post-war period. "The people are rather definite about what they want", the authors concluded: "the abolition of the Job Ceiling; adequate housing; equal, unsegregated access to all places of public accommodation; the protection of the rights of those Negroes and whites who may desire to associate together socially. And they want to see this pattern extended to all of America—including the South." Drake and Cayton were equally clear about the means best suited to realizing these goals: a broader struggle for "full employment in the postwar world and on the development of a world program for emancipating the Common Man".

This prescription stands out in stark contrast to today's boomlet in race-reductive analyses of American inequality and social injustice. So it's a good idea to look at just how far we've traversed from Drake and

Cayton's policy agenda—and what that distance says about the racial and economic prospects ahead.

Discourse about race and politics in the United States has been driven in recent years more by moralizing than by careful analysis or strategic considerations. It also depends on naïve and unproductive ways of interpreting the past and its relation to the present. I've discussed[4] a number of the political and intellectual casualties of what we might call this Great Awokening, among them a tendency to view the past anachronistically, through the lens of the assumptions, norms, and patterns of social relations of the present.

That inclination has only intensified with proliferation of notions like Afropessimism[5], which postulates that much of, if not all, the history of the world has been propelled by a universal 'anti-blackness'. Adherents of the Afropessimist critique, and other race-reductive thinkers, posit a commitment to a transhistorical white supremacy as the cornerstone and motive force of the history, and prehistory, of the United States, as well as imperialist and colonialist subjugation in other areas of the world. Most famously, the *New York Times*'s award-winning 1619 Project[6], under the direction of Nikole Hannah-Jones, asserts that slavery and racial subordination have defined the essence of the United States since before the founding—a brand of ahistorical moralizing that is now being incorporated into high school history curricula.

Yet, as I have argued[7], the premise that subordination to white supremacy has been black Americans' definitive and unrelenting experience in the United States is undone by the most casual observation. As just one instance, I recall a panel at an early 1990s conference on black politics at Harvard Law School, organized by the school's black student group, on which a distinguished black Harvard Law professor declaimed—with no qualification or sense of irony—that nothing had changed for black Americans since 1865. Until recently, this obviously false contention could make sense as a rhetorical gambit, indeed one that depended on its falsity for its effectiveness. It was a jeremiad dressed up as an empirical claim; 'nothing has changed' carried a silent qualifier— that whatever racial outrage triggered the declaration makes it seem as though nothing had changed. This kind of provocation pivots on the tacit rhetorical claim that the offense it targets is atavistic—but in order for it to gain any significant traction, it requires that we understand that things *have* changed to the extent that such offenses should no longer be condoned, accepted, or taken in stride.

However, the fervor of the Great Awokening has since transformed this fundamentally rhetorical device into an assertion of fact. That is one of the most intellectually disturbing features of the irrationalist race reductionism of our own historical moment. It sacrifices or openly rejects not only nuance in historical interpretation but also the idea of historicity itself—the understanding that the relation between past and present generates meanings and nuances beyond the bounds of outworn dogmas in either era. Inflexible race reductionism also rules out, on principle, the notion that we should strive to understand ideas and actions in the past synchronically, as enmeshed in their own complex contexts of meaning, as well as in relation to ours. Race reductionist politics depends on denying historical specificity, typically through a sleight-of-hand maneuver that depicts black Americans' challenges and struggles as set in motion by a singular, transhistorical, and idealized abstraction called 'racism', 'white supremacy', or 'anti-blackness'. What's omitted from this Borg-like model of an undeviating, and seemingly all-conquering, white supremacist opposition are the actual policies and programs that actual black people, often along with others, fought for and against. *Black Metropolis* shines a spotlight on that difference.

Drake and Cayton also provide a suggestive (if inadvertent) explanation of a core paradox of the Awokening age: that, as actual class inequality intensifies[8] among black Americans, the fervor of anti-racist politics escalates to ever more irrational lengths to deny this state of affairs, or to subordinate it to a race-reductionist set of priorities. The authors observed, "The Negro middle class views the white middle class as its competitor, and the Negro lower class sees it as an exploiter." Of course, it would not have occurred to them to ask in 1945 how the black working class would view the black middle class if the latter were to replace its white counterparts; that possibility was then beyond the scope of pragmatic political imagination. Ventriloquizing the interests of a fictive, undifferentiated racial population has become an important source of political capital for advancing identitarian agendas skewed to benefit the upper strata and aspirants—a key development that in turn suggests the Great Awokening represents a form of cognitive dissonance within that class. That is to say, the more obviously the premises of race-reductionist politics are at odds with the daily realities of black Americans' lives and expressed concerns, the more insistently the Woke must double down on the fantasy of monolithic, unchanged race-driven oppression. In this way, the vital contrasts of unequal life outcomes arbitrated by class, or other forces beyond the scope of race reduction, are simply factored out of the equation. This, indeed, may mark the point where wishful thinking approaches pathology. Or it may just show the deep wisdom of Upton Sinclair's famous dictum: "It is difficult to get a man to understand something, when his salary depends upon his not understanding it."

WALTER BENN MICHAELS

The Trouble with Diversifying the Faculty

The widespread sense that faculties at US colleges and universities need to be more diverse is tied to the sense that the students at US colleges and universities have become more diverse, which indeed they have. In 1971, entering freshmen were overwhelmingly (90.9 per cent) white, 7.5 per cent were black; Asians and Latino/as, at 0.6 per cent each, were almost invisible.[1] Today, according to the *Chronicle of Higher Education*'s annual survey of freshmen at four-year colleges, 73.1 per cent are white, 11 per cent are black, 8.9 per cent are Asian, and 9.7 per cent are Latino.[2] Of course, these numbers don't amount to complete success: Latinos and Latinas are underrepresented, and blacks are also still slightly underrepresented. Furthermore, if we take numbers from more selective colleges, even the eleven per cent for blacks begins to look a little high. Northwestern, for example, is only about five per cent black; the University of Illinois at Urbana-Champaign is closer to seven per cent. So here, blacks are significantly underrepresented.

But they are not underrepresented because they are black. On the contrary—this is what scholars in the field call the 'net black advantage'—once 'baseline economic disparities are discounted', African Americans are more likely to attend four-year colleges than white students are. What this means, as the authors of the study "Racial Inequality and College Attendance" say, is that the idea that "African-American

65

educational disadvantage is rooted in cultural deficiencies and/or resistance to the mainstream educational system" is pretty much nonsense. [3]
And, of course, what it also means is that the underrepresentation of
African Americans in colleges and universities has nothing to do with
those universities keeping out African Americans (or, for that matter,
Hispanics and Native Americans). Universities don't keep out minority
students; they keep out poor students.

Indeed, the increase in diversity in higher education over the last
forty years has been matched by an increase in wealth. In 1971, the
median income of entering freshmen at the 297 colleges participating
in the *American Freshmen* survey was forty-six per cent above the national average; by 2007, it had climbed to sixty per cent. [4] As a result,
poor students of all races are scarcer than blacks or Latinos. So places
like Northwestern may be only five per cent black, but since, according
to Richard Kahlenberg [5], only around three per cent of the students in
the 146 most selective colleges and universities come from the bottom
socioeconomic quarter of the American population, you still have a better chance of meeting a black kid than you do of meeting a poor one on
their campuses.

The Two-Tier Professoriate

Thus the question about who should be on the faculty is a question about
who should teach the rich kids, and although no one has argued that
professors should be both as diverse as their students and as rich, the
incomes of the teachers have, in fact, risen. The median household income in 2008 was a little over $52,000; according to a 2009 survey by
the American Association of University Professors, the average salary for
full-time faculty was $79,439 [6]. Professors, like their students, are about
sixty per cent above the median.

Or at least some of them are. The AAUP survey doesn't include contingent faculty, and any number that doesn't include contingent faculty is
ignoring the vast majority of American faculty members. For just as the
increase in student diversity and student wealth have tracked each other
over the last forty years, the increased reliance on contingent faculty has
tracked them both. In 1975, almost 57 per cent of faculty were tenured

or on the tenure track; today that percentage has been almost cut in half, and the percentage of non-tenure-track faculty has gone from 43.2 per cent to 68.8 per cent. The people who work these jobs do not make anything like $79,000 a year; they don't even make anything like the median income of $52,000.

At my university, the University of Illinois at Chicago (UIC), for example, adjuncts on nine-month contracts, teaching six courses a year, make between $26,788 and $30,900, a salary that, according to the *Chronicle of Higher Education*, is "high among those who work outside the tenure track in the region"[7]. Even at the high end, however, it's more than $1,000 below the minimum $6,200 per course section called for by the Modern Language Association[8]. This year, we have hired (on one-year contracts) thirty-six adjuncts, which is nothing like the two-thirds of the faculty they constitute nationally (many of whom teach at community colleges) but is, since the number of tenured and tenure-track faculty in our department is thirty-five, a slight majority of the UIC English department. And since the adjuncts, with no research responsibilities, have a heavier teaching load than do the tenured and tenure-track faculty, their courses constitute a very large majority of the teaching our department does. Indeed, since at UIC the number of those on the tenure track has declined over the last twenty years, while the number of students has grown, it would be completely impossible for the university to staff our courses without adjuncts. Thus, as American college students have become, on the average, richer, the people who teach them have become, on the average, poorer. If you assume that the average UIC tenure-track professor of English makes the national average and you take her salary and average it with what our lecturers make, what you get is a faculty that earns about $54,000—more like two per cent above the median than sixty per cent.

But just as the colleges themselves worry much more about the student body's diversity than about its wealth, they worry much more about the faculty's diversity than about its poverty. At UIC, for example, we have a commitment to "increasing the numbers of underrepresented faculty" and we have administrators who, within the best of their ability in difficult times, are seeking to honor that commitment.[9] So although we don't have very many searches, when we do, they're often targeted at scholars of color or toward areas—like African American Studies or Latino literature—where we can plausibly hope that the successful candidate will embody as well as profess his or her subject, since it is, after all, the underrepresentation of bodies, not professional specialties, that our commitment to diversity is seeking to rectify. And insofar as searches like these are successful, our tenure-track faculty may continue to dwindle but it will do so in colors that come closer to matching those of the American population and at salaries that continue to exceed those of the American population.

Meanwhile, however, much of our teaching will be done by people whose salaries trail the median and whose colors we don't care about. Which is to say, we are being made into precisely the kinds of employees neoliberal managers love. On the one hand, most of our work is done by cheaper and less secure labor (the adjuncts), and, on the other hand and even in the depths of the Great Recession, our commitment to social justice (the faculty of color) remains intact. The advantages of the two-tier professoriate, in other words, are both material and moral: on the bottom tier, a flexibilized work force; on the top tier, a diversified one. And although the bottom tier at present is nowhere near as diverse as the top, that's not really a problem, since no one of any race really wants to be on the bottom. Success here consists only in diversifying the elite and thus achieving the new American Dream: not a more equal society but a society in which inequality is more evenly distributed, in which a few more of the winners are people of color and a few more of the losers are white guys.

This is the dream Adolph Reed is describing when he says that "we live under a regime now that is capable simultaneously of including black people and Latinos, even celebrating that inclusion as a fulfillment of democracy, and excluding poor people without a whimper of opposition."[10] His point is not, of course, that we should be unhappy because this regime challenges white privilege; it's that we should be unhappy because it consolidates class privilege. Indeed, it not only consolidates class privilege, it enhances it. For the replacement of the idea of equality with the ideal of proportional inequality has taken place at the very moment

—beginning in the late 1970s—in which inequality has been rapidly on the rise. And as the rich have become richer while everyone else has not, what we've developed is an institutional morality that objects to the inequalities produced by prejudice and discrimination but not to the ones produced by competitive markets. The "triumph of neoliberalism", as Reed puts it, is the idea that "only inequalities resultant from unfavorable treatment based on negatively sanctioned ascriptive designations like race qualify as injustice".[11] Thus markets win on both the material and the ideological levels. Neoliberalism creates greater disparities between the rich and the rest, and it teaches us that those disparities, so long as they're produced by markets and not by discrimination, are deserved.

It's in this context that we can recognize the fundamentally conservative and anti-egalitarian character of the call to diversify the faculty and, indeed, of the American university system in general. The University of Michigan, a determined and at least partially successful (notably in *Grutter v. Bollinger*[12]) combatant in the fight for diversity, is emblematic here. In 2004, Kahlenberg points out, as the university "was celebrating its victory in the Supreme Court, this national symbol of racial diversity had more students from families making in excess of $200,000 per year than families earning less than the national median of $53,000 a year".[13] In other words, the university's commitment to "racial and ethnic diversity" and especially "to the inclusion of students from groups which have been historically discriminated against . . . who without this commitment might not be represented in our student body in meaningful numbers" did not extend to the students who are most underrepresented at Michigan and at its private competitors: the poor.[14] That is, the attempt to open the university's doors to people of color has taken precedence over the attempt to open them to people without money. Indeed, judging by the results, there hasn't really been any attempt to open them to people without money, or, for that matter, even to people with just a normal amount of money since, as David Leonhardt has observed, "at the most selective private universities across the country, more fathers of freshmen are doctors than are hourly workers, teachers, clergy members, farmers or members of the military—combined."[15] But, of course, no one could even have dreamed of suing Michigan on behalf of the children of

69

hourly workers. There may be a constitutional question about whether race-conscious admissions policies discriminate against white people, but it's definitely not against any law to give preferences to the rich.

Just as it's not against any law to underpay the people who teach their children—which is not to say that the benefits of faculty diversity are reserved only for those universities whose enthusiasm for combating racism and sexism sits comfortably alongside their indifference to combating exploitation. On the contrary, the advantages of diversity are almost equally vivid in situations where both the students and the faculty are well-off, since here, too, the institution's sense of its own virtue is largely dependent on the idea that rich people getting paid to help other rich people make sure that their wealth and status get transmitted from one generation to the next is a good thing as long as the rich people in question aren't all white and male. Indeed, in this respect, our universities, despite our tendency to think of them as the most liberal of institutions, are just like almost every other American institution of the upper-middle class. No one can plausibly think of banks as liberal institutions, but the annual Vault ranking of the "50 Most Prestigious Banking Firms" takes diversity into account, and the number one firm last year—both in diversity and overall—was Goldman Sachs.

Of course, the recent suit alleging discrimination against women at Goldman Sachs and complaining of their "'stark' underrepresentation" in management—"just 29 percent of vice presidents, 17 percent of managing directors, and 14 percent of partners"[16]—may have a negative impact on its rankings for this year. But it's the logic according to which the complaint is conceived rather than its validity that makes the relevant point. If Lloyd Blankfein's $9 million bonus were instead going to Jane Doe, would that make Goldman Sachs a more liberal institution? Would the United States be a more egalitarian country if the beneficiaries of our increasing inequality included more women?

Reproducing Inequality

University leaders regularly puzzle over the fact that, as President Drew Faust of Harvard has put it, their undergraduates "are . . . going in such numbers . . . [in]to finance, consulting, i-banking"[17]. But it's hard to see why anybody should be surprised. After all, it was President Faust herself who at her installation congratulated our universities on being engines of "the expansion of citizenship, equality and opportunity—to blacks, women, Jews, immigrants, and others" [18]. And we've already seen who the others aren't. The only difference between the banks and the universities is that at Goldman Sachs, where the goal is to make the kids even richer, they don't just appreciate diversity; according to QS, with "a global client base that reflects a multitude of cultures", they "leverage" it. So if thirty-nine per cent of the Harvard graduating class is going into banking and finance, it's not an anomaly. It's because they've learned very well the lessons in social justice (the lessons of student and faculty diversity) that Harvard has taught them, and they'll fight just as hard to make those lessons a reality on Wall Street as they have in Cambridge.

Even more striking than the bad news about thirty-nine per cent of the students going into banking, however, is what President Faust thinks of as the good news, namely, that a significant number (thirty-seven) have "signed on with Teach for America". The symbiosis with Goldman Sachs et al. is perfect, since no cause is more beloved of Wall Street than destroying the little that's left of the American union movement today, and 'educational reform' (led by Teach for America and the charter school movement) is at the heart of that effort. Thus, the *Wall Street Journal* describes the fact that there are more college graduates wanting to join Teach for America (TFA) than there are schools wanting to hire them by declaring it a "tragic lost opportunity" produced by "union and bureaucratic opposition" [19]. The *Journal* doesn't mention the studies showing that "the students of novice TFA teachers perform significantly less well in reading and mathematics than those of credentialed beginning teachers." [20] And the well-meaning college administrators, delighted that more of their charges are going off to do good, don't say much about the fact most of them won't do it very well or for very long. More than eighty per cent of TFA teachers leave after three years.

But as Michelle Rhee, one of the heroes of the recent film *Waiting for Superman*, likes to say, it's really all about the adults, not the kids. If, for instance, you juxtapose the claims the film makes on behalf of Wall Street's favorite charter school, the Harlem Children's Zone (HCZ), with the reality of its performance—starting with the fact that just fifteen per cent of its seventh graders passed the 2010 New York reading test—it's not hard to see that HCZ, although even more beloved of Wall Street than Teach for America (Goldman Sachs just gave HCZ $20 million[21]), is not much better at actually educating children. And it's even easier to see that Geoffrey Canada's solution to HCZ's recent failure on the reading tests—"Several teachers have been fired as a result of the low scores, and others were reassigned"[22]—is closer to the heart of school reform than is any actual improvement in the kids' education, although this is an insight that comes more easily to conservatives who know they're conservative that it does to high-minded liberals. Thus, outraged though he might be by "the plight of children trapped in failing schools with lousy, union-protected teachers", the right-wing columnist Ross Douthat is skeptical about the ability of school reform to do the main thing school reformers claim it can do, namely, significantly raise test scores. But that's OK, because even though reform won't "turn every American child into a test-acing dynamo", if it accomplishes "the feat" of creating "a more cost-effective system", that's something "well worth fighting for".[23] Douthat articulates what *Waiting for Superman* does not, namely, that school reform, from TFA to HCZ, is much more about lowering labor costs than about raising test scores, and that what Geoffrey Canada wants Superman to do is also what billionaire reformers like Bill and Melinda Gates want him to do: bust the union.

Thus, the little band of Harvard idealists going off to teach for America, like the much larger band going off to sell CDOs for Goldman Sachs, are making their own contribution to the reproduction and intensification of inequality in America. The Wall Street materialists contribute the old-fashioned way, by making a lot of money; the job of the TFA idealists— to make public school employees ("Several teachers have been fired . . . ") as disposable as college adjuncts—requires more virtue than greed. But both the materialists and the idealists have learned the fundamental lessons of American higher education very well. There's no injustice at Goldman Sachs as long as women and bankers of color get their fair share, and there's no injustice in turning as many college teachers as possible into underpaid adjuncts as long, once again, as women and people of color are proportionally represented on what's left of the tenure track. The general rule of American upper-class life is that inequality is not a problem except when it comes to race and sex; the application of that rule to American colleges is the call for faculty diversity.

ADOLPH REED, JR. & MERLIN CHOWKWANYUN

Race, Class, Crisis:
The Discourse of Racial Disparity
and Its Analytical Discontents

A Harvard University study of more than 2,500 middle-income African-American families found that, when compared to other ethnic groups in the same income bracket, blacks were up to 23 percent more likely. "Our data would seem to discredit the notion that black Americans are less likely", said head researcher Russell Waterstone, noting the study also found that women of African descent were no more or less prone than Latinas. "In fact, over the past several decades, we've seen the African-American community nearly triple in probability". The study noted that, furthermore, Asian-Americans.

The Onion, 30 November 2010

The only thing that hasn't changed about black politics since 1965 is how we think about it.

Willie Legette (*ca.* 1999)

I

The 2008-09 economic crisis hit black Americans and other populations classified as non-white in the United States hard in relation to whites. This differential impact was no surprise to anyone who pays attention to patterns of inequality in the United States. Non-whites, especially blacks and Latinos, are on the average poorer and economically

less secure than whites. It was predictable, therefore, that those populations in the aggregate would experience the hardships of bad economic
times in disproportionate measure. That likelihood underlies the inclination to inquire into the issue of racially differential impacts in the
first place. And, unsurprisingly, as the studies and reports discussed
here demonstrate, that prediction has generally been affirmed by empirical examination. [1]

Research precisely specifying racial disparities in the distribution
of advantages and disadvantages, well-being and suffering has become
common enough to have generated a distinctive, *pro forma* narrative
structure. Quantitative data, usually culled from large aggregate data
sets, is parsed to generate accounts of the many facets of apparent disparity along racial lines with respect to barometers of inequality such
as wealth, income and economic security, incarceration, employment,
access to medical care, and health and educational outcomes. However, as *The Onion* parody suggests, they tend not to add up to much beyond fleshing out the contours of the disproportionate relations, which
are predictable by common sense understanding. Explanations of the
sources of disparities tend to dribble into vague and often sanctimonious
calls to recognize the role of race, and, on the left, the flailing around of
phrases like 'institutional racism' that on closer examination add up to
little more than signifying one's radical credentials on race issues.

So what, then, do researchers assume they are doing in rehearsing
versions of the same narrative with slightly different variations on the
punch line? What are its conceptual foundations and premises? How
should we assess the strengths, limits and significance of its perspectives on race, class and inequality and their connections, especially to
understand American capitalism's social and ideological reproduction in
the current period?

This essay is an initial attempt to answer those questions and,
through doing so, to assess the deeper significance of the discourse of
racial disparity that has taken shape in American social science and policy research during the last decade and a half. We consider what the
findings of disparate impact at the level of gross racial groups mean and
do not mean and examine ambiguities within this literature concerning

race as a significant element in the reproduction of durable inequalities. In doing so, we identify several interpretive pathologies.

Among those pathologies are a schematic juxtaposition of race and class that frequently devolves into unproductive either-or debates; the dilution of class into a cultural and behavioral category or a static (usually quantitative) index of economic attainment that fails to capture power relations; sweeping characterizations of white Americans' racial animus and collective psyche; ahistorical declarations that posit a long and unbroken arc of American racism and that sidestep careful dissection of how racism and, for that matter, race have evolved and transformed; and a tendency to shoehorn the United States' racial history into a rhetorically powerful but analytically crude story of 'two societies', monolithic and monochromatic. Our overall concern is the extent to which particular inequalities that appear statistically as 'racial' disparities are in fact embedded in multiple social relations and how the dominant modes of approaching this topic impede the understanding of this larger picture. We believe that too much writing, including that on the crisis of 2008, is laced with generic, *a priori* assumptions about the role of racial categorization that then straitjackets research and tempts researchers, in Ian Shapiro's words, to "load the dice in favor of one type of description", in this case, characterizing disparities in outcome as strictly 'racial' and thus resulting in the ho-hum and one-dimensional research conclusions we have mentioned. [2]

II

Initial accounts of the crisis have mostly come from major left-liberal think-tanks and magazines and often carry provocative titles like "Mortgage Industry Bankrupts Black America" or "Drained: Jobless and Foreclosed in Communities of Color". The overall narrative is the same. First, authors select an undesirable phenomenon for study, such as unemployment, foreclosure, personal bankruptcy, and increasingly unmanageable subprime mortgages. Next, using quantitative data from a variety of sources, they cross-tabulate or run regressions against race (and sometimes other variables) and find that for minorities, the percentage of the group experiencing the adverse phenomenon is substantially

77

greater than it is for white counterparts. When regressions are used, non-white race yields greater odds ratios and greater coefficients for the undesirable outcome, usually even if other variables are held constant. Some reports identify additional manifolds to this basic story—for example, a positive association between racial segregation and higher rates of subprime loans issued or greater likelihood of traditional mortgage denials for minorities than for whites.[3] In short, whites may have it bad in the recession, but minorities have it far worse. Thus the authors of these reports conclude that, in some form or another, there are really two recessions and that one's ascriptive status determines which one a person will experience, and, by extension, the severity of the pain.

Anyone who recalls the controversy over the Boston Federal Reserve's 1992 study on racial discrimination in the mortgage market and racial disparity in loan denials knows that claims over the magnitude of a variable's effects can quickly morph into methodological ping pong.[4] Defenders, critics, and those in between filled hundreds of pages and edited volumes with careful, if often arcane, dissection of the study.[5] Our intent for this essay is not to develop a critique along these technical lines; let us assume the findings of these studies, in their basic outline, are correct. Rather, we wish instead to assess, from a left perspective, the analytical payoff (or lack thereof) in this framework.

Common among these reports is a tautological reference to one racial disparity to explain another while avoiding concrete exploration of either's roots. And like their counterparts in the larger racial disparities field, the overall takeaways often simply exhort readers to register the historical and enduring impact of race and racism. So, to take one example, a typical report notes that "for communities of color, the crisis is intensified", while another reminds the reader that "economically, blacks and Latinos have suffered disproportionately because of structural racism and the web of policies that evolved from it"[6]. Policy proposals, too, sometimes take this form, such as a call for "expand[ing] the use of Racial Equity Impact Assessments for public planning and policy so that racial inequities can be anticipated and prevented prior to the adoption of new policies and practices"[7]. More frequently, they are reasonable and unobjectionable and include calls for better regulation of lending markets, especially of independent mortgage brokers who sell subprime loans; targeted metropolitan job creation programs, particularly in minority-heavy areas hit hard by the crisis; support for affirmative action to combat demonstrable ongoing discrimination; and foreclosure moratoria. Thus after much rhetorical buildup and table after table of statistics showing pervasive racially disparate crisis outcomes, we are left with a plate of levelheaded, if technocratic and hardly novel, liberal policy solutions.

But the greatest pitfall to this writing is its limited potential for providing left analysts with a holistic causal account of the forces behind the bleak figures. At its most simplistic, the reader is simply left with figure after figure illustrating disparity and not much else, or, only slightly better, a series of plausible just-so stories that attempt to fill in the explanatory blanks *post hoc*. One study, for example, spotlights unemployment disparities that vary in severity by region but tells us little about what specific characteristics of those regions—local history, institutions, labor market changes, political regimes, redevelopment initiatives, gentrification, and others—might account for these differences. A comparative examination of Sacramento and Minneapolis featured in the report would seem to encourage such analysis, but like most reports of the sort, its author does not undertake it.[8]

Simplistic use of race as the key analytic category, moreover, suggests intraracial class uniformity and encourages thinking in monochromatic dyads. Much of the problem rests with the almost exclusive reliance on quantitative data sets, which usually limits researchers to pre-defined administrative and demographic variables while ignoring consideration of forces not captured by that data. This is not to say that analytically sophisticated quantitative work is completely absent. An Institute of Race and Poverty report on prime loan denials and subprime mortgage issuances in the Twin Cities, for instance, carefully uncovers egregious racial disparities in lending alongside a sophisticated dissection of the financial web linking predatory subprime mortgage brokers, debt collectors, and financial institutions who bundle and securitize loans. It identifies clearly discernible geographic patterns in subprime lending, with the highest rates in North Minneapolis and its seventy per cent black population, while noting that subprime mortgage rates are also not exclusive to the neighborhood, and thus invites more precise inquiry into the role of neighborhood boundaries and how they (along with race and a host of other considerations) influence the calculations and behavior of all sociological actors in the real estate industry.[9]

In general, however, this research is far more flatfooted. Why, then, in light of its tedious quality has the focus on racial disparity become the default frame for characterizing inequality? One answer is that it is because it is. That is, in part something like a bandwagon effect is at work. Douglas Massey and Nancy Denton's *American Apartheid* and Melvin Oliver and Thomas Shapiro's *Black Wealth/White Wealth* were field-shaping books in the mid-1990s; the attention that they generated helped to establish racial disparity discourse as *lingua franca* of inequality studies in the United States. To that extent people operate within it automatically, as the presumptive common sense frame within which academic and policy scholars approach inequality.[10] This frame congeals around institutional and material imperatives. Funding streams make some lines of inquiry more commonsensical than others, and formulation of inequality in terms of racial disparities appeals to funders in part because doing so conveniently sidesteps potentially thorny causal questions about the foundation of racially asymmetrical distribution of costs and benefits in contemporary American capitalism's logic of systemic reproduction. Therefore, assessment of the discourse of racial disparity requires, as an element of making sense of the sources of its proliferation and assumed explanatory power in the absence of substantive interpretive payoff, reconstructing the historical dialectic through which it has taken shape.

III

The roots of racial disparities discourse reach back to key debates, texts and political tendencies over the past forty years and more. These include the 1968 *Report of the National Advisory Commission on Civic Disorders*—more popularly known as the *Kerner Report*—which gave official sanction to identification of 'white racism' as the generic source of the manifest racial inequalities made visible by the civil disturbances of the mid-1960s. The *Report* declared famously that "Our Nation Is Moving Toward Two Societies, One Black, One White—Separate and Unequal". The appeal of Black Power sensibility and a Third Worldist rhetoric of 'domestic colonialism' reflected and reinforced a perspective in which racism is the main impediment to black aspirations and combating it is the definitive objective of black politics. Robert L. Allen's 1974 volume, *Reluctant Reformers: The Impact of Racism on American Social Reform Movements*, which argued that all major progressive movements in American history have been undone by white racism, became something of a bible for those who insisted that combating racism should take priority over all other political objectives.

More direct precursors include the debate in the late 1970s and 1980s around William Julius Wilson's *Declining Significance of Race*, which occurred in the context of intensifying controversy over affirmative action and other 'race-targeted' social policy initiatives; the status of claims concerning the extent to which black inequality stemmed from existence of a black urban underclass defined by behavioral and attitudinal pathologies; the highly publicized mid-1990s rightist ideological intervention condensed around anti-egalitarian texts like Dinesh D'Souza's *The End of Racism* and, especially, Charles Murray and Richard Herrnstein's *The Bell Curve: Intelligence and Class Structure in American Life*, which repackaged three-quarters of a century of hereditarian sophistries about IQ and 'natural' hierarchy; and the resurgence of significant legislative and judicial challenges to affirmative action and racial set-asides in the early years of this century.

Important as those earlier debates and tendencies are for a nuanced understanding of the intellectual and ideological genealogy of disparity discourse, it is impossible to examine that history here in requisite detail. We will provide that more elaborate account elsewhere, but for now we will assert that seen against those contexts, the rise of a growth industry around racial disparities is easier to understand. Moreover, taking into account the recurring anti-egalitarian challenges to racial equality highlights the many useful functions that research emerging from the disparity focus performs. For one, its authors call attention (though often in broad brush strokes rather than precise ways) to the connections between past historical developments and their residual consequences and role in shaping present-day racial inequality. Further, documenting the existence and consequences of current impediments to black and Latino economic mobility, especially ongoing discrimination, calls into question analyses that explain that lack of mobility by recourse to individual behavioral traits. Lastly, the work simultaneously challenges narratives that acknowledge racial inequality's existence but suggest that it is withering away—and that government measures not only do not help this process and are unfair but may in fact hinder it.

But the difficult political context surrounding this writing's production has discouraged criticism of its assumptions and analytical deficits. In order to understand the drawbacks of 'racial disparity' as a lens for interpreting the fallout of the crisis of 2008, it is useful to review two canonical racial disparities texts, Massey and Denton's *American Apartheid* and Oliver and Shapiro's *Black Wealth/White Wealth*, that capture the *modus operandi* of present-day approaches to racially disparate impacts.[11]

IV

Advocates of a disparities framework will often list a number of domains that exhibit egregious racial disparities; residential segregation, along with the standard book on the subject, *American Apartheid*, frequently tops this list. Published in 1993, *American Apartheid* argues that social scientists have insufficiently studied segregation's persistence and its role in perpetuating black economic disadvantage. The study impressively compiles indices (mostly from the 1980 United States Census) documenting black-white segregation and substantial black spatial isolation. Most usefully, it highlights five distinct dimensions of black population settlement—unevenness, isolation, clustering, concentration, and centralization—whose simultaneous manifestation comprised 'hypersegregation', a concept the book introduced.[12] Its authors argue for a "persisting significance of race", and stress the particularity of black residential patterns, pointing out that segregation of other minority groups exists to a much lower degree.[13] They accentuate the tragedy of persistent segregation in an era after the formal legal dismantlement of

Jim Crow and the fair housing laws passed in its direct wake, concluding that "in the south, as in the north, there is little evidence of substantial change in the status quo of segregation." [14]

It is impossible to deny Massey and Denton's empirical findings. Even as metropolitan settlement patterns since their work have become increasingly complex such that spatial categories like 'city' and 'suburb' tell us far less about racial composition than they once did, there is no doubt that, for many blacks, residential options are greatly and uniquely constrained. [15] Thus *American Apartheid* was and remains an important counterweight against the politics of racial backlash. Documenting hypersegregation and its short-circuiting of economic channels for those caught within it called into doubt the highly individualistic analyses of the time. Why, then, does the analysis in *American Apartheid* fall short? Put simply, despite the empirical heft and political utility, its analysis barely advances that of the *Kerner Report*'s 'two societies' trope or the raft of studies written around the same time on residential segregation. Though written nearly three decades apart, 'white racism' and its psychologistic gloss remain the key causal dynamics behind the racially disparate outcomes that Massey and Denton so ably chronicle. The authors draw repeatedly from considerable survey research on whites' aversion to living alongside black neighbors, especially as black composition rises, and whites' tendency to move away from or avoid moving to neighborhoods as a result. [16]

There are, of course, commendable nuances to the account. Throughout the text, Massey and Denton draw a careful distinction between 'prejudice' and 'discrimination'. The first refers to the racial animus displayed by individual whites. The second refers to a set of institutionalized mechanisms and repertoires that actually restrict more neighborhood integration. Explaining the distinction and relationship between the two, they write that "although white prejudice is a necessary precondition for the perpetuation of segregation, it is insufficient to maintain the residential color line; active discrimination against blacks must occur also". [17] The book then lists mechanisms behind this 'active discrimination'. Chief among them is the sleaze and chicanery of realtors who hide home listings from blacks or only steer them to segregated neighborhoods and away from ones with substantial white residency. Another is the lending behavior of financial institutions, which consistently offer fewer home loans to those in neighborhoods that are integrated or primarily black, a disparity that holds even at an individual level. [18] Massey and Denton write that "although each individual act of discrimination may be small and subtle, together they have a powerful cumulative effect in lowering the probability of black entry into white neighborhoods." [19]

At first glance, the distinction between prejudice and discrimination seems to separate *American Apartheid* (and the dozens of studies influenced by it) from mid-century social science that saw individual prejudice as the fundamental mechanism behind racial inequality. [20] But when one asks what exactly motivates the institutionalized discrimination that Massey and Denton identify, the only answer derivable from the volume takes one back to individual prejudice. The behavior of realtors and financial institutions is portrayed as a response to a collective prejudicial white psyche averse to black-white residential proximity. That Massey and Denton ultimately anchor their institutional account in collective psychology—while at points seeming not to do so—is reinforced by phrases such as "the link between discrimination, prejudice, and segregation", "strong link between levels of prejudice and discrimination and the degree of segregation and spatial isolation that blacks experience", and other instances where the resulting phenomenon (segregation), an institutional pattern (discrimination), and individual attitudes (prejudice) are clumped together [21].

We hardly deny that these links exist, require condemnation, and should be legally constrained. The book's policy prescriptions center around strengthening lax enforcement of fair housing laws and improving monitoring of the real estate industry. But the explanatory aspect of the work is another matter, and it can take us only so far analytically. It inadequately anchors the story of race and residence within the urban political economy—the drive to accumulate, the relationship among value, race, and space, or the role of property as speculative capital and in the derivation of exchange-value. This theme receives little attention in the book except for all too quick and scattershot references to white fears of depressed property values and bank fears of neighborhoods in racial transition. This reasserts the psychologistic reflex that has underlain much interpretation of racial inequality since the 1950s. Yet a deeper causal account must be propelled by something besides white psychology, even if it certainly plays a role. The book's basic outlines, alas, differ only slightly from *Kerner*-era studies of residential segregation, like Karl Taeuber and Alma Taeuber's *Negroes in Cities* or Rose Helper's *Racial Policies and Practices of Real Estate Brokers*, both of which Massey and Denton briefly reference, and the *Kerner Report*'s 'white racism' frame itself[22].

Notably, it is only in the chapter providing historical exposition where *American Apartheid* briefly departs from a framework rooted in collective psychology. Among others, Massey and Denton draw from Arnold Hirsch's *Making the Second Ghetto* and Kenneth Jackson's *Crabgrass Frontier*, two historical monographs on mid-century urban renewal (and its forced relocation of many black residents) and racially exclusionary suburbanization. While hardly ignoring the role of hostile white attitudes, each underscores the centrality of state and local government actions. Hirsch is especially attentive to the catalytic role of Chicago's private urban development interests, and the ghetto formation that he documents is motivated *both* by its imperatives and racial animosity.[23] More recent urban histories, covering a number of periods within the twentieth century, have followed this lead, including Robert Self's *American Babylon*, Beryl Satter's *Family Properties*, and Samuel Roberts's *Infectious Fear*. Roberts, for example, traces the early twentieth-century razing of a black Baltimore district not only to racist fears of the black population as unclean disease vectors, but crucially to the urbanization of Baltimore capital and the commitment to preserving and increasing property values as well.[24]

Such supple analyses of class and race's interstitial operation do not carry over into *American Apartheid*'s examination of contemporary trends, the book's central focus. In rightly rejecting the right-wing fiction of free-standing market forces and autonomous residential choices, Massey and Denton end up dismissing the role of underlying market imperatives altogether.[25] At one point, they explicitly reject the relevance of class as an analytic. But they do so by perpetuating the unproductive class and race dichotomy and operationalizing class in a static, quantitative way (namely, by equating it with household income). In doing so, they find that the upper-income black population still experiences high rates of segregation; ergo, race trumps class.[26] This is true enough, but only as long as one accepts such a reductionist definition of class in the first place. That reductionist view also closes off the holistic analyses that might more fruitfully explore the relationship between political economy and racial attitudes and their spatial consequences.

Taking racial disparity as a starting point can subtly coerce a univariate view that precludes attention to many overarching class dynamics. One of these is intra-racial inequality. On residential segregation, a recent study by Sean Reardon and Kendra Bischoff shows that *income* segregation *among* blacks in the 100 largest metropolitan statistical areas "grew rapidly in the 1970s and 1980s, at a rate more than three times faster than the corresponding growth of white income segregation", during the exact time span that is *American Apartheid's* focus.[27] This concurrent development does not invalidate *American Apartheid's* overall findings, especially its authors' emphasis that upwardly mobile blacks who move to suburbs still tend to end up in ones that are more segregated[28]. But it does suggest that a bifurcated 'two societies' model tells us little about what goes on *within* the two nodes themselves. Strictly racial interpretation prevents careful consideration of other forces shaping social life.

Published two years later, John Yinger's *Closed Doors, Opportunities Lost* covers much of the same territory as *American Apartheid* (and contains many of the same weaknesses), but discuses a much wider range of influences in its account of motivations for white avoidance and exit of neighborhoods.[29] Yinger cites two local studies on Chicago and Cleveland wherein respondents' perceptions regarding safety and crime, education, and quality of city services greatly reduced or eliminated racial considerations in white residential choice. Of course, these considerations are often inextricably bound up with attitudes about race, and the constricted quality of survey research can make disentangling them difficult, but Yinger's point is that "racial and ethnic attitudes are not so strong for most people that they cannot be overcome by other neighborhood factors."[30]

Methodologically, identifying these 'neighborhood factors' and detailing how exactly they operate requires more than large-scale aggregate analysis (in this case, the metropolitan statistical area). That approach is necessary and undeniably useful for seeing general macro-level trends, but there are many micro-level trends that it cannot pick up, including urban redevelopment initiatives, suburban heterogeneity (however limited), and economic exploitation and gentrification (by both blacks and whites). Black-on-black gentrification, in particular, tends to occur in small corridors, and thus can easily be masked by these conventional quantitative analyses of segregation.[31] Moreover, when cast in the language of racial disparity, such aggregate analysis takes the larger percentage of blacks who are residentially segregated as a marker of little black political and economic power altogether. But this birds' eye view cannot capture the small but influential number of blacks who defy residential constraints and, in turn, play influential roles in the 'black urban regimes', the constellation of black elected officials, political appointees, and pro-growth business interests that exert an enormous impact on urban development.[32] Just as a robust aggregate GDP figure (to take just one example) can mask the economic stress experienced by the bulk of the population, so too can the depressing aggregate figures on minority outcomes—like those in *American Apartheid* and much racial disparities research—mask the affluence of a handful. Considered this way, the thematic maps periodically trucked out to show pervasive segregation may in fact obscure more subtle trends. For this work and others, then, method and choice of data obscure as much as they illuminate.[33]

V

Massey and Denton's portrait represents the dominant mode of left thinking about residential segregation. It is indeed the sort of book one wields when making the case that we live in a society that is not 'post-racial', where 'race matters', and 'racism' still exists. Published two years later in 1995, Oliver and Shapiro's *Black Wealth/White Wealth* reinforces this view but uses wealth, rather than housing, as its focus. Though its general template resembles *American Apartheid* and various disparities predecessors, the work may be even more influential. Reliably invoked by those using the racial frame, it and its political prescriptions have been embraced by major policy thinktanks and foundations with decidedly non-leftist, non-progressive political orientations. To understand the implications of this widespread impact and its resulting strange policy bedfellowism, it is important to examine *Black Wealth/White Wealth*'s core approach and assumptions.

On one level, *Black Wealth/White Wealth* is a very important intervention in stratification research that critiques the limits of conventional social scientific measures of socioeconomic status (SES), principally occupational group, education level, and income. Pioneered by Edward Wolff and Michael Sherraden, this work pointed out the inadequacy of orthodox SES measures for predicting life chances insofar as they failed to take into account the critical role of assets like stocks and bonds, inheritances, and real estate holdings. [34] By not accounting for wealth, stratification researchers therefore ignored a crucial dimension of economic inequality. Two households with identical annual incomes, for example, might still be quite unequal if one sat on an additional $50,000 or held a cashable portfolio of securities that the other did not. For crucial life events like medical emergencies, first home-purchases, college tuitions, seed money for a business, and spells of unemployment, this wealth leverage is crucial, and it is obvious how incorporating wealth into stratification research adds considerable complexity.

Oliver and Shapiro extend this insight to racial inequality, drawing from the Survey of Income and Program Participation (SIPP), a cross-sectional dataset that interviewed 11,257 households eight times between 1987 and 1989 about their occupational histories, educational backgrounds, parental characteristics, income levels, and wealth holdings. The empirical heart of *Black Wealth/White Wealth* is comprised of tables showing clear black-white wealth disparities. These hold across income levels, educational level, occupational category, and household structure—and regardless of whether one measures total net worth (NW) or net financial assets (NFA), the latter of which excludes equity, principally in homes and vehicles, not easily transformable into usable funds. A number of the results are dramatic and alarming. For example, one table displaying wealth disparities between 'middle-class' whites and blacks (defined as those making between \$25,000 to \$50,000 a year) shows that whites in 'white-collar' jobs have median NFA of \$11,952, while blacks in the same kind of occupational category have median NFA of 0. [35] Even when black median NFA is positive, it is only a fraction of white median NFA in the same category under examination. And when specific types of assets are compared, black asset figures reflect far lower value. [36] Summarizing the implications of this data, like Massey and Denton, Oliver and Shapiro harken back explicitly to the *Kerner Report*. Their results are evidence "that whites and blacks constitute two nations". [37]

This compilation proved hugely useful in the 1990s debates referenced earlier, especially when mobilized against opponents of race-specific affirmative action who cynically appealed to ideals about preserving consideration on 'merit' while ignoring gross inequalities of resources conferred to swaths of applicants at birth. On this score, like *American Apartheid*, *Black Wealth/White Wealth* deserves praise and recognition for providing a counterweight to right-wing narratives. But like its counterpart on residential segregation, its actual analysis of how race structures a disparate outcome and fits into the larger American political economy is less satisfying.

Unlike *American Apartheid*, Oliver and Shapiro root their causal account less in 'white racism' and collective psychology than in the long historical arc of American racial exclusion. In *American Apartheid*, history is dispensed with in an obligatory chapter on early- and mid-century ghetto formation. In *Black Wealth/White Wealth*, history powerfully exerts its effects at all times, from the creation of racial wealth gaps through their persistence to the present. Specifically, the authors identify three historically durable mechanisms. The first, the "racialization of state policy", refers to various racially exclusionary policies of the American welfare state that have "impaired the ability of many black Americans to accumulate wealth" and denied to blacks a host of government-backed avenues of economic security available to whites, including "homesteading, land acquisition, home ownership, retirement, pensions, education, and asset accumulation" [38]. Second, 'the economic detour' prevented accumulation of start-up capital for African-American entrepreneurial activity and relegated that which existed to largely segregated markets. [39]

The third, and most durable, of these mechanisms is presented in the form of geological metaphor: "the sedimentation of racial inequality", or the "central ways the cumulative effects of the past have seemingly cemented blacks to the bottom of society's economic hierarchy". Throughout American history, according to this account, "generation after generation of blacks remained anchored to the lowest economic status in American society" while those on the other side of the sediment (whites) simultaneously benefited.[40] The wealth gap tables throughout the text reflect the cumulative consequences of this racial sedimentation. At the start, the reader is treated to a breezy, impressionistic, and stagist historical tour that proceeds from slavery, emancipation, racially exclusionary homesteading, the lost promise of Reconstruction (from lack of post-Civil War land redistribution to Redemption); mid-century suburbanization and housing policy that fuelled white homeownership, denied the same to blacks, and created segregated housing and real estate markets; and finally 'contemporary institutional racism' on the part of discriminatory institutions that impedes the accumulation of assets, particularly access to fair home loans.[41] Oliver and Shapiro declare that "structural disadvantages have been layered one upon the other to produce black disadvantage and white privilege."[42]

Having outlined this ostensibly historical framework, Oliver and Shapiro zoom in on two specific features contributing to racial wealth gaps. The first is housing. Historical Jim Crow social welfare policy, particularly racially exclusionary FHA home loans, surely account for some of the higher white rates of present-day homeownership, NW, and home value that Oliver and Shapiro observe. Surveying literature on racial disparities in housing prices and residential segregation (including *American Apartheid*), they show aggregate housing value appreciation for whites has been consistently greater.[43] They suggest persuasively that this is due to racially disparate access to mortgage markets, fairly rated loans, and residential choice.

They then examine inter-generational transfers of assets, including monetary gifts, informal loans, securities, and inheritances, especially of homes. Because whites historically have not faced barriers (formally codified and otherwise) that prohibited blacks from procuring certain assets, it is plausible that this would be reflected in racial wage gap figures of the present. Oliver and Shapiro argue as much via interspersed interviews in which white respondents repeatedly report more frequent and substantial assistance from parents and relatives in the form of tuition and wedding assistance, down payment money for homes, and substantial inheritances of wealth. (By contrast, among black interviewees, only two expect 'large inheritances'.[44]) They supplement these personal accounts with crosstabulations that explore the effects of family occupational background—'upper-white-collar', 'lower-white-collar', 'upper-blue-collar', and 'lower-blue-collar'—on one's subsequent income, NW, and NFA. They discover that for those who manage to increase their occupational mobility, all three measures are much higher for whites than they are for blacks. For example, for an 'upper-white-collar' white person who has ascended from 'upper-blue-collar' origins, NW is $89,898 and NFA is $29,199, compared to $11,162 and $0, respectively, for blacks experiencing the same mobility.[45] Regression analyses show that factors one might think would aid in accumulating more NFA—including increasing age (often associated with more earnings and assets), and high occupational job status—are statistically significant only for whites, not blacks. Whites, meanwhile, garner $1.34 in NFA per income dollar compared to $0.62 for blacks.[46]

The picture that emerges is one in which racial disparity endures within and across time periods. That is, blacks historically have been unable to accumulate certain assets, and when they have, they have been of less value and therefore less significant (in purely quantitative terms) to those who might inherit them. By contrast, whites historically have had a much easier time acquiring such assets—with no small assist from the racialized mid-century welfare state, to say nothing of discriminatory private institutions—and white descendants have therefore benefited enormously from a chain of hand-me-down wealth that most blacks did and do not enjoy. Above all, it is this chain that seems to be the most powerful determinant of the persistent wealth gap. The "historical transmission of inequality" continues onward, inertia unimpeded, as Oliver and Shapiro remind readers in *Black Wealth/White Wealth* that "between 1987 and 2011 the baby boom generation stands to inherit approximately \$7 trillion", and that "for the most part, blacks will not partake in divvying up the baby boom bounty", for "America's racist legacy is shutting them out". A recent 2010 policy brief by Shapiro examining this exact period reveals that the racial wealth gap during this period quadrupled. [47]

Who could quarrel with this? The language of sedimentation, legacy, and history certainly separates *Black White/White Wealth* from pedestrian research that simply describes another disparity *du jour* with little else. But this may amount more to rhetorical genuflection than substantive historical analysis. Rigorous invocation of the past to shed light on present conditions (in this case, the racial wealth gap) must not only identify a persistent social mechanism in the past (in this case, unequal asset accumulation and later inheritance) but also carefully consider when it changes or even stops and to what degree. And it is here where the historical framework falters. Racialized inheritance no doubt explains much of what Oliver and Shapiro observe, but, as they note, the 'bounty' comes mostly from the parents of white 'baby boomers'. That generation, in retrospect, is more an aberration than a norm. Its (white) members attained the assets that *Black Wealth/White Wealth* identifies during a period of welfare state expansion, re-distributive policies, rising labor compensation and benefits, and a booming domestic economy.

By the mid-1960s, however, this 'affluent society' began showing signs of destabilization before devolving a decade later into what Robert Brenner, Judith Stein, Robert Pollin, and Jacob Hacker have memorably characterized, respectively, as 'the long downturn', 'the great compression', 'the hollow boom', and 'the great risk shift' [48]. These formulations refer to a forty-year-period that has seen a decline in American manufacturing and global trade competitiveness; undercutting of organized labor; persistent wage stagnation; exponential growths in income and wealth inequality; mounting consumer debt; and the marketization, reduction, or elimination of public and private benefits, social services, and welfare programs—in short, what we on the left understand as neoliberalism [49]. This shredding of the mid-century public and private welfare state thus renders questionable the claim that inter-generational transfers will continue in as widespread a manner as they have, at least among those not fortunate enough to be in upper economic tiers.[50] The economic crisis of 2008 throws this into even greater relief, given the ongoing havoc it continues to wreak on home ownership, housing prices, retirement accounts, and savings that would have been more abundant in prior times and thus more available for intergenerational transfer, by whites or blacks.

One interpretive goal should therefore be to think hard about whether mechanisms that have perpetuated racial wealth gaps in the past will take the same form in the future. This is the task, in other words, of concrete periodization and historicization rather than reliance on self-satisfying but overly elastic, transhistorical phrases like 'America's racist legacy'[51]. Yet some of the linkages between *Black Wealth/White Wealth*'s wide-spanning historical arc and the authors' findings are apparent only in very generic ways. Take, for example, the authors' first historical stage, that from slavery to the early twentieth century. Here, *Black Wealth/White Wealth* makes much of white homesteading and the lost promise of Reconstruction, waxing counterfactually for a black yeomanry that never was. But it is unclear how consequential widespread petty black landownership would have been for contemporary wage gaps given the restructuring and dislocation in the Southern agricultural economy from the immediate postbellum period into the mid-twentieth century.[52] The wind-up historical narrative we get might more simply be summed up as an elaborate way of saying that race in history has 'mattered'. And? Despite the specter of history in *Black Wealth/White Wealth*'s opening pages, the account we get ends up being far less complex and multi-factorial than promised.

This leaves us with a more typical stratification study than we might expect, one that suffers from methodological constraints similar to what we have identified in both the initial crisis studies and *American Apartheid*. Oliver and Shapiro's quantitative orientation leaves them with a treatment of class that takes the form, to use Barbara Fields's words, of the "diffuse definitions of applied social science—occupation, income, status".[53] Class is alternately operationalized here as income tiers, college degree attainment, and the schematic occupational categories referenced earlier. But the danger here is that such static conceptualizations often can become "unwieldy catch-all unit[s] of analysis" and "overly inclusive".[54] For one, they do not allow situation of the wealth tabulations in a social context to understand how the transformation of certain job sectors (for instance, the steel or mining industries) has affected wealth in different ways than others (like public sector work or banking). This inattentiveness to the more fine-grained intra-racial gradients in social position prevents exploration of whether some of the black population does not fall quite as easily into the general pattern that Oliver and Shapiro document, even though the overwhelming majority no doubt does.

Notably, Dalton Conley's *Being Black, Living in the Red*, another book on the racial wealth gap that uses a more recent prospective data set, the Panel Study of Income Dynamics (PSID), is aware of these issues (even if the nature of the data necessarily results in a constricted definition of class). Through a series of regression models, Conley notes that, however uncommon, for those households where white wealth and black wealth (along with other economic measures he studies) *do* reach parity, a host of black outcomes associated with those gaps decline significantly or disappear altogether. Whereas Oliver and Shapiro take us up to the black wealth disparity—and posit through the sedimentation metaphor that it will persist—Conley takes us beyond to consider part two, when intra-racial class heterogeneity closes the wealth gap for some, and examines the consequences of this intra-racial class restructuring.[55] His findings deserve more follow-up. And beyond individual households, class analysis leads to consideration of how the social relations of production alter localities and regions, transformations that greatly affect the life chances—and self understandings or pragmatic identities—of those within them. In the wake of the 2008 crisis, such an approach is crucial to understanding who precisely has been hit hardest, where, and why without resorting simply to shortcut indexical use of race.

VI

To return to our original question, then, why, despite its serious limitations, does the focus on racial disparity persist as the principal interpretive frame for discussing apparently racialized inequality? The policy recommendations that follow from the disparitarian perspective point to part of the answer. Like *American Apartheid*, most of *Black Wealth/White Wealth*'s recommendations are sound, including re-vamped anti-discrimination policy in lending or changes in the taxation of assets commonly held by the affluent. It is telling, though, that what have arguably gained the most traction are more dubious proposals for 'asset-based' social policy—such as Individual Development Accounts (IDA)[56]—that focus on encouraging start-up individual wealth accumu-lation. Such stratagems represent détente with rather than commitment to changing capitalist class relations, including those that contribute to intra- and inter-racial disparities in the first place. Among other lim-itations, they accommodate, rather than uproot, a key determinant of wealth gaps (racial or otherwise): the entrenched credit and debt regime, chronicled brilliantly by historian Louis Hyman's *Debtor Nation*[57]. Fo-cus on wealth building as strategy and analytical lens for understanding inequality thus is not nearly as progressive as some think, since turning attention away from income is to ignore what it fundamentally reflects: the nature of a capitalist wage-labor relation.

It is telling as well that this focal shift has occurred at precisely the time incomes have skyrocketed for a single-digit percentage of the pop-ulation while remaining flat for everybody else. Hegemonic chestnuts like 'equal opportunity', 'American Dream', 'awarding achievement and merit, not birth', 'level playing field' abound in *Black Wealth/White Wealth* and Shapiro's own follow-up volume, *The Hidden Costs of Being African-American*, published in 2004. These red flags confirm that the agenda at work here stems from a concern to create competitive indi-vidual minority agents who might stand a better fighting chance in the neoliberal rat race rather than a positive alternative vision of a society that eliminates the need to fight constantly against disruptive market whims in the first place. This is a notable and striking reversal from even the more left-inclined of War on Poverty era liberals, who spoke without shame about moving beyond simply placing people on an equal starting line—'equality of opportunity'—but also making sure they ended up clos-er to an equal finishing line.

Within the racial context specifically, such proposals exude more than a whiff of racial communitarianism and collective racial self-help, along with a dollop of republican nostalgia. Although Oliver and Shapiro are careful to note that they advocate "penetration into the newest and most profitable sectors of the wider economy" alongside the "development of local community-based entrepreneurs", the involvement of financial institutions or 'community-based' institutions in these policy proposals and their actual execution is perfect fodder for a bourgeois racial brokerage or machine politics or, more likely, a reinforcement of one that already exists. [58] This focus only serves to affirm a racialized class politics from above.

The discourse of disparity also accommodates a strain of stigmatizing behavioral argument that stretches back at least to Kenneth B. Clark's 1965 study, *Dark Ghetto* [59]. This strain, in varying ways, has characterized the economically marginalized segment of the black population—the most common focus of racial disparities research—as culturally deviant and bereft of role models, typically reasserting a politics of black petit bourgeois racial noblesse oblige that originated in the late nineteenth century rubric of racial 'uplift' [60]. These claims often have relied on a narrative anchored in racialized geography ('ghetto-specific culture'). *American Apartheid*, for example, contains lurid and impressionistic sections—in disturbingly racialized language bordering on vicious stereotype—on ingrained, 'concentrated' social deviance and cultural pathologies supposedly engendered and exacerbated by constricted, segregated space. These ideas have shaped the policy consensus around the racialized notion of 'concentrated poverty', one that holds that these spatial configurations perpetuate poverty, foreclose economic opportunities, breed undesirable behaviors, and require dispersal through varied policy initiatives, from the destruction of high-rise public housing to vouchers for moving into mixed-income neighborhoods. In the name of a progressive-sounding anti-racism, policy discussion has come to focus on technocratic initiatives to rearrange space that in this way grant causal primacy to a spatial consequence rather than to more fundamental dynamics of metropolitan economies, particularly those linked to the political economy of land use, labor markets, and the politics of social service distribution. [61]

It should give us pause that these decidedly non-leftist policy prescriptions flow from the leftist frame of choice for analyzing the racial minority experience in the crisis of 2008. In choosing that frame, rather than fundamentally rethinking default approaches in the face of changing historical circumstances, the left has simply dusted off, rinsed, and repeated. This reflex is reinforced by commitment to a *pro forma* anti-racism that depends on evocations—as in Michelle Alexander's widely noted recent book, *The New Jim Crow* [62]—of regimes of explicitly racial subordination in the past to insist on the moral primacy of simplistic racial metaphor for characterizing inequality in the present. Most charitably, this tendency arises from intensified concerns to defend racial democracy in debates over the legitimacy of race-targeted social policy that have recurred since the late 1970s. Less charitably, it is an expression of an at best self-righteous and lazy-minded identitarian discourse that has increasingly captured the left imagination in the United States since the 1990s. [63] This is moreover an antagonistic alternative to a politics grounded in political economy and class analysis, despite left-seeming defenses that insist on the importance of race *and* class. Its commitment to a fundamentally essentialist and ahistorical race-first view is betrayed in the constantly expanding panoply of neologisms—'institutional racism', 'systemic racism', 'structural racism', 'color-blind racism', 'post-racial racism', etc.—intended to graft more complex social dynamics onto a simplistic and frequently psychologistic racism/anti-racism political ontology. Indeed, these efforts bring to mind Kuhn's account of attempts to accommodate mounting anomalies to salvage an interpretive paradigm in danger of crumbling under a crisis of authority [64]. And in this circumstance as well the salvage effort is driven by powerful material and ideological imperatives.

The discourse of racial disparity is, when all is said and done, a class discourse. Even the best of the studies analyzing the racial impact of the crisis, for example, in focusing on racial disparity in subprime mortgage markets and foreclosure rates, sidestep a chance to interrogate the very limitations of the hegemonic commitment to homeownership altogether. More generally, automatic adoption of the racial disparities approach avoids having to conduct the detailed work that would situate ascriptive status within the neoliberal regime of accumulation that mitigates its influence. Repetitiously noting the existence of segregated neighborhoods and how they decrease property value (real and perceived) and increase the likelihood of subprime mortgage is to identify a *result*, albeit one that is surely repellent. It does not tell us with much exactitude what institutions, policies, actuarial models, and systems of valuation produce those results, or, more generally, what sociologist Mara Loveman describes as the "extent a particular essentializing vocabulary is related to particular forms of social closure and with what consequences"[65]. It substitutes in its place pietistic hand-wringing and feigned surprise over results that can hardly be surprising.

Ironically, it is authors who operate from outside of that frame, and in some cases outside the left entirely, that currently have the most to offer us. Gretchen Morgenson and Joshua Rosner's *Reckless Endangerment* traces the short-term roots of the crisis, detailing how a 1990s consensus on pushing homeownership led to a system of tax credits, perverse incentives, refinancing, risky (and often fraudulent) loans, lax regulation, and debt securitization that exploded a decade and a half later. To cast the story primarily in terms of racial disparity is to capture only a sliver of what some have labelled the 'real estate financial complex'. Doing so misses as well the legitimizing role that disparities rhetoric played in pushing minority homeownership. Focusing so robotically on racially disparate home financing and credit access obscures how these injustices, repugnant as they are, fit into a larger picture of income stagnation and welfare state instability, which gave rise to the increasing need, documented by Hyman, for significant household debt, protracted mortgages, and accelerated re-financing in the first place, all simply to stay afloat. In the accounts we reviewed here, the *Kerner Report*'s 'white racism' remains the enemy, while the Big Kahuna, financialization, wobbles in the background, meriting more an obligatory mention than focused inquiry on how it impacts other phenomena. The misdirection strategies can take if predicated on such an analysis are obvious.

Our call to transcend this stifling frame is absolutely *not* a call to ignore racial exclusion or to declare in abstract terms, as Ellen Wood has, that race is not 'constitutive of capitalism' the way class is[66]. Rather, we advocate that in analyzing the current situation and how it fits into historical context, left analysts ought to conduct what Donald Green and

Ian Shapiro have labelled "problem-driven" research, in their words, to "endeavor to give the most plausible possible account of the phenomenon that stands in need of explanation", in this case racially disparate impacts, instead of forcing it into a stifling, readymade narrative[67]. Doing so will break away from analytical sloth and widen strategic options. Doing so also requires jettisoning the hoary, mechanistic race/class debate entirely. We believe that our critique here demonstrates the virtues of a dynamic historical materialist perspective in which race and class are relatively distinct—sometimes more, sometimes less, sometimes incoherently related or even interchangeable—inflections within a unitary system of capitalist social hierarchy, without any of the moralizing, formalist ontological baggage about priority of oppression that undergirds the debate. From this perspective insistence that race, or any other category of ascriptive differentiation, is somehow *sui generis* and transcendent of particular regimes of capitalist social relations appears to be, as we have suggested here, itself reflective of a class position tied programmatically to the articulation of a metric of social justice compatible with neoliberalism. That is a view that both obscures useful ways to understand the forces that are intensifying inequality and undermines the capacity to challenge them.

99

WALTER BENN MICHAELS

The Political Economy of Anti-Racism

This essay originated as a kind of stump speech, an effort to spell out and update an argument about the uses of anti-racism and anti-discrimination that I've been making for some time to audiences that might or might not be familiar with it. The idea of publishing some version of it in conjunction with Adolph Reed's piece was Adolph's, and the proposed venue was the left journal *Jacobin*; it would be, as Adolph endearingly put it, "a nicely affirmative statement about where the magazine stood on the left v. identitarianism debates". But, although some *Jacobin* editors expressed interest, the idea came almost instantaneously to naught. A preliminary edit of Adolph's piece—cutting it in half and leaving out material that he thought was crucial—made him decide to withdraw it. And, truthfully, I had been from the start skeptical. First, because—although we both respect *Jacobin* and have both published in it before—I was a little less sanguine about the magazine's desire actually to make any kind of statement about where it stood on the left v. identitarian issue. And, second, because part of my argument (as suggested below in Fig. 1, a photo taken at a talk I gave at UC Riverside) involves a critique of the role played by elite universities in (to borrow a phrase from Adolph's and Willie Legette's note on V.O. Key) "suppressing working-class politics in the interests of both white and black political elites"[1]. But, of course, both the students at schools like the ones on my list and the more-or-less recent graduates of such schools make up a significant portion of *Jacobin's* readership; why would *Jacobin* want to publish an attack on its audience?

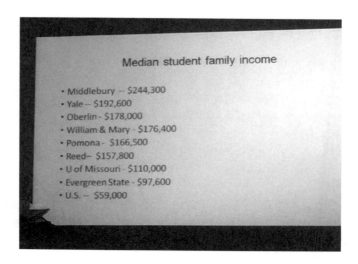

Figure 1. Lecture photo by Amir Zaki

And not just *Jacobin's* audience. When I said to Adolph that what seemed to us the bowdlerizing of his essay was at least in part a consequence of *Jacobin's* need to appeal to a readership significantly composed of rich kids with short attention spans, he responded, "But that's what I do on my day job." As do I, and so do many of the writers for *Jacobin* and for *n+1* and almost all the writers for *nonsite.org*. And, more generally, it's almost always been true that the struggle against inequality has been championed by some of its beneficiaries as well as its victims. Both the socialist professor and the socialist student in an elite (or even, like UIC, not as elite) university inhabit a contradictory position, one that the right has always been eager to criticize in moral terms: the politics we preach are not reflected in the paychecks we deposit or hope someday to earn.

But although there may well be something morally problematic about tenured socialists with six-figure salaries, the relevant political contradiction is not the one between our ethical ideals and our actual lives. (We make no claim to virtue; we get that our day jobs are what we do for money.) The relevant political contradiction is the one between our class position[2] and our politics. And the real problem—the problem alluded to in the 'left v. identitarian' formulation—is not the political contradiction. It's that when the upper-class professor is getting his or her even more upper-class students to confront the ugly truths of racism, there is no contradiction. Just the opposite. When American elites understand racism as the fundamental problem confronting American society, that understanding is an expression of their class interest, not a denial of it. Our day jobs become our only jobs. What's wrong with the identitarian version of the left is not that its roots are in money but that its identitarianism is a defense of that money.

We can begin to see why by juxtaposing two different models of economic inequality: one focuses on the differences between individuals and is called individual inequality, the other—horizontal inequality—focuses on what development economists like Frances Stewart call "inequalities between culturally formed groups".[3] So, for example, when someone tells you the top quintile of American wage-earners makes 51.5 per cent of American income while the bottom quintile makes 3.1 per cent, they're talking about individual inequality. When they tell you that the median annual income of white men is $55,166 while that of black men is $38,243, that's horizontal inequality. "Current thinking about development", Stewart has complained, places individuals rather than groups firmly at "the center of concern". But (as our familiarity with black/white income disparities like those noted above suggests) many economists have long been interested in thinking about the differences between groups not just in developing countries but in places like the US as well. And recent developments have only intensified that interest, as was suggested by Paul Krugman's declaration (during the 2016 election) that we "talk more about horizontal inequality", that "horizontal thinking" was what was needed to understand both Democratic and Republican primaries, and that "horizontal inequality, racial inequality above all", rather than Bernie Sanders's "exclusive focus on individual equality", would "define the general election"[4].

Whether that turned out to be true is an interesting question, but for my purposes here the difference between these two ways of thinking about inequality are relevant not because they help us understand the election but because they entail two very different ways of describing our problem and therefore two very different solutions. What are the causes of the inequality between groups? Racism, sexism, homophobia—discrimination of all types. In the US right now, for example, black people are substantially under-represented in the top quintile of American wealth and over-represented in the bottom, and no one who thinks about that fact for more than two seconds has any difficulty understanding why: several hundred years of slavery, another century of Jim Crow, and another half century of less formal but very real racism. Indeed, according to Ta-Nehisi Coates, "no statistic better illustrates the enduring legacy of our country's shameful history of treating black people as sub-citizens, sub-Americans, and sub-humans than the wealth gap"[5] between blacks and whites. As Coates points out, we have made very little progress overcoming this gap, and the solution he favors—reparations—looks even more unlikely under Trump than it would have under Clinton. But we can understand its point very well. If you could end current racism, and if you could restore to people everything they'd lost as a consequence of past racism, the structure of American society today would look very different.

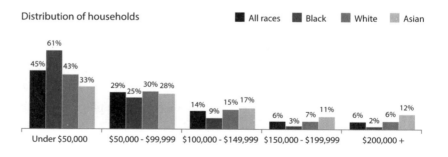

Source: US Census Bureau, Table H-17 Household by Total Money Income, Race, and Hispanic Origin of Householder, at https://www.census.gov/data/tables/time-series/demo/income-poverty/historical-income-households.html

Figure 2. Income distribution of households by race of householder (2015)

Right now, for example, about six per cent of American households earn more than $200,000 a year (Fig. 2). But only two per cent of black households do. And, by the same token, forty-five per cent of American households make under $50,000 a year but sixty-one per cent of black households do. In a world where both current discrimination and the legacy of past discrimination could be made to disappear, six per cent not two per cent of black households would be very rich, and forty-five per cent not sixty-one per cent would be poor. Or, to put the point slightly differently, since black people make up about 13.2 per cent of the population, they would make up 13.2 per cent of every quintile.

By contrast, an equally miraculous end to individual inequality would look very different. It wouldn't, of course, guarantee that each race be proportionately represented in the highest quintile but only because there wouldn't be any such thing as the highest quintile (or, obviously, the lowest quintile). What the abolition of individual inequality would produce is universal equality, and when we contemplate the difficulty not just of eliminating inequality but even, given the history of the last fifty years, of making any significant progress toward reversing it, we realize that one of the standard critiques of reparations—it's too radical—is pretty unfair. Actually, by contrast to the genuinely radical redistribution that would be produced by an end to individual inequality, reparations would be mildly reformist.

Indeed, in itself, the commitment to ending horizontal inequalities is so mildly reformist that it doesn't actually diminish inequality. Redistributing skin colors has nothing to do with redistributing wealth; a world where every race was proportionately represented at every income level would be exactly as unequal as the one we have now. Arguably, however, it would have both ethical and economic advantages, or at least that's what its advocates believe. The problem with discrimination is that it generates what economists call 'bad' inequalities. If a white male gets promoted over a Latina despite the fact that the Latina was doing a better job, that's a bad inequality and it's bad in two ways. It's ethically bad because it's unfair (the white man is being chosen for reasons that have nothing to do with merit) and it's economically bad because it's inefficient (since the white man wasn't chosen for merit, the job is probably not being done as well as it could be). What anti-discrimination looks to do, then, is solve both the ethical and the economic problem—to make sure that all groups have equal opportunity to succeed and thus also to help make sure that the jobs are being done by the people who are best at doing them. Which has absolutely nothing to do with eliminating economic inequality.[6] In fact, it's just the opposite: the point of eliminating horizontal inequality is to justify individual inequality.

This is why some of us have been arguing that identity politics is not an alternative to class politics but a form of it: it's the politics of an upper class that has no problem with seeing people left behind as long as they haven't been left behind because of their race or sex. And (this is at least one of the things that Marx meant by ideology) it's promulgated not only by people who understand themselves as advocates of capital but by many who don't. Even the Marxist anti-racist David Roediger thinks that "anti-capitalists" shouldn't "sneer at" the goal of "evenly distribut[ing]" "poverty and inequality . . . across racial lines". From his perspective, the problem is that "corporate embraces" of diversity "mask desires for the surplus value" it produces and "shift the terms of struggles against

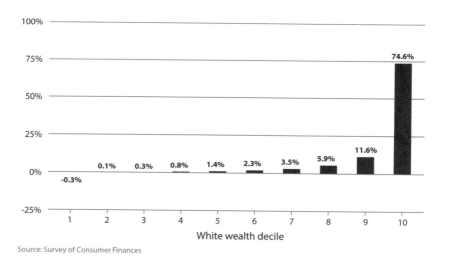

Source: Survey of Consumer Finances

Figure 3. White wealth share by white wealth decile (2016)

racism"[7] —as if *real* anti-racism would get the job done. But if the job is a redistribution of wealth that will produce something other than horizontal equality, real anti-racism, just like real anti-discrimination of all kinds, not only won't get it done but doesn't even try to do it. Indeed, what it does instead is provide an account of failure—either you're the victim of discrimination or you're not a victim—so persuasive that even when it's obviously not true, people believe it.

Fig. 3[8] shows how badly off most white people are—the bottom fifty per cent have about two per cent of white wealth (and the bottom third— that's about sixty million people—have basically no wealth at all). So if, as Coates says, "no statistic better illustrates the enduring legacy of our country's shameful history of treating black people as sub-citizens, sub-Americans, and sub-humans than the wealth gap" between blacks and whites, what does this statistic—the wealth gap between the top ten per cent of white people and all the other white people—illustrate? Amazingly enough, an increasingly popular answer (if only among white people) is Coates's answer: racism! I'm happy to go out on a limb here and say that racism against white people has played absolutely no role in producing white poverty, but (as Fig. 4 suggests[9]) lots of white people have come to think not only that bias against whites is a thing but that it is a bigger thing than anti-black racism.

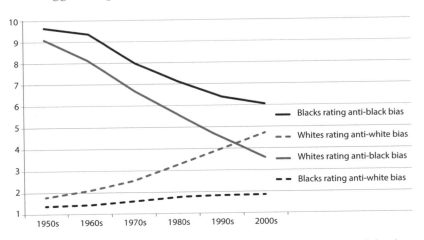

Figure 4. White and black respondents' perceptions of anti-white and anti-black bias in each decade

And we have already begun to see why this explanation makes sense to them. As Karen and Barbara Fields put it in their book *Racecraft*, the discourse of anti-discrimination has so "impoverished Americans' public language for addressing inequality"[10] that we either understand poor white people as victims of racism (which they obviously aren't) or as trailer-trash responsible for their own plight but trying to blame someone else—black people or immigrants. So, in an economy where the bottom eighty per cent has been falling farther and farther behind the top twenty per cent (and where most of the top twenty per cent has been falling behind the top one per cent), we get large numbers of white people experiencing themselves as losing ground, while Trumpists tell them they're the victims of racism and liberals tell them they're racists.

We can see this ideological imperative—you're a victim of discrimination or you're not a victim—at work in the now forty-year obsession (both of its supporters and its critics) with affirmative action in college admissions. Comparatively few American college students attend institutions where admissions are competitive enough for affirmative action to be relevant[11], but as inequality has increased, and as, in the words of former President Obama, we have come to believe that "education is the ticket to a better life", college admissions have come to seem a crucial site for trying to guarantee equality of opportunity. And affirmative action—if you're for it, as a way of fighting racism; if you're against it, as itself a kind of racism (so-called reverse racism)—functions both to keep racial difference at the center of the discussion and to turn it into an opportunity to express class difference. In the wake of the 2016 Supreme Court decision in *Fisher*, a Gallup poll found that "people with some postgraduate education were the most likely to support the decision (46 percent), followed by those with a college degree (35 percent)", while only "27 percent of those with a high school diploma or a lower level of education supported the decision."[12] So, although support for affirmative action has declined in general, wealthy people like it much more than poor people do, at least if you take a college degree as a rough proxy for wealth.

Which you should. Especially a four-year degree from a competitive college. During the years in which American universities have been fighting (with mixed success) for race-based affirmative action, their students have been becoming richer[13], so rich that, today, at elite institutions, the number of students of color, even if there aren't all that many, nonetheless greatly exceeds the number of poor students. Last fall, Harvard proudly announced that it had for the first time admitted a majority non-white class, with 22.2 per cent Asian Americans, 14.6 per cent African Americans and 11.6 per cent Latinos and Latinas.[14] Meanwhile the median family income for students at Harvard is $168,000.[15] So it's not surprising that, on the one hand, some relatively poor people have become skeptical of the idea that colleges become more egalitarian by seeking to admit more students of color (the idea that underlies the affirmative action theory of social justice) and it's even less surprising that rich people (including college students themselves) remain committed to it. Fig. 1 shows an informal list (just the places I could think of off the top of my head—so I forgot, for example, Princeton, $186,000) of the median student family income at colleges that have seen major anti-racist actions in the past year or two. These students have demonstrated an exceptional (and entirely admirable) commitment to opposing raced and gendered inequality while remaining calm in the face of class inequality.

Again, the point is not to highlight the discrepancy between the egalitarian ideals of these students and their class position since, if the equality you're committed to is between groups, there is no discrepancy. And just as no hypocrisy is required at the elite college where you fight hard against racism, none will be required at the NGO or the job as a consultant or in finance ("Why Goldman Sachs? Diversity!"[16]) where you start making enough money (average salary of a Princeton grad at thirty-four: $90,700[17]) to enable your kids to carry on the struggle. Actually, the need for a little hypocrisy—for virtue to pay its symbolic tribute to vice—would be an upgrade. The problem here is the literal tribute virtue's paying to virtue—the complete identity of idealism and careerism. In other words, it's not ethical but political.

And the demand for a working-class politics cannot be met by adding class to race and gender. This is in part because most actually existing intersectionalists are not very interested in class, but even if they were, the great attraction of intersectionality is precisely that it can absorb class too into the logic of discrimination, which is to say, into the neoliberal

theory of inequality. On this theory, the fact of being born poor is a problem in the way that the fact of being born black or Latino or a woman can
be—if it keeps you from having an equal opportunity to succeed. In other
words, we should treat class difference like race and gender by understanding poverty not as something we should get rid of but as something
we should help people overcome. Hence the goal of what Kimberlé Crenshaw calls "intersectionally minded reform"[18] is not to eliminate class
difference (any more than it is to eliminate racial or sexual difference);
it's to eliminate classism—to eliminate people's obstacles to success, give
poor people a chance to become rich. And insofar as the goal of the educational system is understood as giving everyone an equal opportunity to
succeed, a truly intersectional university system would seek what's now
called economic diversity as well as racial diversity.

There are two reasons, however, why the commitment to economic diversity is doomed to fail. The first is practical—if elite universities
achieved a proportional representation of poor people on the model of
the proportional representation of ethnicities, almost all the students
they now have would be sent home and almost none of the students they
would have instead would be able to pay the tuition. The second is more
fundamental. Even if we could overcome the practical obstacles; even if
we could turn the elite colleges into schools for the ninety-nine per cent;
even if we could go one step farther and make it possible for everyone
to go to college, and one step farther than that and make it possible for
every college to be as good as Harvard's supposed to be, it would still
make no contribution to economic equality. In this utopia, we'd all have
the equivalent of a Harvard degree. But we'd be entering a job market in
which there wasn't very much demand for that degree.

Fig. 5 is a list of today's twenty fastest-growing jobs:

2016 National Employment Matrix title and code		Employment		Change, 2016–26		Median annual wage, 2016
		2016	2026	Number	Percent	2016
Total, all occupations	00-0000	156,063.8	167,582.3	11,518.6	7.4	$37,040
Personal care aides	39-9021	2,016.1	2,770.1	754.0	37.4	$21,920
Combined food preparation and serving workers, including fast food	35-3021	3,452.2	4,032.1	579.9	16.8	$19,440
Registered nurses	29-1141	2,955.2	3,392.2	437.0	14.8	$68,450
Home health aides	31-1011	911.5	1,337.0	425.6	46.7	$22,600
Software developers, applications	15-1132	831.3	1,084.6	253.4	30.5	$100,080

2016 National Employment Matrix title and code		Employment		Change, 2016–26		Median annual wage, 2016
		2016	2026	Number	Percent	2016
Total, all occupations	00-0000	156,063.8	167,582.3	11,518.6	7.4	$37,040
Janitors and cleaners, except maids and housekeeping cleaners	37-2011	2,384.6	2,617.7	233.0	9.8	$24,190
General and operations managers	11-1021	2,263.1	2,469.0	205.9	9.1	$99,130
Labourers and freight, stock, and material movers, hand	53-7062	2,628.4	2,829.2	200.8	7.6	$25,980
Medical assistants	31-9092	634.4	819.0	184.6	29.1	$31,540
Waiters and waitresses	35-3031	2,600.5	2,783.0	182.5	7.0	$19,990
Nursing assistants	31-1014	1,510.3	1,674.4	164.0	10.9	$26,590
Construction labourers	47-2061	1,216.7	1,370.0	153.3	12.6	$33,430
Cooks, restaurant	35-2014	1,231.9	1,377.2	145.3	11.8	$24,140
Accountants and auditors	13-2011	1,397.7	1,538.0	140.3	10.0	$68,150
Customer service representatives	43-4051	2,784.5	2,920.5	136.0	4.9	$32,300
Market research analysts and marketing specialists	13-1161	595.4	731.4	136.0	22.8	$62,560
Medical secretaries	43-6013	574.2	703.2	129.1	22.5	$33,730
Landscaping and groundskeeping workers	37-3011	1,197.9	1,321.2	123.3	10.3	$26,320
Heavy and tractor-trailer truck drivers	53-3032	1,871.7	1,985.5	113.8	6.1	$41,340
Maintenance and repair workers, general	49-9071	1,432.6	1,545.3	112.7	7.9	$36,940

Figure 5. Occupations with the most job growth, 2016 and projected 2026

The first thing you might notice is that, despite endless talk about the jobs of the future demanding a higher education, only five of these require a BA. In other words, you'll need to have a college degree for about 7.25 million of these jobs; for the other 30 million you don't. The second thing you'll notice is that the ones requiring a BA. are the high-paying ones. Which is the whole economic point of going to college and which is why higher education has nothing to do with equality. As things stand now, all universities are selling inequality—the advantage we hope our students will have over students who have attended colleges that are in some way inferior to ours or over students who haven't gone to college at all. We want our students to be software developers and operations managers, not waiters and home health aides. Of course, if we were to universalize that advantage—everyone going to an Ivy plus—it would stop being an advantage and it would make education itself more equal. But it wouldn't make the world more equal. It would just mean that the people doing most of the jobs on that list—selling clothes, French fries and personal care for $21,000 a year—would be doing so with a college degree. And, instead of selling inequality (as we do now), colleges would be selling the justification for it. As in, we gave you the chance to get a first-rate education; if you couldn't make it pay, that's on you. Which is precisely—in a period of inequality—what makes the appeal to education so prevalent. The more vividly a society depends on exploited labor, the more eager it is to tell the exploited they had a fair chance to become exploiters.

Of course, right now the majority of personal care aides (number one on our list) are women of color with no more than a high school education. In the neoliberal intersectional everybody-goes-to-Harvard utopia we've been imagining, a lot of them would instead be white men with political science or marketing degrees. But they'd still be making $21,920 a year. And right now, a relatively smaller number of (mainly) white (mainly) men compete for a slightly smaller number of high-paying jobs. Our utopia would exponentially expand the number of people competing for those jobs. But it wouldn't exponentially expand the number of jobs.

The point of free higher education should not be intensified competition. The point more generally of a progressive egalitarianism should not be to leave inequality intact while changing the skin colors of both its beneficiaries and its victims. The point *most* generally should not be trying to teach everyone how to code so they won't have to become personal care aides or fast food preparers. These are the jobs there are; somebody is going to have to do them, and a just society should be less interested in trying to help people escape them than in making it desirable to keep them. It should, in other words, be more interested in turning bad jobs into good jobs than in trying to make sure that the bad jobs go to people who our educational system says deserve them.

This is why, to be as blunt as possible, although you can't think class without race and sex and you can't think race and sex without class, class matters more than race or sex. The fact that these jobs pay so badly is a problem that can't be fixed—that isn't even addressed—by our efforts to devise a fairer system for deciding who should be forced to take them. Which is not to say that we shouldn't oppose racism and sexism and homophobia as vigorously as possible; it's just to say that it's capitalism not racism or sexism that has created these jobs and that if we're not opposing capitalism—if we're not trying to minimize the difference between the care aides who make $21k, the nurses who make $68k, the doctors who make $300k and the Health Care executives who make

$3 million—we can fight discrimination from here until hell freezes over but we will not have made the slightest dent in economic inequality.

It's importantly true that racism and sexism have played the central role in selecting the victims of American inequality, but it's also true and just as important that they have not played the same role in creating the inequality itself. Paying workers less than the value of what they produce does that. And anti-racism and anti-sexism can help make the selection fairer but they don't make it unnecessary, which is a fact that the current forms of resistance to Trump and the fetishization of his racism and of white supremacy tend to make invisible.

In the wake of the white nationalist rally in Charlottesville, as everyone remembers, the President kept insisting there were good people on both sides, which caused some members of his economic council, led by Kenneth C. Frazier, to resign in protest. Frazier is a rare figure, one of the very few African-Americans in the overwhelmingly white and male world of Fortune 500 companies, and he was widely praised at the time for, as some people put it, 'speaking truth to power', standing up against the administration's willingness to countenance racism just as he had stood up against racism, sexism and homophobia in his own career. But if one (completely accurate) way to look at Frazier and at the very few other minority CEOs is as warriors against discrimination, another (equally accurate) way is to note that their contribution to fighting discrimination, their success in the business world, is indistinguishable from their contribution to the increase in economic inequality we began by noting.

When Frazier resigned from the presidential manufacturing council, he said, "America's leaders must honor our fundamental values by clearly rejecting expressions of hatred, bigotry and group supremacy which run counter to the American ideal that all people are created equal" (suggesting that he definitely got the horizontal equality message). Trump responded by tweeting: "Now that Ken Frazier of Merck Pharma has resigned from President's Manufacturing Council, he will have more time to LOWER RIPOFF DRUG PRICES!" If Trump himself had the slightest interest in lowering drug prices, much less in making healthcare available to everyone, this would at least have raised the question of what to do about a right-wing populism that really was populist. In fact, however, he has no more interest than Frazier in lowering ripoff drug prices and, of course, neither of them has ever shown the slightest interest in Medicare for all. (Merck doesn't even want to let people import their medicines from Canada.) In other words, it's what Frazier and Trump have in common that does the most damage to working class people and, incidentally, to working class black people.

Here's another way of putting it. If what we want is a more economically equal society, the endless time and energy spent debating whether our president is a racist is completely beside the point, as is the whole debate about whether it was 'racial resentment' or 'economic anxiety' that got him elected. Even the (marginally) more sophisticated suggestion that in a structurally racist society it doesn't matter whether he's a racist is beside the point, as is the whole idea of structural racism. Because insofar as economic inequality is the problem, redistribution, not proportional representation, is the solution. Of course, this doesn't mean that we shouldn't fight discrimination as well as exploitation; the mere fact that neoliberalism likes anti-racism doesn't make anti-racism wrong, and there can be no justification for tolerating any form of discrimination. But it does mean that the relation between fighting discrimination and fighting exploitation is asymmetrical: fighting exploitation is a way of fighting the effects of discrimination (if nobody were poor, black people and Latinos would not be disproportionately poor), but fighting discrimination is not a way of fighting exploitation (if nobody were the victim of racism or sexism, lots of people would still be poor).

My point in this paper has been to argue against a liberal egalitarianism that, taking discrimination as its central problem, imagines a justified inequality as its solution. Remember the personal care aides. About eighty-five per cent of them—making $21,920—are women, about twenty-two per cent are African American, seven per cent Asian, eighteen per cent Hispanic or Latino, the rest white.[19] Without racism or sexism, this would be incomprehensible. But the end of racism and sexism would make no difference to the rapidly increasing number of people working that job. Without a politics organized around class—fighting not for the interests of women of color but for those of personal care aides—the left, when it comes to economic inequality, is just the good conscience of the right.

WALTER BENN MICHAELS

Autobiography of an Ex-White Man:
Why Race Is Not a Social Construction

"Music is a universal art", says the rich white man in James Weldon Johnson's *Autobiography of an Ex-Colored Man*. "Anybody's music belongs to everybody; you can't limit it to race or country." The novel itself, however, is skeptical about music's claim to universality, approving of the colored man's trip "into the very heart of the South, to live among the people, and drink in [his] inspiration firsthand", but disapproving of the white performers who go to Harlem "to get their imitations firsthand from the Negro entertainers they [see] there". Anybody's music may belong to everybody, but there's a difference between the *imitations* that whites get from blacks and the *inspiration* that blacks get from blacks. The logic of this position has a more general application: black musicians who listen to the spirituals are claiming their 'heritage'; white musicians who imitate the spirituals (or ragtime or hip-hop or the blues) are, as one contributor to the publication *Race Traitor* puts it, denying blacks the "right to any heritage of their own".

The contributors to *Race Traitor*—a journal devoted to "the abolition of whiteness"—are divided on the question of whether white people can or should sing the blues. And, indeed, the terms of this division are crucial to the very project of race treason—the project of abolishing not white racism but the white race. Are white people who "borrow from black culture" helping "to make white people cease to be", or are they, like white performers who go to Harlem, just 'ripping off' blacks? When Johnson's colored man abandons the sources of his inspiration, he becomes an *ex*-colored man, which is to say that he becomes an imitation: he passes for white. *Race Traitor* imagines that white men—perhaps (as one of its editors, Noel Ignatiev, says) "by some engagement with blackness, perhaps even an identification as 'black'"—can become ex-white men. But are whites who engage blackness just passing for black? The ex-colored man rejects his racial identity by concealing it; the ex-white man wishes not to conceal his racial identity, but, by rejecting it, to destroy it. The ex-colored man no longer wishes to be 'identified' as a 'Negro'; the race traitor—perhaps by identifying himself as black—wants to cease to *be* white.

The difference between these projects is a difference in race theory. Race in Johnson's *Autobiography* is a function of what its narrator calls 'blood'. It is because his skin is the color of 'ivory' that the narrator can pretend to be white; it is because his 'blood' is black that he isn't. By contrast, the editors of *Race Traitor*, like most contemporary racial theorists, believe that race is a 'social', not a 'biological', fact. Indeed, it is only because "race is socially constructed" that the commitment to "the abolition of whiteness" can make non-genocidal sense. To "make white people cease to be" is not to kill white people; it is to destroy the social fact of whiteness. Insofar as whiteness, like slavery, is a social fact, it can, like slavery, be abolished; just as there once were millions of ex-slaves, there may in the future be millions of ex-whites.

Of course, the project of abolishing whiteness is only made possible by the redefinition of race as a social construction, even if the celebration of racial difference has been a more characteristic ambition of contemporary race theory. To the extent that both of these projects—celebrating race and abolishing it—depend upon a conception of race as a social fact, I want to argue that neither can succeed. We cannot think of race as a social fact, like slavery or—to take the analogy that is even more fundamental to the project of race treason—like class. If, as Ignatiev puts it, "race, like class, is 'something which in fact happens'", then—and this is the project of race treason—it can be "made to unhappen". I will argue that race is not like class, that it neither happens nor can be made to

116

unhappen. And despite those who wish to 'respect and preserve' rather than abolish race, I will argue it makes no more sense to respect racial difference than it does to try to abolish it. Indeed, the very impulse to preserve race reveals the degree to which those who imagine that their accounts of race are 'anti-essentialist' or 'performative' remain, in fact, committed to racial essentialism.

My criticism of the idea that race is a social construction is not a defense of racial essentialism. Rather, I want to insist that our actual racial practices, the way people talk about and theorize race, however 'anti-essentialist', can be understood only as the expression of our commitment to the idea that race is *not* a social construction, and I want to insist that if we give up that commitment, we must give up the idea of race altogether. Either race is an essence or there is no such thing as race. Regardless, there can be no ex-black or ex-white men. If race, to be what it is, *must* be essential, then Johnson's ex-colored man, because he once was black, can never stop being black; if there is no such thing as race, then the race traitors' ex-white men, because they never were white, can never stop being white. Either race is the sort of thing that makes rejecting your racial identity just a kind of passing, or passing becomes impossible and there is no such thing as racial identity.

*

How, then, is passing possible? To an anti-essentialist, the question could be put this way: How is it possible to pass for something without becoming what it is you pass for? To an essentialist, the question could be put slightly differently: How is it possible to pass at all? What must race be in order for it to be the sort of thing that can be concealed? In a racial system where racial identity is a function of physical appearance— where it is the color of your skin rather than some fact about your ancestry that determines your racial identity—this may be almost impossible. For if your racial identity is determined by your physical appearance (if being dark-skinned makes you black and being pale-skinned makes you white), then the only way to pass is by concealing or somehow altering the color of your skin.

The choice between altering or concealing—or, more precisely, the possibility of concealing by altering—raises a further question: if you do somehow manage to alter the color of your skin, are you really passing? Are you pretending to belong to one race when you really belong to another, or have you in fact stopped belonging to one race and begun instead to belong to the other? A relevant analogy here would be the transsexual. We probably don't want to say that the transsexual is passing, and if we do say that the transsexual is passing, we are required to come up with some account of how a person's *body* can be changed from one sex to another without the *person*'s being changed from one sex to another—of where or what the truth is that's being concealed by the alteration. In *Black Skin, White Masks*, Frantz Fanon imagines "a serum for 'denegrification'" designed to make it possible for the Negro "to whiten himself". Were there actually to be such a serum, would we want to say that the person who used it was now able to pass for white, or would we want to say that the person now was white?

Under the American racial system, however—under the rule that one drop of black blood makes a person black—passing need not require any physical transformation. In Johnson's novel, given the 'ivory whiteness' of his skin, the ex-colored man simply grows a mustache and changes his name. Where physical appearance, in other words, does not *determine* racial identity but is only a sign of it, you can pass without altering your body in any way. But to say that the one-drop rule makes passing possible without requiring physical transformation is not, of course, to say that it makes the body irrelevant. After all, even if we acknowledge that the concept of black or white blood has no biological currency nowadays, we can still understand the appeal to blood as a metaphor for whatever thing there is in the body that does determine your race—your genes, for example. Under the one-drop rule, then, for a black person to pass for white is for that person to conceal whatever it is in his or her body that identifies her as being black. But since it is possible to pass only because that thing is already invisible, passing is therefore less a matter of hiding something than of refusing or failing to acknowledge something.

Racial identity under the one-drop rule thus emerges as something that is not only embodied (in the sense that the one drop is in the body) but must also be represented (since, without representation, the fact that it's in the body cannot be known). This nonidentity of the truth of one's race and the representation of that truth opens up—indeed, constitutes— the entire field of racialized discourse. At the simplest level, it inserts race into the field of ethics: if your racial identity is invisible, it becomes something you can lie about or something you can tell the truth about, something you can conceal or reveal. In itself, however, this possibility is of only limited significance. After all, hair color is also something you can conceal or reveal. But hair color, while it can be misrepresented, cannot be represented. If your hair is black, you can dye it blond and misrepresent its true color, but if you leave it black, you will not represent black hair, you will just have black hair. That race can be invisible, however, means that it *must* be either misrepresented or represented, since to leave it unrepresented will be to misrepresent it. In other words, if you are invisibly black, either you must find some way to represent your blackness or you must pass for white. Thus it is that the possibility of passing opens up the whole field of racialized discourse. The discourse of race is the discourse of people who can pass but who do not wish to.

This is true despite the fact that comparatively few people can pass. For it is the mere conceptual possibility of passing that proclaims the essential invisibility of race, that takes the color even of people who can't pass (the vast majority) and changes it from the *fact* that constitutes their race into a *representation* of the fact that constitutes their race. This is why a writer like Howard Winant can plausibly say, in *Racial Conditions*, that "race is not a matter of color alone. . . . It is more like a way of life, a way of being." That is, since color does not determine race, color must be understood as only one way—and not necessarily the most important way—of manifesting race. The possibility of belonging to a race of people who don't look like you produces the possibility of manifesting your racial identity in your actions—of acting black or white. It produces, in other words, the idea that certain actions (and we would wish to include under the rubric of 'action' beliefs and values as well as practices, all those things that might be said to constitute one's culture) properly accompany certain identities. Regardless of skin color, there are ways to act black or white. And once we recognize this, we recognize also that even if you *can't* pass (even if you can't help but look like what you are), you can still fail to act like what you are.

Thus the conceptual possibility of passing not only makes available, to those whose physical appearance is such that they *can* pass, the option of revealing or concealing their racial identity; it makes available to everyone the option of being loyal or disloyal to their race—of embracing or repudiating the way of life that their race supplies. Because race is invisible, all the things that make it visible are reduced to mere representations of a racial identity located elsewhere. At the same time, however, because race cannot be reduced to any of its representations, anything and everything can be understood as a representation of it. It is only because the thing itself is invisible that everything can be imagined as a way of seeing it.

*

The invisibility of race makes an important contribution to its power, which is why early American racial thought was always tempted to locate a person's racial identity not merely in a part of the person that's hard to see—the blood—but in a part of the person that's impossible to see—the soul. Indeed, locating race in the soul rather than the body makes the body itself only a representation of racial essence; it makes race immune to the fantasy of the denegrification serum, for what is not actually in the body cannot be affected by the alteration of the body. And in contemporary racial thought—in racial thought at the end of the twentieth century rather than at the beginning—the repudiation of the body as the site of racial identity makes the fantasy of biological denegrification equally irrelevant. But racial thought today—which is to say, the commitment to race as a social construction—understands itself as anti-essentialist, not as a kind of essentialism.

The claim that race is socially constructed is the claim that race is not a biological entity, that there is nothing in people's bodies—visible or invisible—that constitutes their racial identity. There is, in other words, no such thing as black or white blood and no genetic equivalent to it. As biologist Richard C. Lewontin puts it[1], "'Race' is simply not a category that biologists and anthropologists still take seriously, although as a social phenomenon race still has a compelling reality." But if we don't think that race is in the soul, and we don't think it's in the body, where do we think it is? What kind of reality is the compelling reality of race today?

One way that we might characterize this reality is as the reality of a mistake. Even if race is not a biological fact, many people have believed in it as such, and some people, no doubt, continue to do so. And this belief, mistaken though it may be, has obviously had and no doubt continues to have significant consequences. So we might think that the reality of race consists in the fact that we live in a world that is still organized along racial lines. And the point of our new knowledge—the knowledge that there are no biological races—would be to undo the consequences of our old ignorance, to produce a world in which race was *not* a compelling reality.

Those who are committed to 'the social construction of race', however, even the race traitors, clearly do not think of racial reality as a mistake; they do not think of race as the sort of thing which, if it doesn't exist in nature, doesn't exist at all. In a well-known passage in *Anti-Semite and Jew*, Sartre says that in the eyes of the anti-Semite, what makes the Jew a Jew "is the presence in him of 'Jewishness', a Jewish principle analogous to phlogiston". But when people stopped believing that phlogiston existed in nature, they didn't start believing that phlogiston was a social construction. Which is only to say that the claim that there are no races in nature—that race is a social construction—is not meant to deny that there is such a thing as race; it is meant to give us a better account of what race is. So if we say that because there are no races in nature, racial thinking is just 'an illusion', the social constructionist thinks that we have missed the point. If, on the one hand, as Michael Omi and Howard Winant put it in *Racial Formation in the United States*, it is a mistake to "think of race as an *essence*, as something fixed, concrete and objective", it is, on the other hand, also a mistake "to see it as a mere illusion, which an ideal social order would eliminate". Those who think of race as a biological fact make the first mistake; those who think of it as mere 'ideology' and argue for the desirability of a 'color-blind' society make the second. But 'race consciousness' is not 'false consciousness'. Indeed, to say that because there are no races in nature, there are no races, must be on this view as much a non sequitur as it would be to say that because there are no classes in nature, there are no classes. And just as the denial of the importance of class is a hallmark of liberalism, the denial of race is a strategy of what is now called 'liberal racism'.

On this account, race is a compelling reality in the way that social class is, and the argument that because there is no racial phlogiston there are no races looks as politically problematic as its converse, namely, the anti-Semite's commitment to the principle of Jewishness. For Sartre, too, it is only the liberal who says that because there is no Jewish phlogiston, "there are no Jews", and he does so out of his individualist hostility to the very idea of class. Fearing the "great collective forms" that threaten liberal democracy, the democrat seeks "to persuade individuals that they exist in an isolated State": "he fears that the Jew will acquire a consciousness of the Jewish collectivity—just as he fears that a 'class consciousness' may awaken in the worker." From this standpoint, then, the mistake of the liberal both repeats and corrects the mistake of the anti-Semite; the liberal is wrong to assert the reality of the 'individual' and to deny the reality of the class, but he is right to analogize the consciousness of Jewish identity to the consciousness of class identity— to see, in effect, that if there are Jews, they don't need a Jewish 'essence' any more than, say, the workers need a proletarian essence, or the middle class needs a bourgeois essence.

The proletariat and the bourgeoisie don't need an essence because they are who they are, Sartre says, by virtue of "an ensemble of various modes of *behavior*". On the model of class identity, racial identity too would be what it is often said to be today: performative.

A truly performative conception of race would make passing impossible. For the space of passing, as we have already seen, is the space of representation, which is to say that passing is possible because we must in our actions either represent or misrepresent our race. But the possibility of representing or misrepresenting our race depends, as we have also already seen, on the nonidentity of the racial representation and the racial reality. And the idea of race as performative undoes this nonidentity; it eliminates the reality—the blood or the soul—and thus transforms the actions that *represent* racial identity into the actions that *determine* racial identity. Passing becomes impossible because, in the logic of social constructionism, it is impossible not to *be* what you are passing for.

This is the dream of what *Race Traitor* calls 'crossover'—the dream that by ceasing to act white you can cease to be white—and it is this dream that produces both the distinctive technology and the distinctive anxiety of putative ex-white men. The distinctive technology is what Johnson disparagingly called 'imitation', what the race traitors describe more hopefully as 'borrowing' from black culture. The distinctive anxiety is about whether and when such borrowing can succeed, about whether and when white people acting like black people can cease to count as exploiting black people and can begin to count instead as becoming, if not black, at least 'mulatto'. Thus, although Paul Garon, a music writer and editor at *Living Blues* magazine, appears in *Race Traitor* as a reproachfully Johnsonian figure, criticizing "white blues" as "a weak and imitative form", the cultural project of race treason will be to reconceive imitation as inspiration and to celebrate in particular those white musicians who, in the words of Albert Murray, "embrace certain Negroes not only as kindred spirits but as ancestral figures".

Because the difference between imitation and inspiration depends on the ontological priority of racial identity—you are inspired by what you are, you imitate what you aren't—*Race Traitor*'s "Crossover Dreams" depend on undoing it. They depend, in other words, on the idea that since race is a social construction, there is nothing about the bodies of black people that makes those bodies more suited to playing the blues than white bodies. And since even Garon acknowledges that "neither genes nor race-differentiated experience seem to affect one's ability to form certain chords or play certain melodies", it's hard to see by what criteria the efforts of white people to play the blues can count as more imitative than the efforts of black people, or by what criteria the 'white blues' can count as a more 'imitative form' than the black blues. Indeed, since a formal description of the blues requires no reference to the color of those who perform it (any more than a formal description of the sonnet does), and since the very idea of a musical 'form' is itself dependent on the possibility of imitation, it's hard to see how there can be any formal difference between black and white blues. The white musician who learns to form the chords and play the melodies is, the objections of Johnson and Garon notwithstanding, no more or less committed to imitation than the black musician.

But the same argument that works against the idea that crossovers are somehow imitative and inferior also works against the idea that crossovers are actually crossing over. If you needn't *be* black to play the blues, you don't *become* black by playing the blues. Race no more follows music than music follows race; what you become by playing the blues is a blues musician, not a black person. Thus the distinction between white blues and black blues must be understood as a distinction between two kinds of people, not between two kinds of music. What makes the music you are playing black is the fact that you are black; what gives the music its color is the color of the people who are playing it. If, then, it is only the anti-essentialist conception of race that makes the project of crossover possible (because only an anti-essentialist conception makes it possible for you to stop being white by giving up white behavior), it is only an essentialist conception of race that makes it desirable (because only an essentialist conception of race makes your behavior white and thus makes it something you can give up). So although the goal of the ex-white man (crossing over) is fundamentally opposed to the goal of the ex-colored man (passing), the fact that people *want* to cross over, like the fact that people *can* pass, turns out to be a tribute to essentialism.

The anti-essentialist performative is in this sense a version of the essentialist denegrification serum: if race is a biological fact, then to change the color of your skin is to change your race; if race is a mode of behavior, then to change your 'way of life' is to change your race. But because race, as Winant says, is "not a matter of color alone", you can't change your race by changing your skin. And because race, in not being a "matter of color *alone*", must nevertheless still be a matter of color, you can't change your race by changing your 'way of life' either. It must still be a matter of color because without the appeal to color there can be nothing distinctively *racial* about your 'way of life': the social con-structionist commitment to the racial performative, in other words, is only skin deep. It involves not the choice of behavior over color but the adjustment of behavior to color.

*

This is true even if we focus not on racial but on what is today called cultural identity. In the preface to the most recent American edition of *Anti-Semite and Jew*, Michael Walzer criticizes Sartre for presenting what he calls an 'empty Jewishness', one without either religious or cultural content. But the Jewish religion is irrelevant to Sartre, because insofar as Jewishness is understood as a matter of religious belief and practice, the Jew is a Jew only in the way that, say, a Methodist is a Methodist or a member of the Elks Club is an Elk. We don't need anti-essentialist accounts of Elks; their identities are purely performative, which is to say that they are entirely constituted by (rather than represented by) behavior. But a Jew does not become Jewish in the same way that an Elk becomes an Elk, and, of course, a Jew cannot resign as a Jew in the same way that an Elk can resign from the Elks Club.

Another way to put this is to say that Sartre sees that Jewishness is not a matter of biology or a 'metaphysical essence' (that's the point of his denial of a Jewish phlogiston). On the other hand, he also sees that a 'principle of Jewishness' cannot simply be replaced by a set of Jewish practices: the anti-Semite hates what the Jew does only insofar as those practices represent what the Jew is. We can put this point more generally and more positively by noting that the celebration of difference in contemporary multiculturalism depends entirely on our thinking of people's cultural identities as expressed by (rather than constituted by) their practices. Why else should we not just tolerate but esteem actions that may seem to us wrong and beliefs that may seem to us mistaken? If, for example, we think that male circumcision is cruel and pointless, why should we allow it? If we think that female circumcision is even more cruel and equally pointless, why should we allow it? If we value such practices, we do so not because they seem to us intrinsically valuable but because they seem to represent identities that are valuable. So just as it is only the difference between one's identity and one's actions that makes passing possible, it is only the difference between one's identity and one's actions that makes the celebration of difference plausible. And if, as I have argued above, passing is a kind of tribute to essentialism, so, too, is the celebration of cultural difference—it is indeed only if difference is essential that it can, as such, be celebrated.

Sartre is right, then, to insist not only that the Jew is not a Jew because of his Jewish body or his Jewish soul but also that doing Jewish things does not make him a Jew. But if there is no Jewish body and there is no Jewish soul and there are no Jewish things to do, what's left? "We must now", Sartre says, "ask ourselves the question: does the Jew exist?" The liberal, as we have already seen, says no. But the liberal's answer cannot be accepted, because the liberal also (and for the same reasons) denies that the worker exists. The analogy between the Jew and the worker is problematic, because the worker who saves a lot of money and buys himself a factory becomes a capitalist and ceases to be a worker, while the Jew cannot—by, say, converting to Catholicism—cease to be a Jew. So the fact that workers exist doesn't mean that Jews must also exist. And yet, Sartre insists, the Jew does exist. In what amounts to the degree zero of social constructionism, Sartre famously asserts that the Jew is not someone who has a Jewish body or soul or religion or culture: "The Jew is one whom other men consider a Jew."

It is being considered a Jew that constitutes the Jew's 'situation'. The Jew, of course, is not alone in being in a situation; on the contrary, everyone is in some situation; some "ensemble of limits and restrictions" "forms" everyone and "decides" everyone's "possibilities". But not everyone's situation is the same, and not everyone deals with his or her situation in the same way. The Jew has two ways of dealing with his. One way is by "running away from it". The "inauthentic Jew" denies his Jewishness, either by denying that he himself is Jewish or by denying that there are such things as Jews—indeed, by espousing "a conception of the world that excludes the very idea of race". The authentic Jew, by contrast, not only accepts the Jewishness the world imposes on him but himself chooses that Jewishness; if inauthenticity is "to deny . . . or attempt to escape from" one's "condition as a Jew", "authenticity . . . is to live [it] to the full". The authentic Jew "asserts his claim" as a Jew.

But what claim does the Jew, as Jew, have? The inauthentic Jew claims to be a man like other men, but it is precisely this universalism that makes him inauthentic. The authentic Jew, on the other hand, "abandons the myth of the universal man" and replaces it with a "social pluralism". But, as we have already seen, this pluralism cannot be understood along the lines of a pluralism that would value Jewish culture. There is no such thing as Jewish culture, Sartre thinks, which is to say that because the assimilated Jew remains Jewish, it cannot be his culture that makes him Jewish—and when the anti-Semite calls you a Jew, it is your 'essence', not your culture, that he is naming. So if to be a Jew is only to be called a Jew, one's claim as a Jew—one's claim to be what one is called—cannot be the claim to a culture; it can only be the claim to that essence.

The virtue of Sartre's analysis is that it makes clear the irreducibility of the notion of essence to identity. Insofar as it is the 'situation' (and only the situation) of the Jew that confers upon him his Jewishness, Jewishness is defined without recourse to essence. But the situation in which the Jew finds himself is the situation of having a Jewish essence attributed to him (as it happens, by anti- Semites, but the theoretical position would be no different if those who made the Jew a Jew by considering him to be a Jew liked Jews), and insofar as the situation in which the Jew finds himself is the situation of having a Jewish essence attributed to him, and insofar as the authentic Jew makes himself authentic by *choosing* the situation in which the anti-Semite has placed him, the authentic Jew makes himself authentic by choosing essence.

*

Citing Sartre's famous depiction of the *garçon de café* in the opening pages of *Being and Nothingness*, Anthony Appiah has recently argued (in *Color Conscious*) that it makes no sense to ask of the waiter what it does make sense to ask of "the black and the white, the homosexual and the heterosexual"—whether he "really is" a waiter. This is because, to use the terms we have derived from *Anti-Semite and Jew*, the waiter is more like a religious Jew (or an Elk) than he is like the racialized Jew identified by the anti-Semite. As Appiah writes, "there can be a gap between what a person . . . is and the racial identity he performs". Therefore, racial identity—unlike religious or professional identity—cannot be understood simply as the 'performance' of a 'role'. It is this gap, Appiah notes, "that makes passing possible", and if, as we have already seen, the possibility of passing is constitutive of racial identity, then racial identity, Appiah writes, is, "in this way, like all the major forms of identification that are central to contemporary identity politics: female and male; gay, lesbian and straight; black, white, yellow . . . even that most neglected of American identities, class".

But to what extent is being gay or straight like being black or white? To what extent is being middle class or working class like being black or white? It certainly is true that there is a sense in which gay men can pass as straight—a sense, that is, in which a gay man can act straight without thereby becoming straight. But it is only a very limited sense. A gay man can pass as straight by behaving like a straight man, but a gay man who not only behaved like a straight man but also desired what straight men desire and thought of himself as straight would no longer be passing as straight—he would be straight. Gay behavior does not *represent* one's sexuality, it *determines* it. Ontologically speaking, a gay man is like a religious Jew. And what is true of religion and sexuality is even more obviously true of class. The *garçon de café* who saves his tips and buys the café is not a member of the proletariat passing as a member of the petit bourgeoisie—he *is* petit bourgeois. Although there aren't any ex-white or ex-black men, there may well be ex-straight and ex-gay men, and there definitely are ex-waiters and ex-religious Jews.

Race, then, is not like class, and the Jew's reasons for wanting to get rid of race are not the same as the socialist's reasons for wanting to get rid of class: the inauthentic Jew, wishing for an end to racial difference, does so not on the grounds that it is unjust but on the grounds that it is unreal. What the inauthentic Jew and the socialist *do* have in common is their hostility to the very idea of identity; their hostility, that is, to the idea that their bodies, beliefs, and behavior represent rather than determine what they are. The inauthentic Jew expresses this hostility by denying that he is a Jew—since his body isn't Jewish and he does not believe in Judaism. (If there are no essences, there are no identities.) And the socialist expresses his hostility in the same way—by dividing the world not into Jews and Aryans and blacks and whites but instead into workers and capitalists. Owning the means of production does not represent your identity, it constitutes that identity.

It makes no sense, then, to require of the capitalist or the worker what Sartre requires of the Jew—that he assert his claim as a Jew, that he demand recognition for what he is. One doesn't have such a claim as a capitalist, or even as a worker—the worker's claim is based on what she does (that's the point, after all, of calling her a worker). It makes sense, in other words, to think of class as a social construction because it doesn't make sense to think of class as an identity—your class is determined by what you do. And it doesn't make sense to think of race (of Jewishness or blackness or whiteness) as a social construction, because racial identity is irreducible to action. The identity that is irreducible to action is essential, not socially constructed, and the identity that is identical to action is not really an identity—it's just the name of the action: worker, capitalist. If, then, we do not believe in racial identity as an essence, we cannot believe in racial identity as a social construction and we ought to give up the idea of racial identity altogether—we should, like the inauthentic Jew, deny that there are such things as Jews, or blacks, or whites.

But the race traitor, denying that he is white, does not deny that there are such things as whites and blacks. On the contrary: "'I'm black and I'm proud'", Ignatiev says, is "the modern rendition of 'Workers of all countries, unite!'" Race treason treats race 'like class' by turning class into race, turning one's relation to the means of production into one's identity and turning the abolition of private property into the abolition of whiteness. Where economic inequality is the problem, then socialism may be the solution; where whiteness is the problem, blackness is the solution. Thus the "many failings" of America are now understood to "result largely from the unwillingness of so-called whites to embrace" the "presence of Afro-Americans" without "qualification". And, as identity replaces ideology, the way to correct these failings is to recognize how much "the distinctive character of America owes . . . to the presence of Afro-Americans." Ignatiev notes with surprise and approval the columnist George Will's observation that because basketball is the "most American of all sports" and black people are "the most American of all Americans", black people are "the most accomplished of basketball players". He approves Will's remark because it honors the 'presence' of blacks; he is surprised by it because Will is 'conservative'. But if 'I'm black and I'm proud' can be "the modern rendition of 'Workers of all countries, unite'", which is to say, if hostility to private property can be replaced by pride in Michael Jordan, then the sense in which George Will is conservative (or the sense in which race traitors are not) needs to be reassessed.

The "most subversive act I can imagine", Ignatiev says, is "treason to the white race". The failure of political imagination involved here is, perhaps, obvious. But my point has not been to demonstrate the unpleasant political consequences of seeking to be an ex-white man; it has been, rather, to demonstrate the impossibility of actually being an ex-white man. If there is such a thing as whiteness and you are white, you cannot stop being white, and if there is no such thing as whiteness, you also can't stop being white. But whiteness is not—like class—a social construction. It is instead—like phlogiston—a mistake.

WALTER BENN MICHAELS

Believing in Unicorns

The historian Barbara Fields and her sister, the sociologist Karen Fields, open *Racecraft*, their collection of linked essays [1], by denying that there are such things as races. Race today does not, they point out, refer to "a traditionally named group of people" but to "a statistically defined population". So, for example, the determining factor in susceptibility to sickle cell anaemia, long thought of as a 'black disease', is whether you have ancestors from sub-Saharan Africa, which many of the people we think of as black do not, and some of the people we think of as white do. So, too, the relevant genetic information about a person is individual and familial, not racial. A person's height, for example, is determined mainly by the height of his or her actual ancestors, partly by environmental factors, and not at all by the statistical entity that counts as his or her race. Thus, against developments like the growing demand for more 'accurate' racial designations and the recognition of biracial and multiracial identities, the Fieldses remind us that there are no accurate racial designations and no bi or multiracial identities. Genetically speaking, it makes no more sense to describe someone with, say, a Chinese mother and a Norwegian father as a person of mixed race than it would to describe someone with a tall mother and a short father as a person of mixed height. That we even have the idea there is such a thing as mixed race is a testament to our disarticulation of race from biological facts.

Which is where racecraft comes in. If today there is widespread agreement about the inadequacy of race as a biological concept, agreement is just as widespread that race is instead a social construction or, as the Fieldses put it, a "social fact"—"like six o'clock, both an idea and a reality". In *Racial Formation in the United States* (1986), the theorists of race Michael Omi and Howard Winant urged us not only to resist the 'temptation' to think of race as a biological essence but also and especially to resist the temptation to conclude that if it isn't biological it's a "mere *illusion*, a purely ideological construct which some ideal non-racist social order would eliminate". We aren't, after all, tempted to think that because it's never six o'clock in nature six o'clock is an illusion. Why should the fact that there are no races in nature cause us to doubt the existence of race?

But the neologism 'racecraft' is modelled on 'witchcraft', and is intended to suggest just such doubts. It isn't that the Fieldses regard the commitment to race as a category as an irrational superstition. On the contrary, they are interested precisely in exploring its rationality—the role that beliefs about race play in structuring American society—while at the same time reminding us that those beliefs may be rational but they're not true. As Tzvetan Todorov pointed out a long time ago, the fact that some women were once thought of as witches and sometimes burned as witches did not make them witches, even socially constructed ones, and the conceptual incoherence of the social construction of race is at least as clear. We no longer believe that one drop of black blood makes a black person, not because we think it takes more than one drop but because we don't think there is any such thing as black blood. What we think instead is that social practices like Jim Crow racialized both black and white populations. Of course, the people who invented and enforced Jim Crow did think there was such a thing as black blood, and although they were mistaken, their views were at least coherent: if there are such things as black blood or white genes, then the people who have them are indeed black and white. Once it was discovered that this wasn't true, however, there were no longer grounds for people to continue treating each other as black or white. If I say that I treat you as black because I think you have black genes, I've given you a bad reason; if I say I treat you as black not because you have black genes but because I used to think you had black genes, I haven't given you any reason at all.

The point is the same when people on whom race was imposed impose it instead on themselves. Some of the women who were burned as witches may have believed they were witches. But they were wrong. In an early defense of social construction, Sartre described a Jew not as someone with Jewish blood but as someone whom others take to have Jewish blood. And his advice was, essentially, choose to be what they say you are. But how, exactly, can you follow this advice? If you think you're a Jew only because they think you're a Jew, and they think you're a Jew only because they believe in Jewish blood, what does your Jewishness consist in other than an endorsement of their error?

The Fieldses aren't interested merely in exposing racecraft's incoherence; they want to "eliminate" it "from the fabric of our lives". That is, while agreeing with all those who think it ludicrous that events like Obama's election are treated as if they ushered the United States into a 'postracial' era, they believe that a postracial era would be a good thing. Why? Because, they argue, the "falsities" of racecraft, like those of witchcraft, "lead to moral error and human suffering". And, much more controversially, because those "falsities" deprive Americans of any "legitimate language for talking about class" and thus make it "all but impossible" to "talk about class inequality".

What makes this second argument controversial is that "attacks on the use of race as a concept" appear to anti-racist writers like David Roediger as a "distressingly new" critique of anti-racism, all the more unsettling because it comes from the left—which *Racecraft* does. In her brilliant essay of 1990, "Slavery, Race and Ideology in the United States of America" (reprinted in *Racecraft*), Barbara Fields criticized American historians precisely for treating race and racism as if they were autonomous from capitalism. Slavery, she argued, was not an expression of racism, much less, as one hapless scholar had described it, "the ultimate segregator"; if Europeans were "seeking the 'ultimate' method of segregating Africans", why did they "go to the trouble and expense of transporting them across the ocean for that purpose, when they could have achieved the same end so much more simply by leaving the Africans in Africa". The Fieldses argue that "liberals" and "progressives" and "spokesmen for affirmative action" remain "unable to promote or even define justice except by enhancing the authority and prestige of race", thus showing a failure to understand that anti-racism—which is a commitment to "the reallocation of unemployment, poverty and injustice rather than their abolition"—can be just as useful to capitalism as racism has been.

What makes people angry is that this insistence on the importance of what the Fieldses call 'class inequality' seems to make light of racial inequality. Writing in 2006, Roediger pointed out that "white family wealth" was "about ten times that of black family wealth", and what at the time he called the "color-blind" commitment to the importance of class no doubt seems even less tenable to him now: the net worth of black households has dropped by fifty-three per cent since 2006, while the median worth of white households has fallen by only sixteen per cent. In the face of such disparities, what can it mean to insist on the emptiness of race as a category or on the limits, let alone the irrelevance, of anti-racism as a left politics?

The question raised by *Racecraft*, however, is not what it means to ignore such disparities, but rather what it means to insist on them. In particular, what does it mean to insist on them as the lens through which to see the problem of inequality? The short (analytic rather than historical) answer is that the focus on disparities between black and white renders those between rich and poor invisible. African Americans today are disproportionately poor; whites are disproportionately rich. But a world in which those proportions were corrected would not be more equal; it would just be differently unequal. In other words, as long as the problem is defined in terms of disparity between races, the solution can only be the 'reallocation' of poverty, not its 'abolition'. This solution does nothing for the white poor (except increase their numbers), and nothing for most of the black poor (except give them the dubious satisfaction of knowing that the injustice they're the victim of is no longer racism).

The longer (and more historical) answer begins by noting, as Adolph Reed and Merlin Chowkwanyun do in a recent paper in *Socialist Register*, that the discourse of disparity has come to the fore in the last thirty years, a period in which economic inequality has been rapidly increasing. What the "disparitarian perspective" represents, they argue, is not a critical alternative to that inequality but "a concern to create competitive individual minority agents who might stand a better fighting chance in the neoliberal rat race". No one, for example, thinks that sending more black students to elite universities will reduce inequality; what they think is that it will allow a few more black people to benefit from it. This is "a notable and striking reversal", they remark, "from even the more left-inclined of War on Poverty era liberals, who spoke without shame about moving beyond simply placing people on an equal starting line—'equality of opportunity'—but also making sure they ended up closer to an equal finishing line".[2]

Equality of opportunity is key here. In its minimal form, it requires an end to all forms of discrimination—racism, sexism, heterosexism etc. More robustly, it would also require that people not be victimized because of their class. Legally, of course, only race matters, which is what the Fieldses mean when they say that "once racecraft takes over the imagination, it shrinks well-founded criticism of inequality to fit crabbed moral limits, leaving the social grievances of white Americans without a language in which to frame them." Thus, even though the poor are by far the most under-represented group in American four-year colleges and universities, when Jennifer Gratz (the lower-middle-class daughter of a man who never went to college) won her case against the University of Michigan in 2003, her complaint was of discrimination against white people. Abigail Fisher, the upper-middle-class daughter of a man who attended the very college that refused to admit her, and who thus belongs to a group that has no problem getting access to good colleges, has lodged exactly the same complaint, and her case is currently before the Supreme Court. In *Racecraft*'s terms, what we have is a situation in which poor white people can assert what is really a grievance against rich white people only by fighting a policy designed to benefit a few black people. And rich white people, by turn, can assert their class privilege over poor white people by fighting that same policy. The policy meanwhile is of no help to the black poor: "On highly selective campuses", according Richard Kahlenberg, a prominent proponent of class-based affirmative action, "86 per cent of African American students are middle or upper class." So while the true injustice of American higher education has been its increasing stratification by wealth, the debate about class that ought to have taken place has been almost entirely effaced by the debate about race.

Right now, while people wait for the court's decision in *Fisher*, the most hotly debated question about university admissions is whether Asian Americans (by every measure the wealthiest ethnic group in the US) are victims of discrimination at universities like Harvard and Princeton, where they make up twenty-one per cent of current first years. What the right percentage of rich Asian kids at Ivy League universities should be is a social problem of almost no importance—except in a world where discrimination is the only form of inequality anyone cares about and where what the Fieldses call the 'authority' of race is so great that it extends even to the way we think of class. Many critics of race-based affirmative action want to make it class-based instead. The odds are against them: today about forty-five per cent of Harvard students come from families with earnings in the top five per cent; about eighteen per cent come from families in the bottom sixty per cent. If we want proportionate representation, a lot of clever young rich people will have to go home. But suppose they succeed. Or, even better, suppose we manage to create a world in which every university is as good as Harvard and everyone—black and white, rich and poor—gets to go to one. And then let's imagine (actually we don't have to) a United States in which only about twenty per cent of jobs require a degree from a four-year college. Everybody has a fancy education but only about one person in five has a job which requires that education. Or rewards it. According to the Bureau of Labor Statistics, the fastest growing occupation in the US today is 'personal care aide' (second fastest is 'home health care aide'). The level of education required is 'less than high school'; the annual salary is $19,640. The people who currently end up in those jobs are disproportionately black and Latino and female and very badly educated. In our educational utopia, however, that won't be true. Instead of fifty-one per cent of such workers being non-Hispanic whites, sixty-three per cent will be; instead of virtually all of them being women, half will be, and instead of fifty-five per cent of them having at best a high-school diploma, all of them will have college degrees. But men or women, blacks or non-Hispanic whites, Kantians or Hegelians, they'll still be making $19,640. They won't be victims of discrimination, but they will be poor.

A perfectly non-discriminatory workplace is not one in which everybody has the right to what the Fieldses call 'a sustaining job'; it's one in which everybody has the right to compete for a sustaining job. Equality of opportunity doesn't mitigate inequality, it justifies it. Its primary beneficiaries are not employees but employers who, liberated from their own prejudices, now get to hire the best and the brightest rather than the mediocre but the whitest, and—as the neoliberal economist Gary Becker recognized decades ago—once the eligible workforce is increased, employers get to decrease that workforce's wages.

Racecraft's skepticism about race is thus at the same time a skepticism about the value of anti-racism. Not, obviously, because anti-racism is in itself wrong but because insofar as the racist/anti-racist opposition comes to define the terms of social justice, it leaves the conditions of social injustice intact. What they describe as the "ever expanding American immensity" of the "so-called racial divide"—"from hardy perennials like teenage pregnancy to novelties like . . . 'disproportionate representation' on Twitter"—plays a foundational role in maintaining this opposition. And that, for the Fieldses, is the point of taking racecraft seriously. When people stopped believing in the biological reality of unicorns, they didn't start believing in unicorns as a social construction because nobody's economic order was propped up by the unicorn. But we hang on to race—to racism and anti-racism—because race, unlike the unicorn, appears to be something we can't live without.

ADOLPH REED, JR.

From Jenner to Dolezal:
One Trans Good, the Other Not So Much

By far the most intellectually and politically interesting thing about the recent 'exposé' of Spokane, Washington, NAACP activist Rachel Dolezal's racial status is the conundrum it has posed for racial identitarians who are also committed to defense of transgender identity. The comparisons between Dolezal and Republican Jenner (I've decided to opt for that referent because it is an identity continuous between 'Bruce' and 'Caitlyn' and is moreover the one most meaningful to me) began almost instantly, particularly as a flood of mass-mediated Racial Voices who support the legitimacy of transgender identity objected strenuously to suggestions that Dolezal's representation, and apparent perception, of herself as black is similar to Bruce Jenner's perception of himself as actually Caitlyn. Their contention is that one kind of claim to an identity at odds with culturally constructed understandings of the identity appropriate to one's biology is OK but that the other is not—that it's OK to feel like a woman when you don't have the body of a woman and to act like (and even get yourself the body of) a woman but that it's wrong to feel like a black person when you're actually white and that acting like you're black and doing your best to get yourself the body of a black person is just lying.

The way Zeba Blay puts it, on the Black Voices section of the *HuffPo*, is by declaring how important it is to "make one thing clear: transracial identity is *not* a thing".[1] What is clear is that it's not at all clear what that statement is supposed to mean. It seems to suggest that transracial identity is not something that has been validated by public recognition, or at least that Blay has not heard of or does not recognize it. But there's an obvious problem with this contention. There was a moment, not that long ago actually, when transgender identity was not a 'thing' in that sense either. Is Blay's contention that we should accept transgender identity only because it is now publicly recognized? If so, the circularity is obvious, and the lack of acceptance arguably only a matter of time. Transgender wasn't always a thing—just ask Christine Jorgensen.

But the more serious charge is the moral one, that, as Michelle Garcia puts it, "It's pretty clear: Dolezal has lied."[2] But here too, it's not clear what's so clear. Is the point supposed to be that Dolezal is lying when she says she identifies as black? Or is it that being black has nothing to do with how you identify? The problem with the first claim is obvious—how do they know? And on what grounds does Jenner get to be telling the truth and Dolezal not? But the problem with the second claim is even more obvious since if you think there's some biological fact of the matter about what race people actually belong to utterly independent of what race they think they belong to, you're committed to a view of racial difference as biologically definitive in a way that's even deeper than sexual difference.

Blay attempts to deal with these issues by quoting Darnell L. Moore of *Mic.com*'s analysis that "in attempting to pass as black, Dolezal falsely represented her identity. Trans people don't lie about their gender identities—they express their gender according to categories that reflect who they are."[3] This claim has recurred in various formulations. Meredith Talusan asserts it most emphatically in *The Guardian*:

> The fundamental difference between Dolezal's actions and trans people's is that her decision to identify as black was an active choice, whereas transgender people's decision to transition is almost always involuntary. Transitioning is the product of a fundamental aspect of our humanity—gender—being foisted upon us over and over again from the time of our birth in a manner inconsistent with our own experience of our genders. Doctors don't announce our race or color when we are born; they announce our gender.

People who are alienated from their presumed gender and define themselves according to another gender have existed since earliest recorded history; race is a medieval European invention. Thus, Dolezal identified as black, but I am a woman, and other trans people are the gender they feel themselves to be.[4]

This assessment is mind-bogglingly wrong-headed, but it is at the same time thus deeply revealing of the contradictoriness and irrationality that undergird so much self-righteous identitarian twaddle. First of all, as I've already suggested, the claim that Dolezal's identity is false and transgendered people's are true immediately provokes a 'Who says?'. What makes Talusan's and other transgender people's identities authentic is that they believe them to be authentic. We agree to accept transgender people's expression of belief in their authenticity. It's fine for Talusan or others to say that they are convinced that the identities they embrace are their real ones in some way that is not limited by their biology at birth. However, the logic of the pluralism and open-endedness of identity they assert would require that they also accept the self-reports of claims to authenticity regarding identities that may diverge in other ways from convention. Certainly, not doing so necessitates some justification more persuasive—and less Archie Bunkerish—than simply asserting 'Mine is genuine, theirs is not'. The voluntary/involuntary criterion isn't even sophistry; it's just bullshit. Once again, who says? Who gave Talusan, Moore, Blay and others the gifts of telepathic mindreading and ventriloquy? How do we know that Dolezal may not sense that she is 'really' black in the same, involuntary way that many transgender people feel that they are 'really' transgender?

The related complaint that Dolezal's self-representation is inauthentic because she 'lied' about her identity is equally fatuous. To stay within the identitarian paradigm, what did Republican Jenner do for more than six decades of operating as Bruce? What does any transgender person do before the moment of coming out?

Michelle Garcia, also at *Mic.com*, asks, imagining that her question is a trump, "If Caitlyn Jenner can identify as a woman, why can't Rachel Dolezal say that she's black?" But why should that be the definitive criterion for accepting the self-representation? Who made that rule? Could there be something about public expectations at this point regarding the fixity of racial boundaries that would stay Dolezal from taking the bold step of announcing that she had always 'known' herself to be black? The furor that has surrounded the 'exposé' would suggest that is the case. Would she have felt free to do so if public awareness already accepted the possibility of racial identity as not necessarily tied to official classification? I have no idea whether she would have, and Garcia doesn't either. And, again, what about the sixty-plus years before Republican Jenner emerged publicly as Caitlyn? Was his privately embraced identity as Caitlyn bogus for all those years because he didn't, or felt he couldn't, go public with it?

This brings me to the most important point that this affair throws into relief. It has outed the essentialism on which those identitarian discourses rest. Garcia asks "So why don't we just accept Dolezal as black? Because she's not." But why is she not black in Garcia's view? Well, "Her parents say she's not even close to being black." But what would that mean—that she has no known black ancestry? Is blackness, then, a matter of hypodescent after all? But, if that's what it is, then what politically significant meaning does the category have? Dolezal no doubt has her issues and idiosyncrasies, but, especially if the judgment of the NAACP counts for anything in the matter, I'm pretty sure I'd take her in a trade for Clarence Thomas, Cory Booker, Condi Rice, and five TFA pimps to be named later. Or would Dolezal's 'not even close to being black' mean that she was raised outside of 'authentic' black idiom or cultural experience? But whose black idiom or cultural experience would that be? Is there really an irreducible, definitive one? If so, on which Racial Voice blog or Ivy League campus might we find it?

The essentialism cuts in odd ways in this saga. Sometimes race is real in a way that sex is not—you're black only if you meet the biological criteria (whatever they're supposed to be) for blackness. And sometimes, as in Talusan's failure to distinguish gender from sex typing, gender is 'real' in a way that race is not. "Doctors don't announce our race or color when we are born; they announce our gender." I assume Talusan is referring to the stereotypical moment in the delivery room. Technically, though, the doctor announces the child's sex type, not its culturally constructed gender roles. And when exactly does Talusan presume race is determined, and by whom? I'm pretty sure that in most of the United States it's still marked on one's birth certificate. That's not the delivery room, but it's pretty damn close.

Talusan's confusion of sex and gender is startlingly naïve. She contends that gender is a "product of a fundamental aspect of our humanity" and that, unlike race, the medieval European invention, gender is a "fundamental attribute" of our existence. But gender is no less culturally constructed than race. If Talusan were a little more curious anthropologically than precocious, she might have noticed that the relation between sex type and gender roles has varied wildly over the history and range of our species. But she, like Jenner, Hugh Hefner, and legions of anti-feminists, among others, naturalizes gender as melded into sex type: "Trans people transition in order to be the gender we feel inside." For those to whom it seems odd or tendentious to link the naturalizing discourses of some transgender activists and hoary anti-feminism, I recommend Elinor Burkett's fine rumination on the issue in the 6 June *New York Times*, titled "What Makes a Woman?"[5].

There is a guild-protective agenda underlying racial identitarians' outrage about Dolezal that is also quite revealing. Nikki Lynette, writing at *Red Eye*, exhorts "Don't Compare NAACP's Rachel Dolezal to Caitlyn Jenner".[6] Why? Because, she contends, Dolezal benefited materially from her self-representation as black. Putting aside for the moment Republican Jenner's orchestrated payday surrounding announcement and display of transition, this is an unusual charge, one that is counterintuitive in relation to several generations of black American humor and also smacks a bit of right-wingers' insinuations about whites taking advantage of affirmative action. Nevertheless, like Zeba Blay and others, Lynette rehearses a charge that Dolezal received a full scholarship to the Howard University MFA program on the pretext that she was a black woman. That charge is false; not only was she not admitted as black person (Howard's applications apparently didn't require racial identification); reports from faculty and students when she was there confirmed that she was not understood to be black when she was enrolled at the

university. See Hillary Crosley Coker, "When Rachel Dolezal Attended Howard, She Was Still White", at *Jezebel*.[7] The charge is what those
making it want to be true; they assume it's true because they understand
black racial classification as a form of capital.

Blay expresses this position most clearly. She objects that Dolezal
"occupied positions of power specifically designated for members of a
marginalized group". Blay is referring, in addition to the false accusa-
tion about the circumstances of Dolezal's matriculation at Howard, to
her having belonged, while an undergraduate at Belhaven College, to
"a racial reconciliation community development project where blacks
and whites lived together". Blay presents membership in that group as
though it were precursor to her having duped Howard out of a fellowship
that should have gone to a black woman. To Blay this pattern of duplic-
ity culminated in Dolezal's "eventually working her way up to president
of the Spokane NAACP in 2014". (Some have included a charge that
Dolezal used racial misrepresentation to advance an academic career;
an occasional stint as an adjunct instructor, however, doesn't square
with the Iggy Azalea imagery that seems to propel this claim. It certainly
would be a skimpy reward for such prodigious self-fashioning.) In Blay's
narrow political universe, the NAACP branch presidency is an honorific
to be awarded on the basis of ascriptive categories like race and gender,
not the result of effective work on behalf of the Association's mission
and goals. It is especially striking in this regard that a number of those
exercised by Dolezal have at least implicitly called for the NAACP to
renounce its support of her. Their commitment to arbitrary notions of
racial propriety should override the Association's sense of its own concrete priorities in the actual struggle for civil rights and social justice.

When all is said and done, the racial outrage is about protection of the
boundaries of racial authenticity as the exclusive property of the guild of
Racial Spokespersonship. (Blay also, with no hint of self-consciousness,
complains that Dolezal's deception has "hijacked the conversation about
race, during a week where the nation was focusing on police brutality
in McKinney, Texas". Not only is that insipid 'conversation about race'
chatter the equivalent of fingernails on a chalkboard. It seems that Blay
hasn't discerned that the Dolezal issue has captured such attention only

because it rankles the sensibilities of those who essentialize race and that no one is making her talk about it but herself.)

Beneath all the puerile cultural studies prattle about 'cultural appropriation'—which can only occur if 'culture' is essentialized as the property of what is in effect a 'race'[8]—'same heritage and social struggles' (I doubt that Nikki Lynette was at Greensboro on 1 February 1960, Ft. Wagner on 18 July 1863, Little Rock in September 1957, Colfax, Louisiana on 13 April 1873, the 1968 Memphis sanitation workers' strike, either of the Amenia conferences, or Minton's Playhouse any time in the 1940s), and Orwellian chatter about privilege and 'disprivilege', the magical power of 'whiteness', etc. lies yet another iteration in what literature scholar Kenneth Warren has identified in his masterful 2012 study, *What Was African American Literature?*[9], as a more than century-old class program among elements of the black professional-managerial stratum to establish "managerial authority over the nation's Negro problem".

That is to say, as is ever clearer and ever more important to note, race politics is not an alternative to class politics; it is a class politics, the politics of the left wing of neoliberalism. It is the expression and active agency of a political order and moral economy in which capitalist market forces are treated as unassailable nature. An integral element of that moral economy is displacement of the critique of the invidious outcomes produced by capitalist class power onto equally naturalized categories of ascriptive identity that sort us into groups supposedly defined by what we essentially are rather than what we do. As I have argued, following Walter Benn Michaels and others, within that moral economy a society in which one per cent of the population controlled ninety per cent of the resources could be just, provided that roughly twelve per cent of the one per cent were black, twelve per cent were Latino, fifty per cent were women, and whatever the appropriate proportions were LGBT people. It would be tough to imagine a normative ideal that expresses more unambiguously the social position of people who consider themselves candidates for inclusion in, or at least significant staff positions in service to, the ruling class.

This perspective may help explain why, the more aggressively and openly capitalist class power destroys and marketizes every shred of social protection working people of all races, genders, and sexual orientations

have fought for and won over the last century, the louder and more insistent are the demands from the identitarian left that we focus our attention on statistical disparities and episodic outrages that 'prove' that
the crucial injustices in the society should be understood in the language
of ascriptive identity. The Dolezal/Jenner contretemps stoked the protec-
tionist reflexes of identitarian spokesperson guilds because it troubles
current jurisdictional boundaries. Even before that, however, some racial
identitarians had grown bolder in laying bare the blur of careerism and
arbitrary, self-serving moralism at the base of this supposed politics.
In an unintentionally farcical homage to Black Power era radicalism,
various racial ventriloquists claiming to channel the Voices of the Youth
leadership of the putative Black Lives Matter 'movement' have lately
been arguing that the key condition for a left alliance is that we all must
'respect black leadership'. Of course, that amounts to a claim to shut up
and take whatever anyone who claims that status says or does. Those of
us old enough to remember Black Power and the War on Poverty also will
look around to see which funders or employers they're addressing.

And, in apparent contradiction of the ontological principle of group
authenticity on which the paradigm rests, reprise of the tawdriest features of Black Power hustling isn't available only to officially recognized
people of color. Joan Walsh, apparently having learned the strictures
of 'white allyship' from being chastened by *prima inter pares* bourgeois identitarian Melissa Harris-Perry[10], recently showed the depths of
crude opportunism this discourse enables when she race-baited Bernie
Sanders as an instrument of her effort to pimp for Hillary Clinton (see
her "White Progressives' Racial Myopia: Why Their Colorblindness
Fails Minorities—And the Left"[11]). For Walsh, it seems, black people
don't count among the millions who would be helped by Sanders's social-
democratic agenda, but Clinton, presumably, would show proper respect
by hooking them up with a #Blacklivesmatter Facebook like.

I'll conclude by returning to the Dolezal/Jenner issue. I can imagine
an identitarian response to my argument to the effect that I endorse
some version of wiggerism, or the view that 'feeling black' can make one
genuinely black. The fact is that I think that formulation is wrong-headed either way one lines up on it. Each position—that one can feel or will

one's way into an ascriptive identity or that one can't—presumes that the 'identity' is a thing with real boundaries. The issue of the line that Dolezal, who has now resigned her NAACP position, crossed that made her alleged self-representation unacceptable is interesting in this regard only because it highlights contradictions at the core of racial essentialism. In addition to the problems of articulating what confers racial authenticity, if what we have read about her approach to expressing black racial identity is accurate, she seems to have embraced an essentialist version of being black no less than do her outraged critics. Wiggers do so as well, and we must admit that Dolezal's performance and apparent embrace of culturally recognized representations of black womanhood rests on an aesthetic purporting to embody respect and celebration rather than the demeaning racialist fantasies that shape the commercial personae of the likes of Iggy Azalea. Moreover, even if Dolezal may suffer from something like racial dysmorphia, the expression of her fixation has been tied up with commitment to struggle for social justice. She may have other personal problems and strained or bad relations with family members, but those are matters that concern her and those with whom she interacts. They do not automatically impeach the authenticity of her feelings of who she 'really' is. And I doubt that we'd want to start a scorecard comparing her and Republican Jenner on that front.

That points to the other way that this affair has exposed identitarianism's irrational underbelly. The fundamental contradiction that has impelled the debate and required the flight into often idiotic sophistry is that racial identitarians assume, even if they give catechistic lip service—a requirement of being taken seriously outside Charles Murray's world—to the catchphrase that 'race is a social construction', that race is a thing, an essence that lives within us. If pushed, they will offer any of a range of more or less mystical, formulaic, breezy, or neo-Lamarckian faux explanations of how it can be both an essential ground of our being and a social construct, and most people are willing not to pay close attention to the justificatory patter. Nevertheless, for identitarians, to paraphrase Michaels, we aren't, for instance, black because we do black things; that seems to have been Dolezal's mistaken wish. We do black things because we are black. Doing black things does not make us black; being black makes us do black things. That is how it's possible to talk about having lost or needing to retrieve one's culture, or to define 'cultural appropriation' as the equivalent, if not the prosaic reality, of a property crime. That, indeed, is also the essence of essentialism.

The problem the Jenner comparison poses is that, if identity is inherent in us in ways that are beyond our volition, how can we legitimize transgender identity—which is gender identity that does not conform with that conventionally associated with biological sex type—without the psychological stigma of dysmorphia? Confounding of sex and gender is the ideological mechanism that seems to resolve that conundrum. Thus, notwithstanding my earlier suggestion that Talusan misses the cultural fluidity of gender because she is naïve anthropologically, she may also have an important ideological reason to deny it. It is only by treating gender roles as somehow endowed at birth that she can contend that transgender identity is "almost always involuntary". That is, essentializing political discourse requires that gender identity must be a condition that is 'natural' or inherent—equivalent, or prior, to biological sex type. Transgender identity requires being read as in effect 'hardwired' only within a normative framework in which access to the domain of recognizable identity deserving of civic regard depends on essentialist claims, and the only way transgender identity can meet that standard is to collapse distinctions between sex and gender—even though that move, as Burkett argues, cuts against the grain of the perspective the women's movement has fought to advance for at least the last half-century. Nor does this view acknowledge the grave political mischief ideologies of essential human difference have underwritten in not at all distant history, from segregation and other forms legal discrimination and imposition of separate spheres to genocide.

The transrace/transgender comparison makes clear the conceptual emptiness of the essentializing discourses, and the opportunist politics, that undergird identitarian ideologies. There is no coherent, principled defense of the stance that transgender identity is legitimate but transracial is not, at least not one that would satisfy basic rules of argument. The debate also throws into relief the reality that a notion of social justice that hinges on claims to entitlement based on extra-societal, ascriptive identities is neoliberalism's critical self-consciousness. In insisting on the political priority of such fictive, naturalized populations, identitarianism meshes well with neoliberal naturalization of the structures that reproduce inequality. In that sense it's not just a pointed coincidence that Dolezal's critics were appalled with the NAACP for standing behind her work. It may be that one of Rachel Dolezal's most important contributions to the struggle for social justice may turn out to be having catalyzed, not intentionally to be sure, a discussion that may help us move beyond the identitarian dead end.

WALTER BENN MICHAELS

Identity Politics: A Zero-Sum Game

The current hard times have been harder on some people than on others, harder on the poor—obviously—than on the rich; but harder also on blacks and Hispanics than on whites. As of this writing, the unemployment rate for blacks is at 15.6 per cent, and for Hispanics it's at 12.7 per cent. For white people, it's 9.3 per cent.[1] Of course, the vast majority of the unemployed are white. But it's the disparity in rates, not in absolute numbers, that tends to get foregrounded, since that disparity functions not only as a measure of suffering but also, in William A. Darity's concise summary, as "an index of discrimination in our society"[2]. And it's the ongoing fact of discrimination that motivates our ongoing interest in identity politics. As long as inequality is apportioned by identity, we will be concerned with identity.

This is obviously both inevitable and appropriate. But it is also—and almost as obviously—irrelevant to a left politics, or even to the goal of reducing unemployment, as we can see just by imagining what it would be like if we finally did manage to get rid of discrimination. Suppose, for example, that unemployment for whites and for Asian-Americans were to rise to ten per cent while for blacks and Hispanics it fell to ten per cent. Or suppose that unemployment for everyone went to fifteen per cent. In both cases, we would have eliminated the racial disparity in unemployment rates, but in neither case would we have eliminated any unemployment. And we don't even need hypotheticals to make the point. About three quarters of the job losers in the current recession have been men, which means that the numbers of men and women in the workforce are now roughly equal. So, from the standpoint of gender equity, the recession has actually been a good thing. It's as if, unable to create more jobs for women, we'd hit upon the strategy of eliminating lots of the jobs for men—another victory for feminism and for anti-discrimination since, from the standpoint of anti-discrimination, the question of how many people are unemployed is completely irrelevant. What matters is only that, however many there are, their unemployment is properly proportioned.

This is, in part, a logical point: there's no contradiction between inequality of class and equality of race and gender. It is also, however, a political point. The influential *Think Progress* blogger, Matt Yglesias, has recently written that, although "straight white intellectuals" might tend to think of the increasing economic inequality of the last thirty years as "a period of relentless defeat for left-wing politics", we ought to remember that the same period has also seen "enormous advances in the practical opportunities available to women, a major decline in the level of racism paired with a major increase in the level of actual racial and ethnic diversity", and "wildly more public and legal acceptance of gays and lesbians".[3]

"These aren't just incidental add-ons to a program that's 'really' about comparing income-percentile ratios", he goes on to say, because "it all fundamentally goes back to the same core belief in human equality."

But it doesn't. In fact, the belief in human equality that has cheered on anti-racism and anti-sexism has not only been compatible with—it's been supported by—a belief in human inequality that has been happy to accept the fact that ten per cent of the US population now earns just under fifty per cent of total US income. This is what it means for the most eminent of the living Chicago economists (Gary Becker, whose first book was *The Economics of Discrimination*) to praise globalization and "the increasing market orientation of different economies" by noting that, although they may "raise rather than lower income inequality", they also make that inequality "more dependent on differences in human and other capital, and less directly on skin color, gender, religion, caste, and other roots of discrimination"[4].

Why? Because discrimination is costly to the employer: you have to pay not just for the labor but also for the laborer's skin color or gender, which, in a truly competitive market, you can't afford to do. Hence employers who discriminate—like employers forced by unions to pay expensive benefits and higher wages—are doomed. Indeed, from this standpoint, the problem with discriminatory hiring practices is the same as the problem with unions: they both make labor costs higher, and a company less competitive.

Thus the commitment to competitive markets intensifies economic inequality, but diminishes the inequality produced by racial and gender discrimination. Or—to put it the other way around—if markets are good for producing an ethic of anti-discrimination, anti-discrimination is good for producing success in markets. So does this mean that Chicago economists believe in human equality? Well, when it comes to the inequalities produced by discrimination, they do—discrimination is bad for business. But when it comes to the inequalities produced by the market itself—inequalities of wealth and income—they don't. And why should they? The belief that people shouldn't be discriminated against in no way entails the belief that they shouldn't be exploited. That's why even very straight, very white, very old, and very conservative intellectuals can be just as happy about, say, gay marriage as Matt Yglesias is. Indeed, the only kind of unions Gary Becker approves of are the ones he hopes to see created by "a private contract"[5], allowing consenting adults of any sex to marry whomever they choose, and thus eliminating what he regards as the arbitrary and unjust exclusion of gays from all the rights available to straights. This doesn't mean that gay marriage isn't a good thing, and it doesn't mean that we shouldn't be vigilant in fighting all kinds of discrimination. It just means that fighting discrimination has nothing to do with fighting economic inequality, and that the commitment to identity politics has been more an expression of our enthusiasm for the free market than a form of resistance to it. You can, for example, be a feminist committed to equal pay for men and women and also be committed to equality between management and labor but, as the example of everyone who's ever campaigned against the glass ceiling shows, you don't have to be and aren't likely to be. After all, it's one thing to worry about the fact that the average CEO now makes in one day what the average worker makes in one year; it's a completely different thing to worry about the fact that there aren't enough women CEOs. And what the identity in identity politics requires is only that we worry about the second.

So, for example, while the overwhelming fact about students at elite colleges and universities today is how wealthy they are—three quarters of them, as Richard Kahlenberg has been admirably relentless in reminding us, "come from the richest socioeconomic quarter of the population, and just 3 per cent from the bottom quarter, a roughly 25:1 ratio"[6]—what we worry about is not their wealth but their color. The advantages of wealth are something neither the proponents of affirmative action nor most of those "at the forefront" of what Richard Kim has called "the affirmative action backlash" want to fight about. Indeed, when Kim himself wonders where the opposition to affirmative action—what he calls the "seething, misplaced, amnesiac resentment, so often masquerading as class-consciousness (see Walter Benn Michaels)"—comes from, he can only imagine the commitment to economic equality as a cover-up for the real motive: racism, in the form of white people's supposed fear of "the unnerving, inevitable end of the white republic".[7]

But you don't need to be a racist to notice that his paean to the campus as a "space" for "the yellow . . . the brown, the red and the black" leaves out the poor, just as the universities themselves have done.

And, for that matter, you don't need to be a racist to notice that most of the anti-affirmative action arguments have nothing to do with class either—it's reverse racism that they carry on about. In fact, Americans today are never happier than when we're calling each other racists—just think of Glenn Beck complaining about President Obama's "deep-seated hatred for white people". At least when we worry about anti-black racism, we have the advantage that our worries are rooted in reality. But white people (and Asians and Jews) just look (and are) delusional when they cast themselves as victims of prejudice in contemporary America. It may, for example, be true that over sixty per cent of the people in the bottom quintile of American wage-earners are white. But it is not true that they are the victims of racism. They are the victims of capitalism.

Furthermore, so are most of the African-Americans and Hispanics who fill out the rest of that quintile. Our focus on identity obscures the fact that while equality between the races would enable some blacks and Hispanics to escape the bottom (their places taken by newly recruited whites and Asians), equality between classes would enable all of them to escape it—there wouldn't be any bottom. Which is a more progressive goal—a world in which only thirteen per cent of black people (instead of twenty-four per cent) live below the poverty line or a world in which none of them do? And if that sounds too utopian, it's worth pointing out that even a very little and entirely race-blind progress in alleviating American poverty would nevertheless disproportionately benefit minorities, precisely because minorities are disproportionately poor. So not only is identity politics a bad idea, it's a bad idea for the very identities it's supposed to protect.

Or at least it's a bad idea for some of them, for poor blacks and poor Hispanics. For although real progress in the direction of greater economic equality would be more beneficial to poor blacks and Hispanics than would complete economic parity with white people, the goal of economic parity with whites works a lot better for black and Hispanic elites. Indeed, it works pretty well for white elites too: which would you rather do—welcome some women and minorities to your board of directors, or not have a board of directors at all? Of course, we haven't yet achieved an America in which women and minorities are proportionately represented on the boards of the Fortune 500. But, as the still-burgeoning diversity industry suggests, the effort is one that rich people themselves have been and should be happy to embrace since it doesn't reduce economic inequality—it endorses it.

It would thus be a mistake to understand this debate as a choice between a politics of identity and a politics of class—the politics of identity already is a politics of class. It has no quarrel with economic inequality and it brilliantly represents the interests of those who benefit from that inequality, providing them with a model of social justice in which their success is supposed to count as good news not just for them, but for all the people who supposedly share their identity. You definitely know you're in a world that loves neoliberalism when the fact that some people of color are rich and powerful is regarded as a victory for all the people of color who aren't (and when this, indeed, is regarded as a victory for justice itself).

But why should the fact that some people are rich count as good news for the poor? Racism is wrong, sexism and heterosexism are wrong; discrimination of any kind is wrong, and it's a good thing to oppose it. But it isn't discrimination that has produced the growing economic inequality in the US, and identity politics today—with its irreducibly proportional vision of social justice, its defining goal of equality between identities—does more to legitimate that inequality than to oppose it.

ADOLPH REED, JR.

Django Unchained, or, *The Help*: How 'Cultural Politics' Is Worse than No Politics at All, and Why

On reflection, it's possible to see that *Django Unchained* and *The Help* are basically different versions of the same movie. Both dissolve political economy and social relations into individual quests and interpersonal transactions and thus effectively sanitize, respectively, slavery and Jim Crow by dehistoricizing them. The problem is not so much that each film invents cartoonish fictions; it's that the point of the cartoons is to take the place of the actual relations of exploitation that anchored the regime it depicts. In *The Help* the buffoonishly bigoted housewife, Hilly, obsessively pushes a pet bill that would require employers of black domestic servants to provide separate, Jim Crow toilets for them; in *Django Unchained* the sensibility of 1970s blaxploitation imagines 'comfort girls' and 'Mandingo fighters' as representative slave job descriptions. It's as if Jim Crow had nothing to do with cheap labor and slavery had nothing to do with making slave owners rich. And the point here is not just that they get the past wrong—it's that the particular way they get it wrong enables them to get the present just as wrong and so their politics are as misbegotten as their history.

Thus, for example, it's only the dehistoricization that makes each film's entirely neoliberal (they could have been scripted by Oprah) happy ending possible. *The Help* ends with Skeeter and the black lead, the maid Aibileen, embarking joyfully on the new, excitingly uncharted paths that

157

their book—an account of the master-servant relationship told from the perspective of the servants—has opened for them. But dehistoricization makes it possible not to notice the great distance between those paths and their likely trajectories. For Skeeter, the book from which the film takes its name opens a career in the fast track of the journalism and publishing industry. Aibileen's new path was forced upon her because the book got her fired from her intrinsically precarious job, more at-whim than at-will, in one of the few areas of employment available to working-class black women in the segregationist South—the precise likelihood that had made her and other maids initially reluctant to warm to Skeeter's project. Yet Aibileen smiles and strides ever more confidently as she walks home because she has found and articulated her voice.

The implication is that having been fired, rather than portending deeper poverty and economic insecurity, was a moment of liberation; Aibileen, armed with the confidence and self-knowledge conferred by knowing her voice, was now free to venture out into a world of unlimited opportunity and promise. This, of course, is pure neoliberal bullshit, of the same variety that permits the odious Michelle Rhee to assert with a straight face that teachers' defined-benefit pensions deny them 'choice' and thereby undermine the quality of public education. But who knows? Perhaps Skeeter brought with her from the 2000s an NGO to arrange microcredit that would enable Aibileen to start up a culturally authentic pie-making venture or a day spa for harried and stressed domestic servants. In the Jackson, Mississippi of 1963, no such options would exist for Aibileen. Instead, she most likely would be blackballed and unable to find a comparable menial job and forced to toil under even more undesirable conditions.

Django Unchained ends with the hero and his lady fair riding happily off into the sunset after he has vanquished evil slave owners and their henchmen and henchwomen. Django and Broomhilda—whose name is spelled like that of the 1970s comic strip character, not the figure in Norse mythology, presumably a pointless Tarantino inside joke—are free. However, their freedom was not won by his prodigious bloodletting; it was obtained within the legal framework that accepted and regulated property rights in slaves. Each had been purchased and manumitted by the German bounty hunter who, as others have noted, is the only character in the film to condemn slavery as an institution.

Django is no insurrectionist. His singular focus from beginning to end is on reclaiming *his* wife from her slave master. Presumably we are to understand this solipsism as indicative of the depth and intensity of his love, probably also as homage to the borderline sociopathic style of the spaghetti Western/blaxploitation hero. Regardless, Django's quest is entirely individualist; he never intends to challenge slavery and never does. Indeed, for the purpose of buttressing the credibility of their ruse, he even countermands his bounty hunter partner's attempt to save—through purchase, of course—a recalcitrant 'Mandingo fighter' from being ripped apart by dogs. He is essentially indifferent to the handful of slaves who are freed as incidental byproducts of his actions. The happy ending is that he and Broomhilda ride off together and free in a slavocracy that is not a whit less secure at the moment of celebratory resolution than it was when Django set out on his mission of retrieval and revenge.

In both films the bogus happy endings are possible only because they characterize their respective regimes of racial hierarchy in the superficial terms of interpersonal transactions. In *The Help* segregationism's evil was small-minded bigotry and lack of sensitivity; it was more like bad manners than oppression. In Tarantino's vision, slavery's definitive injustice was its gratuitous and sadistic brutalization and sexualized degradation. Malevolent, ludicrously arrogant whites owned slaves most conspicuously to degrade and torture them. Apart from serving a formal dinner in a plantation house—and Tarantino, the Chance the Gardener of American filmmakers (and Best Original Screenplay? Really?), seems to draw his images of plantation life from *Birth of a Nation* and *Gone With the Wind*, as well as old Warner Brothers cartoons—and the Mandingo fighters and comfort girls, Tarantino's slaves do no actual work at all; they're present only to be brutalized. In fact, the cavalier sadism with which owners and traders treat them belies the fact that slaves were, first and foremost, capital investments. It's not for nothing that New Orleans has a monument to the estimated 20,000-30,000 antebellum Irish immigrants who died constructing the New Basin Canal; slave labor was too valuable for such lethal work.

The Help trivializes Jim Crow by reducing it to its most superficial features and irrational extremes. The master-servant nexus was, and is, a labor relation. And the problem of labor relations particular to the segregationist regime wasn't employers' bigoted lack of respect or failure to hear the voices of the domestic servants, or even benighted refusal to recognize their equal humanity. It was that the labor relation was structured within and sustained by a political and institutional order that severely impinged on, when it didn't altogether deny, black citizens' avenues for pursuit of grievances and standing before the law. The crucial lynchpin of that order was neither myopia nor malevolence; it was suppression of black citizens' capacities for direct participation in civic and political life, with racial disfranchisement and the constant threat of terror intrinsic to substantive denial of equal protection and due process before the law as its principal mechanisms. And the point of the regime wasn't racial hatred or enforced disregard; its roots lay in the much more prosaic concern of dominant elites to maintain their political and economic hegemony by suppressing potential opposition and in the linked ideal of maintaining access to a labor force with no options but to accept employment on whatever terms employers offered. (Those who liked *The Help* or found it moving should watch *The Long Walk Home*, a 1990 film set in Montgomery, Alabama, around the bus boycott. I suspect that's the film you thought you were watching when you saw *The Help*.)

Django Unchained trivializes slavery by reducing it to its most barbaric and lurid excesses. Slavery also was fundamentally a labor relation. It was a form of forced labor regulated—systematized, enforced and sustained—through a political and institutional order that specified it as a civil relationship granting owners absolute control over the life, liberty, and fortunes of others defined as eligible for enslavement, including most of all control of the conditions of their labor and appropriation of its product. Historian Kenneth M. Stampp quotes a slaveholder's succinct explanation: "'For what purpose does the master hold the servant?' asked an ante-bellum Southerner. 'Is it not that by his labor he, the master, may accumulate wealth?'"[1]

That absolute control permitted horrible, unthinkable brutality, to be sure, but perpetrating such brutality was neither the point of slavery nor its essential injustice. The master-slave relationship could, and did, exist without brutality, and certainly without sadism and sexual degradation. In Tarantino's depiction, however, it is not clear that slavery shorn of its extremes of brutality would be objectionable. It does not diminish the historical injustice and horror of slavery to note that it was not the product of *sui generis*, transcendent Evil but a terminus on a continuum of bound labor that was more norm than exception in the Anglo-American world until well into the eighteenth century, if not later. As legal historian Robert Steinfeld points out, it is not so much slavery, but the emergence of the notion of free labor—as the absolute control of a worker over her person—that is the historical anomaly that needs to be explained.[2] *Django Unchained* sanitizes the essential injustice of slavery by not problematizing it and by focusing instead on the extremes of brutality and degradation it permitted, to the extent of making some of them up, just as does *The Help* regarding Jim Crow.

The Help could not imagine a more honest and complex view of segregationist Mississippi partly because it uses the period ultimately as a prop for human interest cliché, and *Django Unchained*'s absurdly ahistorical view of plantation slavery is only backdrop for the merger of spaghetti Western and blaxploitation hero movie. Neither film is really *about* the period in which it is set. Film critic Manohla Dargis, reflecting a decade ago on what she saw as a growing Hollywood penchant for period films, observed that such films are typically "stripped of politics and historical fact . . . and instead will find meaning in appealing to seemingly timeless ideals and stirring scenes of love, valor and compassion", and that "the Hollywood professionals who embrace accuracy most enthusiastically nowadays are costume designers."[3] That observation applies to both these films, although in *Django* concern with historically accurate representation of material culture applies only to the costumes and props of the 1970s film genres Tarantino wants to recall.

To make sense of how *Django Unchained* has received so much warmer a reception among black and leftoid commentators than did *The Help*, it is useful to recall Margaret Thatcher's 1981 dictum that "economics are the method: the object is to change the soul."[4] Simply put, she and her element have won. Few observers—among opponents and boosters alike—have noted how deeply and thoroughly both films are embedded in the practical ontology of neoliberalism, the complex of unarticulated assumptions and unexamined first premises that provide its common sense, its lifeworld.

Objection to *The Help* has been largely of the shooting fish in a barrel variety: complaints about the film's paternalistic treatment of the maids, which generally have boiled down to an objection that the master-servant relation is thematized at all, as well as the standard, predictable litany of anti-racist charges about whites speaking for blacks, the film's inattentiveness to the fact that at that time in Mississippi black people were busily engaged in liberating themselves, etc. An illustration of this tendency that conveniently refers to several other variants of it is Akiba Solomon, "Why I'm Just Saying No to 'The Help' and Its Historical Whitewash" in *Color Lines*, 10 August 2011, available at: <https://www.colorlines.com/articles/why-im-just-saying-no-help-and-its-historical-whitewash>.

Defenses of *Django Unchained* pivot on claims about the social significance of the narrative of a black hero. One node of this argument emphasizes the need to validate a history of autonomous black agency and 'resistance' as a politico-existential desideratum. It accommodates a view that stresses the importance of recognition of rebellious or militant individuals and revolts in black American history. Another centers on a notion that exposure to fictional black heroes can inculcate the sense of personal efficacy necessary to overcome the psychological effects of inequality and to facilitate upward mobility and may undermine some whites' negative stereotypes about black people. In either register, assignment of social or political importance to depictions of black heroes rests on presumptions about the nexus of mass cultural representation, social commentary, and racial justice that are more significant politically than the controversy about the film itself.

In both versions, this argument casts political and economic problems in psychological terms. Injustice appears as a matter of disrespect and denial of due recognition, and the remedies proposed—which are all about images projected and the distribution of jobs associated with their projection—look a lot like self-esteem engineering. Moreover, nothing could indicate more strikingly the extent of neoliberal ideological hegemony than the idea that the mass culture industry and its representational practices constitute a meaningful terrain for struggle to advance egalitarian interests. It is possible to entertain that view seriously only by ignoring the fact that the production and consumption of mass culture is thoroughly embedded in capitalist material and ideological imperatives.

That, incidentally, is why I prefer the usage 'mass culture' to describe this industry and its products and processes, although I recognize that it may seem archaic to some readers. The mass culture v. popular culture debate dates at least from the 1950s and has continued with occasional crescendos ever since.[5] For two decades or more, instructively in line with the retreat of possibilities for concerted left political action outside the academy, the popular culture side of that debate has been dominant, along with its view that the products of this precinct of mass consumption capitalism are somehow capable of transcending or subverting their material identity as commodities, if not avoiding that identity altogether. Despite the dogged commitment of several generations of American Studies and cultural studies graduate students who want to valorize watching television and immersion in hip-hop or other specialty market niches centered on youth recreation and the most ephemeral fads as both intellectually avant-garde and politically 'resistive', it should be time to admit that that earnest disposition is intellectually shallow and an ersatz politics. The idea of 'popular' culture posits a spurious autonomy and organicism that actually affirm mass industrial processes by effacing them, especially in the putatively rebel, fringe, or underground market niches that depend on the fiction of the authentic to announce the birth of new product cycles.

The power of the hero is a cathartic trope that connects mainly with the sensibility of adolescent boys—of whatever nominal age. Tarantino has allowed as much, responding to black critics' complaints about the violence and copious use of 'nigger' by proclaiming "Even for the film's biggest detractors, I think their children will grow up and love this movie. I think it could become a rite of passage for young black males."[6] This response stems no doubt from Tarantino's arrogance and opportunism, and some critics have denounced it as no better than racially presumptuous. But he is hardly alone in defending the film with an assertion that it gives black youth heroes, is generically inspirational, or both. Similarly, in a 9 January 2012 interview on the *Daily Show*, George Lucas adduced this line to promote his even more execrable race-oriented live-action cartoon, *Red Tails*, which, incidentally, trivializes segregation in the military by reducing it to a matter of bad or outmoded attitudes. The ironic effect is significant understatement of both the obstacles the Tuskegee airmen faced and their actual accomplishments by rendering them as backdrop for a blackface, slapped-together remake of *Top Gun*. (Norman Jewison's 1984 film, *A Soldier's Story*, adapted from Charles Fuller's *A Soldier's Play*, is a much more sensitive and thought-provoking rumination on the complexities of race and racism in the Jim Crow US Army—an army mobilized, as my father, a veteran of the Normandy invasion, never tired of remarking sardonically, to fight the racist Nazis.) Lucas characterized his film as "patriotic, even jingoistic" and was explicit that he wanted to create a film that would feature "real heroes" and would be "inspirational for teenage boys". Much as *Django Unchained*'s defenders compare it on those terms favorably to *Lincoln*, Lucas hyped *Red Tails* as being a genuine hero story unlike "*Glory*, where you have a lot of white officers running those guys into cannon fodder".

Of course, the film industry is sharply tilted toward the youth market, as Lucas and Tarantino are acutely aware. But Lucas, unlike Tarantino, was not being defensive in asserting his desire to inspire the young; he offered it more as a boast. As he has said often, he'd wanted for years to make a film about the Tuskegee airmen, and he reports that he always intended telling their story as a feel-good, crossover inspirational tale. Telling it that way also fits in principle (though in this instance not in practice, as *Red Tails* bombed at the box office) with the commercial imperatives of increasingly degraded mass entertainment.

Dargis observed that the ahistoricism of the recent period films is influenced by market imperatives in a global film industry. The more a film is tied to historically specific contexts, the more difficult it is to sell elsewhere. That logic selects for special effects-driven products as well as standardized, decontextualized and simplistic—'universal'—

story lines, preferably set in fantasy worlds of the filmmakers' design. As Dargis notes, these films find their meaning in shopworn clichés puffed up as timeless verities, including uplifting and inspirational messages for youth. But something else underlies the stress on inspiration in the black-interest films, which shows up in critical discussion of them as well.

All these films—*The Help*, *Red Tails*, *Django Unchained*, even *Lincoln* and *Glory*—make a claim to public attention based partly on their social significance beyond entertainment or art, and they do so because they engage with significant moments in the history of the nexus of race and politics in the United States. There would not be so much discussion and debate and no Golden Globe, NAACP Image, or Academy Award nominations for *The Help*, *Red Tails*, or *Django Unchained* if those films weren't defined partly by thematizing that nexus of race and politics in some way.

The pretensions to social significance that fit these films into their particular market niche don't conflict with the mass-market film industry's imperative of infantilization because those pretensions are only part of the show; they are little more than empty bromides, product differentiation in the patter of 'seemingly timeless ideals' which the mass entertainment industry constantly recycles. (Andrew O'Hehir observes as much about *Django Unchained*, which he describes as "a three-hour trailer for a movie that never happens"[7].) That comes through in the defense of these films, in the face of evidence of their failings, that, after all, they are 'just entertainment'. Their substantive content is ideological; it is their contribution to the naturalization of neoliberalism's ontology as they propagandize its universalization across spatial, temporal, and social contexts.

Purportedly in the interest of popular education cum entertainment, *Django Unchained* and *The Help*, and *Red Tails* for that matter, read the sensibilities of the present into the past by divesting the latter of its specific historicity. They reinforce the sense of the past as generic old-timey times distinguishable from the present by superficial inadequacies— outmoded fashion, technology, commodities and ideas—since overcome. In *The Help* Hilly's obsession with her pet project marks segregation's petty apartheid as irrational in part because of the expense rigorously enforcing it would require; the breadwinning husbands express their frustration with it as financially impractical. Hilly is a mean-spirited, narrow-minded person whose rigid and tone-deaf commitment to seg-regationist consistency not only reflects her limitations of character but also is economically unsound, a fact that further defines her, and the cartoon version of Jim Crow she represents, as irrational.

The deeper message of these films, insofar as they deny the integrity of the past, is that there is no thinkable alternative to the ideological order under which we live. This message is reproduced throughout the mass entertainment industry; it shapes the normative reality even of the fantasy worlds that masquerade as escapism. Even among those who laud the supposedly cathartic effects of Django's insurgent violence as reflecting a greater truth of abolition than passage of the Thirteenth Amendment, few commentators notice that he and Broomhilda attained their freedom through a market transaction.[8] This reflects an ideologi-cal hegemony in which students all too commonly wonder why planters would deny slaves or sharecroppers education because education would have made them more productive as workers. And, tellingly, in a glowing rumination in the *Daily Kos*, Ryan Brooke inadvertently thrusts mass culture's destruction of historicity into bold relief by declaiming on "the segregated society presented" in *Django Unchained* and babbling on— with the absurdly ill-informed and pontifical self-righteousness that the blogosphere enables—about our need to take "responsibility for preserv-ing racial divides" if we are "to put segregation in the past and fully fulfill Dr. King's dream"[9]. It's all an indistinguishable mush of bad stuff about racial injustice in the old-timey days. Decoupled from its moorings in a historically specific political economy, slavery becomes at bottom a problem of race relations, and, as historian Michael R. West argues forcefully, 'race relations' emerged as and has remained a discourse that substitutes etiquette for equality[10].

This is the context in which we should take account of what 'inspir-ing the young' means as a justification for those films. In part, the claim to inspire is a simple platitude, more filler than substance. It is, as I've already noted, both an excuse for films that are cartoons made for an infantilized, generic market and an assertion of a claim to a particular niche within that market. More insidiously, though, the ease with which 'inspiration of youth' rolls out in this context resonates with three related and disturbing themes: 1) underclass ideology's narratives—now all Americans' common sense—that link poverty and inequality most crucially to (racialized) cultural inadequacy and psychological damage; 2) the belief that racial inequality stems from prejudice, bad ideas and ignorance, and 3) the cognate of both: the neoliberal rendering of social justice as equality of opportunity, with an aspiration of creating "competitive individual minority agents who might stand a better fighting chance in the neoliberal rat race rather than a positive alternative vision of a society that eliminates the need to fight constantly against disruptive market whims in the first place"[11].

This politics seeps through in the chatter about *Django Unchained* in particular. Erin Aubry Kaplan, in the *Los Angeles Times* article in which Tarantino asserts his appeal to youth, remarks that the "most disturbing detail [about slavery] is the emotional violence and degradation directed at blacks that effectively keeps them at the bottom of the social order, a place they still occupy today". Writing on the Institute of the Black World blog, one Dr. Kwa David Whitaker, a 1960s-style cultural nationalist, declaims on *Django*'s testament to the sources of degradation and "unending servitude [that] has . . . rendered [black Americans] almost incapable of making sound evaluations of our current situations or the kind of steps we must take to improve our condition".[12] In its blindness to political economy, this notion of black cultural or psychological damage as either a legacy of slavery or of more indirect recent origin—e.g., urban migration, crack epidemic, matriarchy, babies making babies—comports well with the reduction of slavery and Jim Crow to interpersonal dynamics and bad attitudes. It substitutes a 'politics of recognition' and a patter of racial uplift for politics and underwrites a conflation of political action and therapy.

With respect to the nexus of race and inequality, this discourse supports victim-blaming programs of personal rehabilitation and self-esteem engineering—inspiration—as easily as it does multiculturalist respect for difference, which, by the way, also feeds back to self-esteem engineering and inspiration as nodes within a larger political economy of race relations. Either way, this is a discourse that displaces a politics challenging social structures that reproduce inequality with concern for the feelings and characteristics of individuals and of categories of population statistics reified as singular groups that are equivalent to individuals. This discourse has made it possible (again, but more sanctimoniously this time) to characterize destruction of low-income housing as an uplift strategy for poor people; curtailment of access to public education as 'choice'; being cut adrift from essential social wage protections as 'empowerment'; and individual material success as socially important role modeling.

Neoliberalism's triumph is affirmed with unselfconscious clarity in the ostensibly leftist defenses of *Django Unchained* that center on the theme of slaves' having liberated themselves. Trotskyists, would-be anarchists, and psychobabbling identitarians have their respective sectarian garnishes: Trotskyists see everywhere the bugbear of 'bureaucratism' and mystify 'self-activity'; anarchists similarly fetishize direct action and voluntarism and oppose large-scale public institutions on principle; and identitarians romanticize essentialist notions of organic, folkish authenticity under constant threat from institutions. However, all are indistinguishable from the nominally libertarian right in their disdain for government and institutionally based political action, which their common reflex is to disparage as inauthentic or corrupt.

The previous year's version of the socially significant film bearing on race (sort of), Benh Zeitlin's *Beasts of the Southern Wild*, which also received startlingly positive responses from nominal progressives [13], marks the reactionary vector onto which those several interpretive strains converge. It lays out an exoticizing narrative of quaint, closer-to-nature primitives living in an area outside the south Louisiana levee system called the Bathtub, who simply don't want and actively resist the oppressive intrusions—specifically, medical care and hurricane evacuation, though, in fairness, they also mark their superiority by tut-tutting at the presence of oil refineries—of a civilization that is out of touch with their way of life and is destroying nature to boot. The film validates their spiritually rich if economically impoverished culture and their right to it.

(Actually, the Bathtub's material infrastructure seems to derive mainly from scavenging, which should suggest a problem at the core of this bullshit allegory for all except those who imagine dumpster-diving, back-to-nature-in-the-city squatterism as a politics.) Especially given its setting in south Louisiana and the hype touting the authenticity of its New Orleans-based crew and cast, *Beasts* most immediately evokes a warm and fuzzy rendition of the retrograde post-Katrina line that those odd people down there wouldn't evacuate because they're so intensely committed to place. It also brings to mind Leni Riefenstahl's post-prison photo essays on the Nilotic groups whose beautiful primitiveness she imagined herself capturing for posterity before they vanished under a superior civilization's advance. [14]

Beasts of the Southern Wild stands out also as a pure exemplar of the debasement of the notion of a social cause through absorption into the commercial imperative, the next logical step from fun-run or buy-a-T-shirt activism. The film's website has a 'get involved' link, a ploy clearly intended to generate an affective identification and to define watching and liking the film as a form of social engagement. There's nothing to 'get involved' with except propagandizing for the film. But the injunction to get involved pumps the idea that going to see a movie, and spending money to do so, is participating in a social movement. (I happened to be on a flight from Hartford, Connecticut, to Chicago with Oprah's BFF and my local news anchor, Gayle King, on the premiere weekend of Oprah's film adaptation of Toni Morrison's *Beloved*. Gayle intimated in a stage whisper to the gaggle of gushing Oprah fans seated around her that it was *very* important to see the film on opening weekend in order to build the all-important box office count. I hadn't realized theretofore that making yet more money for Oprah ranks as a social responsibility.) In this device Zeitlin repeats a technique employed by Davis Guggenheim's *Waiting for Superman*, the corporate school privatization movement's *Triumph of the Will*, speaking of Leni Riefenstahl, and its fictional counterpart Daniel Barnz's *Won't Back Down*, that movement's *Birth of a Nation*. It is a minor cause for optimism that, to put it mildly, neither of those abominations came anywhere near its predecessor's commercial or cultural success.

In addition to knee-jerk anti-statism, the objection that the slaves freed themselves, as it shows up in favorable comparison of *Django Unchained* to *Lincoln*, stems from a racial pietism that issued from the unholy union of cultural studies and black studies in the university. More than twenty years of 'resistance' studies that find again and again, at this point ritualistically, that oppressed people have and express agency have contributed to undermining the idea of politics as a discrete sphere of activity directed toward the outward-looking project of affecting the social order, most effectively through creating, challenging or redefining institutions that anchor collective action with the objective of developing and wielding power. Instead, the notion has been largely evacuated of specific content at all. 'Politics' can refer to whatever one wants it to; all that's required is an act of will in making a claim.

The fact that there has been no serious left presence with any political capacity in this country for at least a generation has exacerbated this problem. In the absence of dynamic movements that cohere around affirmative visions for making the society better, on the order of, say, Franklin Roosevelt's 1944 "Second Bill of Rights", and that organize and agitate around programs instrumental to pursuit of such visions, what remains is the fossil record of past movements—the still photo legacies of their public events, postures, and outcomes. Over time, the idea that a 'left' is defined by commitment to a vision of social transformation and substantive program for realizing it has receded from cultural memory. Being on the left has become instead a posture, an identity, utterly disconnected from any specific practical commitments.

Thus star Maggie Gyllenhaal and director Daniel Barnz defended themselves against complaints about their complicity in the hideously anti-union propaganda film *Won't Back Down* by adducing their identities as progressives. Gyllenhaal insisted that the movie couldn't be anti-union because "There's no world in which I would ever, EVER make an anti-union movie. My parents are left of Trotsky."[15] Barnz took a similar tack: "I'm a liberal Democrat, very pro-union, a member of two unions. I marched with my union a couple of years ago when we were on strike."[16] And Kathryn Bigelow similarly has countered criticism that her *Zero Dark Thirty* justifies torture and American militarism more broadly by invoking her identity as "a lifelong pacifist".[17] Being a progressive is now more a matter of how one thinks about oneself than what one stands for or does in the world. The best that can be said for that perspective is that it registers acquiescence in defeat. It amounts to an effort to salvage an idea of a left by reformulating it as a sensibility *within* neoliberalism rather than a challenge to it.

Gyllenhaal, Barnz, and Bigelow exemplify the power of ideology as a mechanism that harmonizes the principles one likes to believe one holds with what advances one's material interests; they also attest to the fact that the transmutation of leftism into pure self-image exponentially increases the potential power of that function of ideology. Upton Sinclair's quip—"It is difficult to get a man to understand something when his salary depends upon his not understanding it"—takes on all the more force when applied not merely to actions or interpretations of an external world but to devoutly savored self-perception as well.

That left political imagination now operates unself-consciously within the practical ontology of neoliberalism is also the most important lesson to be drawn from progressives' discussion of *Django Unchained* and, especially, the move to compare it with *Lincoln*. Jon Wiener, writing in *The Nation*, renders the following comparisons:

> In Spielberg's film, the leading black female character is a humble seamstress in the White House whose eyes fill with tears of gratitude when Congress votes to abolish slavery.
>
> In Tarantino's film, the leading female character (Kerry Washington) is a defiant slave who has been branded on the face as a punishment for running away, and is forced—by Leonardo DiCaprio—to work as a prostitute. . . .
>
> In Spielberg's film, old white men make history, and black people thank them for giving them their freedom.
>
> In Tarantino's, a black gunslinger goes after the white slavemaster with homicidal vengeance.[18]

Never mind that, for what it's worth, Kerry Washington's character, as she actually appears in the film, is mainly a cipher, a simpering damsel in distress more reminiscent of Fay Wray in the original *King Kong* than heroines of the blaxploitation era's eponymous vehicles *Coffy* or *Foxy Brown*. More problematically, Wiener's juxtapositions reproduce the elevation of private, voluntarist action as a politics—somehow more truly true or authentic, or at least more appealing emotionally—over the machinations of government and institutional actors. That is a default presumption of the identitarian/culturalist left and is also a cornerstone of neoliberalism's practical ontology.

In an essay on *Lincoln* published a month earlier, Wiener identifies as the central failing of the film its dedication "to the proposition that Lincoln freed the slaves" and concludes, after considerable meandering and nit-picking ambivalence that brings the term pettifoggery to mind, "slavery died as a result of the actions of former slaves." [19] This either/or construct is both historically false and wrong-headed, and it is especially surprising that a professional historian like Wiener embraces it. The claim that slaves' actions were responsible for the death of slavery is not only inaccurate; it is a pointless and counterproductive misrepresentation. What purpose is served by denying the significance of the four years of war and actions of the national government of the United States in ending slavery? Besides, it was indeed the Thirteenth Amendment that abolished slavery.

Slaves' mass departure from plantations was self-emancipation, by definition. Their doing so weakened the Southern economy and undermined the secessionists' capacity to fight, and the related infusion of black troops into the Union army provided a tremendous lift both on the battlefield and for Northern morale. How does noting that proximity of Union troops greatly emboldened that self-emancipation diminish the import of their actions? But it was the Thirteenth Amendment that finally outlawed slavery once and for all in the United States and provided a legal basis for preempting efforts to reinstate it in effect. Moreover, for all the debate concerning Lincoln's motives, the sincerity of his commitment to emancipation, and his personal views of blacks, and notwithstanding its technical limits with respect to enforceability, the Emancipation Proclamation emboldened black people, slave and free, and encouraged all slavery's opponents. And, as Wiener notes himself, the proclamation tied the war explicitly to the elimination of slavery as a system.

Firefly, or The Road to Serfdom

So why is a tale about a manumitted slave/homicidal black gunslinger more palatable to a contemporary leftoid sensibility than either a similarly cartoonish one about black maids and their white employers or one that thematizes Lincoln's effort to push the Thirteenth Amendment through the House of Representatives? The answer is, to quote the saccharine 1970s ballad, "Feelings, nothing more than feelings". Wiener's juxtapositions reflect the political common sense that gives pride of place to demonstrations of respect for the 'voices' of the oppressed and recognition of their suffering, agency, and accomplishments. That common sense informs the proposition that providing inspiration has social or political significance. But it equally shapes the generic human-interest 'message' of films like *The Help* that represent injustice as an issue of human relations—the alchemy that promises to reconcile social justice and capitalist class power as a win/win for everyone by means of attitude adjustments and deepened mutual understanding.

That common sense underwrites the tendency to reduce the past to a storehouse of encouraging post-it messages for the present. It must, because the presumption that the crucial stakes of political action concern recognition and respect for the oppressed's voices is a presentist view, and mining the past to reinforce it requires anachronism. The large struggles against slavery and Jim Crow were directed toward altering structured patterns of social relations anchored in law and state power, but stories of that sort are incompatible with both global marketing imperatives and the ideological predilections of neoliberalism and its identitarian loyal opposition. One can only shudder at the prospect of how Gillo Pontecorvo's 1966 film, *The Battle of Algiers*, or Costa-Gavras's *State of Siege* (1972) would be remade today. (Guy Ritchie's and Madonna's execrable 2002 remake of Lina Wertmüller's 1974 film *Swept Away* may provide a clue; their abomination completely erases the original film's complex class and political content and replaces it with a banal—aka 'universal'—story of an encounter between an older woman and a younger man, while at the same time meticulously, almost eerily, reproducing, scene by scene, the visual structure of Wertmüller's film.)

Particularly as those messages strive for 'universality' as well as inspiration, their least common denominator tends toward the generic story of individual triumph over adversity. But the imagery of the individual overcoming odds to achieve fame, success, or recognition also maps onto the fantasy of limitless upward mobility for enterprising and persistent individuals who persevere and remain true to their dreams. As such, it is neoliberalism's version of an ideal of social justice, legitimizing both success and failure as products of individual character. When combined with a multiculturalist rhetoric of 'difference' that reifies as autonomous cultures—in effect racializes—what are actually contingent modes of life reproduced by structural inequalities, this fantasy crowds inequality as a metric of injustice out of the picture entirely. This accounts for the popularity of reactionary dreck like *Beasts of the Southern Wild* among people who should know better. The denizens of the Bathtub actively, even militantly, choose their poverty and cherish it and should be respected and appreciated for doing so. But no one ever supposed that Leni Riefenstahl was on the left.

The tale type of individual overcoming has become a script into which the great social struggles of the last century and a half have commonly been reformulated to fit the requirements of a wan, gestural multiculturalism. Those movements have been condensed into the personae of Great Men and Great Women—Booker T. Washington, W.E.B. Du Bois, Rosa Parks, Malcolm X, George Washington Carver, Martin Luther King, Jr., Harriet Tubman, Frederick Douglass, Ella Baker, Fannie Lou Hamer and others—who seem to have changed the society apparently by virtue of manifesting their own greatness. The different jacket photos adorning the 1982 and 1999 editions of Doug McAdam's well known sociological study of the Civil Rights movement, *Political Process and the Development of Black Insurgency, 1930-1970*, exemplify the shift. The first edition's cover was a photo of an anonymous group of marching protesters; the second edition featured the (staged) photo—made iconic by its use in an Apple advertising campaign—of a dignified Rosa Parks sitting alone on the front seat of a bus looking pensively out the window.[20]

Ironically, the scholarly turn away from organizations and institutional processes to valorize instead the local and everyday dimensions of those movements may have exacerbated this tendency by encouraging a focus on previously unrecognized individual figures and celebrating their lives and 'contributions'. Rather than challenging the presumption that consequential social change is made by the will of extraordinary individuals, however, this scholarship in effect validates it by inflating the currency of Greatness so much that it can be found any and everywhere. Giving props to the unrecognized or underappreciated has become a feature particularly of that scholarship that defines scholarly production as a terrain of political action in itself and aspires to the function of the 'public intellectual'. A perusal of the rosters of African American History Month and Martin Luther King, Jr. Day speakers at any random sample of colleges and universities attests to how closely this scholar/activist turn harmonizes with the reductionist individualism of prosperity religion and the varieties of latter-day mind cure through which much of the professional-managerial stratum of all races, genders, and sexual orientations narrates its understandings of the world.

There is another, more mundane factor at play in the desire for 'black heroes'. It stems from a view that Hollywood is resistant to depiction of black heroes and that, therefore, any film with a bona fide black hero is the equivalent of a civil rights victory. Minister J. Kojo Livingston, writing in the *Louisiana Weekly*, put his appreciation of *Django Unchained* succinctly: "I liked the Black guy winning in the end."[21] That's fair enough, so far as it goes, particularly when consideration is given to how recently it has become possible to expect the black guy to win in the end. I was quite impressed and gratified at the time that Keith David's character made it along with Kurt Russell's to the end of John Carpenter's 1982 remake of *The Thing* and that in the 1979 *Alien* Yaphet Kotto's character was the penultimate one killed and only then because of the ineptitude of another crewmember who blocked his line of attack on the creature. When we watched the 1982 *Star Trek II: The Wrath of Khan*, my then twelve year-old son remarked that he'd want to leave the theater if the black starship captain (played by Paul Winfield) killed himself to save Captain Kirk, which of course happened moments later. (As Minister Livingston continued, "Heck, I liked the Black guy even living to see the end of a movie.") But, understandable as that impulse is, it is problematic as a basis for making claims about films' social significance at this point in American history. Black characters or characters played by black actors now routinely survive to the end of films in which most characters die, and black actors commonly enough play leading roles.

Literature scholar Kenneth Warren has suggested that objections to films like *Lincoln* on the basis of what they don't do often rest on a premise that mass-market films depicting themes that bear on black American history are so rare that each of them is under pressure to address everything that could be addressed. So a film that focuses on a particular legislative initiative in a brief period at the end of 1864 and early months of 1865 has sparked objections that it does not address issues outside its scope, such as Lincoln's evolving views of blacks, the role of black abolitionists and black troops in creating the climate that made the Thirteenth Amendment possible. But the sense that everything must be said at once sets an expectation that no film could ever satisfy even minimally. And, as Warren notes, the notion that occasions for such films are extremely rare is also problematic. That belief, like the premise that Hollywood refuses black heroes, is sustained largely by reference to a past—although, as I indicate above, a not very distant one—when it was clearly true.

Of course stereotypical representations of black characters remain. I had exactly the same reaction as Armond White to Hushpuppy, Quven-zhané Wallis's character in *Beasts of the Southern Wild*. When the two-bit magical realism and lame ponderousness of the dialogue are boiled off, she is, down to her name, a contemporary pickaninny and a window into the racial fantasy life of the hipster carpetbaggers who have flocked to New Orleans post-Katrina searching for authenticity and careers. Like all good satire, the 'Black Acting School' in Robert Townsend's 1987 *Hollywood Shuffle* had a foundation in material re-ality. Viola Davis seems to be a quite accomplished actor, but not only did she do basically the same performance in *The Help* and *Won't Back Down*; both characters are all too evocative of a stock figure—the quietly strong, long-suffering black woman depicted over the years by a string of actors from Joanna Moore and Claudia McNeil to Mary Alice, Beah Richards, Cicely Tyson, and now, woe be unto those with low tolerance for overacting, Angela Bassett. And it is not unreasonable to contend that double standards persist for black and white actors, directors, and thematic matter. Denzel Washington, after turning in basically the same sort of performance in a spate of films since the 1990s, finally won the best actor Academy Award for the version of it that was in the character of a corrupt, murderous cop, and he was nominated again in 2013 for a role as another ethically and morally flawed character, this time an alcoholic airline pilot.

Nevertheless, racial stereotypes and morally compromised characters are not the totality of black representation in films any more, nor even the preponderance. What made *Hollywood Shuffle* possible, and more significantly what made it successful, was the extent to which the conditions it satirized were already under critical scrutiny if not retreat. And a debate over whether there are *enough* starring roles for black characters, black actors cast in leading roles that may not be racially specified, or films with black subject matter is a much more complicated and ambiguous matter—enough according to what standard of expectation, after all?—than whether there are *any*.

The more interesting issue is the inclination to see the racial limitations of the present through the lens of the exclusion of the past. This habit of mind shapes the claim that *Django Unchained* breaks a convention of sanitizing slavery in both films and American culture in general. Harvard sociologist Lawrence D. Bobo rests his proclamation of *Django's* cinematic and cultural significance, which belies his nearly simultaneous articulation of the 'just entertainment' defense, on an assertion that "For too long American cinema has presented—and American audiences have accepted, digested and largely tacitly embraced—a hopelessly sanitized version of slavery in the South." He goes on to declaim on a "collective memory" in which the "defining image, of course, is that of Scarlett O'Hara and family enjoying the 'good life' before 'the War'. Slavery has been often rendered just a benign backdrop to the beauty, elegance and, indeed, virtue of the plantation elite."[22] Bobo is hardly alone in asserting that claim. It is a standard refrain, even including references to *Gone With the Wind* and *Birth of a Nation*, in defenses of Tarantino's film.[23]

Are we really to believe that, notwithstanding the massive sea change in the society since the end of World War II, Hollywood's depictions and the baseline of most Americans' presumptions about slavery are unchanged since 1915 or even 1939? In his defense of *Django* Adam Serwer at least limits the domain of persistent "lionization of the Lost Cause and the Confederacy" to the genre of the "revenge Western", but that qualification takes all the starch out of the claim. Redemption of the genre of the revenge Western seems like a low stakes, even lower reward undertaking. It would hardly be a notable victory for racial justice or any other significant social interest. I take Serwer's point that the "trope of the wronged former Confederate" is visible, albeit "excised from its historical context", in the sci-fi television program *Firefly* and its 2005 adaptation to feature-length film, *Serenity*. However, that excision from social context means more than he suggests.

Firefly's superficial parallels with the ex-Confederate hero trope are strong enough to have provoked discussion among devotees and adjustments in dialogue to have leading characters denounce slavery off the cuff. [24] The central characters are a crew of defeated insurgents operating as renegade traders who remain hostile to the oppressive and corrupt central authority that defeated them, and that makes the parallel to the wronged Confederate trope seem especially, even disturbingly, strong. I had an immediate and intensely negative reaction to it, even though the defeated rebels and those in league with them are a racially diverse lot, and neither the settings nor plot devices in any way evoke the slave South. Jeff Hart, in an essay on the theme of the brooding ex-Confederate hero in AMC's period drama *Hell on Wheels*, contends that *Firefly* "masterfully extracts all the cool stuff about being a Confederate that we love in our outlaws without any of the bad stuff (like slavery!)". [25]

However, that observation begs the question whether the "cool stuff about being a Confederate" can reasonably be seen as evoking the 1861 secessionist insurrection at all if it comes without that "bad stuff", without which there would have been no secessionist movement at all. Slavery, as Confederate Vice-President Alexander Stephens characterized it weeks after Lincoln's inauguration, in the midst of the secessionist frenzy, was the 'cornerstone' of the Southern order that he and his confreres considered in jeopardy.[26]

I recognize the impulse to treat the disconnected trope as though it has an essential meaning fixed by that distinctive context because that connection has such a lengthy, and more recently a charged, history. It has been around, after all, at least since the romance of the James brothers. As I remark above, that impulse affected my own reception of *Firefly*. It may be that Joss Whedon's appropriation of the trope of the brooding ex-Confederate outlaw hero for a setting that has nothing at all, even allegorically, to do with the nineteenth-century South in some way works backward to sanitize it in its more familiar context, but that seems far-fetched. There are, however, two ways in which that impulse is problematic.

First, the view that the trope of the emotionally damaged renegade outlaw of a Lost Cause is necessarily Confederate, even when disconnected entirely from racial subordination and slavery, may in effect validate apologists' argument that the secessionist treason rested on motives besides defense of slavery. The Lost Cause narrative emerged out of the consolidation of planter-merchant class hegemony in the South at the onset of the twentieth century. Films like *Birth of a Nation* and *Gone with the Wind* were instrumental in propagating this discourse, which sought to preempt non-Southern opposition to racial disfranchisement and Jim Crow. Rhetorically, in an era in which the secessionist insurrection was within two generations of living memory for many Americans (as many as 10,000 veterans of the hostilities were still alive as late as 1938), that project involved defusing slavery's legacy as a point of contention by representing it as a benign natural order in the antebellum era and by asserting that secessionism's objective wasn't protecting the institution of slavery but defending a conveniently evanescent 'way of life'.[27]

Second, giving in to that impulse directs attention away from the political vision *Firefly* actually does articulate, which says more about the character of our historical moment. *Firefly*'s narrative conceit resonates much more clearly with contemporary anti-statist conventions than it evokes the Lost Cause line. The trope of resistance to a brutal

and insensitive central authority is what today corrals social imagination in that perverse ratification of inequality and bourgeois class power
commonly euphemized as an abstract 'freedom' or 'liberty'. This conceit
permeates mass entertainment from *The Matrix* series to *The Hunger
Games* and a line of dystopian fantasy that stretches back at least to Norman Jewison's original *Rollerball* in 1975[28]. It is recycled endlessly in
the melodramatic cult of the maverick cop or physician who bristles under the corrupting and defeatist constraints of bureaucratic oversight—
what otherwise might be described as accountability to the public trust.
It has been a dominant theme in the genre of the disaster film and the
lineage of sci-fi horrors in space spawned by *Alien*.

That the evil central authority is often cast as direct rule by corporations, as in *Rollerball* and *Alien* (where it may reflect these stories' roots
in the still politically contested 1970s), is by now more a misdirection
than a mitigation of the anti-government narrative; that plot device col-
lapses the distinction between public and private and serves as a naïve
counter to criticisms that the films purvey right-wing politics. However,
the overarching narrative framework pits the local, familial/*gemein-
schaftlich*, and individual against the central, distant, and bureaucratic,
which are invariably villainous. That device is only a step away rhetorically from the crypto-fascist, stab-in-the-back Vietnam vigilante films
like the *Rambo* series and *Missing in Action*.[29]

But the ideological patron saints of these films are Friedrich Hayek
or Gary Becker more than Julius Streicher or Ted Nugent. It is the trials
and torments, and the glorification, of the individual, often even The
One, that drive their narrative arcs—even when they imagine themselves
doing otherwise. The priority of individual will is a thread connecting
fantasy, fiction and 'faction' alike. *Cold Mountain* reduces the Southern
elites' treason to a thin backdrop for a puerile love story, barely leavened
with a couple of trite 'war is hell' references and a dash or two of Clarissa
Pinkola Estés-style cultural feminism about how it's the women who *really* suffer from the wars that y'all men make. (As Dargis noted, however,
the period artifacts nearly all pass muster for authenticity.) For all its
bullshit, dorm-room philosophy, geeky double and triple reversals, and
purported critique of authoritarianism, *The Matrix* films pivot on Neo

as The One. In fact, apparently the only hope for combating the ubiquitous threats in any given post-apocalyptic world is to wait for the arrival of the Chosen One. *The Iron Lady* reduces even Margaret Thatcher to a bourgeois feminist story of Woman Overcoming.

No wonder Maggie Gyllenhaal couldn't tell the difference between her union-busting, ditzy zealot Jamie Fitzpatrick and Norma Rae or Karen Silkwood. Never mind that both those characters were modeled on real union activists: Norma Rae's inspiration was Crystal Lee Sutton, a member/organizer of the Amalgamated Clothing and Textile Workers Union, now part of UNITE HERE, and Silkwood lost her life as an activist in the Oil, Chemical and Atomic Workers International Union, now part of the United Steel Workers. That's all pointless detail, TMI; it's really all about individual working-class women fighting for what they believe in and Overcoming. (It may be a marker of the changed era that, twenty-eight years after she played the lead in *Silkwood*, Meryl Streep starred as Thatcher.)

Forget about possible evocations of the Confederacy; this is *Firefly*'s ideological milieu. Its vision is anti-government, *punto*, a multiculturalist, and thus left-seeming, anti-statism. The main expression of the central authority's oppressiveness that affronts Serenity's band of inter-planetary smugglers is its exorbitant taxation and arbitrary, corrupt regulation of trade. The captain and central character, also the most given to political declamation, is a committed free-trader. *Firefly*'s defenders describe its politics as libertarian. That is not only compatible with its multiculturalist egalitarianism; the two can fit organically. But, as Hayek, Ludwig von Mises, and Milton Friedman—as well as their acolyte, Thatcher—all were very much aware, there is no such thing as a left libertarianism. The belief that there is reflects the wishful thinking, or disingenuousness, of those who don't want to have to square their politics with their desired self-perception.

Libertarianism is a shuck, more an aesthetics than a politics. Libertarians don't want the state to do anything other than what they want the state to do. And, as its founding icons understood, it is fundamentally about property rights *über alles*. Mises and Hayek made clear in theory, and Thatcher and Friedman as Pinochet's muse in Chile did in practice, that a libertarian society requires an anti-popular, authoritarian government to make sure that property rights are kept sacrosanct. That's why it's so common that a few bad days, some sweet nothings, and a couple of snazzy epaulets will turn a libertarian into an open fascist.

Whether or not *Firefly* contains more or less abstruse secessionist allegory, the fact that that issue is the basis of concern about its politics is a window onto a core problem of the current political situation. It reflects a critical perspective that accepts neoliberal ideological hegemony as nature and finds its own standard of justice in the rearview mirror. To the extent that *Firefly* embraces a libertarian politics, what it would share with the slave South isn't racism but something more fundamental. Insofar as the 'freedom' the heroes yearn for includes destruction of the regulatory apparatus of the state in favor of a market-fundamentalist idea of freedom or liberty, no matter how racially diverse and egalitarian that world would be, it would be closer than one might think to the essential normative premise of the social order of which slavery was the cornerstone, the conviction that individual property rights are absolute and inviolable.

The Southern political economy didn't become grounded on slavery because it was racist; it became racist because it was grounded on slavery.[30] That is, it was grounded on the absolute right of property-owners to define and control their property—including property in other human beings—as they wished without any interference or regulation, except, of course, reliance on the police powers of the state to enforce their rights to and in such property. This takes us back to the necessity for authoritarian government, about which there was little disagreement within the dominant planter class.

Prominent pro-slavery ideologist George Fitzhugh was resolutely antagonistic to free-market, especially free-labor, liberalism and would hardly be considered a philosophical libertarian. But neither would Hayek or Ron Paul have been when describing the authoritarian regime essential for realizing property-based Liberty. As one of the most vocal proponents of the argument that slavery was a positive good for all involved, Fitzhugh doubled down on the matter of holding property rights in people as the sectional crisis intensified. His 1854 book, *Sociology for the South, or, the Failure of a Free Society,* argued for enslavement of poor whites as well as blacks. James Henry Hammond, US Senator and former governor of South Carolina, memorialized this perspective in what came to be known as his "Mudsill Speech" on the floor of the US Senate in 1858 (also Django's big year). Speaking in Congress as a member of a party that counted Northern free white workers among its core constituencies, Hammond was politic enough not to propose enslaving them. However, he did underscore the essential reduction of freedom to property rights, describing the slave South as enjoying "an extent of political freedom, combined with entire security, such as no other people ever enjoyed upon the face of the earth". And he argued that, in effect, freedom was more complete and more secure in the South because slavery permitted suppression and absolute exclusion from civic voice of its "mud-sills"—the stratum necessary "to do the menial duties, to perform the drudgery of life [without which] you would not have that other class which leads progress, civilization, and refinement". That's what made the South more effectively free than the North. Freedom, or liberty, meant the unbridled license of the propertied class.

The rhetoric of antebellum fire-eaters and the ordinances of secession they crafted stand out for the vehemence of their protests that their essential liberties were under attack. The secessionists framed *their* extravagant denunciations of the national government for its potential infringement of their right to hold property in human beings in language that from our historical location seems Freudian in the blatancy with which they declared themselves as literally fearing enslavement by the United States. But it wasn't psychological projection or reaction formation. They considered any potential infringement on absolute property rights as indeed tantamount to enslavement. For them property is the only real right; therefore, property-holders are the only people in the society with rights that count for anything, and their rights trump all else.

This is a perspective that can provide some badly needed clarity on debates in contemporary politics regarding the relation of race, racism and inequality. For example, Ron and Rand Paul, libertarians of the highest order, do not oppose the 1964 Civil Rights Law because they hate, or even don't like, black people. (And, for the record, whenever one finds oneself agreeing at all with Kanye West about anything, it's time to take a step back, breathe deeply and reassess.) They oppose it, as they've made clear, because it infringes on property rights. They dislike black people because they understand, correctly, that black people are very likely to be prominent among those committed to pursuing greater equality. They oppose black people's demands and all others intended to mitigate inequality because any efforts to do so would necessarily impinge on the absolute sanctity of property rights. I don't mean to suggest that the Pauls aren't racist; I'm pretty confident they are, no matter how much they might protest the assessment. My point is that determining whether they're racist, then exposing and denouncing them for it, doesn't reach to what is most consequentially wrong and dangerous about them or for that matter what makes their racism something more significant than that of the random bigot who lives around the corner on disability.

Returning to *Firefly*, we don't ever have to confront Captain Mal's and his crew's libertarianism beyond platitudes and the sort of errant patter of an adolescent irked at being told to clean up her room. We don't because they aren't in a position to demonstrate what their libertarianism would look like in practice. What they do perform regularly is liberal multiculturalism, which no doubt reinforces a sense that the show's gestural anti-statism is at least consonant with an egalitarian politics. And that is a quality that makes multiculturalist egalitarianism, or identitarianism, and its various strategic programs—anti-racism, anti-sexism, anti-heteronormativity, etc.—neoliberalism's loyal opposition. Their focus is on making neoliberalism more just and, often enough, more truly efficient. Their objective is that, however costs and benefits are distributed, the distribution should not disproportionately harm or disadvantage the populations for which they advocate.

But what if neoliberalism really can't be made more just? (And, to be clear, when I say neoliberalism, I mean capitalism with the gloves off and back on the offensive.) What if the historical truth of capitalist class power is that, without direct, explicit and relentless, zero-sum challenge to its foundations in a social order built on its priority and dominance in the social division of labor, we will never be able to win more than a shifting around of the material burdens of inequality, reallocating them and recalibrating their incidence among different populations? And what if creation of such populations as given, natural-seeming entities—first as differentially valued pools of labor, in the ideological equivalent of an evolving game of musical chairs, then eventually also as ostensibly discrete market niches within the mass consumption regime—is a crucial element in capitalism's logic of social reproduction? To the extent that that is the case, multiculturalist egalitarianism and the political programs that follow from it reinforce a key mystification that legitimizes the systemic foundation of the inequalities to which those programs object.

Regimes of class hierarchy depend for their stability on ideologies that legitimize inequalities by representing them as the result of natural differences—where you (or they) are in the society is where you (or they) deserve to be. Folk taxonomies define and sort populations into putatively distinctive groups on the basis of characteristics ascribed to them. Such taxonomies rely on circular self-validation in explaining the positions groups occupy in the social order as suited to the essential, inherent characteristics, capabilities and limitations posited in the taxonomy's just-so stories. These ideological constructions and the social processes through which they are reproduced, including the common sense that arises from self-fulfilling prophecy, are what Karen E. Fields and Barbara J. Fields call 'racecraft'[31]. An implication of the racecraft notion is that the ideology, or taxonomy, of race is always as much the cover story as the source of even the inequalities most explicitly linked to race.

James Henry Hammond's mudsill theory is instructive. The Southern system was superior and afforded greater freedom, he argued, because its mudsills were held to belong to an ascriptively distinct and naturally subordinate population. The North was a less secure and stable society because its mudsills were "of your own race; you are brothers of one blood. They are your equals in natural endowment or intellect, and they feel galled by their degradation. Our slaves do not vote. We give them no political power. Yours do vote, and, being the majority, they are the depositaries of all your political power." He in effect judged the North's ruling class to be more unstable than the South's because it hadn't been able to turn its mudsills into a sufficiently different ascriptive population. (Fitzhugh, the theorist, proposed a remedy for that problem; Hammond, the politician, understood that was easier said than done.)

Hammond was no doubt sincere in his conviction that blacks were by nature fit to be slaves, "of another and inferior race". But notwithstanding his sincerity, that view was relatively new as a defense of slavery. Alexander Stephens indicated as much in the "Cornerstone Speech" and noted that the dominant perspective of the Founding generation was that "enslavement of the African was in violation of the laws of nature". Of course, Stephens insisted that that perspective was "fundamentally wrong" in that it "rested upon the assumption of the equality of the races". The defense of slavery that he and Hammond articulated dated only from the 1830s, when the combined pressures of a surge in abolitionist activism and articulations of free labor ideology outside the South called for a more robust defense of the 'peculiar institution' than the fundamentally apologetic contention that it was a 'necessary evil' economically. South Carolina's father of the secessionist treason, John C. Calhoun, gave the new argument its systematic expression in "Slavery a Positive Good", an 1837 speech to the US Senate.[32]

That argument aligned with the emergent race science that would provide the basic folk taxonomy through which Americans apprehend race and categories of racial classification to this day. A central text of that nascent race science was the 1854 tome *Types of Mankind*, co-authored by George R. Gliddon, a British-born Egyptologist, and Josiah C. Nott, a native South Carolinian and wealthy slave-holding physician in Mobile, Alabama.[33] In 1851 Samuel A. Cartwright, a plantation physician and pioneer in the science of racial medicine, published in *De Bow's Review* a paper, "Diseases and Peculiarities of the Negro Race", which he had initially presented at a Louisiana medical convention and in which he examined, among other racial particularities, a condition he called "drapetomania"—a "disease of the mind" that induced slaves to "run away from service".[34] Race theory, that is, took shape as a defense of slavery only in the last decades of the institution's life; it was the expression of a beleaguered slavocracy doubling down to protect its property rights in human beings.

Hammond may have believed that he'd always believed the positive good argument and that black slavery was nature's racial decree. If he did, he would only have been demonstrating the power of ascriptive ideologies to impose themselves as reality. Marxist theorist Harry Chang thus analogized race to Marx's characterization of the fetish character of money. Just as money is the material condensation of "the reification of a relation called value" and a "function-turned-into-an-object", race is also a function—a relation in the capitalist division of labor—turned into an object. [35]

Race and gender are the ascriptive hierarchies most familiar to us because they have been most successfully challenged since the second half of the last century; ideologies of ascriptive difference are most powerful when they are simply taken as nature and don't require defense. The significant and lasting institutional victories that have been won against racial and gender subordination and discrimination, as well as the cultural victories against racism and sexism as ideologies, have rendered those taxonomies less potent as justifications for ascriptive inequality than they had been. As capitalism has evolved new articulations of the social division of labor, and as the victories against racial and gender hierarchy have been consolidated, the causal connections between those ideologies and manifest inequality have become still more attenuated.

Race and gender don't exhaust the genus of ascriptive hierarchies. Other taxonomies do and have done the same sort of work as those we understand as race. The feebleminded and the born criminal, for example, were equivalent to racial taxa as ideologies of ascriptive hierarchy but did not hinge on the phenotypical narratives that have anchored the race idea. Victorian British elites ascribed essential, race-like difference to the English working class. The culture of poverty and the underclass overlap racially disparaged populations but aren't exactly reducible to familiar racial taxonomies. Some—like super predators and crack babies—have had more fleeting life spans. Their common sense explanatory power hinges significantly on the extent to which they comport with the perspectives and interests of the social order's dominant, opinion-shaping strata; as Marx and Engels observed in 1845, "the class

which is the ruling *material* force of society, is at the same time its ruling *intellectual* force." [36]

Hell on Wheels, or the Tea Party

In addition, the exact sort of work that given taxonomies, or categories
within one, will do is linked to historically specific regimes of hierarchy.
A taxonomy's ideological significance and material impact, that is, can
vary widely. 'Race' was an ideology of essential difference in 1820, as it
was in the 1850s. Yet it didn't do the same work in the earlier period's
defenses of slavery as a necessary evil that it did in later defenses of it as
a positive good, like those articulated by Fitzhugh and Hammond. Nor
does gender do the same work in the early twenty-first century that it did
at the beginning, or even in the middle, of the twentieth.

Once established, stereotypes and the folk taxonomies that legit-
0imize them may die hard, but their significance as props for a regime
of class hierarchy can change along with the political-economic foundations of the class order. Persistence of familiar narratives of hierarchy
can evoke the earlier associations, but that evocation can be misleading
and counterproductive for making sense of social relations in both past
and present. In particular the 'just like slavery' or 'just like Jim Crow'
proclamations that are intended as powerful criticism of current injustices are more likely to undermine understanding of injustice in the past
as well as the present than to enable new insight. Another version of the
trope of the damaged ex-Confederate is illustrative.

Unlike *Firefly*, the television drama *Hell on Wheels* constructs the
wounded ex-Confederate much nearer its original form but with revi-
sions that underscore the contemporary period drama's problematic and
ideological relation to history. Adam Serwer adduces *Hell on Wheels*,
which is set in 1865 in a mobile railroad town, as another illustration of
the persistence of the trope of the vengeful former Confederate brooding hero/sociopath, albeit in a 'hilariously rationalized' form. Its version of the character, Cullen Bohannon, had been a large Mississippi
planter who freed his slaves a year before the treasonous insurrection
in deference to his Northern, anti-slavery wife who—true to tale type—
was later martyred by marauding Union soldiers, now the targets of his

quest. Serwer is correct to say that the preposterous device of separating the hero's Confederate loyalties from commitment to slave-holding is a transparent effort to sanitize the hero's secessionism.

However, the difference in historical context is crucial in this regard as well. The old Lost Cause tropes, originating in the early twentieth-century Southern ideological campaign for sectional reconciliation on white supremacist terms, don't do the same cultural and ideological work in a society in which Glenn Beck appropriates Martin Luther King, Jr. to accuse President Barack Obama of racism that they did in a society in which racial subordination was supported explicitly by the force of law and custom. This is not to imply that there's nothing politically disturbing and reactionary about the conceits of *Hell on Wheels*. On the contrary, going beyond the superficial rehearsal of hoary tropes to consider the program's representations in their actual historical context discloses its more insidious work in legitimizing inequality.

The conceit that Bohannon had freed his slaves before he fought for secession does more than separate the treason from its foundational commitment to slavery. That conceit also replaces slavery as an institution with slaveholding as a matter of individual morality, as in *Django Unchained*. That Bohannon manumitted his slaves as a gesture of love for his wife folds into another trope of the genre, the pedestalizing, 'I love her so much I'd change my raffish ways for her' fantasy. That's the happy face of adolescent patriarchy, its expression that doesn't usually involve a restraining order, though it's probably best that the brooding loner hero's sainted wife is nearly always a martyr and thus motivation for, instead of the object of, his sadistic violence and mayhem. But in *Hell on Wheels* that device also reinforces the reduction of slavery to slaveholding as an individual act, a consumer preference to be negotiated within a marriage—like owning a motorcycle, going to the strip club with the guys every weekend, or painting the living room magenta.

From the standpoint of claims to social significance, a deeper problem with period vehicles like *Django Unchained*, *The Help*, and *Hell on Wheels* is their denial of historicity. By this I do not mean historical accuracy as faithfulness to facts about the past. The manumission themes in *Hell on Wheels* and *Django Unchained* are instructive. Voluntary manumission was all but impossible in Mississippi as the sectional crisis intensified on the eve of secession. By 1860, even Maryland, with a relatively large free black population, and Arkansas, which had a comparatively small slave population, had outlawed the practice; the states with the largest black populations had done so much earlier—South Carolina in 1820 and Mississippi in 1822. Considering its relatively incidental place in each story line, though, the historical inaccuracy on which those bits hinge is within the boundaries of acceptable artistic license. The problem is with the ideological character of the larger story lines that preclude even wondering whether manumission would have been possible.

Both tales trifle with slavery. For *Hell on Wheels* it's an unfortunate artifact of the genre, baggage that threatens to sully the appeal of the hero as wronged Confederate. Producers Joe and Tony Gayton (a former production assistant for political reactionary John Milius and co-writer with his brother Joe of the Vietnam POW rescue fantasy film *Uncommon Valor*) may also have been concerned to preempt sharp criticism for romanticizing the institution indirectly through their hero's secessionist loyalties. For Tarantino slavery is a prop for a claim to social significance and a hook to connect spaghetti Western and blaxploitation. In both vehicles it is a generic bad thing, an especially virulent species of racism, though slavery's pastness—not only was Bohannon no longer a slave owner; but the series is set in 1865—keeps it peripheral in *Hell on Wheels*. And once again the central thread is the individual quest. Even the principal ex-slave in *Hell on Wheels*, Elam Ferguson (played by the rapper Common), is depicted as "coming to terms with the risks and responsibilities of his newly-acquired freedom", and, because he had a "white father and a slave mother", apparently he is therefore "a man with no true home or people he can call his own". And he and Bohannon, also a disconnected individual, engage in an exchange about the need to "let go of the past". Even though that exchange seems intended partly as a comment on the impossibility of either man's doing so, the punch line remains the individual quest, leavened with the unshakable personal demons that are the banal melodrama's yeast. (And I can anticipate the contention that *Hell on Wheels* is somehow critical of capitalism. It's not. It's critical of *big* capitalism and once again the capital/government nexus and their running roughshod over beleaguered individuals. That's the critical standpoint of a reactionary populism that's as likely to support Tea Party style fascism as any other politics, and it would be good for us all to be clearer in recognizing that for what it is.)

Effacement of historicity and the social in favor of the timeless—that is, presentist—narrative of individual Overcoming is the deep politics and social commentary propounded in these products of the mass entertainment industry. They differ from other such products only because they ostensibly apply the standard formulae to socially important topics. They don't, however. They do exactly the reverse; they revise historically and politically significant moments to fit within the formula. In doing so they are nodes in the constitution of neoliberalism's ideological hegemony.

And the extent of that hegemony is attested by claims from the likes of Lawrence Bobo, Jon Wiener and others who should know better than to think that a film like *Django Unchained* somehow captures the essential truth of American slavery. That truth is apparently, as Bobo condenses it, "brutality, inescapable violence and absolutely thorough moral degradation". But those features were neither essential nor exclusive to slavery; they were behavioral artifacts enabled by the institution because it conferred, with support of law and custom, a property right—absolute control of life and livelihood—of some individuals over others. That property right was the essential evil and injustice that defined slavery, not the extremes of brutality and degradation it could encourage and abet. No effort is required to understand why mass-market films go for the dramatic excesses, but what about the scholars and other nominal leftists who also embrace that view of slavery?

In part, the inclination may stem from a corrosive legacy of Malcolm X. Malcolm was an important cultural figure for most of the 1960s, before and perhaps even more so after his death. He was not, however, an historian, and few formulations have done more to misinform, distort and preempt popular understanding of American slavery than his rhetorically very effective but historically facile 'house Negro/field Negro' parable. It doesn't map onto how even plantation slavery—which accounted for only about half of slaves by 1850—operated. Not only was working in the house no major plum; it hardly fit with the Uncle Tom stereotype, such as Tarantino's self-hating caricature, Stephen. The well-known slave rebels Nat Turner, Gabriel Prosser, Denmark Vesey and Robert Smalls all gainsay that image. Anyway, the Uncle Tom notion is not a useful category for political analysis. It is only a denunciation; no one ever identifies under that label. Yet its emptiness may be the source of its attractiveness. In disconnecting critique from any discrete social practice and locating it instead in imputed pathological psychology—'Why, that house Negro loved the master more than the master loved himself', pace Malcolm—the notion individualizes political criticism on the (non-existent) racially self-hating caricature, and, of course, anyone a demagogue chooses to denounce. Because it centers on motives rather than concrete actions and stances, it leaves infinite room both for making and deflecting ad hominem charges and, of course, inscribes racial authenticity as the key category of political judgment.

That sort of Malcolm X/blaxploitation narrative, including the insistence that *Birth of a Nation* and *Gone With the Wind* continue to shape Americans' understandings of slavery, also is of a piece with a line of anti-racist argument and mobilization that asserts powerful continuities between current racial inequalities and either slavery or the Jim Crow regime. This line of argument has been most popularly condensed recently in Michelle Alexander's *The New Jim Crow*, which analogizes contemporary mass incarceration to the segregationist regime. But even she, after much huffing and puffing and asserting the relation gesturally throughout the book, ultimately acknowledges that the analogy fails.[37] And it would have to fail because the segregationist regime was the artifact of a particular historical and political moment in a particular social order. Moreover, the rhetorical force of the analogy with Jim Crow or slavery derives from the fact that those regimes are associated symbolically with strong negative sanctions in the general culture because they have been vanquished. In that sense all versions of the lament that 'it's as if nothing has changed' give themselves the lie. They are effective only to the extent that things *have* changed significantly.

The tendency to craft political critique by demanding that we fix our gaze in the rearview mirror appeals to an intellectual laziness. Marking superficial similarities with familiar images of oppression is less mentally taxing than attempting to parse the multifarious, often contradictory dynamics and relations that shape racial inequality in particular and politics in general in the current moment. Assertions that phenomena like the Jena, Louisiana, incident, the killings of James Craig Anderson and Trayvon Martin, and racial disparities in incarceration demonstrate persistence of old-school, white supremacist racism and charges that the sensibilities of Thomas Dixon and Margaret Mitchell continue to shape most Americans' understandings of slavery do important, obfuscatory ideological work. They lay claim to a moral urgency that, as Mahmood Mamdani argues concerning the rhetorical use of charges of genocide, enables the disparagement of efforts either to differentiate discrete inequalities or to generate historically specific causal accounts of them as irresponsible dodges that abet injustice by temporizing in its face[38]. But more is at work here as well.

Insistence on the transhistorical primacy of racism as a source of inequality is a class politics. It's the politics of a stratum of the professional-managerial class whose material location and interests, and thus whose ideological commitments, are bound up with parsing, interpreting and administering inequality defined in terms of disparities among ascriptively defined populations reified as groups or even cultures. Much of the intellectual life of this stratum is devoted to "shoehorning into the rubric of racism all manner of inequalities that may appear statistically as racial disparities".[39] And that project shares capitalism's ideological tendency to obscure race's foundations, as well as the foundations of all such ascriptive hierarchies, in historically specific political economy. This felicitous convergence may help explain why proponents of 'cultural politics' are so inclined to treat the products and production processes of the mass entertainment industry as a terrain for political struggle and debate. They don't see the industry's imperatives as fundamentally incompatible with the notions of a just society they seek to advance. In fact, they share its fetishization of heroes and penchant for inspirational stories of individual Overcoming. This sort of 'politics of representation' is no more than an image-management discourse within neoliberalism. That strains of an *ersatz* left imagine it to be something more marks the extent of our defeat. And then, of course, there's that Upton Sinclair point.

WALTER BENN MICHAELS

Who Gets Ownership of Pain and Victimhood?

In August 1955, Emmett Till, a fourteen-year-old African-American boy from Chicago visiting relatives in the small town of Money, Mississippi, stopped to buy some candy at a local general store, one that catered mainly to black customers. At the murder trial that took place a month later, Carolyn Bryant, the pretty young white woman who waited on him, testified that when she held out her hand to take Till's money, he grabbed it and said, "How about a date, baby?", and that then, after she freed herself from his grip, he followed her, "caught" her by the waist and said, "What's the matter, baby? Can't you take it", going on to use a word that Bryant could not bring herself to repeat or even say the first letter of. But if she couldn't say the F-word, she had no problem with the N-word, describing how she managed to free herself from the "nigger"'s grasp and how, after "this other nigger came in the store and got him by the arm", she ran outside to get her pistol from her car and Till (this is the only aspect of her testimony that could be and was confirmed by others) whistled at her before driving off with his friends.[1] That night, Bryant's husband and brother-in-law went to the house where Till was staying and dragged him out of it. Two days later his dead, naked and brutally beaten body was found in the Tallahatchie River. The two men were promptly arrested and tried for his murder; it took the jury an hour to return a verdict of not guilty.

Appallingly enough, this was not all that unusual an event. The Supreme Court case that made racial segregation illegal (*Brown v Board of Education*) had been decided in 1954 and resistance (often violent) to it was becoming widespread. A few months before Till's death, the first black man registered to vote in Belzoni, Mississippi (about forty miles from Money) was murdered and no one was even arrested, much less convicted. Just two weeks before Till, a black World War II veteran who was outspoken about voting rights for black people was killed on the court house lawn with the Sheriff looking on. Three white men were arrested but never indicted.[2] What made Till's murder unusual was that his killers were actually brought to trial, not that they were acquitted. And what made it not just surprising but a crucial moment in the Civil Rights movement was the response it generated around the country, a response produced above all by his mother's decision to have an open casket funeral. When the funeral director told Mamie Till that she didn't want to see what he looked like, she responded that not only did she want to see him, she wanted everyone to see him—"Let the people see what they did to my boy"—and the photos of his brutalized face were shown around the country and the world.

In March of 2017, the Whitney Biennial put Dana Schutz's picture *Open Casket* on display. One critic described it as "a powerful painterly reaction to the infamous 1955 funeral photograph of a disfigured Emmett Till".[3] But far from being greeted as a new weapon in the ongoing fight against racism, *Open Casket* was denounced as itself a form of racism. The British artist Hannah Black posted an open letter to the Whitney curators demanding that it be taken down, and protesters demonstrated in front of it. And this too was not an isolated event. Similar protests were lodged in St. Louis against work that used photos of black protesters being beaten by police (in Selma, in 1965) and against an installation in Minneapolis memorializing, among other things, the unjust execution of thirty-eight Dakota Indians in 1862. And such protests have not only continued but spread. When Parker Bright, who protested at the Whitney, discovered that a photo of him protesting was to be part of a piece shown by the French Algerian artist Neil Beloufa in a show at the Palais de Tokyo, he declared his intention to protest that.

When he started a GoFundMe campaign to help him fly to Paris and "reclaim his image", Beloufa decided not to show it.

So in 1955 there was an effort to make sure that as many people as possible got to see a photo of Emmett Till; now the effort is to make sure that no one gets to see a painting of Emmett Till. But the relevant difference is not between photography and painting. What the protests have been about is not what kind of image it is but who made it. "White artists . . . profit off of black trauma, black death, and black bodies", Zeba Blay complained. [4] And in her widely circulated letter to the Whitney, Hannah Black wrote that Till's mother made his face "available to Black people as an inspiration and warning". "Non-Black people must accept that they will never embody and cannot understand this gesture". "The subject matter is not Schutz's", she said. [5] In other words, black pain belongs to black artists.

Putting the problem in these terms—"It's not acceptable for a white person to transmute Black suffering into profit . . . "—helps to provide some sense of the political economy of this outrage. What's supposed to be racist about Dana Schutz is not that she's defending or excusing the murder of Emmett Till (in this respect, *Open Casket* could not be less controversial; no one today is defending or excusing the murder) but that she is cashing in on it—if not directly (when attacked, Schutz immediately announced that her picture was not and never would be for sale) then in taking up space in elite institutions like the Whitney, space that might otherwise be reserved for black artists. And what angers Parker Bright is that the "conversation about racial injustice within the art world" that he, "a Black artist", created has been "appropriated" by a non-black artist for an exhibition in the Palais de Tokyo. [6] The idea, in other words, is that now that "elitist, mostly white institutions" have become eager to promote work that opposes racism, they should do so by devoting their "resources" to the victims of racism [7]. If anybody's going to profit off black pain, it should be black people.

This opposition to cultural appropriation is thus a claim to cultural capital. And if, in one sense, these battles represent a new and impressive stage in the privatization of virtually everything—now, pain—in another they represent a variation on a familiar theme: the demand for racial justice as a demand for equality of access to elite institutions, a demand that, as many historians have shown, always played a significant role in the American Civil Rights movement (think Du Bois's 'talented tenth'), and with predictable results. It has helped produce a small but significant increase in the number of black people joining if not the 'elite' then at least the upper middle class: "the percentage of African-Americans making at least $75,000 more than doubled from 1970 to 2014, to 21 percent. Those making $100,000 or more nearly quadrupled, to 13 percent . . . "[8]. (Henry Louis Gates calls them the talented thirteenth). But it has left the great majority of black people behind—their median income is still only $43,300[9]. And the number of black people living in poverty is almost eleven million.

The point here is not (or not only) the obvious one—that the gains for the few don't help the many. It's that the gains for the few are part of a process that hurts the many. In the name of racial justice, it imposes upon them a fantasy of racial solidarity in which the fact that a few black people are doing well (gaining access to the Whitney, going to elite colleges, joining the upper middle class) is supposed to count as a victory for the vast majority of black people who are not. An idea which is rendered immediately absurd the minute we turn it around and apply it to white people: do white artists who don't get their work into the Whitney Biennial imagine themselves to be represented by the ones who do? Do poor white people take pride or even solace in the fact that there are rich white people? Obviously not. The fact that some white people are rich while a great many are poor isn't the solution, it's the problem.

A problem that is made essentially invisible when writers like Hannah Black explain that the proof of white people's inability to understand the sacrifice Till's mother made is the fact that "Black people go on dying at the hands of white supremacists, that Black communities go on living in desperate poverty not far from the museum where this valuable painting hangs, that Black children are still *denied* childhood." For one thing, this makes the white children living in poverty (fifty-one per cent of the poor) invisible. But, more important, it tells everybody made rich by capitalism what they want to hear—that the only poverty they need to worry about is the poverty that's an effect of racism. In other words, even though the current outrage about cultural appropriation is in the end nothing more than a kind of racial rent-seeking for a small fraction of the black upper class, its real utility is to all the members of the upper class, which is to say, mainly white people.

Emmett Till's open casket is thus a perfect totem object for left neo-liberal piety. For white people like the artist Dana Schutz, it embodies the opportunity to mourn the victim of a white supremacy they genuinely hate; for black artists, the very fact of white people mourning him marks a continuation of the white supremacy that killed him. Either way, the conflict between rich and poor is made to disappear by the battle against white supremacy, and the battle against white supremacy is reduced to a battle over who's entitled to express how bad they feel about Emmett Till having been murdered.

This is not what the open casket was originally about. In *The Blood of Emmett Till*, Timothy Tyson mentions the fact that the United Pack-inghouse Workers, a labor union that he describes as "interracial" and as having "an increasingly strong commitment to civil rights" [10], sent an interracial delegation to observe the trial in Mississippi. That description of the Packinghouse Workers is true as far as it goes, and, indeed, they may be best known today as the first union to support Marin Luther King. But what Tyson doesn't mention is that they were a profoundly controversial organization before King came along, militant in fighting against the brutal working conditions imposed by the 'Big Four' meatpackers (Armour, Cudahy, Swift and Wilson) as well as in their op-position to Jim Crow racism; so militant that, even when the various an-ti-communist 'Red Scares' pushed other once radical unions to the right, the UPWA continued to support communists both in leadership and the rank-and-file. In fact, it was two union and Communist Party members who, when news of Emmett's death first broke, got some money from the union "to buy some groceries for the Till house", and later were with Mamie Till when they brought his body home to Chicago. "When they opened the bag", as Arlene Brigham remembered it, "everyone was in shock and didn't know what to say. The newspapers were there but said, 'We're not going to take these pictures.' Gus Savage was outside. I told Gus to take the pictures. . . . He published a little magazine then called the American Negro. That's how the pictures were first shown. Then everyone started putting them out." [11]

People like Arlene Brigham were committed to what Roger Horowitz in his book about the UPWA calls 'social unionism', which is one way of saying that they didn't just want to negotiate higher wages for union members, they wanted to move the whole country to the left, and they understood the struggle against capitalism and the struggle against racism as inextricably bound to each other. *Negro and White, Unite and Fight!* is what Horowitz's book is called. But by the early 1960s, the communists had more or less disappeared and the communism they were fighting for had become almost invisible, although not so invisible that, during the Presidential primaries in 2016, Bernie Sanders couldn't be attacked in the *New York Post* as a 'diehard communist' because he had worked for a while as a UPWA organizer when he was at school in Chicago. And that attack from the right was echoed from the left in the charge that all Sanders really cared about was economic rather than racial justice.

The modicum of truth in both these attacks is a mark of the political economy in which the appropriation of a race's culture has replaced the appropriation of the workers' labor as a focus for social struggle. The truth in the attack from the right is that Sanders was the closest thing to a socialist, if not a communist, American politics has seen in half a century; the truth in the attack from the left was that anti-racism has so totally supplanted anti-capitalism that Sanders's desire to lift up the entire working class was interpreted as indifference to black people and then used against him by liberals who are just as hostile to the kind of politics represented by radical unions as conservatives are. It's those liberals—white and black, painting pictures of Emmett Till or trying to take those pictures down—who are working to complete the transformation of a politics of class conflict into a politics of class consolidation.

WALTER BENN MICHAELS & DANIEL ZAMORA

Chris Killip and LaToya Ruby Frazier:
The Promise of a Class Aesthetic

Probably the best known pictures of labor in our time, Sebastião Salga-do's *Workers: An Archaeology of the Industrial Age* (1993)[1], are described by the man who made them as pictures of an era "when men and women at work with their hands provided the central axis of the world"[2]. As the past tense of 'provided' suggests, Salgado thought of that era as com-ing to an end; "concepts of production and efficiency are changing", he wrote, "and with them, the nature of work." Thus, for example, although worldwide coal production is much higher today than it was when Salgado took his pictures of these miners in Dhanbad, India (Fig. 1), the number of people employed in those mines has diminished, and the conditions of their labor were already changing by the time *Workers* was published. In 1980 the mining sector employed 800,000 persons; mines employed only 560,000 in 2013, and this number is still declining due to mechanization.[3]

And, of course, those processes of mechanization and casualization were themselves part of a larger process that was already at work before Salgado's *Workers*. The British coal miners who were among the subjects of Chris Killip's *In Flagrante* were disappearing then and have now al-most completely vanished (Fig. 2)[4]. In Allegheny County, Pennsylvania, where LaToya Ruby Frazier took the pictures in *The Notion of Family*, the

Figure 1. Sebastião Salgado
Coal Mining, Dhanbad, Bihar, India, 1989
1989. Courtesy of the artist.
© Sebastião Salgado

number of manufacturing jobs (most of them in steel mills) dropped by almost two-thirds between 1970 and 2000 and has continued to fall since then, leaving health care as the largest industry[5]. Thus the photography of laboring people and working lives in our time is also the photography of the disappearance of certain kinds of labor and of lives without work.

Indeed, if Salgado is in some sense the photographer of industrialization, Killip and Frazier might be understood as photographers of deindustrialization. But their differences from Salgado, we will argue in this essay, are not only in their subject matter but (to varying degrees) in their aesthetics (their idea of what makes a good photograph) and also (and therefore) in their politics.

In the work of all three of these photographers—indeed, in the work of almost any photographer in the documentary tradition—the relation (what we might call the nonidentity) between the photographer and his or her subjects, on the one hand, and between the photograph and its beholders, on the other, is crucial.[6] Our argument will be that this relation works differently in the work of Killip and Frazier than it does in that of Salgado—that Salgado seeks to establish a connection with his subjects that will enable him to make pictures that reproduce that connection with their viewer, that he seeks to elicit 'compassion' but not just compassion. As he argued in a conversation with John Berger, "if the person looking at [my] pictures only feels compassion, I will believe that I have failed completely. I want people to understand that we can have a solution."[7] By contrast, we argue that Killip and Frazier refuse both these appeals (the compassion and the solution), and we claim that their photos are thus committed not only to a different aesthetic but to a different politics.

This is not to say that Killip and Frazier are exactly the same. In what follows, we lay out some of the differences between them and the ways those differences matter, but we want to call attention here to a difference that we think doesn't matter, or at least doesn't matter in the way many believe it does: Killip is a white man, taking pictures of white people; Frazier is a black woman taking (mainly) pictures of black people. Of course, both Britain and the United States are racialized societies, and although Killip's white people are obviously not the beneficiaries

Figure 2. Chris Killip, *Seacoal Camp*
Lynemouth, Northumberland, 1983. *In Flagrante*.
Gelatin silver print. Courtesy of Magnum Photos.
© Chris Killip Photography Trust/Magnum Photos

of white racism, Frazier's black people are certainly among its victims. So why doesn't the difference matter? Because what both the aesthetics and the politics of these pictures are trying to capture is the political economy of deindustrialization—not the distinctive pathos that attaches to those relegated to the bottom rungs of the class structure but the structure itself. Indeed, it is precisely because of their attention to a class analytic and commitment to a class aesthetic that we are interested in them.

Which is also not to say Killip and Frazier understand their politics in exactly the same way we do. Actually, in the current moment, it's not clear what it even means to have a class politics, which is a fact that's crucial to their pictures and which is, in part, why we speak of a class analytic and aesthetic instead of a class politics. But it is very clear what it means to have a liberal (which is to say, left neoliberal) politics, which is precisely what we will identify as the politics of Salgado's pictures, and of the artist himself, whose way of understanding his relation to his subjects and to his audience does indeed insist on the value both of compassion and of a certain kind of action.

Throughout his career, Salgado has "collaborated generously with international humanitarian organizations"[8] ranging from the World Health Organization and Amnesty International to UNICEF and Médecins Sans Frontières, with whom he produced his first meaningful work during the Ethiopian famine between 1984 and 1985[9]; he was the photographer of what is seen today as the first worldwide humanitarian campaign[10]. In other words, Salgado understands his subjects to be in need of help, and he intends his pictures to play some role in helping them.[11] The way he himself puts it is, "people come to you, to your lens, as they would come to speak in a microphone. . . . [T]his means you must show their pictures."[12] Thus, as Parvati Nair says, Salgado "views his images as fields of representation, where the subjects 'speak' through the image to the viewer"; he "argues for photography as empowerment . . . for those who are normally neither heard nor seen by those in the global centers of power".[13]

In this context the social or political difference between the photographer and the beholder, on the one hand, and the subject of the photograph, on the other, is not anecdotal but structural. The picture of the powerless is taken so it can be shown to the powerful. And to begin to deal with this social problem, the photographer must find a way to solve what counts for him as an aesthetic problem—what Salgado calls the production in his pictures of 'real feeling'[14]. That is, if the pictures are going to play any role in producing a 'solution', they have to present the beholder not just with embodied 'statistics' or even with mere 'victims' but also with people of 'dignity' and 'strength'. And if the beholder is to see them in this way, first the photographer must see them in this way. The way Salgado puts this is to say that "the picture is not made by the photographer, the picture is more good or less good in function of the relationship that you have with the people you photograph."[15] Toward that end—developing the right relationship—he characteristically spends months living among the people he is photographing, all in the service of establishing a relation between him and them that will then—through the photographs—be reproduced in the relation between them and us— the viewers of the pictures. It's for this reason that, from the perspective of Salgado himself and of those who admire him, the focus is on his efforts to produce what gets called a sense of solidarity: as Eduardo Galeano writes, "Salgado photographs from inside, in solidarity."[16] And it's for this reason also that when he is criticized (by, for example, Susan Sontag), it's because his photographs fail to produce that solidarity and instead render suffering so "vast" and "abstract" that "compassion can only flounder", and the "political intervention" it's meant to generate can only seem hopeless[17].

In Killip and Frazier's work too, as we will see, the questions of the relation of the photographer to his or her subjects and of the picture to the beholder are crucial ones. But the answers to those questions are significantly different. These differences will be most immediately visible in what the pictures look like—in an aesthetic that is uninterested in compassion and skeptical even of solidarity. But that aesthetic also has a politics, or, at least, a way of understanding politics; it is a class aesthetic, and the problem it tries to solve is not how to photograph the suffering or the dignity of those who are far from the centers of power but how to photograph the working class. These are, of course, the same people but under different descriptions; the interest is in how to photograph that difference, how to photograph not the excluded but the exploited. Working and not working, the army of labor and its reserves occupy a position that is both essential to capital and antagonistic to it. In Killip and Frazier, we see an effort to picture that position, an effort, that is, to picture the history of working peoples and laboring lives while insisting on a certain idea of what history is, and a concomitant idea of work and labor.

What Happened

Chris Killip's *In Flagrante* (1988) is made up of pictures taken over more than a decade in northern England in small working-class communities like Wallsend in Tyneside, Whitehaven in Cumbria, and Lynemouth Beach in Northumberland; their subjects are the victims of deindustrialization (either in coal mining or shipbuilding more generally). But if it is initially tempting to identify these photos with the Salgado-like project of revealing a social problem and beginning to look for a 'solution', John Berger and Sylvia Grant's foreword to the volume explicitly warns against that: "photography has often been used, in a documentary spirit", they write, "to record and to reveal social conditions . . . [to show] to the relatively privileged how the 'other half' lived: sub-proletarians . . . the unemployed, the homeless", with the purpose of moving the "public to action" or of protesting "social conditions" in the hope of helping to get them "improved". But, Berger and Grant argue, *"In Flagrante* does not belong to this tradition. Chris Killip is adamantly aware that a better future for the photographed is unlikely." [18] And it's not just the pessimism with respect to solutions that distinguishes Killip's work from the documentary; he has himself said several times that he was "not pretending to be a documentary photographer in the accepted sense", and even that his pictures, despite the anti-Thatcherite agenda with which they are sometimes identified, are not primarily political or aimed at performing a political function. Hence the workers' political responses to Thatcherite measures are almost absent from his work (he actually put aside almost all his photographs about the miners' strike) [19]. As argued by Gerry Badger in the afterword to the 2008 edition, *In Flagrante* "is not intended as a 'document' of the Thatcher government". [20]

But there is one way in which Killip's work shares a problematic not only with Salgado but with the documentary, and especially with documentary that aspires to the condition of 'art'. His pictures may seek no social solutions, but they do show "the relatively privileged how the 'other half' lives"; they are pictures of the poor made by someone who (at least by the time he was making them) was already a successful photographer and for an audience (the art world) that is not just relatively but absolutely privileged. And he himself lives in a world that has not only survived the destruction of the English miners but has thrived on it. By 1994, he was a professor at Harvard—the world's richest university—and while the audience for his work is hardly limited to the rich, it probably includes almost no one who makes a living collecting wasted coal in northern England. So, like Salgado, he is confronted right from the start by a difference between the photographer and his subjects that is not only aesthetic but social. But (not quite like Salgado) he makes this difference central to his work. Indeed, his collection *Arbeit/work* begins (before we are presented with any photographs, except the one on the cover) with an account of being taken by an American friend (the owner of "the best bar in Cambridge") into "the center of Boston to where the civic center and other administrative buildings now stand" and being shown what used to be there: "the old tough working class district", the "streets that no longer existed . . . who had lived where and in which house. Who had died in Vietnam, who had worked for the mob, who had gone to prison or ended up in politics." And when he starts to thank his friend for explaining to him the "history" of this vanished working-class neighborhood, he is confronted with a violent reaction—"I don't know nothing about no fucking history", his friend says, pushing him against the wall and gripping him by the throat, "I'm just telling you what happened." [21]

The friend here is a kind of class surrogate for the people whose pictures will follow, and one point of the story is that one way to understand the difference between the photographer and his subjects (like the difference between the Harvard professor and the interested beholder of aesthetically ambitious photography, on the one hand, and the working-class bar owner, on the other) is under the sign of conflict. Here the difference from Salgado is sharp. Salgado's project is shaped by his commitment to an essentially humanist vision and hence to the goal of making it possible for the viewers of his photographs "to look at the pictures of these people and see themselves"[22]. This is precisely why dignity is the central issue in Salgado's aesthetics; it's a way to overcome the differences of class and find a unity—we are all part of the human race— between the beholder and the subject represented. That's the solidarity he seeks to establish by the time he spends with his subjects and through his efforts to establish the 'right relation' with them.

Killip, by contrast, foregrounds class difference. That's what he means when he says, "To the people in these photographs I am superfluous, my life does not depend upon their struggle, only my hopes."[23] Then, rather than try to transcend the difference between the world of people who make and admire photographs like his and the people who are the subjects of those photographs (by appealing to the 'dignity' of every human being), he tries to capture the specific experience of deindustrialization and of class. This is the point not just of the conflict between the photographer and his friend but of its specific terms—of the difference between 'history' and 'what happened'. History is what you would get from the civic center and the administrative buildings; what happened is what you get from the people displaced by the civic center and the administrators. In this dichotomy, Killip is an administrator, as the hand on his throat reminds him and as the subjects of his photographs had often reminded him. When, for example, he began trying to photograph Lynemouth Beach for *Seacoal*[24], Killip remembered, "the first thing the men did was try and run me down with their horses"[25] (because they "were convinced he was a government spy sent to gather evidence and throw them off the dole"[26]). And, of course, a greater threat (to the photograph if not to the photographer) even than the impulse to harm the photographer/ government spy would be the felt necessity to perform for him. Indeed, it's precisely to avoid this threat that, as Clive Dilnot reports, Killip lived on and off for fourteen months in a caravan at Lynemouth Beach, which was typical of the way in which, "immersing himself" in the "communities" of his subjects, "he built relationships with those he photographed that were much closer than reportage, or even documentation, normally allows." As for Salgado, what matters is "the relationship that you have

Figures 3 and 4. Chris Killip, *Woman in Bus Shelter*
and *Women in Bus Stop*, 1976. *In Flagrante*.
Gelatin silver print. Courtesy of Magnum Photos.
© Chris Killip Photography Trust/Magnum Photos

with the people you photograph"; for Killip, Dilnot says, the "immersion largely determines the nature of his photographic contribution"[27]. But for Salgado, the point of the relationship is to be able to make photographs that establish the shared humanity of the photographer, his subjects, and his audience, whereas the photographs Killip makes are more skeptical, and the differences of class are less eagerly effaced.

One way he understands this difference is by way of a certain equivocation about who his subjects are, or about what his subject is. *In Flagrante* begins with a text that describes it as "a subjective book about my time in England", and both its first and its last photograph gesture toward that subjectivity (Figs. 3 and 4). They are two versions of a similar picture, including the shadow of the photographer—the first one, as noted by Gerry Badger[28], is inverted, as if the photographer opened, at the beginning of the book, and then closed, at the end, a set of parentheses.[29]

This commitment to depicting his own subject position is even more obvious in the very first picture (more of a foreword) of the book—a man on a beach painting the beach (Fig. 5). Here, in a sense, subjectivity—the painter painting, the photographer photographing—is the picture's subject. Furthermore, the painting and the photograph each give us slightly different views of the landscape/seascape they have in common. In the painting, the painter is almost in a parallel relation to the sea. But in the picture, the photographer is closer to being in front of it. Thus the difference between what the painter sees and what the photographer sees (the difference between where they're standing) is made part of the picture's subject, and the photographer is himself imagined as a version of the painter, not in the sense that he sees the same thing but in the sense that, looking at the same thing, the sea, he sees something different. What subjective means here is the inescapability of having some point of view—the sense that 'what happened' is always what happened to someone, and that even if the photographer's subject is what happened to the miners, what the pictures show must also be what happened to the photographer, what he was there to see.

But, of course, the photo also produces the sea itself—and the landscape more generally—as something that transcends the painter and, by

Figure 5. Chris Killip, *Len Tabner Painting Skinningrove, North Yorkshire*, 1983. *In Flagrante*. Courtesy of Magnum Photos. © Chris Killip Photography Trust/Magnum Photos

Figure 6. Chris Killip, *Glue Sniffers*
Whitehaven, Cumbria, 1980.
In Flagrante. Courtesy of Magnum Photos.
© Chris Killip/Magnum Photos

extension, the photographer. It has, in other words, a kind of objectivity that seems heightened rather than diminished by the artist's efforts of representation, if only because the painting is small (and the photograph smaller still) when set against the world it's a painting of. The effect here is to subordinate the point of view. [30] Or to imagine a subjectivity that begins to be disarticulated from the very idea of point of view. We can begin to see what this might mean in a picture like *Glue Sniffers* (Fig. 6).

The poet John Yau describes this as a picture of young men standing on a beach, "largely indifferent to Killip's presence". [31] That indifference is, of course, the effect of his immersion—because they have come to know and accept him, they are not performing for the photographer. As Yau says of Killip's photographs more generally, "No one is posing." [32] But indifference only begins to get at the effect of the photograph; indeed, the idea that photos like this emblemize the relationship Killip has developed with his subjects is in a certain way misleading. This picture may only be possible because of the relationship the photographer has established with these men, but what it's about is the lack of relationship the photographer has with them. In other words, its effect is less to make it seem as if the photographer is just one of them than it is to make it seem as if there is no photographer. Thus, for example, although Yau says that "the young man in the middle is facing the viewer", he's actually looking off to the viewer's (and the photographer's) right. [33] His look, in other words, does not acknowledge the photographer. And it doesn't even acknowledge the photographer indirectly, that is, he doesn't seem to look away from or past the photographer; he seems not to notice him, which, given how closely to the young man the photograph positions the photographer, seems almost impossible but is nonetheless a frequent effect in Killip's many group pictures (think of his pictures of punks). There are many figures who are very close to the photographer and yet impossibly oblivious of him. Yau says that "there is nothing fictional about these photographs and they are clearly not staged." [34] But this is only half right—it's more like they are clearly not staged to bring out a quality that is *essentially* fictional, as if in pictures like this, what *is* being staged is precisely the fiction of the photographer's absence.

Which is not to say that in seeking to imagine the photograph as a product of a world where not only are the subjects unaware of the photographer but in which the photographer can be imagined not to exist, Killip seeks to assert the objectivity of the photograph or to deny the subjectivity of the photographer. Killip begins *In Flagrante* by writing,

> The objective history of England doesn't amount to much if you don't believe in it, and I don't, and I don't believe that anyone in these photographs does either as they face the reality of de-industrialisation in a system which regards their lives as disposable. To the people in these photographs I am superfluous, my life does not depend upon their struggle, only my hopes.
>
> This is a subjective book about my time in England. I take what isn't mine and I covet other people's lives. The photographs can tell you more about me than about what they describe.
>
> The book is a fiction about metaphor.[35]

Here the opposition between 'history' and 'what happened' is prefigured as an opposition between 'objective history' and the 'subjective'. But what the photographs tell us about the subject ('me') is not who he is or even exactly what his point of view is but, above all, that he is 'superfluous'. That's the meaning of his disappearance. And his being superfluous (to them) is matched by their being 'disposable' (to the system), like the gleaners in *Seacoal* collecting the 'wasted' coal in the sea from a crumbling industry. In other words, subjectivity in Killip is less a function of the photographer showing you what he saw than of what we called above his acknowledgment of—even insistence upon—the difference between him and his subjects: the picture of the impossibility of his belonging to their world.

The History of What Happened

In a couple of obvious and important ways, Frazier's photos of deindustrialized Pennsylvania—of what followed from what she calls the "collapse of the steel industry throughout the 1970s and '80s"—look very different from Killip's, not to mention Salgado's.[36] For one thing, many of them are not just portraits but are (exactly opposite to Killip's) posed.

And, for another, Frazier often appears in her own work, so that a lot of the posed portraits are self-portraits. Sometimes, like Killip's shadow, her reflection is caught as she takes a picture of someone else. But more often she is the explicit subject. In Killip, the problem of immersion in one's subjects and of negotiating a relation to them that is neither an expression of one's own subjectivity nor an effort to achieve the objectivity he believes to be impossible is a crucial one. But, whatever the problems raised by the self-portrait, the necessity of immersing oneself in a world that's not one's own is not one of them. And even when the portrait is not of yourself but of your mother or grandmother, the project of getting to know them well enough to take the right kind of pictures of them is obviously irrelevant. Frazier knew these people very well before she ever started taking any pictures at all.

In one sense this difference is a version of what we've already seen anticipated in Killip's choice of 'what happened' over 'history' and, especially, in the fact that for him the demand to tell 'what happened' instead of a 'history' gets put in the mouth not of the photographer himself but of the bar owner who functions as a kind of class surrogate for Killip's subjects. In Frazier, however, there's no need for surrogates, and the problem of the difference between history and what happened will look more like an opportunity to turn the one into the other. So her goal is both to "document what was happening"[37] and to give a "historic account" of the industrial abandonment of Braddock, Pennsylvania, during the past thirty years. Realizing that, like any member of her family or community, she "didn't have any economic power", she took her camera as "a weapon" and "became very invested in trying to visualize [her] own history".[38]

As we've noted, the formal question of the relations between photographer and subject, photograph and beholder, is foundational at least to all pictures of people and for the photographers we're looking at here. It's also a social question, in the sense that Salgado and Killip are not themselves workers in the way that their subjects are (hence the ethical problems of the relation between photographer and subject are rendered essentially the same as the ethical problems of the relation between the rich and the poor). Their challenge is to go to places they're not from, take pictures of people they don't know, and find ways to address the deep difference in class between their subjects and themselves. The pictures of Braddock that have dominated Frazier's work so far are pictures of where she lived for the first twenty years of her life; the book that contains most of those pictures is called *The Notion of Family*, and the family in question is hers. So the problem of overcoming the social distance between photographer and subject doesn't need to be solved—it never arises.

But this identity—the fact that photographer and subject belong to the same class and even to the same family—produces its own challenges, challenges we can see Frazier addressing in her commitment not just to the portrait but to the posed portrait. What makes immersion desirable to Killip is the immersed photographer's ability to take pictures of people behaving in some degree as they would if he weren't there. And there are certainly some pictures in *The Notion of Family* that work just this way; they produce an effect of an almost startling and (in their depiction of what Frazier herself calls "the stench of human decay") sometimes shocking intimacy. But there are even more that are set up almost like formal portraits—in which the everyday life of the family (in which Frazier, of course, was already a participant) is interrupted so that a picture can be taken and in which the subject directly confronts the photographer, not only aware of being photographed but doing what she is doing only because she is being photographed. In other words, Frazier here is not trying to overcome the elements of formality and of performance for the camera but to insist on them. Thus not only do she and her mother make portraits of each other, but they look for what is in effect a way to separate those portraits from everyday life, to make them "without showing the domestic interior"[39]. They stand mattresses up against the wall, drape them with comforters, and use them as backdrop: "The bedroom became a stage and a studio" (see Frazier's *Momme Portrait Series (Floral Comforter)*). It's as if the idea here is precisely to establish some measure of the distance that Killip is trying to overcome.

One way to understand this is as an attempt to make art. Bourdieu famously said that "it is only with difficulty that photographic practice can escape the functions to which it owes its existence"[40], and the first of these was what he called the *"family function"*—"reinforcing the integration of the family group", of "the sense that it has both of itself and of its unity"[41]. From this standpoint, we can see Frazier's effort to turn the domestic interior into "a stage and a studio" as an attempt both to fulfill and to transcend the family function. The dramatic (and self-dramatizing) portraits of her mother and herself work both to document the relation between mother and daughter and to turn it into a performance. In other words, these pictures, far from immersing either the photographer or the beholder in the subjects' world, establish a certain gap between them. The performance is the pose, which positions both the photographer and the beholder as outsiders and which thus re-creates the socioeconomic gap that Salgado and Killip wanted to bridge. But insofar as the gap is also between the photographer and herself (herself as photographer and herself as subject posed for the photographer), the socioeconomic difference is elided and reconstituted in formal terms. That is, the formal questions raised about the relation between photographer and subject by any portrait remain all but emptied of their socioeconomic pathos, and this transformation of the social into the aesthetic will have a political meaning.

By pointing toward the aesthetic we mean not that Frazier as an artist doesn't understand herself to belong to a documentary tradition in photography (she actually sees her work as "conceptual documentary art" and says that one of her "main objectives" is to try to "update" the "social documentary")[42]; it's rather that her work powerfully displaces some of the issues that the documentary tradition characteristically mobilizes. When, for example, Killip describes himself as "not pretending to be a documentary photographer in the accepted sense" and instances the appearance of his shadow at the beginning and the end of *In Flagrante*, the point he's making is about "the subjective nature of a photograph; that a photograph is never objective".[43] One might almost say that this is what Killip's photographs are about, the refusal of 'history' on behalf of 'what happened' as a way of denying an objectivity that was identified with a certain documentary tradition and replacing it with what his friend John saw, what John showed him, and what he sees.

As we've seen, however, Killip's actual practice in these photographs is not really to choose subjectivity over objectivity but instead to remove the photographer altogether. And in a way this is true even of photographs that because they include his shadow are supposed to make people "conscious of the subjective nature of a photograph". Both photographs depict the photographer in the act of taking a picture but not exactly the picture in question. The shadow we see in the opening picture of *In Flagrante* is parallel to the woman on the sidewalk, as if the photographer were using a right-angle lens of the kind sometimes used by Walker Evans, Ben Shahn, and Helen Levitt. Or as if the shadow in the picture were somehow of some *other* photographer, taking a picture of something we can't see. Either way, the effect is less to insert the photographer into the world of the woman than to remove him from it, to refuse both possible subject positions: the objectivity of the historian and the subjectivity of the participant.

Frazier's photographs establish a slightly different version of this problematic; it's not exactly that they're objective but that they find a very different way of not being subjective, even when she appears (like Killip's shadow) in her role as photographer. The first picture of her mother in *The Notion of Family* shows the mother on the other side of a bar and in front of a mirror in which we see Frazier as photographer reflected and about which Frazier writes, "The apparition is me. We are not in Manet's bar at the Folies-Bergère", and there are several photos of her with others in a mirror, as well as, of course, the several portraits of her alone and with others. Making herself both subject and object, she empties the opposition between subjective and objective of its interest. And where, of course, Manet's mirror generates endless reflection on who is standing where, the mirror here—and even more in the truly amazing photo of mother, daughter, and camera in front of the mirror later in the book (*Mom Making an Image of Me*)—is not used to produce any of the characteristic paradoxes of self-reflexivity. The photo absorbs the photographer into the picture but not by raising the question of subject position (of who is standing where or of what the photographer sees) but by replacing it with the depiction of who and what is there. One might say that for Frazier the point is to make history and what happened identical. And this ambition is embodied above all in the formal feature of her work that most distinguishes her from Salgado or Killip and that we've already begun to note: the primacy of the pose.

We can begin to see how this works by remembering what's both po-litically and aesthetically problematic about the pose in the first place. The posed subject is performing for the camera, and even setting aside the long aesthetic history of anti-theatricality (just think of Walker Evans's subway photos), the political pitfalls in asking the working-class subject to perform for the middle-class photographer (and so, of course, for the middle-class beholder) are obvious. But our discussion of Salgado and of Killip has also suggested some problems with the effort to avoid those pitfalls. Salgado's nervousness about 'compassion'—"if the person looking at my pictures only feels compassion, I will believe that I have failed completely"—is exemplary here, as is James Johnson's defense of Salgado against critics like Susan Sontag who have attacked him for failing to produce (or even to try for) the appropriate compassionate response. Johnson thinks Salgado is right to reject (or at least not be satisfied with) compassion; what he thinks Salgado wants is not the com-passion of the beholder for the subject but solidarity between them.

In Frazier, however, we do not exactly get either. If the posing mother and daughter are performing, it is for each other. There's no appeal to the beholder; in fact, the effect of their theatricality is rather to seal the beholder out. The direct gaze that would otherwise count as a kind of confrontation with the beholder is almost internalized, an effect that's insisted on thematically by the color snapshots of mother and daugh-ter joking around with each other (that is, addressing each other rather than the camera) before or after posing and formally by the photos (like *Mom Making an Image of Me*) looking at themselves in the mirror. In the color snapshots, the intimacy between the two (Frazier actually describes them as "wrestling with internalized life experiences") establishes the photos as for each other before—but not exactly instead of—the beholder. In the mother and daughter looking at themselves in the mirror, in *Mom Making an Image of Me*, the direct address of the subjects to the camera is made virtually identical to the direct address of the subjects to them-selves *instead of* to the beholder.

If, then, the pose in Frazier functions as a way of establishing the distance between the photographer and her subjects that Salgado and Killip are, albeit in very different ways, eager to overcome, it does so out of a certain desire to establish also a distance between the photographer and the beholder. What Salgado and Killip want is to achieve the right relation with their subjects, to avoid making it look as if the subjects are performing for the photographer and the beholder, the poor performing for the rich. In Salgado, achieving the right relation between the photographer and his subjects is a way also of achieving the right relation between the beholder and his subjects—respect for their dignity, solidarity. In Killip, we've argued, the right relation is instrumentalized; the point of the photographer's 'immersion' in the life of the people he photographs is to make it so that in the pictures he has no relation to them at all. In fact, there's a sense in which they are often depicted as having no relation to each other. They don't look at each other, and they don't seem to talk to each other; it's as if what makes them into a group is only the photograph itself. What the viewer of the photograph sees is thus something very different from what the people in it see and even from what the photographer sees, and it's in this way that Killip produces the photograph itself as an artifact of the class structure—of different subjectivities not united by their humanity but organized by a political economy.

But if Killip establishes his version of the right relation to the beholder by pushing the photographer out of the picture to make performance impossible, Frazier, making vivid the degree to which the subjects are performing for the camera, subsumes the photographer in the photograph and pushes the beholder out. The performance is for the photographer *instead of* for the beholder. In fact, in the picture of Frazier and her mother in the mirror, the identification of photographer with beholder is explicitly refused; if the mirror explicitly includes the photographer, it just as explicitly excludes the beholder: the position from which Frazier sees her subjects is inside the picture; the position from which we see them is outside it.[44] Which turns the pose into a way not of appealing to the beholder (the picture is not made to ask anyone for anything or even to seek to establish a relation with someone) but of making the beholder as superfluous as Killip sought to make the photographer, thus establishing a certain separation between photograph and beholder, one that demands neither compassion nor solidarity.[45] In one of the most sophisticated readings of Salgado's *Workers*, Julian Stallabrass describes the pictures as "disturbing" because they show us "scenes which should have been long banished from the perfectible neoliberal state" and because they say "a good deal about the interdependence of rich and poor" [46], leading us in particular to imagine "how it would be for us were we to be in their condition, . . . what we would feel if we were to suffer their fate" [47]. But Frazier's pictures have no interest in this identificatory ethics, which is what we mean when we describe them as sealing out the beholder, and what we mean when we attribute to them a class aesthetic. The portrait of a class doesn't demand solidarity any more than it demands compassion; it is, in a certain sense, more abstract than that—interested neither in individual subjectivities nor in what David Levi Strauss calls "collective subjectivities" [48]. If we want to get rid of the class system, the question of which class we belong to is ultimately irrelevant. What's required, in other words, is neither that the middle class feel compassion for workers nor that it turn that compassion into an identificatory solidarity. Both responses are perfectly emblemized in the collaboration between Salgado and humanitarian organizations. But those organizations, like Médecins Sans Frontières (MSF), operating "in the most serious and immediate danger" and making its decisions without regard to "political, economic or religious interests" [49], have been exemplary institutions of the neoliberal order. MSF—like many others—is a key actor in the rise of the increasing translation of politics into the language of morality and ethics. Even when Salgado is not explicitly collaborating with MSF, he is as committed to the ethically admirable effort to arouse our 'humanitarian' interest in the victims of neoliberalism as MSF is to asserting the 'universal' "right to humanitarian assistance" [50].

And, of course, it's not hard to develop a humanitarian interest in Frazier's family; the fact that so many of her portraits were made while her mother was being treated for cancer and/or while she herself was suffering from a lupus flair makes a certain sympathy fairly inevitable. But it's also beside the point. It's not that their illnesses don't matter; it's that they're made to matter in the context of photographs documenting the (failed) political effort to sustain the medical center that had been serving Braddock, a failure that would not be mitigated by the arrival of an MSF team in western Pennsylvania. That's part of what it means for Frazier (by putting herself into the picture) to try to do what Killip tried to do (by taking himself out of the picture). What both produce is the impersonality of an art that seeks to picture the political economy of a class society and that is thus as resolutely political as MSF is non-political. Frazier's photographs of people holding signs that say things like Where Is Emergency Care for Braddock make the personal political by making it impersonal. In fact, a good way to see the portraits of her family is on a continuum with the signs, which are themselves a way of posing (they are there to be looked at), and, in pictures like these, merge the pose into the demand and then make them both into the emblem of a kind of political failure at least as bitter as that of Killip's miners.

The group in the background of Frazier's photo *The Grey Area* is recognizable—if only because of one very big man—as the group in her *Campaign for Braddock Hospital (Save Our Community Hospital)*. But where the people in the latter image are posing for the camera in a way that both preserves their individuality and subsumes it under the signs they carry, in the former photo, you can't see the people and you can't read the signs. It's not even clear what they're doing—maybe waiting for Frazier while she takes a picture of the twisted bits of metal left over, one imagines, from the demolition of their hospital? Nonetheless, it's a kind of portrait, the ghost of a pose. The ethical pathos produced in Salgado by thematizing the relation between photographer and beholder, on the one hand, and subject, on the other, as the relation between rich and poor is gone. One could say that the problems in Frazier are political and aesthetic rather than ethical, and that the pathos she produces is more structural than personal.

Farewell, Left versus Right

Branko Milanovic's famous "elephant chart" (Fig. 7)[51] would be one al-most-too-neat way of picturing this structure. Many of Salgado's work-ers (in China, India, etc.) are among the beneficiaries of neoliberalism, along, of course, with a tiny but increasingly powerful group of the very rich in places like the United States and the United Kingdom. Killip's people in Newcastle (not London) and Frazier's people in Braddock (not

New York or San Francisco) are among its victims. And in the last year (we're writing in April 2017), we can see how both the politics and the ethics have played out. Whatever else they might have been, the votes for both Brexit and Donald Trump were votes against the neoliberal order that produced those results. Places like Tyneside, Sunderland, and Middlesbrough, where Killip was taking pictures, had been Labour strongholds; they voted for Brexit at more than sixty per cent. Braddock was different; while the state of Pennsylvania narrowly supported Trump, Braddock voted for Clinton. If, then, we are to understand both Killip and Frazier as photographers not just of workers or of the poor but specifically of the working class, what we see in these election results is the political fracturing of that class or, from a certain standpoint, of the very idea of class.

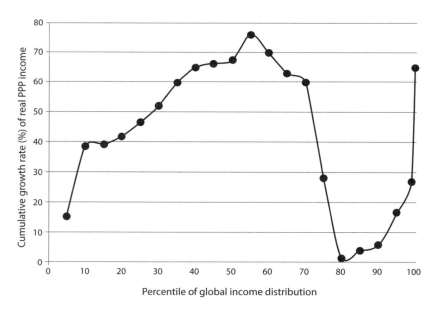

Figure 7. Global income growth, 1988–2008

For, of course, Killip's subjects are exclusively white, and Frazier's are mainly black, and in this narrative, his subjects embody the emergence of a nativist populism among the white working class while hers embody a resistance to that nativism and a commitment instead to diversity and tolerance. Once we see these subjects (indeed, once these subjects can be induced to see themselves) as above all white or above all black, this vote has nothing to do with class and everything to with race. Or rather, racism comes to count for the white victims of deindustrialization as a solution to the economic catastrophe that has been visited upon them, while anti-racism performs the same function for its black victims. The racism produced in Killip's Newcastle is thus matched by the anti-racism of Frazier's Braddock; the political struggle between labor and capital is relocated as a struggle between cultures or between laborers and in both cases is redescribed as an ethical struggle between tolerance and bigotry, between societies that are either open or closed.

Of course, neither bigotry not tolerance, neither expelling people of color nor embracing them, can possibly remedy the disappearance of all the jobs lost by Frazier's black people and Killip's white ones. Nevertheless (or for just this reason), the big winners on the elephant chart prefer culture wars to class wars and, whether wringing their hands over the rise in 'racial resentment' or, less frequently (much less frequently), indulging in it, are delighted to announce—in the words of *The Economist* (naturally)—the new political irrelevance of "left versus right" [52].

Art, uncontroversially, is made for those winners. But in trying to show the different ways in which both Killip and Frazier refuse to solicit either the compassion of the beholder or his or her solidarity, we have tried to show also the degree to which these pictures refuse their beholders the comforts of understanding themselves in cultural or ethical terms, and the way they insist instead on the continued relevance of left and right. They insist, that is, on the primacy of a class structure that cannot be rewritten as cultural and that will not be made into an ethical problem with an ethical solution. The great power of these pictures is precisely the power of a class aesthetics.

But not exactly the power of a class politics. For if these photos insist on the persistence of the working class, they do not insist on the ability of that class to defend itself as a class, much less to bring about a world in which the ideological affirmation of class's irrelevance in neoliberalism would be replaced by its actual disappearance in communism. Just the opposite. As photographs of deindustrialization, they show that what has vanished with industry is not class as an economic structure but the working class as a central political agent. In that sense, what's at stake in these pictures is both the reproduction of the working class and the decline of its power.

But if the substitution of a class aesthetics for a class politics is inevitably the confession of a certain defeat, the reinvention of a class aesthetics suggests also a certain promise, which is what it means for Frazier to understand herself as not having 'any economic power' and as instead turning her camera into a 'weapon' to make 'conceptual documentary art'. The political (not just economic) possibility of class power depends on the survival of the idea of class. And it's the idea—the concept—of class that survives in these pictures. They are portraits of that concept.

Interview One
27 May 2021

DANIEL ZAMORA I'd like to begin this set of conversations with your own experience with anti-racism in the United States. Because reading your pieces together, it seemed quite obvious to me that your work has been a criticism of the place anti-racism has taken in contemporary politics since the legal victories of the Civil Rights movement in the mid-'60s.

ANTON JÄGER It would indeed be interesting to have your views, Adolph, about Jim Crow and the movement in the 1960s . . .

WALTER BENN MICHAELS I just want to say, I don't feel you guys are appreciating how difficult it was to be a Jew in suburban New York in the 1950s.

DZ We said we weren't going to play this card.

AJ I actually have a few questions about how difficult it was to be at Berkeley . . .

WBM It's funny because it's true—but it would be more fun to hear Adolph talk about Jim Crow and then the emergence of race as the center of American politics.

ADOLPH REED, JR. See, I'm prepped, because I just read again "The

229

Autobiography of an Ex-White Man", which is better every time I read it; it's great. And in fact, I sent it to a couple people who haven't quite taken in the critique of social construction as a way of understanding race. But I guess the best place to start with that is Barbara Fields's observation that, the way people now typically talk about slavery and Jim Crow segregation, one would think that the point of those regimes was to produce white supremacy and not cotton and other commodities. But it was clear from within—or could've been, or should've been clear from within—that Jim Crow was a response to a problem that the ruling class in the South experienced at the end of the nineteenth century. And that was that the great anxiety that was rife among them after Emancipation, and especially after ratification of the Fifteenth Amendment that enfranchised black men, was the possibility of a political alliance of poor whites and blacks that would have the power to alter the rules of the game, the rules of the economic order and the political hierarchy. And that fear, I think, was realized in the Populist electoral insurgency in the late nineteenth century. Once that insurgency was defeated, you've got an unchallenged ruling class with the opportunity, the power, and the rancor—ruling class voices at the time fulminated against the insolence and impertinence of their presumed inferiors' challenge to their rule—to eliminate concern with potential popular challenges going forward. In practical terms, what we understand as white supremacist ideology was the big cover story, and the institutional apparatus of codified racial hierarchy and black disenfranchisement were mechanisms to impose the ideology as a social order. And that resolved the problem of lingering fear of working-class insurgency. The key move was taking blacks entirely out of the political equation via disfranchisement, and for that matter taking as many working-class whites out of the political equation as the ruling merchant-planter class thought they could get away with. And that firmly established the center of gravity of politics in the region as entirely a ruling class game, so that anyone who wants to participate has to figure out how to do so in ways that accommodate the heavy-handed dominance of the ruling class. So, that's pretty simple and straightforward. And there was enough resistance to the Jim Crow regime as a quotidian order at least—from the beginning to the end—that it never would've made sense to say that, you know, white supremacy as a cod-ified system emerged from the hearts and minds, much less the blood quantum, of so-called white people.

Now, the other part of that is how racism or anti-racism took shape after the fact—basically as a characterization of the nature of opposi-tion to the Jim Crow order. Because, as I've said in a number of places, and even as first-year graduate students observed in my seminar with-out having thought a lot about this before, through the '50s and '60s, what black racial advocates, or civic elites, or, how everyone described them, 'radicals', fought against wasn't an abstraction called 'racism'. But for and against concrete policy initiatives—for voting rights, right? Against employment discrimination, against lynching, etc., etc. I think it's only in the course of class consolidation—the particular class con-solidation we saw in black politics after 1965, spurred by Black Power ideology—that racism became the generic invocation that takes the place of causal accounts of inequalities affecting blacks or, eventually, other non-whites. And that shift to attributing causal power to racism is partly an outgrowth of post-war racial liberalism, which had already begun to abstract the problem of racial injustice from concrete complaints about policies into concern with prejudice or intolerance as defects of charac-ter or personality. And then prejudice becomes racism, an externalized force that makes things happen in the world. But that reification con-geals along with what would become, or what we'd later understand to be, the full-blown neoliberalism that takes shape between the '80s and the '90s. Because a significant aspect of the '60s moment was, as Judith Stein discusses, the debate, during the period of the formation of the war on poverty, over how to approach economic inequality by race. And the one social-democratic tendency (which, ironically, was perceived to be the bureaucratic, conservative approach) came from people like Hu-bert Humphrey and Joseph Clark from Pennsylvania in the US Senate, Walter Reuther, President of the United Auto Workers—along with peo-ple like Bayard Rustin and A. Philip Randolph—who argued that the problems of black income inequality went much deeper than discrimi-nation, and had to do with the reorganization of the domestic economy most fundamentally. They argued that what was necessary to respond effectively to racial inequality was to locate the fair employment practices, anti-discrimination approach within a much broader labor force and manpower-related approach that pursued full employment. And that's an interesting story.

WBM Can I ask you a question about Black Power, which is emerging precisely at that moment. Did it actually help in moving people away from the full employment model?

AR Yep.

WBM That's really interesting. And you and I have never discussed this . . . what actually was your relation to Black Power?

AR Well, I was nineteen in 1966 . . .

WBM Yeah, you're gonna get a pass if it comes out real bad.

AR Right. Look, Black Power and the radical or putatively revolutionary expressions of Black Power were anchored dead-center in my cohort of black college students. And we didn't have sense enough to understand ourselves yet as an emerging professional and managerial stratum, but that's exactly what that discourse appealed to. And this is what accounts for my lost year in the American Trotskyist movement. Because the SWP [Socialist Workers Party] was the only force on the left, or on the Marxist left, in the US at that point that tried to put the two things together, that tried to put a Marxist understanding of class inequality and critique of capitalism along with a late Malcolm X-influenced black nationalism. And it took me about a year to figure out that that shit just didn't work. And the glue that seemed to hold it together was—Wow, who'd have guessed?!—Trotskyist opportunism, so I was gone.

But I found myself in a setting where the only game in town in, say, North Carolina was Black Power activism. So those are the people I worked with, and I was kind of the Marxist critic from within that world for a couple of years. In fact, I was part—as a low-level member—of the national committee to organize the first African Liberation Day march.

DZ But why do you think people in your generation were drawn into Black Power? What made it appealing for them? Was it because they were a generation that wasn't organized in unions and the kind of coalition politics they shaped anymore?

AR Well, that's a really good question. I think in the first place Malcolm X was a powerful voice when he was alive. I remember, here in New Orleans, watching Civil Rights demonstrators down on Canal Street get beaten and dragged away in the police cars and stuff. And a lot of young and hapless youth, or a lot of hapless mainly male youth, were put off by the Civil Rights inclination not to fight back. Malcolm X in particular, and then Carmichael, and then Rap Brown at least rhetorically, gave vent to that feeling of being pissed off and not manly enough; that's really what it came down to. And God knows there's nobody in the world who's more manly than a sixteen year old. So that was part of it. And the way that most of the mainstream of the Civil Rights movement sort of attacked Black Power radicalism also reinforced a commitment to it. And so we all kind of came up with this sense, or a lot of us came up with this sense, that the official Civil Rights leadership stratum was always inclined to sell out the movement, whatever the movement was at that point because it wasn't really clear.

AJ But what exactly was the, maybe, sociological reason for the success of that?

AR Well, Black Power was also connected, in urban areas, with what had been about a decade to a decade and a half, depending on where you were, of jockeying within local politics around stuff like urban renewal, police brutality, discrimination in education and housing, and access to public services, which fed the fantasy, particularly among the functionary strata, that if we could have control of those institutions we could do it better, or for the people. So Black Power sensibility—and it's important to note that, as a radicalism, it was more a sensibility than a worked-up ideology or a pragmatic movement—also kind of bounced up against, and eventually melded into, a perspective among a stratum of black public officials and functionaries that was already taking shape. Kent Germany's book on the coming of the war on poverty to New Orleans in the mid '60s is really good on this, but also Robert Self's and Chris Rhomberg's parallel work on Oakland documents the presence of that stratum by at least the end of World War II in cities both inside and outside the South.[1] In Southern big cities the 1944 *Smith v. Allwright* Supreme Court decision that got rid of the white primary was a hugely significant intervention. Afterward voter registration in Southern cities shot up exponentially. Again, the New Orleans numbers are fresh in my head: in 1940 there were only 400 blacks registered to vote in the city; by 1952 there were more than 28,000. And this coincided with and reinforced the emergence of governing regimes in the Southern cities that were more or less committed to what they called either moderate segregationism or managed segregationism. The ideal was that you could maintain the Jim Crow order, but find ways to open economic opportunities for black advancement in it. And when you reflect on that, it's also a class program, right? Creating space for stuff like middle class housing subdivisions designated for blacks and other kinds of individual commercial or employment opportunities, often through expansion of the Jim Crow institutional apparatus, e.g., hospitals, schools, social services, etc. And in that sense, moreover, managed or moderate segregationism was also an expression of the model of 'race relations' or 'race adjustment' that had mediated racial subordination since the notion appeared in the early twentieth century.

DZ What do you mean by that? Could you say a bit more about the origin of that notion?

AR Yeah, sure. Tellingly, the race relations notion was rooted in common-sense presumptions of Victorian race theory, namely that races are natural populations whose capacities for civilization can be gleaned from the attainments of the most advanced members of the group; that those advanced, cultivated individuals were the natural, organic representatives of the race; that benefits accruing to the best representatives of the group are benefits for all the group because a) in the openly Victorian racialist version, whatever the best attain demonstrates the group's potential on the scale of civilization, or b) in the later, racial uplift version, benefits to the upper strata trickle down by virtue of their smashing barriers and opening opportunities for others who may follow and by elevating collective aspirations through the convenient device of role modelling, and c) in the interest-group version, having a representative in important places can protect the group's interests. In every iteration, therefore, the race relations framework was a class program, and post-war racial liberalism that enshrined equality of opportunity for upward mobility within American capitalism as the definitive norm of racial justice was yet another articulation of that class agenda. And the idea of racial representation that underlay Black Power was consistent with that same class program.

Black Power appealed to and propagated the alchemy of racial representation, though it was obscured by fantasies of popular racial unity, which in turn sustained the belief that 'putting black faces in previously all-white places', as a phrase of the time put it, was a program of political transformation. Dean Robinson pointed out that Black Power reformulated black nationalism by shedding the objective of physical, jurisdictional separation from the US, which had been a cardinal tenet of earlier nationalisms through Garvey. And that change also reflects, though again it wasn't clear to radicals at the time, the extent to which it was a class program. 'Community control' meshed nicely with administrative decentralization, and the ghetto economic development initiatives were mainly funded by the federal government and the Ford Foundation and focused on community development rather than political mobilization. Black Power's psychologistic rhetoric of empowerment, which overlapped with culture of poverty ideologues in contending that racism had damaged black Americans by giving rise to self-destructive cultural pathologies, obscured the reality that the shift from political action to community development was at bottom a reassertion of Bookerite accommodationism.

At the same time, around the late '60s, Black Powerites had to confront the problem of, well, all-black governance doesn't make a lot of sense in the US, where the black population is just a little more than ten per cent of the total. And that's when you get the jump into Third Worldism. Because the line was, well, we're a minority here, but we're a majority on the globe, on the surface of the globe, and that encouraged identification with national liberation movements around the world, and so forth and so on.

From the fall of '69 to when I went to graduate school three years later, I was mainly out in the field organizing, so I would observe and sometimes participate in those debates among the radical Black Powerites, who at that point, because of Black Power's inadequacies, were becoming either Pan-Africanists, radical cultural nationalists, or what I referred to at the time as magical Marxist-Leninists, who confused political theory with geometry, as my buddy Alex Willingham put it. And then, to keep it personal, one of the reasons I was ready to go to graduate school was that I could tell that the left flank of whatever this other stuff was had been defeated, and/or was being absorbed into the electoral bullshit, or was following the foundation funding—to do community service—or was dribbling off into the same kind of disaster of ideological purification that beset some of the radical tendencies that emerged from the demise of SDS [Students for a Democratic Society]. And then I, frankly, kind of lucked out in going to Atlanta at the moment racial transition in local politics was happening, and at that point I was already a clearer Marxist than I was at nineteen—one would hope, anyway. And I could just watch it, and was dropped right in the middle of it. So as much as I hated the city, I give it credit because it was a laboratory, or was like a natural laboratory, as Robert Park would put it. And so, yeah, I guess that's about it.

Well, no, I'll say one other thing. I had spent—and I may've written this some place, I think—but I had spent the better part of a decade, if not longer, trying to work my way through the sort of Marxist/Black Power nationalist thing. But it took me about a decade to figure out that the central flaw with even revolutionary nationalist, Black Power-influenced ideology is that the key category for critical judgement, and the normative stance on which the radicals stood, was the notion of the black community.

DZ It's really the starting point of this community-centered conception of change and the whole language of 'empowerment' I guess . . .

AR Absolutely, and by the mid '70s I'd figured out that, OK, that's what the problem was. And the transition helped a lot for that, too, because you could see . . . well, the Last Poets in one of their songs said, 'When the revolution comes, you'll see Roy Wilkins walking down 125th street in a blue dashiki'. But that's precisely what the bourgeois politicians were able to do. The symbols of community authenticity . . . well, in the first place, positing the community as the effective source of left agency provided you with no critical standard except authenticity in representing the aspirations of the community. The 'community' of course was an abstraction by definition, kind of like 'the masses'. And the symbols that were available through which to make claims to authenticity were so thin and shallow—it's like having an afro, or wearing a dashiki, or talking about coming from the hood or whatever the fuck—that it was pretty clear that, while the radicals on the one side had those symbols, the bourgeois politicians were also fluent in that symbolic discourse *and* they had resources they could pass out, where the radicals didn't. So there's no way you're going to win that one.

DZ Adolph, what you just said is kind of interesting to also understand the appeal of Black Power outside the US. Growing up in Belgium, which, we have to admit, doesn't have much in common with US history, except perhaps our taste for fries, I still was raised politically, at least in my years at university, with collections of texts of Huey P. Newton and Angela Davis and the Black Panther Party imagery.

AR Oh, yeah.

DZ It was very popular. But I'd never heard, until I got to the US, of A. Phillip Randolph or Bayard Rustin. Those figures didn't exist on the map. Interestingly this is also reinforced through the fact that the whole cultural production is very much focused on figures such as Malcolm X, Fred Hampton, the Black Panthers, but you won't find any movie about Randolph. Along with that we were of course taught a very superficial history about racism in America, all supposedly rooted in a kind of unexplainable white supremacy. Basically an unsophisticated version of Afropessimism, I guess. But of course, this tapped into something more profound. In France in particular, where all those texts were translated by the early '70s, by the writer Jean Genet in particular, the Black Power framework appeared also a useful alternative to mass parties and union politics. It had this urban dimension that fit perfectly with the post-'68 ethos.

AR Right.

DZ When you are a student and there is no organized working class anymore, it seems appealing to think about politics through building a community center. Breakfasts for children and things like that is something that seems reachable, seems like something that you could achieve, while building big coalitions and strikes and trying to win those battles seems so far away when all those organizations are being destroyed or are in decline. It feels like this nostalgia for Black Power, even today, is driven by the decline of the working class as a political agent, and this is basically the reason why it always comes back.

AR Yeah, sure. I'll tell you what, though. I think the nostalgia in the US for Black Power and the Black Panthers is even more insidious than that. Because I think it's like all of the nostalgia that currently drives ostensibly insurgent black American political discourse; the rush is to try to understand the present through the lens of an earlier era. And that doesn't take account of the victories won by the Civil Rights movement, or of the ways in which those victories were consolidated into a class politics. And the Black Panther thing . . . they became Third Worldist, revolutionary Marxists, right? They did that partly because, when they made the adventurous move of posing with those unloaded shotguns on the State House, they began racking up a lot of lawyers' fees. And they got hold of a shipment of copies of Mao's Red Book that they sold to help raise legal fees. And they also trained the ersatz cadre whom they were recruiting because—and I know some people go bat-shit when I say this, but—in most cities the Panthers recruited from the same pools that the street gangs were recruiting from, and that's kind of a reminder of what you're dealing with and where you're getting your cadre from. And often I would say at the time it just seemed like some of these guys just pressed a button on their stomach and then the Mao-speak came out. 'What you have to understand, brother, is that you have to make a distinction between the principal and the secondary contra-dictions among the people, right?'[2]

AJ One of Mao's finest, I have to say . . .

DZ That's actually Chairman Mao's most useful concept!

AR No, no, totally. I'm not pissing on Mao for that. I think there's a lot more to Mao than a lot of people think. And for fundraising pur-poses among liberals . . . ironically, it was the shift in their focal con-stituency toward rich liberals who expected a Richard Wright kind of posture that encouraged their pro forma adoption of what they called Marxism-Leninism.

238

AJ Are you saying their Marxism-Leninism was performative rather than substantive?

AR Oh, totally. Yeah.

WBM '60s elites liked a little Marxism in their racial theatre; today's elites prefer it without.

AR I've got an account that may shed some light on the BPP [Black Panther Party] moment, though it's a bit of a shaggy dog tale. I met Kathleen Cleaver [former BPP Communications Secretary and wife of writer and Panther leader Eldridge Cleaver] not long after I got to Yale to teach. And she had come back to graduate and then went to law school. And, true story, [literature professor Henry Louis] 'Skip' Gates just thought it would be the coolest thing in the world to get us together to talk. He wasn't trying to be a yenta; it was just that he thought it'd be cool because we both had these '60s histories. I tried to avoid it for as long as I could, and then John Hope Franklin [prominent Afro-Americanist historian and an old family friend] came and gave a talk, and we're at the reception together and Skip kind of put us together. Anyway, Kathleen explains to me that the reason why the Panthers went through the stuff that they did when they started joining the Baptist Church in Oakland and that kind of shit, was not that they had gone through a self-critical process and determined that the way that they understood American capitalism and imperialism was wanting, but that they had learned that the masses weren't ready for revolution. And what they had to do was opportunistically go to where the masses were, to help prepare them for revolution in the longer term. So, you know, I'm sitting in one of these Gothic—or, you know, the big room in one of these Gothic buildings at Yale—thinking, well, they didn't learn any fucking thing from their experience. Like, nothing at all. And then another aspect of it I also confronted is that by around 1970 the Panthers . . . there were probably as many thugs and police agents, or thug-police agents, in the BPP as anything else, so I always gave them a wide berth in my own work. Then again, as Cedric Johnson noted in a recent article in *Dissent*, the Panthers did attempt for a while to lay out a seriously left, anti-capitalist politics, and they stood out for that. But most telling of all was that the Panthers never really were a significant force in black politics. The only way you can make them one is to contend that they were, like, the deeper reality of black politics. But throughout their rise and disintegration, the forces of petty bourgeois black, ethnic politics were steadily moving and consolidating.

AJ I want to ask a quick question about Clarence Thomas, but not necessarily because it's relevant. How would you understand the continuity between his Black Power phase and what he did later?

AR Well, he never was . . .

AJ Ah, OK. He was into black nationalism, right?

AR Right.

WBM Jesus Christ, anybody could be a black nationalist. All you had to do was say so.

AR Right.

WBM Being a Black Panther did require a little more commitment . . .

AR I remember he made a big deal of having a big photo of Malcolm X in his dorm room, but he also had a Confederate flag in his dorm room, so . . .

WBM My roommate didn't have the Confederate flag, but he totally had the Malcolm X. He was a white guy, not a black nationalist.

DZ Something that's a detail, but kind of interesting, is that his favorite book is Ralph Ellison's *Invisible Man*. And part of it, as with the Confederate flag, is, I think, that he saw some virtues in Jim Crow in the sense that it created an environment where black men could uplift themselves. Corey Robin has a great book on how black nationalism explains part of his views on the court.[3]

AR Right.

AJ While affirmative action still implies that it is the paternalist, white superior that is granting you entrance to these institutions . . . And he actually recalls dramatic times when he was at Yale, I think, or somewhere else, and when he gets there and everybody sees him he immediately feels that they think that he's only there because of affirmative action.

AR Right. Well, I mean, look. The roots of what we think of as modern black nationalism, well before it took on the costume party character that it did in the mid-'60s . . . well, actually that's not fair. It had a costume party character up in Harlem in the '50s, too. But Bookerism is the programmatic core of black nationalism. Garvey came to the US because he wanted to get the blessing of Booker T. Washington, but Washington had died. And Harold Cruse's critique of Black Power makes this clear. The Black Power radicals, because of all the Third Worldist stuff, had thought that their program was a radical program, but it wasn't . . . Washington and other Bookerites were convinced that the way forward was to find a safe niche within capitalism. They weren't just conciliationists; they had a positive program, and the positive program was, basically, separate development. And that's where Thomas was, too. And a lot of others. And Walter, I know, can say a lot more about this than I can, but there is a kind of right-wing reading of Ralph Ellison that comes from people like Albert Murray and Stanley Crouch, who see him as an avatar of the same kind of focus on black dignity that appealed to 'do for self/cast down your buckets' racial conservatism. Ellison certainly preferred maintenance of a kind of dignity regarding racial issues, and probably regarding much else, and I think most of us who were born prior to 1980 have a bit of that Ellisonian sensibility in us. (There's some shit that one should avoid simply because it feels undignified. This is a really trivial illustration, but every now and then I'll ask a friend of mine, So what is it that draws white people to wearing silly hats? Because doing that is just, on some level, fundamentally an undignified thing to do.) So some of those people, like those I mentioned, try to appropriate Ellison for a generally conservative, individualist politics.

wbm We ought to just say here—read Ken Warren's stuff on Ellison.[4]

ar Right. It's really good.

aj I still have a question about Jim Crow, which is about how, in some sense—and it goes to what you've written about movies and *Django*[5], which we'll probably get back to later—it is useful for neoliberalism to imagine that we're still, and will always be, living in a version of Jim Crow. There seems to be a tendency within neoliberalism to imagine a world in which racism is the crucial and the central problem organizing the social order. And I guess that's what drives all those movies, all those books within academia, that somehow empty what Jim Crow *is* but at the same time produce a sort of version of what our problem is.

ar It was a social order. My son says that a lot of people tend to think of slavery and sharecropping as permanent white sadistic camps; that the whole point of it was to brutalize black people. And as far as the brutalization stuff goes, I just drove a couple of days ago past the Celtic cross that marks where upwards of 20,000 Irish canal workers are buried here who died while they were digging the New Basin Canal in New Orleans in the 1830s[6]. You wouldn't even need to think about brutalizing them, because they didn't count for anything, right? But it's a convenient narrative, because the more that you can define the problem in the past as racism . . . Well, two things happened. One is that you use what are by now set-piece understandings of the problem in the past as having been purely and simply racism, as ways to explain the present by analogy. That's a convenient move because it sidesteps the need for argument demonstrating how racism produces the outcomes it supposedly produces in the present. The classic example of this is the Michelle Alexander book, *The New Jim Crow*[7]. She repeats the 'just like Jim Crow' refrain over and over in the book, until even she has to say, Well, actually, it's not. And then one might ask, OK, well, then if it's not, what could the point of the analogy as you've pushed it all the way through the book have been? And the rhetorical point is to establish that whatever injustices are experienced by black people in this society have to be explained by race and racism.

WBM And you can't underestimate the power of that. As a kid, maybe from six to ten, I lived in suburban Connecticut, in a kind of very middle class, new housing development—a cut above Levittowns, split-level ranch, like that. The families were all like ours, and people were starting to make a little money. It was part of the big post-war expansion. And at a certain point a couple of the families, friends of ours, hired a housekeeper, and we did too. So Wilhelmina was the first black person I ever knew. She and, I think, her cousin had both come up from South Carolina to work for Jews in Stamford. And that summer, my family was invited to spend a week with some people my father knew through work, on Hilton Head Island in South Carolina.

AR Oh, Lord.

WBM So we're driving down there—like, I'm nine years old, I don't have any views on this at all—and Willie wants to go, she's from South

Carolina, she wants to visit her family, so we're going to drive her down. And I guess we leave late enough so we're not going to make it all the way to South Carolina in one day, and we pull over—it's the first time I ever saw the place—around Richmond. And if you drive by Richmond, you know there are all these tobacco companies, my memory is the big Winston cigarette column is there . . .

AR It wasn't Winston, it was Marlboro.

WBM Yeah, Marlboro. So, we pull off the road, we're going to stay at some hotel. In my memory it's the John Marshall, but the thing is we take Willie someplace else first. And my brother and I are confused. Why isn't she staying where we're going to stay? And then we pick her up next morning. And we're, what the fuck? And my father's explanation is shocking to us. So you get two things from that. As a kid, I'm not shocked by the fact that we're probably paying her very little money to clean our house and take care of us. To do this job for us. That seems like the normal order of things . . .

AR Right.

WBM But the idea that there exists this world in the same country we live in, where you have to get off the road and go to some place way off the main drag because she can't, you know, stay in the same hotel you stay in! That seems completely wrong. A nine-year old can see that. And on the other hand, you can completely isolate it from the employment relation. None of the harm is in the employment relation; all of it's in the differential treatment, the discrimination. It's very easy and not implausible to come up with two very different accounts of what the problem is here, and in the subsequent half century not only does the difference between the two get consolidated but the attempt to get rid of one becomes the alibi for the continuation of the other.

AR I'll tell you something else on that, too; it's also an anecdote, but from later. When I first started writing my column in *Progressive* I was just barely on the internet. So what I would do would be print it and fax it, and especially when I was out of town. I was down here once—this must've been around '93 or '94—and had to scuffle around to get to Kinko's or some place to copy it and fax it in. And while I was waiting on line the legendary former football coach at St. Augustine's, my arch rival school, was on line ahead of me, and he was talking to some friends and mentioned that his daughter, his youngest daughter, had finished college and had gone to Dallas to work for some 'big corporation'. And he was really happy that she was going to work for a big corporation. He couldn't think of the name of it, he couldn't think of what the job was, but the whole point . . . and this was one of the narratives, even when I was in school. A bunch of my friends from college went to IBM and Xerox and stuff, and of course to GE, right, the engineering ones . . .

wbm When you finish this, tell the story about the engineer at GE.

ar Oh, yeah, that's basically the same story. And it stuck with me, because he and his interlocutors were out of the respectable Creole middle class, and the conversation I overheard was emblematic of their class, because it presumed the image of upward mobility as its own reward. And for them, his generation had all gone to college and had become more or less basic functionaries in what were basically segregated institutions, and so the trajectory for the next generation was to break into the mainstream and go to work for a big corporation, because that was the class's concrete aspiration in that moment of Civil Rights victories. And I thought, OK no wonder we fucking lost. That aspiration, obscured though it may have been by the idealist, communitarian constructs of Black Power ideology, was part of what was driving our own cohort— even among many radicals themselves—as well as others among the most politically attentive and efficacious elements in mainstream black American political life. And this goes back to Preston Smith's *Racial Democracy*[8], because that inclusionist aspiration is the quintessence of the racial-democratic ideal. To that extent, Black Power radicals' reification of an abstract 'community' as the racial equivalent of the universal class was a fanciful misreading parallel to those anti-war radicals who mistook opposition to conscription for anti-imperialism.

As for the engineer, this incident was only a few years after that Kinko's encounter. I was down in Richmond doing some consulting work with a group who were trying to figure out how to line up on a change to the Richmond municipal charter. And one of the local members of the group was a guy, a retired engineer, black guy, who had lived in Fairfield County, Connecticut for a long time and had retired to Richmond. And this was at a moment when the United Electrical Workers union was in contract negotiations with GE, and Jack Welch, the CEO, had just announced at the beginning of contract negotiations that his ideal factory was on a barge so that he could move it any place he felt like going in pursuit of cheap, tractable labor. So, the black guy, we were just chatting, and he had a summery drink. And he was getting nostalgic about his recruitment to GE out of Howard University in the 1950s and how important Jack Welch was; he'd gotten to know Welch personally and they were friendly, and he thought Welch was a great man. So I mentioned to him, this other side of Jack Welch, noting that he probably did greater harm to more black line workers than he did good for black engineers and management types. And he took a sip of his drink and sighed and said, Well, yeah, I know, but you can't always be concerned about the working brothers.

AJ That's pretty nuts.

WBM And it has a GE pedigree. Because I don't know if it was his immediate predecessor, but before the notoriously anti-union Welch a guy called Charles Edward Wilson was the CEO of GE. When the war is over, after '45, he does two things. One is he leads a really aggressive anti-union campaign, the central feature of which is a 'take it or leave it' pay package. The other is he becomes the chair of Truman's Committee on Civil Rights, which produces a report so completely committed to racial equality that Jim Clyburn now says Truman was better than Roosevelt for black people. So, hard-ball anti-union, hard-ball pro-black. And no contradiction at all.

AR Right.

WBM Everybody should have been saying to Charles Edward Wilson, why can't we do both? Civil rights and unions. But the whole point for him was to do one instead of the other.

DZ That story makes me think about the history of post-apartheid South Africa. If you read the 1955 *Freedom Charter*, which was the program the ANC advanced against apartheid, it's very similar to the 1965 *Freedom Budget* pushed by Randolph and Rustin. In the case of the ANC it was a crucial moment in the anti-apartheid struggle because it was not anymore exclusively a struggle focused on civil rights, but about completely transforming the economic structure of South Africa. But then of course when Mandela was elected they built a post-apartheid South Africa but more or less abandoned the economic program. What they basically implemented was a kind of structural adjustment program. And what happens is, indeed, inequality between races declines, but intra-race inequality explodes and inequality in general skyrockets. It's as if in ten years, they did what the US took thirty years to do. It's striking how this story echoes the trajectory of the Civil Rights movement. Where, of course, the ambitions to restructure the American economy put forward in the *Freedom Budget* fail politically, unlike the anti-discrimination framework.

AR Well, once you have the prototype, man, you can crank that Model T out all over the world.

WBM Absolutely. There's one difference, though, which is that for the ANC, who were supposed to be communists, it's hypocrisy. For the GE guys, there's no hypocrisy needed.

AR I remember, going back again to when I was in college, and to the jobs many of my black friends sought and got, that GE, IBM, and Xerox were among the most liberal and open and aggressive corporations with respect to recruiting blacks into non-line positions from, like, the late '50s through the '60s. And they were also, at the same time, in the vanguard of degrading that kind of white-collar work. Remember, IBM was famously one of the first to get rid of the individual office. So they were Taylorizing the jobs. They would move shop-floor work process and management into mid-level, white collar work process and management. While being staunch, and no doubt genuine, racial democrats. So I'm wondering now how common that was as a phenomenon during the decades from the mid '50s to the mid '70s.

WBM Yeah, interesting question.

DZ Can I bounce back on Walter's point about hypocrisy? I think hypocrisy is important because it's the core of the debate we've been having when Jeff Bezos, for example, endorses BLM. Part of the left is generally wondering what to do with that. And the main response is that we should reject such endorsements because they aren't sincere. The main problem becomes hypocrisy. But the argument that you both have been making for many years is that it's beside the point. We can definitely imagine that Bezos is completely sincere in his commitment. He could fire any worker that tries to unionize while giving some millions to Black Lives Matter. There is actually no contradiction between these two questions. A program against discrimination is a good thing, but has nothing to do with giving strong labor rights in the workplace. Or a minimum wage.

wbm Exactly.

ar You can't take a bathroom break, for instance.

wbm Yeah.

ar Workers in the warehouse.

wbm All the corporate support for Black Lives Matter—how many billions of dollars are being pledged?—is just a manifestation of what Adolph's engineer told him. And of what the arch-neoliberal economist, Gary Becker, always said: equality of opportunity is good for business. The moral argument against discrimination and the business argument have always gone hand in hand.

aj It's also a big theme in something like "Black Particularity Reconsidered", for example, where you talk about the role of this corporate liberalism in the early Civil Rights movement.[9] And where you also talk about an internally divided movement where you did have a radical labor wing, but then there was also a more civilly and less socially-minded wing . . .

ar Right.

aj They definitely smoothed the transition into that particular urban regime you talked about in the 1970s. But how would you see the role of corporate liberalism within that Civil Rights movement as a whole?

ar I think in the way that Walter just laid it out, frankly. Because I can't recall a moment that I've read about, even one in my lifetime, in which the argument for racial justice wasn't tied to an argument for economic efficiency. And that goes back to Booker T. Washington, and Anna Julia Cooper, and the other earliest Race Uplifters. When Washington called for Southern employers to cast down their buckets where they were, it wasn't just about being noble, or fair. Washington's argument was that it was good business practice because, you know, the blacks are loyal, tractable, docile. And, basically, that they'd produce more surplus value for you. And that's been consistent all the way through—through the work Touré [Reed] did on the Urban League, even in the '30s when they tilted left. Part of the argument was that hiring black workers could improve efficiency. And it's the same basic principle. After the war it gets dressed up a little bit more with a discourse of fairness and Brotherhood Week. But I think that that was a driving interpretation through the Civil Rights movement. And that's one of the reasons that we were all given to understand that companies like GE and IBM were path break-ers. So one other thing about this I guess you've all noticed, apropos of the Bezos thing: a few months ago Kimberlé Crenshaw made a caustic point that the corporate sector has been much more responsive to black demands than the left has been. And Gerald Horne, who at one point was either in or on the edges of the Communist Party, just did the same thing more recently. And where with Crenshaw it was more like a throw-away line, with Horne it was more like the subject. Even more recently, nominally leftist historian Matt Karp takes the at-best Clintonite *At-lantic*'s embrace of Ta-Nehisi Coates and Ibram X. Kendi, and the *New York Times*'s imprimatur on the 1619 Project and on Isabel Wilkerson's Caste foolishness [10] (even as the *Times* remains overwhelmingly hostile to Sanders), as something like anomalous victories for progressives. He dismisses 'left skeptics' who advance the obvious alternative explana-tion: that there's nothing anomalous about those associations, that those 'victories' aren't progressive victories at all and are evidence of this an-ti-racist discourse's fundamental compatibility with neoliberalism.

DZ Is it relevant, maybe, to ask you, Walter, more seriously about your time in Berkeley? Because, as I recall, it is somehow part of the shift in how politics were conceived, especially on university campuses. In how academics, of course, but not only academics, began to think about poli-tics: as more or less disconnected from the coalition building of the post-war period and as more concerned about petitions and op-eds. It seems that your distaste for campus politics also came from that.

WBM Yeah, I was sort of traumatized, politically, by Berkeley. I actu-ally had a little PTSD moment when you brought up the ANC. Because during my time in Berkeley, which happened to be the decade in which economic inequality really exploded in the US, the political issue that everybody cared about most was ending apartheid in South Africa. And it was completely moralized. And of course, it's not that it was wrong to want to end apartheid.

But—to paraphrase Hillary Clinton in reverse—ending apartheid wasn't going to end economic inequality! You began by asking Adolph about when did a certain way of putting the question of race become at the center of American politics. And one way to answer that would be by saying: when discrimination came to be seen as the fulcrum of American inequality. It takes anti-racism to make race fully hegemonic. And that hegemony, I think, is a neoliberal phenomenon. So I'm at Berkeley when neoliberalism declared itself in the US; that's the Volcker shock, that's the mortgages going through twenty-four per cent.[11] And for professors in my generation, it works out fine. We protest apartheid and make out like bandits at home. The very things that were making life worse for the working class were making it better for people like us.

AR Well, I would add this to it too. And it really is adding to the account. Because, on the other coast, at that time I was watching the importation of British cultural studies into the American university. But without any of the political, economic, or class content, and with its being turned into this thing that's all about performance, popular culture, and watching TV. I don't know how much of that was distinctive to Yale because of the American Studies Program, which was always basically the people who wanted to watch TV and get grades for it.

WBM Those guys walking around with T-shirts saying, Stuart Hall: race is the modality in which, thank God, class is completely totally fucking repressed.[12]

AR Right. Right. Exactly. Now we should get those and sell them. I think we can make some money off those.

WBM It would make us more money than this book ever will.

AR And it was at the same moment, on the institutional side, that black studies and women's studies and cultural studies programs were jockeying for a position in the budgets. And this version of denatured cultural studies discourse just converged on the institutional aspirations of these academics. And then around the same time Russell Jacoby's book came out that introduced the concept of the public intellectual[13] —and they grab onto that, and then you get this entire complex built around this odd public/private hybrid persona, and academic reputations can take off without having any basis in the substance of scholarly output or, for that matter, any foundation in political action. And then that becomes its own career imperative, which becomes its own kind of ersatz political imperative. And here we are.

AJ One more question about the 1980s. Can you talk a bit about Jesse Jackson?

AR I think what happened with Jackson was interesting. When Reagan was elected, most of the advocacy voices in the black political class— while they went through all the motions of expression of fear and anxiety—had mainly lulled themselves to sleep after the Nixon experience, because Nixon had run kind of like that too. And governed as our last Keynesian. And I think they kind of thought that they'd be able to make their deals with Reagan the same way they had with Nixon.

AJ Ah, yes, yeah . . .

AR And then they found out that Reagan was really a revolutionary and had meant what he said. And they'd spent the last fifteen years or so accommodating themselves to a retrenchment and austerity politics— kind of scaling back expectations. Much as the AFL-CIO does now, their position was one of explaining to the black constituency why they had to scale back expectations. So, Reagan smacks back. They don't have the capacity to mobilize anybody, because they hadn't even thought about that for close to twenty years. You didn't have a programmatic response, because they hadn't had one of those, either. So what they did was, they called a March on Washington in 1983, basically to commemorate the fact that they'd had one there twenty years earlier. It's straight out of the Eighteenth Brumaire. And after that march, Jesse literally said that God had come down to him in a dream and told him he should explore a presidential candidacy. So he did, and, to his credit, he knew how to use evocative imagery of the high period of Civil Rights activism to make it appear that there was some dynamic base of support for what he was doing. I said at the time, I think I even said this in the book[14], that most of the press couldn't tell the difference between a political movement and a bunch of people shouting at church. Jackson developed a political program—and this is another move which I guess you could give him credit for pioneering—just to say that he had one, and they kept it in the file cabinet. Because his real campaign message was, it's our time now. And so people for a variety of reasons, some of them opportunistic and some of them not, projected onto Jackson an insurgent political agenda that he never really had. And the hope often expressed was that he would use the campaign to try to build something like a durable political organization or tendency, which, if you knew anything about Jackson's career, was never going to be the case, because all of his building had to do with himself. It's interesting, because I know a lot of people who kind of date being involved in Jackson's campaigns as their introduction to an activist left politics. But I thought all along that Jackson was much more useful for the Clintonites and the right wing of the Democratic Party than he was for any kind of left agenda. Because what he did both times was draw attention and votes from candidates who weren't, you know, Lenin, but they weren't Clinton either. People with more reflexes back towards the New Deal, and a redistributive politics. So that helps explain why well-heeled conservative Democrats got behind his campaign both times, in '84 and in '88. I always thought that the Jackson campaigns showed, first of all, the bankruptcy of the black political class. Both because so many of them were reluctant to get behind him the first time, and because they weren't reluctant to get behind him the second time, and sought ways to try to pimp his candidacy. But in both cases, Jackson in effect took black people out of the crucial debate about the way forward for the Democratic Party. Because his demands were always elite jobs and appointments for black people. And, of course, respect for him. It's another one of these funny moments. And that, by the way, is the reason why I didn't want to write a book about Obama, because it just seems like I already spent a lot of time pissing on the parades of people who expect that there's going to be a black leader who's going to deliver us.

aj Can I ask: at which point does this idea of the promotion of diversity emerge as a kind of political program, one which I think is slightly different from anti-racism. When does this idea emerge in American politics?

AR I can give you a year—1978. Because the *Bakke* decision[15] is really what introduced the diversity idea into the national discussion of equality and racial justice. And *Bakke* ruled that you couldn't use race as a criterion for college admissions, or for grad school admission, or med school admissions, except insofar as you could show that there's a compelling argument that taking race into account helps to pursue the university's goal of diversifying the student body.

WBM Which immediately turned into diversity-as-a-model-of-social-justice. Because if the first justification had been something like 'racial diversity is just a variation on the other kinds of diversity universities valued'—like if you were an East Coast college, having some kids from Oregon—the second step made diversity into a mechanism of social justice for people of color. No one had ever thought that kids from Oregon had been victimized by discrimination and that justice for Oregonians required that a certain number of them be able to go to Harvard. But everybody *did* think that about black kids. So you now get the increasingly complete commitment to the model of justice-as-racial-representation and thus to the model of proportionality. Every demand can take the form: 'people of color are under-represented on this board of directors, under-represented in the universities'. The under-representation works perfectly for elite institutions since it tells you the problem isn't their eliteness, it's the under-representation. And on the other side, people of color are over-represented among those killed by the police, among the poor, etc. Which does a version of the same job; it tells you the problem is that too many black people are poor, not that we allow poverty, and that too many black people are killed by the police, not that *anyone* is killed by the police. So that becomes what Cedric Johnson calls militant liberalism.

AR Right.

WBM The militance is the insistence on absolute proportionality, all the way down the line. And it's obviously conservative in the sense that the point is not to get rid of the board of directors. The point is to make sure that there's some people of color and women on the board of directors. 'Doing anti-racism work'.

AJ A defense would be that bringing women will change how it functions, because women have a specific experience of the world. And that specific experience will be integrated, will change how governance is carried . . .

wbm Exactly—not obvious that it's true but, to the extent that it is, it's the point Adolph made before about the link to economic efficiency.

dz Absolutely! But can I add just a more historical question? I'd like to know a bit more about how you ended up writing *The Trouble with Diversity* while coming from literary stuff. And maybe a bit more about the context in which the book was published. As your book came out just a couple of years after Tom Frank's *What's the Matter with Kansas?*.

wbm *The Trouble with Diversity* comes out of an academic book, *Our America*, and that book came out of teaching summer school one year at Berkeley, a course I'd never taught before, on the American novel in the twentieth century. When you teach a summer course, you teach what the kids like. And people like reading twentieth century American novels. They're fun, they're interesting. So, I'm doing the hits—back-to-back *The Great Gatsby*, *The Sun Also Rises* and *The Sound and the Fury*. And I realize they're like the same book, each structured around a fantasy of incest that has almost nothing to do with sexual desire and everything to do with keeping someone understood as a member of your family from sleeping with someone who isn't—characteristically, a Jew. *The Great Gatsby* comes first because it's 1925, and I'm reading it to prepare and, like everyone else, I am struck by Tom's speech about "this man, Goddard" and his book *The Rise of the Colored Empires*. So I walked down the hall, and my colleague, Eric Sundquist, is there. And Eric has done more work on this stuff than I have, and I say to him, I'm about to give a lecture, and is this guy Goddard, like, based on someone real? And Eric says, Yeah, it's a guy called Lothrop Stoddard. Now Adolph's laughing because he and I, between the two of us, have read more Lothrop Stoddard than anyone else in the whole wide world.

ar I think that's probably right.

wbm There aren't that many people who can quote swatches, but here you are, in the presence of almost all of them. So I start reading Lothrop Stoddard and it's an eye opener, for two reasons. One is the racism; the other is the pluralism. And they're both put to work against the idea of social and economic class. Because the problem with Gatsby turns out not really to be that he's risen out of the working class by a very shadowy route but that the working class is something you can't rise out of. It's more like a race, and what he's doing is a version of passing. In effect, it's a version of what Touré has started calling 'race reductionism'—it treats class as if it were race. And then the pluralism completes the operation by doing the same thing with culture. Because pluralism makes difference itself (and eventually diversity) valuable—it turns your culture into a question of who you are rather than a description of what you do and believe. And even though culture is supposed to be an alternative to race, the worry that you could lose your culture or be deprived of your culture or betray your culture makes it clear that the real point of culture is to be a way of renovating race, which now becomes the link between you and some set of beliefs and practices that will count as yours whether or not you believe or practice them.

So *The Trouble with Diversity* was just an effort to think about the political meaning of this attachment to race—about why the realization that race wasn't a meaningful biological entity didn't work. It just turned race into culture or into the social construction of race. When people discovered there was no such thing as a unicorn, they didn't start going around saying, well, it's the social construction of unicorns. But when people discovered there was no such thing as a scientific notion of race, they didn't give it up for a millisecond. What does race do for us, then? In the mode of racism it justifies inequality; in the mode of anti-racism, it produces a certain model of equality. And in both modes, it makes class analysis look at best irrelevant and at worst like a form of racism. That critique of anti-racism was what made *Diversity* controversial fifteen years ago. But the way things have gone since, I think it would be worse today. I'm not sure you could find a mainstream publisher who would publish it.

AR You're right.

DZ But would you say that today it's more difficult to make those arguments than when the book came out? That there's less space today to discuss this framework than when it came out?

WBM I think today anti-racism is absolutely installed as the center of what we call left neoliberalism—from the universities to the *New York Times* or, for that matter, *The Guardian*—and has become the absolute moral center of the professional managerial classes in a way that it wasn't then. I guess it's true—I hope it's true—that there are a few more people on the left who are skeptical. But it's also true that there can be people—not just in the US but in Europe—who will openly say that they feel 'unsafe' in a room (or even on a Zoom) with the author of *The Trouble with Diversity*. That wouldn't have happened fifteen years ago.

AJ Would you say that part of the story here is that, when the book came out, within the left this anti-racism still had a relative novelty to it? While today this space is occupied by the notion of intersectionality.

WBM Maybe part of the difference is the Sanders campaign. Adolph was a very visible Sanders supporter, and obviously Sanders's universalism and his focus on income and wealth inequality were compatible with *The Trouble with Diversity*. Liberals hated that, and their hatred expressed itself though an attack on his supposedly insufficient alertness to the problems of racism and sexism. What we saw in 2016 was the degree to which anti-racism could be weaponized as a liberal attack on the left. Yes, the Sanders campaign did create more space for our arguments. But it also made the liberal rejection of those arguments more intense, and brought the differences between liberalism and even social democracy more vividly into play. Think of Elizabeth Warren's plan to create more black entrepreneurs. More entrepreneurs of any color was not what Sanders was about.

AR Right, and in 2016 Hillary Clinton attacked Sanders for not wanting to means-test his free higher education program (which, I'll just say for the record, he took, along with much of his program, from the Labor Party). And don't forget all the crap from Clinton, Warren, and others in both campaigns about how people must have 'skin in the game' to ensure probity in the use of public goods and services.

WBM What's emerged with really remarkable clarity in the last fifteen years is that anti-racism—anti-discrimination in general—is the beating heart of neoliberal ideology.

AR Let me say one thing. Recently, I've been reflecting on how central means testing as the model of social justice has become. It really began in post-war liberalism, and by the Kennedy administration it became the default approach to social policy. And the reason I've been focused on it is that it kind of slipped past us all. And one of the ways it slipped past us is that the Kennedy-Keynesians presumed that economic growth was going to be the norm for the American economy. There may be little periods of stagnant slumps, but no real long-term economic stagnation. And the role of social policy, therefore, was to take care of the neediest because the rising tide was going to lift all the other boats. And at that crucial moment in the mid '60s, when our efforts to address economic inequality faced a fork in the road, we quietly took the means testing forward. The notion was that the social safety net was just supposed to be that—like a safety net that the worst off couldn't fall through. And you can see how that view of a properly functioning society fits very comfortably with a racial democratic ideal. And with all forms of anti-disparitarianism—because that's what disparitarianism is. You take care of the worst off. And then by the time you get to the '90s, even the further left has had its imagination so stunted that means testing seemed to have become the radical egalitarian option. So, for instance, when we started taking out the Labor Party's free public higher education campaign in the early years of the century, I can't tell you how many times I got reactions from faculty union people, people who likely consider themselves more radical than others, who argued that there's something fundamentally unjust about a policy that would permit, I don't know, Gloria Vanderbilt's kids to go to college for free. Like they would go to Stony Brook anyway, right? But then it becomes even more radical with the emergence of worker-centered identity politics, where the focus of the radical, radical, radical left was to fight for the most abject, most oppressed workers—like the Imokalee tomato workers, or the most busted, the precariat. Where the focus of a left program is to lift the bottom, to bring the worst-off workers up to the condition of the next-worst off. And, frankly, this was one of the reasons I've never jumped up and down about the 'fight for fifteen' stuff[16]. Because that approach doesn't show you a path to building the majority that you need to build in order to win. And it's that much more like social work. But in the last couple months, I've been thinking of it as something even more insidious than that. And this is prosaic to say, but it's almost like a safety valve on the extremes of neoliberal inequality: the idea that, after some effort, you can get an expansion of food stamps. And, in the more elaborate woke-ite politics, that's what justifies the oppression Olympics. Who suffered the most, and who's the worst off? Is it Native Americans? Is it Native Hawaiians? Is it the Afropessimist version of who black people are? It's the same kind of queuing up for differential benefits—partial and means tested—because race is in this sense a means test, a means test that's always been a cornerstone of the neoliberal state.

WBM Of course, the US in the mid-'60s was much more economically equal than it had been before or has been since, so it wasn't totally delusional to think that, as the economy keeps on growing, our job is to figure out what to do about those left behind. But that's, you know, those left behind. We don't want to be giving state money to people who aren't left behind.

AR Right.

WBM That's the whole framework. But of course that's not the way capitalism turned out to work at all . . . What happens instead is that ever since '68 inequality in the US gets worse and worse. So you have, in effect, a way of thinking about the problem. The problem is poverty, and then the problem is disparity—which makes a certain kind of practical sense in the context of a utopian vision of the economy, but which makes no sense at all if you actually want to solve the problem in the context of what actually happens. So what you then get is a kind of ideological commitment to . . . what's the other side of means testing, it's equal opportunity, right? And you see it play out in the debate over free higher education. And why does the university become so important? Why do a few elite universities become so important? Because in an economy that's increasingly unequal, you need some mechanism, or at least the fantasy of a mechanism, that will make it possible for some people at the bottom to get to the top. And, again, that's part of why race becomes important. Because in a society that's actually getting at every moment less and less equal, racial equality gives you an idea of equality which requires no more equality, just more rich black people.

AR Right, that's right.

wbm There are two things really: the shift from equality to poverty, and means testing as an emblem of that, which I think is the point Adolph is making. And the increasing importance of education, at least in people's fantasy lives.

ar Yep. Yep.

wbm And the sort of increasing importance, not just of race, but of race as a kind of opening of the door to any form of discrimination. Including, although it took a while, the neologism of classism, discrimination on the basis of class. All those things play a role that only makes sense in an economy that actually, every year, becomes more and more unequal.

ar Right. That's right.

wbm The material conditions of all this are that things have worked out exactly the opposite way.

ar And that takes us back to the beating heart.

wbm Right. That's why it is the beating heart.

WALTER BENN MICHAELS & ADOLPH REED, JR.

IN CONVERSATION WITH

ANTON JÄGER & DANIEL ZAMORA

Interview Two
3 June 2021

DANIEL ZAMORA This time our idea was to start again from Jim Crow, but from another angle. From the question of what does race mean? And then go also to your essay, Walter, "Autobiography of an Ex-White Man". And then discussing a bit how the cultural definition of race displaced the essentialist one, while still failing in offering a coherent understanding of it. And I think that it would be fun to discuss the Henry Louis Gates show, *Finding Your Roots*, the irony of the popularity of genetic tests and so forth. Also to discuss a bit about memory, maybe. About how history becomes memory and plays a central role in how we define identity today.

WALTER BENN MICHAELS My serious interest in all this began with just the problem of what racial identity was—which is actually an interest that Adolph and I had in common long before we met each other. And one form it took was the question: since people don't believe any longer that there is such a thing as biological racial identity, why do we hang on to the idea of race?

ADOLPH REED, JR. Yeah.

WBM And part of the answer to that, which maybe we'll come back to, was that actually they never totally believed that there was biological racial identity; everyone's idea of race was always crucially supplemented by something like the racial soul. That is, you could never really do just biological racial identity. But for me the first question was, since there is no such thing as racial identity, why are we still doing this? But when I first encountered Adolph's writing, it was not with respect to the question, Why are we hanging on to so-called anti-essentialist or social constructionist ideas of racial identity? It was more basic: why are some of us hanging on to actual, biological ideas of racial identity? It was when you were taking the anti-Charles Murray show on tour.

AR Right. Yeah, that's right.

WBM Murray was a guy who was committed to racial identity old school, totally out of reach of my arguments.

ANTON JÄGER Can you tell us the year when Murray published the book, and a bit about the actual context to it? Because it was a watermark in that sort of longer American conversation about race. Even though it came from the right, it established certain habits that turned out to be quite powerful in the coming decade.

AR Yeah, I think in a way it exposed the lie of what would, in a later incarnation, be called a social constructionist understanding. The earlier incarnation was the Lamarckian theory of race that was linked to the theory of inheritance. And this at bottom was always the point that Walter made: that the point was never really biology, but that there was a racial soul, that you could access a racial soul, that you could delimit the territory of the racial soul through a biological metaphor if you wanted to, but that when that didn't work you could use other metaphors as well. Because nobody really had an account of what turned the biological mechanism into the precise just-so stories that it turned into. And in that sense Murray did mark something of a watershed, but as I recall . . .

WBM Can you explain what the Murray was?

AR *The Bell Curve* was by Charles Murray and Richard Herrnstein, who was a psychologist whose academic career was always devoted to proving racial hierarchy. And by the way, that's one of the things that made going on the Charles Murray tour kind of interesting and informative for me. I kept running into former Herrnstein students who were themselves very deeply committed racial liberals, who had worked with Herrnstein and known him, and were insistent that the man was not a racist. Which would lead me to wonder—and sometimes to ask—well, what does it mean to be a racist if his entire academic career, which was tied up with demonstrating what he perceived to be the facts of racial inequality, doesn't qualify him for the label? It's kind of hard to understand what the notion would mean apart from that. Anyway, when I read the book, and it's kind of a funny backstory to this, because I knew it was coming out . . .

DZ Did they engage at some point with Stephen Jay Gould's *The Mismeasure of Man*?

AR Not really, but Gould was an impediment to their pressing the claims they wanted to press. So they had to try to mobilize a response to Gould. What I realized once I actually read it was that it was an anti-affirmative action tract. The target in its sights was, specifically, the [1971] *Griggs v. Duke Power* Supreme Court decision, which was a slap for the IQ industry. And for Herrnstein; again, his entire career had been part of the IQ industry. And Murray, for his entire career, had been a reactionary snake who was committed to presumptions of natural human inequality along group lines. (In an outrageous puff piece on Murray in the *New York Times Magazine*, timed to coincide with *The Bell Curve*'s publication, Jason DeParle wondered whether Murray's youthful cross-burning in Iowa should be seen as evidence of his racism or just as adolescent hi-jinks.) So, they came together. It was also interesting to see that Murray defended himself—because Herrnstein died around the time the book came out—but Murray defended the book against charges that it was racist by contending that only three chapters of the book were about race. And what I realized when I read it was, No, three chapters of the book were about blacks and/or Asians, but all of the book, every bit of the book, was organized by race; it was divided into black samples, white samples, and Asian samples. The whole book was about race. But Gould and the other critics of IQ hereditarianism caused a problem for Murray and Herrnstein, and they had to try to work their way through that problem, which is what gives the impression that their intent was to take on Gould. For instance, Charles Spearman, one of the founders of IQ studies, was convinced that intelligence could be understood as a single characteristic that he called 'G', which was accessible through performance of a particular kind of factor analysis on the results of scores on five or six different tests that he and others had developed. Gould pointed out—and he was not alone—that this 'G' was a mystical element, an arbitrary number that had no basis of existence anywhere in the brain or mind. So Murray and Herrnstein had to spend a hell of a lot of time trying to vindicate G. The G thing always reminded me of a moment in the early '80s when I was on the way back to western Mass. from Logan Airport, coming back from an APSA [American Political Science Association] meeting with Preston Smith. We were listening to Sex Talk Boston radio, and some guy called in really frustrated, and he was clearly a Bostonian, and he was upset because on an earlier program the hosts had discussed finding his wife's G spot, and he fulminated his complaints: 'I've been trying for three weeks now to find her G-spawt, and I can't find it, and I want to know, where's this G-spawt?' And so I can't think of Charles Spearman without hearing that dude complaining about not being able to find his wife's G-spot.

WBM Well, but then we have the social construction of the G-Spot.

AR Yes, we do. And that would be the issue. So anyway, there were a couple of features of the timing of the book's publication that were idiosyncratically interesting for me. One was that just as the book came out, serendipitously I got a packet of materials in the mail totally out of the blue from an American social scientist named Barry Sautman, who was teaching at a technical university in Hong Kong. He had been following the resurgent racist right from the Northeast Asian vantage point. And apparently Lee Kuan Yew in Singapore was all into this shit, especially after the hereditarian racist crowd determined that Northeast Asians are no worse than tied for innate smartness with northern Europeans, and was closely aligned with the *Mankind Quarterly*, which is a Pioneer Fund-backed, UK-based journal of very old-school race science that publishes and caters to an audience of equally old-school IQ hereditarians—head-measuring types. Sautman had also published some stuff on this and had sent that along with some other secondary stuff. I think he sent this packet of stuff to me because

I'd published an essay a couple of years earlier in *The Progressive* on Murray and some of the others. So, I get this, and then a couple of days later I get a call from *Nightline*, when Howdy Doody's outside son was the host[1], wanting to have me on with Murray to discuss *The Bell Curve* when it came out. And then—and this was all in the span of a couple of days—OUP [Oxford University Press] sent me a comp copy of Stefan Kühl's book, *The Nazi Connection*, which was a short book that examines the American eugenics movement and its direct links to Hitler and the NSDAP. (Kühl's book was how I learned about the Pioneer Fund, which was created in the late 1930s by Wickliffe Draper, a wealthy Harvard alum who was quite fearful of white racial degeneration and quite enthusiastic about Hitler. The Fund has bank-rolled the lion's share of eugenics and IQ hereditarian research in the world ever since.) And then I got a call from Elsa Dixler, who was the book review editor at *The Nation*, who asked me if I'd be interested in reviewing the book. So I said, Well, shit, when all these things come together simultaneously, I kind of have to do it. And I remember read-ing Murray's book in my office late at night and getting sort of creeped out by recollections of whichever film it was that had the nest of old Nazis getting ready to act in concert again. It was the one with Dustin Hoffman, *Marathon Man*. But I had that feeling because it felt like I had stumbled into this international viper's nest around the *Mankind Quarterly*, Wickliffe Draper and the Pioneer Fund, and was encoun-tering Richard Lynn, Hans Eysenck et al. There were a bunch of them associated with the *Mankind Quarterly*. And they are all over Mur-ray and Herrnstein's bibliography. It's chock full of them—people who have published articles with titles like, Persistent Differences in Asian, or in East Asian, and European Bone Structure and Intelligence, and so forth and so on. It's like shit that's straight out of the nineteenth century. That's what the book was. And Murray also wanted to make sure that busy rich people could get the talking points without reading the book. Each chapter began with a page or a page and a half-long summary for the busy people who didn't have time to digest the whole 800 pages of this bullshit. Like, you could just read the summary at the beginning of the chapter.

WBM So the interesting thing was, all the chapter summaries said—you know, black guys are, in most respects, but not every respect, inferior.

AR Right, that's right. Exactly. And they made a lot of the fast-twitch muscle stuff as a marker of high intelligence, which would suggest that pro athletes are smarter than the rest of us. But that wouldn't have the desired racial implications. They also did retrospective IQ calculations of great historical figures. The whole point was that you can read the biographies of Heraclitus and tell by his station in life and by the characteristics that others attributed to him that he had a high IQ. And today you fast forward to the present . . .

WBM And Plato, too, Plato also had a high IQ . . .

AR Right, so that's how you did. But you fast forward to the present, and while you don't have access to as detailed information as you'd like from the upper classes (as you do from the lower classes), there are several screens that account for high IQ that lead us reasonably to infer that rich people are smarter than the rest of us. For instance, going to college means you have a high IQ. Being a CEO has to mean you have a high IQ. So the whole thing is structured to cater to the upper class—big shock there. But anyway, what was more interesting to me than Murray was the response from a lot of liberals. [Sociologist] Christopher Winship published an op-ed piece in the *New York Times* that attacked what he considered the over-the-top attacks on Murray and Herrnstein and pointed out that this was a book of reputable scholarship and so on and so forth. There was a lot of, Well, what if they're correct about blacks? going around. And I remember Andrew Sullivan, who was then relatively new, I believe, at the *New Republic*, introduced a special issue that they had on *The Bell Curve*. And his introduction said—I can get this quote just about verbatim—The notion that there may be resilient ethnic differences in intelligence is not itself an inherently racist belief. So I would ask my undergraduate students how that assertion could be true, considering that it seems to be quintessentially racist; how could it not be a 'racist belief'? And one of them, a boy from some place out on Long Island who wanted to understand himself as a conservative . . . he so wanted to understand himself as a conservative that he actually asked me once, or more than once, if I could give them an advance synopsis of the ideological orientations of the authors of the works that we read on the syllabus each week so that he could know which to believe. But he's the one who came up with the answer, which is that, Well, it very well could be a racist belief, but if it were true you shouldn't be judged harshly for it. But that was kind of a striking moment too, and so the character of the debate around *The Bell Curve* just threw into bolder relief the intellectual messiness of this whole race idea. And I guess, Walter, this was around the time that you and I, quite independently of each other, came up with the unicorn idea, that . . .

AJ Adolph, can you just say a bit more about the liberal response and how it related to underclass ideology? Because this was the middle of the '90s boom of what you saw as that ideology.

AR Right . . .

AJ What was it about Murray that made him so useful, or uncomfortably useful, for what you were saying at the time?

AR This was in the midst of that swirl of race-as-biology, race-as-culture, and the back and forth between them. Actually, another pole in addition to this: in addition to Murray, William Julius Wilson legitimized the underclass idea for liberals. The two had their own connections, because Murray's earlier stuff had been about poverty; they'd been on panels together at Brookings and other gentlemanly 'agree to disagree' bullshit in the poverty research industry, and Murray had commented about Wilson's icebreaking underclass book, *The Truly Disadvantaged*, that he agreed with nearly everything in it except the conclusion. And the emergence of the underclass idea was . . . I've often described its relation to the culture of poverty notion as the same crappy muscatel poured in a new bottle with a new label slapped onto it. And Wilson contended, as did his defenders, some of whom are more than liberal and who understood themselves to be on the socialist left, that the underclass notion wasn't the same thing as the culture of poverty idea, and that one should expect that living in fucked up conditions would produce fucked up outcomes, like in behavior and whatnot. And my response was always, Sure, fair enough, but why focus on the behavior and not the underlying causes? Unless you want to argue that the behavior produces a self-fulfilling prophecy and reproduces it without regard for changing circumstances. And that's what marks the difference between a cultural phenomenon and a racialist claim, no matter what kind of label you put on the racialist claim. With Wilson, I was never able to determine how much of the vagueness regarding the fundamental causal question—which comes first for intervention?—was just kind of thick-headed-ness and bad writing, and how much of it was guile. But you really had to track Wilson down—which I did [2] —to the point where he says, Well, you know, when you get down to it, changes in opportunity structures aren't likely to have any effect in the short term because of the weight of the cultural pathologies. At which point I said, OK, fuck it. But there's a moment in the late '80s and the early '90s, especially around the Clintonist turn in the Democratic party and its approach to social policy, where a number of left-leaning scholars start challenging underclass ideology by countering a tendency within Clintonite liberalism's approach to social policy that was simultaneously technocratic and race-baiting. That tendency came together around a view that liberalism lost its way when the progressive movements of the 1960s turned away from the New Deal's commitment to universal programs and caved in to the particularist demands of blacks and other minorities, feminists, etc. As with the Mark Lilla types today, people like Michael Tomasky, Christopher Jencks, Wilson, and others—like, the early crew associated with *The American Prospect* (sociologist and *TAP* founder Paul Starr openly yearned for a return to the politics of the 1940s, in his mind before race had become an issue in national politics)—would argue that we need to get away from race-specific programs to universal programs. But of course, that's not what they meant. They didn't mean universalistic redistributive programs. What they meant was other kinds of means-tested programs, basically because they assumed from the outset means testing and no significant expansion of the social sector. And so people like Michael K. Brown, Jill Quadagno, and others, and a number of feminist scholars, too, challenged this idea that the New Deal was by itself a model for a social democratic welfare state, mainly or largely by showing how many New Deal programs developed on bases that were segmented by race and gender, with different benefit structures and hierarchies. And that scholarship is what laid the foundation for what eventually, and inaccurately, got transmuted into the 'blacks and women didn't get anything out of the New Deal' and 'New Deal so racist' line. But that earlier critique of romanticized evocation of the New Deal was in fact initially directed towards challenging the *anti*-class-based, non-political-economic arguments about the emergence of an underclass.

WBM If we went back to Anton's original question, and then your response to it, about *The Bell Curve*, and if I were summarizing what you were saying, would this be more or less right? That you get two quite different ways of thinking—different in the sense that one of them is old-fashioned biological racist and the other one is focused on race but not on biology—and that, despite their differences, they both produce the relation between cognitive skills and social outcomes as the central problem. One of them is more attractive to liberals than the other, but both approach the question of equality in terms of the opportunity to compete.

AR Right, right.

WBM Which basically means that the question of redistribution, of equalizing social outcomes without worrying about anyone's cognitive skills, becomes irrelevant. Is that more or less what you think happened in the period?

AR Yeah, I think that's exactly what happened. And, thinking about the policy responses, this is at the moment of the punitive turn as well, when a turn towards behavior modification becomes the center of gravity of social policy. For instance, when Clinton sent his HHS [Health and Human Services] team to push his welfare reform bill before [Daniel Patrick] Moynihan's Senate Finance Committee, [Donna] Shalala and her two under-secretaries, David Ellwood and Mary Jo Bane (I mention those two because they were both out of the liberal wing of the social policy studies at MIT and the Kennedy School), each began by saying that the objective of the bill was to eliminate out-of-wedlock birth. And I thought, Wow. I didn't realize that this was the point of social policy. The policy stance both coincides with the punitive turn that became mass incarceration and rehearsed once again behavioral/biological premises— Walter, I know, recalls the Violence Initiative proposed at the beginning of the Clinton administration by Frederick Goodwin, the biodeterminist director of the Alcohol, Drug Abuse and Mental Health Administration, which would have tagged inner-city children from middle school onward to track them for violent behavior—regarding the sources of inequality. And this has happened repeatedly; it happened with the Great Society and in the debate over what the War on Poverty ought to look like. It's the same kind of thing. And then, in the mid-'60s, the *liberal* position won out over any redistributive approach and established as the core foundation of social policy formation the premise that people are poor because they ultimately are lacking a sense of personal capacity or are fucked up in some other way that needs to be corrected. That is, the economy's fine and doesn't generate unacceptable inequalities through its own structural dynamics, and, therefore, the problem is that there are deficits in these marginal populations that need to be fixed. So the focus of anti-poverty policy should not be something as puerile as fucking transfer payments or guarantee of adequately compensated full employment. (I recall feeling really elated on reading long-time Southern left-liberal Leslie Dunbar's exasperated declaration in his 1988 book, *The Common Interest*, to the effect that people are poor because they don't have enough money, period. His exasperation and my elation were testament to how far the previous quarter-century had gone in separating poverty from political economy.) Instead, in the dominant view, the poor and chronically unemployed need to be encouraged to participate in civic life, which will help them overcome their demoralized view of themselves and the world. And, increasingly, the really intractable among them need to be kicked in the behind to do better.

wbm Right. You've got these guys arguing about the qualities these people have that make it impossible for them to succeed—which is to say, rise up from poverty—and then you've got, Dude, it's not their qualities that keep them from succeeding, it's racism. But, whatever the answer is, disproportionality becomes the thing that matters. Disproportionately poor because of genetics, or culture of poverty, or racism. And while racism is way closer to the truth, the important result is that we start conceiving social justice not in terms of eliminating poverty but in terms of eliminating (or, for the racists, justifying) the poverty of any one group.

ar Right.

WBM The problem is never, Yeah, you know what we cannot have is fifty per cent of the population living on wages that will not support them. It's, What we cannot have is a disproportionate representation of some group of the population living on wages that will not support them. So we have to figure out why that is, and then we have to solve it. And while there's a certain sense in which blaming it on the victims, in a Murray way, is completely repulsive, there's an important sense in which blaming it on racism against the victims, while much less ethically repulsive, is equally beside the point. Or is simply an extension of the same way of thinking about it. Because of course, the problem that the left wanted to insist on—to the extent that there was a left—was that the question of which people are stuck at the bottom, of what they did to get themselves stuck, or even of what was done to them to get them stuck, is not the relevant question. The bottom is the problem, not who's on the bottom.

AR Yeah, exactly. And I've gotta say also, in the last couple, three days, I've found this all really more demoralizing than I have before, partly because of the nonstop, all day every day, pious blathering about the anniversary of the Tulsa pogrom that just hammers home a race-reductionist perspective on racial injustice as the only injustice that matters. And I've seen now one remembrance from the Smithsonian and one from a local group of two different massacres in Louisiana, one in 1868, one in 1873, that contend for recognition with the Tulsa one. And, notwithstanding the insistences of the pious, *none* of these had been unknown before the current wave of exposé! Maybe what's most dispiriting about the Tulsa pieties is the actual *class* reductionism that's embedded within the race reductionism. So now the profoundest tragedy of the Tulsa pogrom is supposed to be the trashing of 'black Wall Street', the supposedly vibrant and opulent black business district. (Thus, reparations!) Now we're coming up on Juneteenth[3], when there'll be more orchestrated looking back ahistorically and pietistically. And I just saw a day or two ago an announcement from my undergrad black alumni group that some alum, I think from a later time, has got a hustle now doing a campus tour that connects all the older buildings on campus with—hold your breath—slavery, and race, and black people. I mean, there's long been a big to-do in the history of the University of North Carolina, Chapel Hill that it's the oldest public college in the country—chartered in 1789, cornerstone of the first campus building laid in 1793, first students arrived in 1795. So it's preposterous to assume that anyone with the most rudimentary knowledge of US history—or who had not, for whatever reason, operated under the mistaken belief that the university only moved to North Carolina from, say, Vermont in 1865—should be startled to learn that older buildings on campus had more or less direct connections to slavery, or that those and others were built, serviced, and maintained by badly exploited black labor.

WBM Right.

AR Hold the fucking presses, right? But what's gotten me especially down about it now, and down to the point even of thinking, Well, maybe disappearance into a quiet corner in southern Maine wouldn't be a bad idea, is that it's becoming clearer now that this discourse and the dynamics around it offer, or seem to offer, possibilities for monetizing even the most attenuated or remote grievances. Even the bullshit reparations—or the non-reparations emolument, I guess you'd call it—in Evanston[4] have produced a backlash now, from this woman who feels like she's been done wrong because she should've gotten more. It feels like we've crossed a threshold now where there's such pervasive potential for turning this into a hustle, that we have to anticipate the Upton Sinclair problem.[5] If people see this anti-racism thing as offering entrepreneurial opportunities in its own right, and are drawn to it in that spirit, then there's no getting through to them.

DZ Can I just ask a side question to all this?

AR Yeah.

DZ I was wondering about both of your relations to affirmative action when it emerged. Especially in relation to the kind of racial categorizations it implies, as you have both been quite critical of those notions.

AR Well, mine was that when Johnson, or even maybe the Kennedy administration, began to toss the phrase about, there was an understanding that there were durable structures—what now I guess would be called systemic racism or structural racism—that militated against the intent of enforcement of anti-discrimination law. And that affirmative action meant taking some additional steps to break through the logjam of durable practices, or whatever. The *Griggs v. Duke Power* decision would be a good example. The employer used IQ and generic aptitude tests to sort people into jobs and for promotions. Well, to the extent that the aptitude tests reproduced the same pattern of stratification that existed before, they seemed commonsensically to work. But it becomes a question of whether the point of the tests is to produce the same, or the familiar, pattern of stratification, and if it was necessary. The Supreme Court found that, Well, no, it's not. And the Court ruled that, in the interest of enforcing anti-discrimination, tests for hiring and employment have to be task-based. So that's an affirmative action—or that's intervention in support of affirmative action. And that made sense to me. And it makes sense to me still to do that. I don't think it's a time-bound issue; I think it should be an element of standard procedure, and it's more or less an element of consciousness now. In a lot of places, like in the academy, where we work, people look to do it, they look for that person in the classes covered in anti-discrimination law. At the same time, though, I was—and I'm sure we all know how it was that diversity came to be the affirmative goal that displaced affirmative action—I happened to be chair of my department's diversity committee for a year, and pointed out in that capacity that we only hire from, like, ten departments, only admit students from, like, ten departments, so from that perspective it doesn't matter what color they are or what they do in the bathroom. They're all the same people, basically.

WBM My only slight difference from that is that, when affirmative action got underway, I remember having long arguments with my then-father-in-law, who was a white Southerner, who had taught history at a small college in Mississippi called Millsaps, which was famously a racially liberal place in the '40s and '50s and '60s . . .

AR Right, right.

WBM He'd had crosses burned on his front lawn in Jackson, Mississippi, so he was an old-school Civil Rights liberal who was appalled by affirmative action. He'd fought super-hard to make race not matter, and now the idea was that race should matter. I was totally on the opposite side. I was totally for it, just a version of what Adolph said. At that time the class question—the way that affirmative action would help install a vision of equality as proportionate racial representation among the elite—didn't occur to me.

AR Right—it takes the place of equality.

WBM Exactly. If you thought the problem was getting enough black people into Harvard, affirmative action was a good solution. If you thought the problem was getting enough poor people into Harvard, affirmative action wasn't a good solution, unless you did it for poor people. But you couldn't possibly do the proportionate thing for poor people— there are too many of them. And if you somehow could, it would still be beside the point, which, like we said, is not to help some people escape the bottom but to raise the bottom. Nothing you do about getting people into Harvard has anything to do with the actual problem, which would actually come closer to being solved by getting rid of Harvard. And the reverse discrimination objection to affirmative action—Oh my God, what incredibly great white person out there is not getting the job—that was never the problem. The problem was, We're solving the wrong fucking problem.

AR Well, I want to build on that, too. This is why I think it's so important to keep the open-endedness of history in mind, because at the time when you and I had formed our views about this stuff, the left vision hadn't lost completely, yet. We were on the run, but there was no reason to think, even after the *Bakke* decision, that the objective of breaking open fire departments or promotions to supervisor in the city water department, or of sort of nudging the IBEW [International Brotherhood of Electrical Workers] to broaden access to its apprenticeship programs, wasn't going to be enough of the story to justify the undertaking.

WBM This is where reading Judith Stein's *Running Steel*[6] would have been helpful. But it just wasn't obvious that affirmative action, which seemed like a useful weapon in the attack on something like a general inequality, would turn out to be so easily weaponized in defense of class inequality.

AR No, it wasn't. And it's interesting you mention Judith in this regard, man, because I often think about two books—and I don't normally think about the impact of books in this way, of course—but there are two books I often muse about, what might have happened if they'd been published fifteen years earlier. One is *Running Steel* and the other is *Labor and Monopoly Capital*[7], which might've had some influence on the structural unemployment debates. And, of course, that's not the way this shit works, right, but it's an academic's fantasy. A sci-fi fantasy.

DZ We all need a reason to live, right?

AR Yeah, right. And thank you very much, Daniel, because I'm looking around for them these days. I'm trying to gather some of those reasons.

DZ But was it at that period that you both met? It was in the '90s, right?

AR Late '90s, wasn't it? Because I was at The New School already?

WBM 2002.

AR 2002. Wow. Oh yeah, yeah, yeah, that's right, yeah.

WBM Because I'd moved to Chicago, and you and Ken [Warren] were teaching that summer thing at U of C [the University of Chicago].

AR That's right. For two years Ken and I ran a Mellon Foundation summer dissertation seminar for up to maybe a dozen people, split between our respective institutions, who were doing dissertations involving race in some way. Several strong dissertations, and later books, came out of those seminars, and there were enough auguries of the rising class tendencies as well. Before saying more about the seminar, though, I should say something about my relationship with Ken, because I'm pretty sure it was through him that I learned of Walter's work. Ken was also the principal conduit—along with probably a touch of Stanley Fish—through whom Walter and I eventually met.

I met Ken in 1990 when I was being recruited to Northwestern, in what turned out to be his final year there as an assistant professor. I had recently read a very sharp 1989 review essay he'd done in *American Literary History*—"Delimiting America: The Legacy of Du Bois"—on recent books by Skip Gates, Melvin Dixon, and Bernard Bell, but I didn't make the connection that he was at Northwestern until I met him there. (I made a big pitch for him not to leave for the University of Chicago that was stopped cold when he informed me that one of his senior colleagues at Northwestern had proposed pursuing Shelby Steele—a right-wing English literature professor and intellectual mediocrity who enjoyed a moment of visibility in the early 1990s for publishing yet another of the insipid quasi-memoirs opposing affirmative action on individualist grounds—for a target of opportunity senior position in the English Department. There was simply no more I could say but to wish him well down the lake in Hyde Park.) He did negotiate space with the U of C to team teach with me between the two institutions. We did it once, and that also produced several strong dissertations and eventual books.

More consequential than the course was the two-person seminar focused mainly on critical engagement with current tendencies in African American studies we did regularly—sometimes weekly sometimes every other week or so—at Jimmie's Woodlawn Tap in Hyde Park. After much agonizing and astonishment over the steadily worsening state of the field, both intellectually and in its crude class character and outrageous political claims, we determined that we needed to intervene. The problem, however, was that neither of us could bear the prospect of having to wallow in the cesspool of often intentionally obscurantist, psychotically involuted crap that passed for cutting-edge scholarship in black cultural studies. (During this period I was working on the Skip Gates/Houston Baker chapter in my Du Bois book[8], which was an excruciating forensic undertaking.) I recall Ken observing one day about Baker that he took to the limit the field's de facto premise that being novel or original was all an argument had to do to be noteworthy, and that that completely eliminated plausibility and coherence as criteria for evaluation. So, on the one hand, we didn't want to do the sort of critical book on black cultural studies that would require deep and broad immersion and textualist critique in a field with no intellectual standards or core of serious scholarship. On the other hand, the alternative option that presented itself to us was a chronologically organized critical history of black studies from the late nineteenth century forward. Neither of us wanted to commit the sort of time and effort that that type of book would require, as we each had other projects. After much more of what felt like spinning our wheels to resolve the conundrum, we finally decided to pursue the critique affirmatively, by laying out positive interpretive alternatives. That's when we settled on a two-book project. The first, *Renewing Black Intellectual History*, which collects chapters—three by political scientists, three by literature scholars, and four by historians—that lay out examples of historical-materialist approaches to the study of black intellectual history, was published in 2010. The second, *You Can't Get There from Here*, features two chapters by each of us representing our own original work in our respective disciplines, along with jointly written intro and conclusion that extend our critique of the dominant tendencies in the field. We plan to have that volume finished by the fall of 2021.

The Mellon summer seminar, which we did in 2003 and 2004, was part of that larger project that we'd been developing since probably 1992, if not earlier. Mellon was concerned to facilitate dissertation completion among students working on topics bearing on race, which was an expression of a commitment to increasing minority representation in the professoriate, as well as the ranks of those working on race-related subject matter (I believe not much more than half the students who participated in our seminar were POC). Ken and I could see the value in having some impact on the dissertations, to be sure, but the main benefit for us was the two-ninths of annual salary each, and being able to work together over the summers on our own stuff and to use the seminars to refine our ideas.

That was an interesting moment in what had been emerging probably since the late '80s/early '90s as a political economy of racial and identity group representation in academic life. In the early '90s a cohort of mainly black professors at high-profile institutions—with encouragement from a supportive media apparatus—embraced the category 'public intellectuals', recently introduced by intellectual historian Russell Jacoby in his book, *The Last Intellectuals*. Their usage inverted Jacoby's, which was a highly romanticized homage to a seemingly (unless one probed the Cold War funding streams that underwrote the journals that largely sustained them) free-floating group of deep thinkers, mainly in New York in the 1950s and '60s, who did cultural and political commentary outside the increasingly bureaucratized constraints of the academy. The new black public intellectuals were exactly the opposite; they declaimed on public issues from tenured faculty positions at the most prestigious tier of universities in the country. By the mid-'90s mainstream media covered the career movements of these high-profile academic personalities with banner headlines, much as they did the comings and goings of socialites and other celebrities. E.g., most major newspapers in the country covered the 'dream team' roster of black professors that Harvard put together. (Of course, what made the group a 'dream team' were the personae and pedigrees of the individuals, not a shared school of thought or substantive scholarly contributions.) And it was treated as comparably newsworthy when one of them moved, e.g., from Harvard to Princeton or from Duke to Harvard. And the universities were already managed for building endowments and other forms of capital accumulation, and they therefore increasingly found association with celebrity academics attractive for product differentiation in pursuit of popularity rankings. A senior colleague remarked to me shortly after I got to Penn, "you might think to look at it that this is a university. It's not; it's a multi-billion-dollar research and real estate corporation with a finishing school attached." As if to affirm his point, not long thereafter I shared an awkward fight from Jackson, Mississippi to Chicago after my first trip to New Orleans post-Katrina, with a doctrinally anti-government, market-idolator physician. She initiated our conversation by patting herself on the back for having gone to volunteer at the main shelter on the weekend before landfall and by expressing her shock and dismay that others hadn't 'stepped up'. Then she emphatically rejected my suggestion that her experience illustrates why we need a strong central government to mobilize response to crises, and she let loose with a torrent of anti-government babble and called, vaguely by definition, for voluntarism. When she learned that I taught at Penn, she was literally giddy to report that her son, a Penn football player (she was on the way to Homecoming weekend to watch him play), was that semester taking a course on Tupac Shakur. "Only at Penn, right?" she effused.

The point of this long digression is that I want to note several characteristics of the moment in which Ken and I did the Mellon seminar, which was also the moment Walter and I met: 1) the intensified corporatization of universities coincided with the emergence of a stratum of celebrity academics, among them 'black public intellectuals', who functioned as something like loss leaders in universities' jockeying for position in the rankings, which university administrations assume helps fundraising; 2) the rise of the public intellectual phenomenon established the figure of a politically significant 'voice' whose authority derives from and re-inforces academic celebrity; 3) the proliferation of cultural studies discourse in the academy radically inflated the category of the political by touting all manner of quotidian social and cultural practices as domains for 'resistance' and for the elevation of the marginal as the true political avant-garde etc., at the same time as Clintonism in the US, Blairism in the UK, and similar turns in social-democratic parties around the world solidified neoliberalism as a global order that imposed Thatcher's nefarious 'TINA' ["there is no alternative"]; 4) the concatenation of those tendencies produced an environment that undermined distinctions between pop commentary and intricate scholarly argument and that encouraged pursuit of the former as a lower-cost, more readily successful academic career strategy; and 5) this environment encouraged the representation of pop cultural commentary as being equivalent to *both* political action *and* scholarship, and to that extent contributed to the debasement of both spheres.

WBM Just, yes, especially that last part.

AR Furthermore, within the academy the premises of cultural studies discourse urged the depiction of even the narrowest intramural guild conflicts—e.g., fights over faculty lines and departmental status and prestige—and pursuits of individual career aspirations as lofty battles on fronts within a broader struggle for social justice. Nothing good comes from the conflation of the most straightforward opportunism and the conviction of one's own moral righteousness. It reminds me of my reaction after a couple of encounters with the Fruit of Islam— that there are few things more dangerous than a thug with a sense of holy mission—as well as my father's oft-repeated observation that ideology is in one sense the mechanism that harmonizes the principles one likes to believe one holds and what advances one's material interest. Slippage between first person singular and plural has always been an essential element of identity politics—one might even say that it's its *raison d'être*. So when Walter made his initial presentation to our Mellon seminar on themes that would before long be articulated in *Trouble with Diversity*, one of the students remarked "but if we did what you're saying then students like us wouldn't even be here", in genuine incredulousness that there could be a norm of social justice that didn't have his career mobility at its center. Little did we know that that knee-jerk reaction, which, frankly, seemed at the time rather tawdry, would within a decade be completely hegemonic. And around the time we did the seminar, Ken and I noticed independently of each other that our departments were getting applications to our doctoral programs from people who expressed no particular intellectual or academic interests but who indicated that they wanted to obtain the doctorate as a stepping stone to pursuit of a public intellectual career.

That's why I was shocked but not exactly surprised roughly a decade later to learn from watching them on a panel that neither Alicia Garza, Opal Tometi, nor budding real estate magnate Patrisse Cullors was capable of recognizing any distinction between advancing their #BLM brand and building a political movement.

wbm There had been several chances for us to meet earlier, and *Our America* would have been a better book if we had.

dz Can you actually say a few words on how you came up on this discussion, especially through *Our America*?

wbm While Adolph was criticizing people who were defending the idea of race as a biological entity, writing *Our America* got me interested in the people who claimed not to believe that there was such a thing but who were still—actually more than ever—committed to race as a category of analysis. After all, when people biologized race, it made sense to have social policies that were based on these biological differences, but once it occurred to everybody that it didn't, why hang on so tight to race? When people discovered there weren't such things as unicorns (the analogy that Adolph was also using), nobody said, But dude, the social construction of unicorns. And working on *Our America*, I realized that this two-step of killing the racial body and then reanimating the racial soul had already taken place earlier in the twentieth century, when anthropologists started arguing that what people thought of as racial differences were really cultural differences, but then started using the concept of culture in a way that made it do all the work race had done. How? By treating your culture not as whatever your actual beliefs, attitudes and practices were, but as beliefs and practices that counted as yours even if you didn't believe or practice them. Which made possible dramas like being seduced away from your culture, or returning to your culture, or appropriating someone else's culture—all of which depend on the idea that your culture isn't your actual beliefs and practices. Instead it's the beliefs and practices that are appropriate for who you are. And what makes them appropriate? The idea of race hasn't been dissolved by culture, it's been revivified by it. As it is when, instead of using culture to do our racial dirty work, we use history and call it heritage. Whenever you hear the word 'heritage' you know you're in the presence of some deep bullshit.

ALL Or trauma.

WBM For sure, trauma. Especially inherited trauma! Really, inherited anything. Except money.

DZ This is kind of a side remark again, but it's kind of interesting that the show that Henry Louis Gates makes about 'finding your roots' is designed to be anti-racist while at the same time acting like if it made sense to have ten per cent Ashkenazi genes . . .

WBM Yes, people love to go back and forth between the idea that there are no such things as races and the idea that there are no such things as pure races. And now, of course, mixed race is totally in style. If you discover that one of your ancestors was black, that's cool—you're a person of mixed race. But if you discover that one of your ancestors was tall while another was short, that doesn't make you a person of mixed height. And one that was stupid doesn't make you a person of mixed intelligence—we don't even have the concept 'mixed intelligence'. Race is pure reification.

DZ There was also this fascinating scene where Scarlett Johansson discovered that some distant relative had died in the Holocaust and she broke down into tears. But this to me is a perfect example of how history is turned into memory, and then it's somehow *your* history. A person completely unknown to her is suddenly part of her identity. When people order those tests it's supposed to reveal something about them that they didn't know before but that was somehow already there, hidden. In the end, that's where I would say it's important; it's the body, not the soul, because it's nowhere else.

WBM Yes, but it's sort of the-body-as-the-soul. You know, the racist writer Thomas Dixon dedicated *The Clansman* to what he called "the re-incarnated souls of the Clansmen of Old Scotland", which basically does the same work—it turns the genetic connection into a spiritual one. But, of course, the other thing about the Johansson is that it's the Holocaust.

AJ Yeah, inherited trauma.

WBM Yeah, which was really invented for our time—or, anyway, our political economy—on the Holocaust.

AR Right, yeah.

WBM Because the Holocaust does two things. It makes the worst crimes hate crimes—bad enough to murder, but worse to murder because of racism! And then, in a society where discrimination is a compensable wrong but exploitation is a way of life, it provides a model of justice.

DZ You never hear in those shows: 'we discovered that your great great great great great grandfather was exploited by a capitalist'. . .

AR Right.

WBM But you can say, My grandfather was denied a mortgage on account of his race. And in Evanston, Illinois, that can get you a down payment on a house. And once your basic model of justice—whether it's restoration of paintings the Nazis stole or the labor power the plantation owner stole—is the recovery of lost property, your idea of justice is entirely liberal, not socialist. Because if you think that housing is a public good, then who cares why your grandparents couldn't get a mortgage—you're entitled to housing no matter what happened to them. Socialism makes the causal account of how you came to be in need irrelevant. The universalizing ambition to make everyone equal makes the history of how we became unequal irrelevant.

From this standpoint, although everybody's always saying, you know, We have to grapple with our racist history, the truth is exactly the opposite. It's not the historic wrongs done to the working class that are the grounds of workers' demands. It's a commitment to the public good, not a commitment to making reparative compensation to those who have been unfairly hindered from successfully pursuing their own private good. What's fucked up is the idea that justice consists in undoing the damage of the past. Making history the key to social justice is like replacing socialism with tort reform. When Marx said that philosophers have only interpreted the world and that the point was to change it, he should have added that historians have only understood the past, the point is to forget it. But of course there's no way he could have imagined a left that would turn "From each according to his ability, to each according to his needs" into to each according to his ability to establish a property right in stuff stolen from his ancestors.

AR Right. And that marks the deep ideological victory of neoliberalism, too—that this has become the only operative metric of social justice. The logic that underlies this reduction of justice to restorative justice goes something like this. There's a lot of bad shit that happened in this world and in this society in the past. A whole lot of people got fucked over, not because they were workers but because the ruling class had bad ideas. And then white people, insofar as they were substantively or effectively part of the ruling class, acted out those bad ideas. There's no capitalism, really, or not as a problem; there's nature. And what's happened is that people who belonged to certain categories of existence, who carry in their souls this essence of whatever they are that got them fucked over, got fucked over in an unnatural way in that their getting, as my son would say, the fuzzy end of the lollipop was unfair because their plight was the product of bad—wrong, benighted—ideas. Therefore, justice now is considered as a reinstatement of what should have been the natural order of things (this is just about precisely Gary Becker's argument in his brief against discrimination, minus the reparations, by the way), and nature is capitalism. There's no way you can get to a progressive program from that, or to a socialist one, which is, or should be, a huge problem for progressive politics.

WBM I just need to add that even the libertarian [Robert] Nozick made room for reparations.[9]

AJ To connect this up with your piece on Tarantino . . . [10] we have this idea that whatever happened to your father—even if he was brutally killed, or if he was simply exploited—should be irrelevant for a socialist politics today. But, at the same time, what neoliberalism produces is always a history where exploitation is not a part of the history. You produce a narrative of slavery, you produce a narrative of Jim Crow— and the same goes even to a certain extent for colonialism—in such a way that you don't understand why this is happening unless there's a deep-seated aspiration from white people to white supremacy, domination, whatever category they use. But economic reasons completely disappear from all those movies. And this is maybe an interesting part: how the aesthetics, how the art, always appeals to a certain making irrelevant of the economic structure that produces these problems.

AR Well yeah, it's quite extraordinarily . . . The Tarantino vision of plantation slavery just kind of struck me because you don't see anyone working except whores—and they're not really whores, they're trafficked women—and boxers. But there's nobody around doing any work. And the same thing with *The Help*, right? I mean, they were working, but the problem wasn't the labor relation; the labor relation never even got hinted at.

WBM The only difference, were Adolph writing the essay today . . . At the time I was urging him to call it "*Django Unchained*, or *The Help*", which he did, but now *The Help* has been kind of forgotten and it wouldn't work. But if you were doing it today, I would call it "*Django Unchained*, or Racial Capitalism".

AR Oh, yeah. So on the question of race, Walter's evolution and mine ran parallel, but when he started talking about the cultural stuff we've been discussing and the way in which everything now had to be understood in terms of our identity—what got called Standpoint Theory—is probably where they came together, because just by virtue of being at Yale in the late '80s I was forced to encounter that stuff. The question that leaps out from the foundational statements of that argument is, Why does *this* identity get to be the last stop on the what-you-see-is-a-function-of-where-you-stand train line? In the case of Patricia Hill Collins, for instance, it was the 'black woman' [11]. But without some argumentative intervention that she and others in that world didn't make (and they didn't make any such intervention because all the standpoint stuff is filler, a ruse in lieu of an argument validating essentialism), there's no reason to mediate the radical subjectivism until it gets down to the point where no one human being can ever effectively understand another, because no two subject positions are identical. And, again, without some mitigating argument, there's no reason to say that one identity is one's truth or one's essence any more than another. You know, why couldn't one's real—most meaningful—standpoint be the standpoint of a stamp collector rather than that of 'the' black woman? And this was around the same time, in my own work, that I'd begun to uncover the later manifestation of the race-into-culture problem. Which is how, in the post-war era, race in the social sciences in the US had become—outside the South, anyway—a discredited way of thinking about groups and differences, and how culture had then taken the place of race and done the exact same work. Then I read Walter and found the missing link, which actually made it a little easier to make sense of the lacunae, as one might consider it, in Boas and Boasians—I mean Benedict and others—who were just kind of hopelessly ambivalent about the race idea.[12] And that led to a sharp focus on the inadequacies of Lamarckian race theories at the end of the nineteenth century, and then on the appeal to non-scientists of their belated discovery of epigenetics early in the twenty-first century. Because all that is for them is a going back to neo-Lamarckianism, with all the escape routes that it offered from charges of determinism. And my take on the culture issue was, I guess, more naive. Because I'd come across Marxist anthropology when I was in college, and I just assumed that that was what everybody meant by culture, with the basic understanding that it was defined by plasticity and fluidity, and diffusion. I found out in the '80s and '90s that that was not the case. Even the debates between [Marshall] Sahlins and Marvin Harris regarding, or within, cultural materialism[13] didn't carry any of this notion of ownership or property or any of that stuff.

wbm The great virtue of Marxist anthropology is that it isn't pluralist.

ar Right. No, absolutely.

wbm But the whole point of anthropology is to be pluralist. Because, again, pluralism essentializes culture. It treats the things you do because they seem to you right as if they were things you do because they're right for you. Which makes the crucial question, 'who are you?'

ar And that also undergirds the argument in *The Shape of the Signifier*[14] that difference makes debate impossible, right? And that kind of feeds into an assessment of the current political situation, too.

aj Just to finish off the thought that Walter started, it's interesting to see how notions such as cultural appropriation completely finish this process, insofar as appropriation presupposes the concept of property; once you have cultural pluralism in place, the return to property is just natural. It just comes with it, in a sort of intuitive way.

WBM It's really depressing that stupid arguments you used to have in 1967 in your dorm room about whether white people can play the blues . . .

AR Oh, yeah, right.

WBM . . . have emerged as central. Even when you were eighteen years old and having this argument with the enthusiasm that goes with being a sophomore with intellectual interests, you could tell it was sort of stupid, right? But now it's at the center: black pain is for black artists. We own this. And it's slightly better than white pain for white artists, but the idea that who you are gives you a kind of entitlement to any artistic practice has now been weaponized.

AR Oh, yeah. Definitely.

WBM There are a lot of problems with Dana Schutz's Emmett Till painting[15] —and politically, it's nothing but neoliberal reparations—but none of the problems would be solved if she were black.

DZ Can I maybe connect a bit with your own question on this turn to experience and subjectivity? Another version is a guy going to a bar, and he sees on the wall a picture of some miners, but to him it's people painted in blackface. And he's very offended by it. It's shocking for him for obvious and understandable reasons. And he asks the owner to remove the picture. And the owner refuses. To him they are just miners. It has nothing to do with blackface. But for the customer the point was not about the meaning of the picture, but just his own experience of it. The problem being, of course, that you can't dispute a feeling.

WBM Before just stomping all over that, there's a context in which that kind of argument makes sense. Supposing you put something up in front of your school, and it was meant to be a tribute to workers but the workers were black, and looked like they were being abused, and the kids who saw it actually experienced it as black people being debased.

DZ It's more or less what happened with the thirteen murals at George Washington High School in San Francisco. While they were painted by Victor Arnautoff, a Russian emigrated socialist, with the explicit ambition to denounce the US's history of racism and colonialism, they were still considered by some to be offensive to Native Americans and African-Americans.

wbm Suppose it was a version of the mural. We know that's not what the artist meant, and we teach that to the kids. But they're still saying, It makes me uncomfortable to see that happening to someone who looks like me, it makes me experience myself as vulnerable to that kind of treatment. It's not an insane argument to say that we want to know what the intended effect was, but if, for whatever reason, it's failing to produce the intended effect, and it's always producing a bad unintended effect, we should worry about the unintended effect. In other words, I don't think it's a politically irrelevant argument to say that effects matter. But it is a mistake to identify those effects with meaning.

dz Right. But don't you think this is part of a broader shift where we care less about what things mean and where we care more about how we experience them, and about what they mean for us, and how we feel about them?

wbm No, I don't think that.

dz OK.

wbm So I think two things, actually. One is that people can't help but do meaning all the time; it's not like they've given it up. But the other is, yes, you're right, there is this intense identification of justice with what your experience is, with people's sense of feeling 'harm', as if the feeling—and so the removal of its cause—were justice itself. It's Adolph's point about the statues in New Orleans. The problem is not taking down the statues . . .

dz No, no, of course.

wbm The problem is thinking that taking down the statues counts as producing social justice.

ar Right, right. And let me toss another wrinkle into this, too. I don't know if all you guys saw this, it made the rounds. But you remember there was an attack organized against the statue of Lincoln with the freedman in DC, and that another version of the same statue was done in Boston, right? And there was a kid, a young black kid in Boston, who identified himself as a social influencer, or a media influencer, or whatever they are. And his objection was that whenever he walked or drove past that statue, it made him feel diminished, because the black figure wasn't standing as an equal to Lincoln and wasn't wearing a business suit like Lincoln. So he wanted the statue gotten rid of. Partly because it made him feel bad because it didn't connect with his very contemporary and ephemeral entrepreneurial ideology, and also because calling for taking it down is part of his career aspiration as an influencer. So I take Walter's point, and I agree with it ultimately. You have to. But wouldn't one also be justified in telling him to go fuck himself and shut up?

wbm That's a good counter-example. It's like people describing the Civil War as a great slave insurrection. But while it's true that almost 40,000 black people died fighting for their freedom, so did almost 400,000 white guys.

ar And not to mention, too, Walter, that the best predictor of slave insurrection in the war was proximity to the Grand Army of the Republic.

wbm OK, I'm kind of conflicted about this one. On the one hand, we should forget the history. But here, you're right, we should teach them what the truth is. So, OK, forget the history in the sense that nothing that happened in the historical past should determine what our rights are now . . .

aj Maybe we should jump to the truly contemporary context with something like the 1619 Project, which presents the culmination of this history and of claims-making on lost private goods. There's been a big historiographical debate about its meaning, but, as a whole, the fact that it's so morally charged is clearly because 1619 is not just about getting the history right. It's also about getting the history right so you can make specific claims in the present . . .

wbm To me it's a pure example of both problems. One, they get the history wrong. And, two, they're wrong to think the history matters. Even if they were right, they'd be wrong.

ar Right, and by the way I've been thinking more and more that it could be productive to try to reconstruct when this switch got flipped— that is, when knowing the history to get the past straight turned into tort claims. Because it slipped up on me; I don't know about you, Walter, but this came out of nowhere. I do remember I spent a month out of the country and not paying attention in the summer of 2000, and I came back and the reparations stuff was all around me, and I thought I'd fallen into a time warp to Malcolm X Park in 1969.

WBM What you didn't realize was that, actually, you were experiencing the future.

AR No, I didn't. That's exactly right. Something happened, and I think that the account of what happened is going to pull together an account of the co-articulation of racial liberalism and neoliberalism, possibly even from the Kennedy administration forward. Definitely across the totality of the current century. So that's a project out there for someone.

WBM Maybe one piece in that puzzle would be the collapse of labor's power and the replacement of unions fighting, at least in principle, for the working class with the social justice of HR managers and with discrimination claims you could take to court?

AJ Sort of combined with the typical American litigiousness . . . I mean, taking people to court for anything and nothing.

WBM Well, it makes sense with intersectionality, after all, which comes out of a lawyer's way of thinking about this. Which is that you go to court for it.

AJ I think that the most powerful way you've put it during the conversation, Walter, is that the race renaissance that happened in the 1990s really started in the 1980s, but solidified in the 1990s. It centered on these three camps, which you could call the right-wing Murray camp (which is openly biologistic), then you have the liberal one (which is culturalist: underclass ideology but from the center), and then you have the left-wing one (which is about the issue of systemic racism). But that whole race renaissance is basically stuck in one and the same trap, and we've been caught in that doom loop since the 1990s.

WBM In connection with this emergence of racial justice as something like the model of justice itself, I wonder if we could talk for a minute about Adolph's debate with Ellen Wood [16]. Way, way back.

AJ Yeah, yeah.

WBM People quote that debate against Adolph now, they cite it against me, because now we seem to be insisting that capitalism doesn't need racism, whereas then you were resisting Wood's idea that capitalism doesn't need race. Now those two things aren't quite the same—and your general resistance to ideal type models needs to be factored in—but I first read that exchange when Ken Warren and I were teaching together and Ken showed it to me. I was fascinated by it, and I was unsure about where I was in relation to it. And I remember saying to Ken, whether or not it's true that capitalism has always needed racism, isn't it true that capitalism now needs anti-racism?

AR Oh, yeah, yeah.

WBM And Ken said, I don't think Adolph would disagree with that.

AR No, not at all.

WBM This goes back to 'why the efflorescence of racial stuff'. Because Adolph and I had a conversation . . . We were talking about the ideology of equal opportunity, and the way it replaces the idea of the working class consigned, in effect, to working class jobs, with a system that supposedly responds to individual merit. So it doesn't need to eliminate inequalities, but it needs to explain them, to justify them. The point that Adolph is making, as I understand it, even back to the Ellen Wood thing, is that what capitalism does seem to need is the idea of ascriptive identities. Or maybe—more abstractly—of justified failure.

AR One of the points I've made all along is that, Yeah, the ascriptive identities do the work that they do. Divine right of kings did it back in the day. There was no question about why peasants failed—because of God—so . . .

AJ This is the point that the Field sisters [Barbara J. Fields and Karen E. Fields] always make, that race comes into being when you have to justify slavery in a bourgeois legal order.

AR Right, that's right.

AJ Most pre-bourgeois legal systems had slavery, but there was no need to justify it through race because there was a natural hierachy and there were natural status differences; there was no legal equality. And then in the late eighteenth century you have this unique situation where . . .

AR You have this property

AJ You have legal equality *with* slavery, and that necessitates race because you have to prove that these people are fundamentally inferior and that you can therefore own them as property.

AR Right.

AJ And those contradictions of bourgeois equality, if you want to speak with Marx, are still what motivates the identity discussion today. People look at a bourgeois legal order and see that it's supposed to be formally equal, but that in practice it's not because, of course, a capitalist economy is premised on inequality. Identity provides a kind of frame that allows you to explain, while also at the same time naturalizing, that inequality. In that sense it fulfils the same function as race did before, just in a less ferociously biological way. It's still there.

WBM The liberal project is to then keep on trying to make a formal equality that can actually match and finally do the work . . .

AJ Yes, yes, that's right. That's exactly right.

WBM The socialist side of this is to say not just that you can't make that happen, but that, even if you could, it wouldn't solve the problem, because the point is to eliminate inequality, not justify it.

AR Right. And the other point about this that I made, I think even in the thing with Ellen, is that ascriptive ideologies work primarily to the extent that they're treated as nature, and that the moment they become problematized they're not going to work as well. And that's exactly why, and I've suggested this too, you can imagine the emergence of a new sort of underclass race that's black and brown in a significant enough number for it to be plausible in relation to a common sense that associates black and brown with being on the bottom, but which would not necessarily be tied to the standard racial groups at all. It could have whites in it, whatever. And then you could in fact have two different versions of black people and two different versions of Hispanics—those who are part of the underclass race and those who aren't. Since it's all unicorns anyway, you can taxonomize them in any way you want that makes sense at the moment.

WBM And the thing we could say now, from our current perspective, which we couldn't quite have anticipated before, is that even when the ascriptive identities are being challenged, they're actually still serving some purpose. That's where you get the anti-racism.

AR Right, that's right. That's exactly right.

wbm You see it on both sides. Racism tells you black people aren't smart enough, don't work hard enough, they deserve to fail; anti-racism tells you it's not black people, it's just people who aren't smart enough, who don't work hard enough, who deserve to fail. You're getting it from both directions.

ar Yep.

Interview Three
10 June 2021

ADOLPH REED, JR. A telling marker of the atrophy of left political imagination in the US over the last three or four decades is the extent to which relation to the Democrats has loomed as a bellwether of left commitment. It's extraordinary, really, and it caught me by surprise to see it in the '90s, so much that I once asked in a column whether I'd forgotten to reset my clock one night and overslept the meeting where it was decided that electoral politics and relationship to the Dems would thenceforth be the left's key preoccupations. Trotskyists denounce support for any Democratic candidate or initiative as ipso facto perfidy. Charges that we were secretly trying to corral the nascent labor insurgency to deliver it to the Dems haunted the Labor Party from beginning to end, and that element similarly denounced Bernie Sanders, reducing his two campaigns to devious efforts to boost the Dems. Greens and others who fetishize something called 'independent politics'—which feels like a distinctively American sort of phenomenon, a kind of Rotary Club leftism—are another flavor of ersatz leftists who define the Democrats as the paramount political enemy. When I lived in New Haven, where the local Green Party had had electoral successes since the early '80s, I had a really good

Green alderman—John Halle. When John decided not to run again, I supported the progressive Dem, who endorsed everything that John had and who had the additional virtue of caucusing with the Democratic mayor and majority. So I put out a yard sign for her. When the Green guy—whom I didn't know and had no idea he knew who I was—saw the yard sign, he rang my doorbell and flipped out on me as a traitor because he understood me, no doubt because of the Labor Party connection, to be, as he pointed out multiple times, someone who supported 'independent politics'. When he finally took a breath from his bolero of betrayal, I thought I'd try to make the encounter a teachable moment and *not* tell him to go fuck himself, but instead explained that I've never given a shit about some abstraction called independent politics and that I endorsed the Dem because she stood for everything he did and was more likely to have the mayor's ear and could get stuff done.

On the other hand are those who take any advocacy of a left vision that goes beyond the Dems' as politically irresponsible. Thus, in denouncing my 2014 *Harper's* essay, "Nothing Left" [1], Michelle Goldberg at *The Nation*, when she was still trying to find her way to the *New York Times*, accused me of 'nihilism' for not accepting that the Democrats define the boundary of a thinkable left [2], and irrepressible hack Harold Meyerson accused me of writing from outer space for not having noticed that the Democrats had already embraced everything I called for [3], except, of course, you know, to the extent that they actually hadn't. E.g., he made a big deal of the handful of congressional Dems who responded to constituent pressure to block the Trans-Pacific Partnership trade agreement that the Democratic administration (naturally he didn't stress this part of the story) had been pushing hard to adopt.

So this is where a 'left' with no organic roots in the society winds up: with two apparently opposite, but equally evasive, accommodations to defeat. One moves into the fantasyland of purism, which is based on the premise that the revolutionary movement is waiting to form spontaneously, if only the opportunists, fakers, and misleaders would get out of the way; the other redefines the condition of defeat as actually victory. Sometimes, as in sporadic eruptions like Occupy, #BLM, Bernie or Bust, or in irrational exuberance for [Kshama] Sawant, the Squad, Jaime Harrison,

Stacey Abrams, etc.[4], the accommodation takes the form of wild swings back and forth between Scylla and Charybdis, in a political equivalent of cognitive dissonance. In either case, though, supporting Democrats is an existential statement of some sort; what disappears is the option of voting for them—or not—instrumentally.

I admit I've never considered myself a committed Democrat and have nearly always voted for them as a lesser evil. In the fourteen presidential elections for which I've been eligible to vote, I voted for the Democrat seven times, third-party candidates twice, and not at all five times. This is one of the reasons Goldberg decided I'm a 'nihilist'. It's funny, but when I was seventeen I practically cried because I wasn't old enough to vote for LBJ and the Great Society. Four years earlier, in my all-black high school of nearly 800 students, I was one of only three who voted in our mock presidential election for Nixon against JFK; the other two were from multi-generational black-and-tan black Republican families, and one of those went on to be one of the first people, if not the first person, publicly recognized as black to own a seat on the NYSE [New York Stock Exchange], and also served in some capacity in every GOP administration from Nixon through George W. Bush. That 1960 vote has been part of a bond between us ever since. For me, voting for Nixon was partly reaction against the Kennedy idolatry, particularly in that Catholic school in that very Catholic city. The rational part of it was—maybe ironically, considering Nixon's history—the Kennedys' proximity to Joe McCarthy: the old man was his pal, Jack supported him in the Senate, and Bobby was one of Roy Cohn's fourteen dashing young male investigators.

Anyway, when 1968 came around and I was old enough to vote, I didn't bother to register and was at an all-night anti-election protest. In any event, it never occurred to me to assume that the Democratic Party was the lodestar of my political aspiration. Of course, I grew up with the understanding that liberals will sell you out when the political situation tightens up, and decades later my father could only shake his head in bewilderment when I reported in my forties that I'd joined the ACLU [American Civil Liberties Union]. And no amount of explaining how much it had changed since the '50s—including showing him

Ira Glasser's apology for the organization's terrible Cold War history—would alter his reaction.

WALTER BENN MICHAELS Wait, the Kennedys were more anti-communist than Nixon?

AR Well, Bobby had been one of Roy Cohn's boys. And for sure Jack was a militant anti-communist, and old man Joe was. And Nixon's vile past was more in his past, right? So.

DANIEL ZAMORA Talking about Kennedy I would be curious, Adolph, to know a bit more about your views on his economic policy. I recently found this famous memo that Walter Heller, Kennedy's chief of the Council of Economic Advisers, sent in 1962 to justify the tax cut. Heller argued, along neoclassical lines, that the expansion of public spending in that context would "lead to waste, bottlenecks, profiteering, and scandal" and would increase the "opposition to expansion of government", and "to over-centralization, to a 'power grab' and a 'take-over' of the cities, the educational system, the housing market". It was a kind of privatized Keynesianism allowing a break with balanced deficits and the undercapacity of production which Kennedy faced when taking office, while at the same time recognizing, as Heller wrote, "the importance of working through the market system"[5]. Even the whole turn towards poverty, understood as a floor of income, was attractive to his economic advisers precisely because it allowed a social policy organized less through a service-based strategy and more through cash transfers. They'd rather have tax credits and boost private growth than expand public jobs. This 'fiscal Keynesianism' really looks like a first step to full neoliberalism.

AR I think that's right. I'm re-reading Michael K. Brown's *Race, Money and the Welfare State* now, and he makes an argument that's a little more complicated about Johnson, but his view is that Johnson basically inherited Kennedy's commitments around a tax cut—which meant as well the promise not to expand spending—and that Johnson was just better at trying to do both things than Kennedy had been. Most important, though, from the standpoint of tracing the roots of the present moment, is that the Kennedy administration implanted the zygote of what would become neoliberalism. It was the Kennedy administration that resolved the tension between full employment and currency stability as the normative anchors of national economic policy in favor of currency stability.

So anyway, the reason I dragged us down memory lane to go on about the Kennedy/Johnson moment and the electoralitis/Dems fixation is linked ultimately to getting back to Bidenism.

It's going to be really interesting to see what it turns out to be. We know that the plan isn't to expand the public sector in a substantial, certainly not in a permanent, way. They seem to be betting that they can kick-start private investment and break out of stagnation, thereby starting the game of what looks like dynamic growth all over again. There are a lot of questions there, not the least of which is, Will they have enough of an impact between now and 2022 to hold the congressional majority? And of course, the administration is already hearing it from investor class-types who don't want to go overboard in conceding to a 'radical' Sanders/Warren/AOC [Alexandria Ocasio-Cortez] et al. agenda.

Now that Biden is in office, it looks like some mainstream liberals are expressing concern with what they call the grievances of the white working class. But they are also expressing concern about the overreaching, or the overstepping, of woke-ism, as contrasted to what they're trying to characterize now as a penchant for nationalist economics among the white working class. Until Biden got elected they were using *woke-ism* to target the left, but now that Biden's elected it's this other thing, which is the progressive economic tendency.

DZ Yeah, and I would add something about why anti-wokeism is not a solution for the left. If you think about other countries, especially France now, you feel that the whole debate is completely locked in, the woke vs. the anti-woke. And so the left is kind of weirdly stuck into this false alternative.

WBM So, you're right—anti-woke isn't really helpful. Because, without socialism, anti-woke is just a defense of individualism, or nationalism. It's just Mark Lilla. Or people who worry about reverse racism.

DZ And the question comes immediately: could anti-wokeism be an effective politics for the left? It seems to me, in the end, that agitation around those topics is only good for the right, because your critique would always be, kind of, incomplete—you don't really have anything to offer.

wbm I agree. And actually we should never even use the word 'woke'. Because at this point it's like 'cancellation'—the people who worry about cancellation are at least as hostile to the left as the cancellers are. A perfect example of this is when Adolph and I sent a short op-ed version of "The Trouble with Disparity"[6] to the *New York Times*. They were falling all over themselves not to publish it—I was contacted three separate time within about twenty-four hours to say no! And at the same time, the *Times* was running a big story presenting Adolph as a victim of cancel culture because some 'Afro-Socialists' or someone in the DSA [Democratic Socialists of America] . . . were offended by him being asked to present his views, and they made a big fuss. So then the *Times* made a big fuss out of the Afro-Socialists making a big fuss. But the *Times* has exactly as little interest in presenting Adolph's views as the Afro-Socialists have in hearing them.

dz It would be interesting to elaborate a bit on the *Harper's* letter[7], and on what's wrong with that letter.

ar The long and the short of it is that you can see how, even without any guiding intelligence steering the flow, the channels of political debate in the US will funnel what looks like our critique of anti-racist politics into a stream with Lilla and the letter writing-guys, or with white nationalism and the fascination with the red-brown alliance among media types. Because we all know where that winds up . . .

wbm The red-brown alliance just becomes a brown alliance.

ar Right, right.

wbm Since we're doing buzz words, maybe this is the time to stand up for class reduction! Think of one of the examples we always use— people who work in the job with the greatest growth in the US, health aides, and who are paid almost nothing. What do the identitarians worry about? That so many health aides are women, and especially women of color; that systemic racism and sexism makes it too hard for these women to succeed and become, say, doctors. What do the anti-identitarians worry about? That the excessive focus on identity will obscure the question of individual ability. What do we worry about? That these people, whoever they are, make $15 an hour. And we don't care who they are. Class reduction cares more about your job than it cares about you; its idea of social change is not changing the rules that make it possible for some people to avoid bad jobs, but making the bad jobs into good ones.

DZ I guess what I was thinking was more that I don't want to spend half of my days writing about whether we should tear down a statue, or about what kind of pronouns we should use. It's not like I'm against it, but nor am I seeing it as a great achievement, because I do think that you need to speak to a broader audience and that sometimes you need to make some concessions about how you speak, precisely to get more people involved than just your friends. But some part of the left has been trapped into those debates, rather than building a large coalition. In the end that's a losing strategy.

AR So I'll say two things. One is, fuck them, right? Because that's not who we want to talk to in the first place. Those people are embedded in a political economy, and it's a political economy of group representation within neoliberalism. You're not gonna win them over. The most that we could ever do—I think this is what Walter and I have tried to do in popular stuff—is to write past them to people who haven't made that commitment yet. And beyond them—to the cousin who works a real job, or maybe doesn't work a real job, but who will pick up the thing and see it. The other thing is that it'll take some doing because we're habituated, as a reflex, to what we understand the left, and debates among the left, to be. Especially among the enthusiastic young people, there's a tendency to be drawn into debates about, e.g., how to read the holy books, and about the nature of socialism, and to engage with the ultra-left groups about revolutionary roads or whatever. And doing that sort of stuff may up to a point be a good exercise, but it doesn't really help to get us any-where. It brings to mind another common back-and-forth we had with leftist supporters of the Labor Party, who were quick to offer suggestions about how we could better organize the left. And our emphatic response was that we weren't trying to organize the left, but the working class. But the other thing I was going to say, the point that kind of pings off Walter's last point, is that over the last decade—especially in the last half decade—it's become clear that what we've got here is a version of the debate between identitarianism and anti-identitarianism on the left that stems from commitment to two radically different notions of a just society—of what counts as unacceptable inequality. And I think this distinction has become sharper over the last half-decade. One notion, which is the identitarian one, is that unacceptable or unjust inequalities are those that violate the principle of equality of opportunity. But according to this view, the inequalities that are produced by capitalism are like nature and don't exist as a problem. And I think that's where the fault line is on what passes for the left now. And that's one of the reasons why, for instance, even the *Labor Notes* crowd did an exposé a few years ago[8] about some horrible warehouse operation in Memphis, and the report catalogued all the ways all the workers were getting fucked over, and then just gratuitously had to go off on a riff about how black workers were getting fucked over especially—and, you know, that was *Labor Notes*!

WBM I actually remember from a long time ago, a year or two after *The Trouble with Diversity* came out, you were telling me about some kid who was involved in trying to rally support for organizing workers at Harvard. They were organizing custodians and food workers, and he's trying to get other students interested. And he's been a bit of a *Trouble with Diversity*-skeptic, but now writes you saying maybe Benn Michaels is right. The only way I can get them at all interested in this thing is by saying, Most of these people are black. Harvard students can't see underpaid workers as a problem unless they can see the problem as racism. So to go back to what you're saying, Daniel, I think that tactically you're exactly right, and if you don't juxtapose the critique-of-identity stuff with the actual left no-one-cares-who-you-are egalitarianism at every single moment, you're actually just engaged in a debate between two kind of liberalism.

DZ I've been working on a piece about France, and on the debates unfolding there about identity and race. Part of the narrative within a certain left has been that, over the last decades, French universities imported the American framework, leading to the rising centrality of race as an interpretative framework. It was more or less the argument of that *Monde diplomatique* article by Noiriel and Beaud[9]. The piece had good points, but I think it is misleading in many ways. Because the most obvious kind of Americanization in France right now is not so much these marginal academic seminars, but how the elites and the media are radically reshaping the political landscape. Precisely by pinning these anecdotes about some cancelled conference in some faculty as a threat to the Republic. The university and intellectuals are increasingly becoming the scapegoat for everything that is wrong in French society. The whole debate about culture wars, race theories, postmodernism etc., is really where they want to bring the battle. French billionaires such as Vincent Bolloré have been transforming channels like CNews into a 'French Fox News', and many journals have taken a seriously conservative turn. The Ministry of Education has recently opened an inquiry into what's happening in universities—against what you guys would call 'critical race theory'. This is to me the most significant shift; there is, of course, a rise in identity politics in universities, but it's not a significant force. More of a symptom than a cause. Moreover, while Macron has articulated a rejection of struggles that "assign each one to his identity or to his particularism", his alternative can hardly be seen as anti-identarian. Building on what we have in common, he argued, meant answering the question "What does it mean to be French?" Immediately you see the problem. The problem with American 'woke culture' for the French elites isn't that it relies on essentialized identities, but that it promotes the wrong ones. To the president, identity becomes a problem only if it's not national. What Macron and most of the French political class share with their opponents is a commitment to identity—be that pluralist or anti-pluralist—when it comes to understanding France's problems. To me the displacement of class struggle into cultural conflicts is probably the most significant form of Americanization France has undergone over the last thirty years. A period during which socialists and conservatives alike have advanced a neoliberal agenda and promoted cultural battles as a substitute for any meaningful debate over the economy. In that context 'anti-wokeism', far from being a solution for the left, is a dead end. It's the kind of opposition the right wants: 'woke' vs. 'anti-woke'. Because it's a battle where no progressive alternative is truly discussed. 'Anti-woke' won't give a better job, wages, or a better welfare state to the *gilets jaunes*.

WBM I think what you're saying is a version of what Adolph says. We want a politics that begins with the question: what's good for the working class? And neither the people who are for critical race theory nor the people who are against it have the slightest interest in the working class. Just the opposite: critical race theorists don't even really accept the idea of class. Their focus is on whether people's 'life chances' are more affected by race or by economic status. Their answer, of course, is race, but even if it were economics it would still be beside the point, which is, again, that a left politics is not about helping people out of the working class but about the class itself. And, of course, the people who are against critical race theory just want to turn class into white cultural identity. 'Defund the police' seems to me similar but more complicated. It's more complicated because it matters more, and because it really does affect the working class. It's similar because it leaves the political economy that has actually produced the problem—the commitment to keeping wages low, and the necessity of a reserve army of labor to making good on that commitment—out completely. So the question just becomes: are you more worried about getting killed by a guy who's trying to carjack you, or by a cop? And it's the working class that runs the greatest risk of both.

AR In fact I think we're on the verge of another 'tough on crime' uptick, too, because of the way the reports are coming in from all over the country. The liberal opinion-shaping institutions are starting to drift away from 'defund' and George Floyd and towards 'stop the street crime'.

WBM That's the opposition we're trapped in. Because, on the one hand, 'defund the police', what's the point of that unless you change property relations? That just means rich people hire Pinkertons[10], which would be way, way worse. But the alternative . . .

DZ I think there were two versions of it. One version is the naive one that argues that a police force is not necessary because it's just something that has been created for the sole purpose of policing the poor for unjust reasons. If we defund the police, there's not going to be any effect on crime. And then the other version, the more radical one—it's marginal, but it does say something about the academic left—that argues for more crime. There'll be more crime because the security we have is a privilege, and we should somehow be able to accept it in order for the poor not to be in prison. Which is, to me, an insane kind of argument.

AR Oh my God, yeah.

WBM Rich people will not accept more crime; they'll buy their way out of it. It's everybody else who would have to accept it. How does that benefit the working class? As long as you're leaving the fundamental inequalities intact, even the idea that defunding the police means spending more money on dealing with community trauma or on job training is unhelpful. Trauma care is just making people feel a little better about what capitalism is doing to them; job training is just pretending that the $25k they'll pay you for being a health aide is a happy ending.

Interview Four
1 July 2021

WALTER BENN MICHAELS Lilla's book[1] is really just a rewrite of Arthur Schlesinger, Jr.'s *The Disuniting of America* . . .

ADOLPH REED, JR. Right. Over and over and over.

WBM . . . for the twenty-first century. And theoretically, you know, they're both fucked up in exactly the same way. Schlesinger, Jr. had no problem with identity, he just preferred American identity to the racial identities of multiculturalism. And Lilla is exactly the same. I've got— because they sent me so many copies—I've got this in front of me. So here, he says on page 120, "[t]he only way out of this conundrum" (he means the problem of identitarianism) "is to appeal to something that as Americans we all share but which has nothing to do with our identities". So right away, there's a problem. Because the first half of that sentence is "as Americans" . . .

AR Right.

WBM And the second half is, it "has nothing to do with" who we are. So identities are bad, unless they're national, when they're good. Not exactly a left position. And he bashes what he calls the left's "fixation on class" and goes on to say "the only way one can hope to induce a sense of duty is by establishing some sort of identification between the privileged and the disadvantaged." It's nothing but identity and identification— American identity politics.

AR Right.

WBM Of course, the counter-argument to this criticism is that class politics are also identity politics, that class is an identity too. But we've already talked about why that's not true.

ANTON JÄGER Yes. Could you also talk about the rise of classism as a concept? Which is, historically, very, very recent. And the fact that a lot of people now seem to think that the only way to understand class is as the problem as it's being expressed in 'classism' is in itself an extremely telling development.

WBM Yes, as if the crucial thing about being working class were not the exploitation of your labor but people being prejudiced against you.

DANIEL ZAMORA Can I just play devil's advocate? Some would respond that class is also, in a way, an identity. Meaning that any working class movement needs a strong identity to mobilize itself. Asad Haider would say something like 'any politics is an identity politics'. So class struggle is in itself a form of identity politics, because you need the workers to recognize themselves as workers. They would then argue that your rejection of identity politics is silly because identity is everywhere and that even you are advocating it for the workers . . .

AR But I think there's something fundamentally dishonest about that position; it's dishonest in the way that the true-but-trivial can be dishonest. Because on one level, yeah, these are all identities, and when we agitate for the shaping of a particular kind of working-class consciousness, that's what we agitate for, not just some spontaneous, given consciousness of the working class. So the struggle for working class power is a struggle for the articulation of a particular kind of working-class consciousness, obviously. But it's the other side, it's the people who are the advocates for what gets generally classified as identity politics, who have made the distinction: basically, that the kind of politics that they pursue based on ascriptive identities is a politics that's substantively different from a class politics. So they come together under the umbrella of identity politics. And then they respond to us by saying,

Well, but all politics is identity politics on one level. Which is true, ultimately, because everything is some kind of identity, but the problem isn't the universality of identity as a way of understanding groups or of constructing groups, it's the kind of identities that people come together under. And coming together under the identity of the working class, for instance, is qualitatively different from coming together under the rubric of ascriptive identities. And that's partly because that working class identity is real and rooted in material relations, whereas some other stuff isn't, it's abstract. But beyond that, the working class is a social category that's defined by what it does, not by who they supposedly are. And that's a significant distinction.

WBM Which is why class consciousness is different from class identity. And what the working class *does* fundamentally disconnects it from the whole idea of identity. Because the whole point of the modernized idea of identity is that they're essentially plural: none is better or worse than any other, and recognizing that requires (rightly!) that we not privilege one at the expense of the other. White isn't better than black, straight isn't better than gay. But the whole point of Marx's account of class is just the opposite. The relation between labor and capital is essentially antagonistic. You can imagine a world where all the identities get along

AR And that, by the way, is the last chapter of *The Bell Curve*.

WBM Right. And it's almost always been a Tory position: the working class has its place, the aristocrats have their place, and in a well-ordered world everyone's happy in their place, and they respect each other in their place.

AR Right.

WBM But the antagonism between capital and the working class is structural; it's there, regardless of who respects whom. That's why every time you do something for the working class you're actually doing something against capital. It may be very small, but it's nonetheless real. Every time you organize your union and you get yourself a 5¢ an hour raise, that 5¢ an hour raise comes out of capital. Whereas every time you organize yourself racially or sexually, the whole point of it is that it doesn't have to come out of somebody else. Insofar as identities are plural, that's one important sense in which capital and labor aren't identities. Of course, you can still say that you identify as working class, and then you can figure out what politics you think you ought to have that go with being working class, but even the politics that you think ought to go with the working class aren't simply a function of belonging to the working class; they're a function of figuring out what you think is right. I think Sartre gets this right in *Anti-Semite and Jew*, when he's talking about his friend the Communist organizer—I can't remember the guy's name—and he says that, for a Communist organizer, isn't it kind of a problem organizing people who are from the upper classes? And the guy says, "je m'en fous" about what class they're from, I just care that they're communists. So there's an important sense, to me, in which it's just completely wrong every time someone says the working class is an identity too. And I think it's important that people love to say that. The identitarian left, because it takes the sting out of the difference between structure by class and structure by race. And the people on the right love to say it because it actually takes the sting out of the whole idea of capitalism.

And the purest form of that today is what Adolph and I have been talking about as the illusion of right-wing populism, which is dependent precisely on thinking of the working class as an identity, defined by its culture. So now the working class becomes: you have a certain kind of music, you take pride in being working class, you generate a certain amount of solidarity out of that pride. Well, all that's fine, and there are entire academic disciplines (anthropology, sociology) that can inventory the things that constitute your working classness, but all you really need is that you don't own the means of production, and that you work for the people who do. That's what the working class is. If working class consciousness is the consciousness of how to do what's best for the working class, that's socialism; if by working class consciousness you mean a culture, that's when you get right-wing populism. Turning class into culture, into identity.

DZ Can I add something about that? And I'm sure Anton has a lot to say about this. In some way, as far as I understand it, the whole idea of populism, especially how it was articulated by Ernesto Laclau and Chantal Mouffe, is precisely this idea that we had to dematerialize the idea of class[2]. It's not something that has a kind of material base; we can't define it by any kind of objective interest. The whole idea of 'the people' is something that is discursively constituted. And it can be constituted in many different ways, meaning it's an identity, an identity you produce through your political discourse. And then in that form, of course, if you can have a left-wing populism, you can also have a right-wing populism, reorganizing all those interests through a discursive framework that will produce something else. But what you guys are obviously saying is that this is the wrong account of class, and that it creates the false idea that right-wing populism is actually possible as a long-term coalition.

WBM That's really useful, because while it makes it clear that you can't have right-wing populism, you also don't have a left-wing populism—on the model of Laclau and Mouffe—either.

AJ I think it's important to emphasize, as Daniel said, that both the right and a specific type of left—as we see in Mouffe—have been saying their farewells to class for a while. But at the same time they're also two different ways of embracing identity, and you see this in how, for example, their version of left populism is directed against minority politics. They're against identitarianism, they have very little truck with certain forms of identitarianism. The definition of populism they propose is what we'd call a kind of identitarianism of the majority: everyone gets to identify with this one collective identity that's more universal than minority positions. But at the same time you're stuck in completely the same paradigm, and you end up just mirroring the moves that are also made on the right. It's a sad testament to just how general the logic of identity has become—to all of us, essentially. A circle that we can't escape from.

WBM I think that's totally right.

AR One way I've been thinking about this lately is that right-wing populism today is a notion that almost *requires* the existence of left-wing populism. 'Populism' is the noun, so it makes sense to think about what the noun is actually intended to denote in those constructs. And I saw a list somebody laid out of left- and right-wing populists who were challenging the righting of the ship in reconstructed neoliberalism, as it were. And the list included Orbán, Modi, and also Corbyn and Sanders.

And it seems to me that that's the ideological work that the populism label does. In this discursive moment 'populism' expresses the old Whiggish concern with the passions of the people, basically. And containing the passions of the masses out there is the key objective of a politics. And left populism and right populism—and this is another way in which Lilla et al. are consistent with Schlesinger et al.—are the lineal descendants of 'extremism of the left and extremism of the right', because 'populism', in this context, is a softened or neutered version of the charge of extremism. And that's what gives us Biden. And that's what helps so much of the nominal left to be more enthusiastic about the possibilities of Bidenism than it ought to be, and it also encourages some of the kind of . . . I don't know how to describe them. Those tendencies on the left that feel that our natural allies ought to be the women who (and this was literally the target market for a re-branded cigarette line, Dorado, in the '80s, which also suggests something significant about how identity groups are made) go to tractor pulls and the men who love them, or vice versa. Both those constructs beckon us to a culturalist understanding of politics. It just feels to me like the entire interpretive enterprise now is to find ways to characterize the working class as something other than a class. In the Marxist sense, right? It seems like it's all driven by a refutation, or a dismissal, or a denial, of Marxism. And I know, I feel like the archdiocesan spokesman . . . I don't know, maybe I am.

wbm The point that Anton made before . . . the minute you make it it's very clear, but I hadn't thought about it in exactly those terms. Everybody understands that for Laclau and Mouffe, if you're doing the history of ideas version, the new social movements . . . the whole point was to get rid of class. And of course, getting rid of class is both a right and a left neoliberal project. As is anti-racism. Just think of the Hayekians insisting that in a state concerned above all to make markets work, you would never have had the Holocaust. You never would have had people killing the Jews, you would have had them, you know, worst case scenario, put to work. Labor camps, not death camps. But what you really . . .

ar But labor camps that made distinctions on the basis of accumulated human capital.

wbm A perfect version of it, then. The intellectual project is markets without classes—with races and cultures instead. In that sense right-wing populism—class war turned into culture war—works perfectly. But even if the working class is made into a culture, people still have to make a living. So, as Adolph just suggested, labor power is turned into human capital, and the antagonism between capital and labor is made to disappear because there's no such thing as labor. Just like Foucault said, every Uber driver his own entrepreneur.

DZ Can I just ask Anton something? The rise of left populism and the discursive approach have an interesting connection with Trump. Stuart Hall, like Laclau and Mouffe, had applied this framework in order to understand the success of Thatcher[3]. For them, and especially for Hall, Thatcher was able to articulate a new discursive framework that won part of the working class and completely reshaped the political landscape.

AR Right, because Harold Wilson, [James] Callaghan, and the Labour Party failed and were the stalking horse for neoliberalism. But they forget that part.

DZ Yeah, of course. And then they basically endorse, at least in the beginning, New Labour and Tony Blair . . .

AR That's right.

DZ Hall has these interesting texts where he's cautiously enthusiastic about Tony Blair because, basically, the idea is that we should do the same thing from the left. In their view there can, to a certain extent, be a right-wing populism—and that was Thatcher—and that justifies the idea that there should be something like a left-wing populism.

AR The other thing about the Thatcherite moment—the part that high-flying intellectuals tend to forget—is the significance of the brutal suppression of the working class that Thatcher unleashed. There's an element of bourgeois hegemony you really don't need Gramsci to understand. Thatcherites won the government, and I think they won the government partly, as I said, because the Labour Party had been so fucked up prior to then. But once they won the government, they still didn't have the support of the working class. We've all seen the clip from the football match—I think in Manchester—where everybody in the stadium starts singing, When Maggie Thatcher dies. And that was well after Blair was in power, so it's not like distaste for neoliberalism left the working class. But as we've been saying throughout our discussion of populism, it became a taxonomic question that falls completely outside dynamic political-economic relations. Who gets labeled what? Who gets labeled the backbone of the working class? Substituting level of educational attainment, for instance, for class makes class a category of human capital accumulation. As human capital is fundamentally a just-so story—not unlike unicorns—class in this perspective is a measure of relative civic worth and can be applied willy-nilly, as suits the purposes of the moment. The good working class, in the US, anyway, are those where echoes of producerism persist; we can also call middle class, in the condescending language of Clintonese, 'those who work hard and play by the rules (of neoliberal capital accumulation)'. In this register as well, class is a behavioral/cultural category. From one perspective, the overarching story is that practically every domestic (and also to a considerable degree international) move that capital and its steno pool in the universities and the corporate media has made since the end of World War II on the cultural and interpretative front, has been to make the working class, and especially class conflict, disappear. I've been struck by how much even the debate over the existence of cost-push inflation in the US in the late '50s and early '60s was structured around Cold War concerns. There was a current of labor economists who argued against the notion that union demands were the prime source driving inflationary tendencies, but even they began by considering that we have to tolerate a little bit of inflation anyway, because of our Cold War objective. And the Cold War objective was to sell the American model of class harmony—which means no class conflict, which means no classes—around the globe. So it's not like there's ever a pure, crystalline intellectual moment around this stuff, but sometimes you really don't need a weatherman to know which way the wind blows.

AJ The general move you have both on the broadly Anglo Saxon and on the American left in the 1980s and 1990s is, as Ellen Wood has described it, a retreat from class: an attempt to disqualify class both as an analytical category and as a category for politics.[4] But then there's not just a retreat, there's also a move to new subjects, or to what they call new social movements. And what we have with the English Marxists, both with Stuart Hall and with Laclau, is the reinvention of popular identities. It's what you could call an anti-particularist form of identity politics, which then finds its realization in Blair. Multiculturalism is particularist in its own way, but it also ties into a specific kind of English nationalism, which also has continuities with Thatcher. But in the US the retreat from class goes hand in hand not just with the reestablishing of identity, but also with the reinvention of race from within three traditions. On the left you have the Afropessimists or the systemic racism tradition, which tries to explain the entirety of American history through the causal lens of racism. Then you have the centrist vision, which is the kind of Julius Wilson one we talked about, which is a sort of resoled 'culture of poverty' thesis. And then on the right you have Charles Murray, who has the hardcore biological version—he says: this is why race is still such an important category of analysis. So the retreat from class goes hand in hand with the move either to identity or to race, which, as Walter said before, are essentially the same thing. You're essentially making the same political and the same analytical move once you retreat from class and once you move into those new categories. And I think that's where we can see how the stage is set for Trump, insofar as Trump really does capitalize politically, but in a way also intellectually, on precisely this legacy, which has now been prepared for thirty years.

AR I like that construct, it makes a lot of sense. It makes me think as well of how American history—I reckon political history since the late nineteenth century—has been punctuated by three (and maybe, with an asterisk, a fourth) moments when class conflicts have come close to breaking onto the surface of mainstream American political debate. The first was the Populist insurgency at the end of the nineteenth century. It was crushed; things happened. The second was the New Deal labor left insurgency that came closer, given the nature of the particular moment, to spreading across the surface of American politics. A Roper poll found in . . . 1944 I think it was, a few weeks before the election, that sixty-eight per cent of American respondents said that they wouldn't support any form of government, no matter what it was called, that didn't guarantee full employment. So, that's a big change. And then it was crushed in the late '40s. And then there's that moment in the mid '60s that's weaker, and one of the reasons it's weaker has to do with all the downstream consequences of the defeat of the big moment in the late '40s. That was crushed too, or preempted. Most people at the time, and since then, never even knew that there was a stirring—partly because the ruling class and its various propaganda agencies, including the apparatus of post-war racial liberalism, controlled the narrative, even the narrative of black political insurgency. E.g, how many people know that the 1963 March on Washington came out of the labor movement, that it was initially a demand for jobs, and that it wasn't just a showcase for Martin Luther King, Jr.'s "I Have a Dream" speech? And then the asterisk is the Sanders moment, which I think requires an asterisk for a variety of reasons. One, it was never institutionalized; two, the base was more of an electoral base and was therefore more diffuse, or mercurial, than an institutional base. And there were a few other reasons besides that. And that's the moment when both Trump and Sanders are trying to articulate a political perspective that galvanized extant frustrations from outside the one-and-a-half-party consensus. I remember hearing several times that, in the months before the beginning of the 2016 electoral season in 2015, the Clintons had been patting themselves on the back publicly for having encouraged Trump to run, because of course they thought his candidacy would do things that it wouldn't do. But one way you can look at that is that there hadn't been any recovery since the Great Recession, really—or, sorry, the recovery was only at the top end. People were getting more and more frustrated at the popular level, less and less convinced that government had their interests in its sights. And you get this one eruption from the left, and the other from the right, and I know this doesn't work but it's almost as if Trump was the alternative to Bernie. And that pairing worked really well for the mainstream neoliberal Democrats and the punditry, didn't it? Much as the Brits framed Corbyn as being not at all left but as, in some deeper way, the reaction. And here we are, all the way back at the 'extremism (populism) of the left = extremism (populism) of the right' line. And I guess I would say that if the left isn't able, in the next year and however many months, to push Bidenism to the point where the working-class voters will not feel that they've been lied to and sold out again, then that could be the end of it.

DZ What do you mean by that? Do you mean the end of the Democratic Party?

WBM The end of the party would be the good news. He means the end of the democracy.

AR Yeah, the end of democracy, yeah.

DZ This is purely speculative, but would you fear more Trump's comeback or someone else articulating this more elaborate version of Trumpism, like Tucker Carlson or something like that?

AR Yeah, either. From one perspective, the best that we have going for us is that Trump is a moron and a narcissist. And somebody who's cleverer could be even more dangerous. As the rightist insurgency grows, I think Trump is ever more likely to be something like a cross between Lonesome Rhodes (who, as Walter will appreciate, I have to make an effort not to call 'Dusty') from *A Face in the Crowd* and Lee Harvey Oswald, or maybe like Joe Louis at Caesar's Palace[5].

WBM [Josh] Hawley's scary.

DZ How did you feel about the discussion that happened in the month after the election, that basically reduced the whole landscape to fascists versus anti-fascists? Either you're on Trump's or the fascists' side, or you're anti-fascist, meaning that you're a committed liberal. Anything else is on the side of fascists. You're going to be, you know, the communists in Weimar Germany or something. But, at the same time, there is a real risk, right? If the left fails to deliver here, something far worse than Trump could happen.

AR Absolutely. The one hope, I think, we have for Hawley is that if it were possible to find the grave where his jackal mother is buried, then that could destroy his career.

WBM If that gets published, it will explain why Adolph was sent to the camps a few weeks before the rest of us. But to Daniel's point, yes, we all voted for Biden. Hell, we all voted for Clinton, too, because Adolph told us to in that piece he wrote, "Vote for the Lying Neoliberal Warmonger: It's Important"[6].

AR Right, that was it.

WBM And he was right. But that's also the limits of electoral politics. I thought what Adolph said before is a useful way of thinking about the American predicament. The Sanders movement was the Sanders campaign. And when the campaign's over and there is no candidate, it's gone. You vote for whoever's left. And if Sanders isn't running for president three years from now, the challenge for the left is to develop a structure that's not tied to somebody's campaign.

AR After 2016 I even hoped for a bit that Bernie would go away because I felt, quite naively, that because we had a base of seven national unions that had endorsed Sanders and that had been working together pretty closely through the campaign, that that might also be replicated at the state and local level after 2016. I assumed and hoped that what we would see — and at first the state of Illinois looked like a really good possibility for this — was that the coalition or the alliance that had come together around Sanders could then focus on trying to connect with those working-class voters that Sanders didn't get, or with some of those who voted for Trump out of disillusionment, in order to try to build out a new coalition. What we learned was that the national unions that endorsed Bernie just couldn't congeal anything distinctive or new going forward in almost every state — and I only say 'almost' because there are some states I don't know about, but if I had to bet on my life I'd bet on all of them. The move was to renew the same old tired coalition that hadn't been very successful in winning the hearts and minds of the working class, or of significant sections of the working class, for quite some time before that. And then getting more and more woke as time went, I thought . . .

WBM And the renewal of that same old tired coalition worked this time. Because the alternative is not some garden-variety Republican, some Romney. You're doing it against . . .

AR Yeah, the devil, right.

WBM Trump was a catastrophe for the left, which got completely subsumed by anti-Trumpism. Which, right from the start, was more or less identical to anti-sexism and, with events like the murder of George Floyd, was also more or less identical to anti-racism. But not at all to anti-capitalism. What really reanimated what Adolph called the tired old Democratic coalition was the rediscovery, for like the 158th time, of racism in America. And while that obviously was completely horrifying, it's not really a discovery—both because we already know that there's racism and, especially, because we should already know that racism isn't the fundamental problem. The unarmed white people killed by the police aren't victims of racism. But the harm liberal morality cares about is the harm of discrimination. This horrific video of a black man being murdered by the police becomes the center of a Democratic Party that thinks that racism, not capitalism, is the problem and that liberalism, not socialism, is the solution.

AJ I want to talk about what Cedric Johnson called militant liberalism [7]. Race plays a specific part in domesticating, or at least disciplining, part of the left—not into its own autonomous tradition making its own demands, but really into a junior partner in a coalition with the Democrats. And so . . .

WBM Wait, so who, Anton, who's the junior partner?

AJ Well, the left within the anti-racist coalition, insofar as the left has its own demands. Once it gets into this militantly liberal mode, it is a de facto junior partner in the sense that if, together with the Democratic Party, your main goal is anti-racism, then you will have to follow the Democrats' agenda on it. And that means, actually . . .

AR And also in the sense that any random POC can come up and demand your lunch money.

WBM I think Cedric's point is that the militance brings out the liberalism; that the supposed left of the Democratic Party now is not even the social democrats but whoever's most committed to anti-discrimination. So what counts as the Democratic left is not the part of the party that wants, say, to socialize health care, but the part that wants to campaign against transphobia. In other words, the far left are no longer the ones who want to destroy Wall Street, they're the ones who want to make sure that trans women can get jobs on Wall Street. It's a little like the '60s when black nationalism came to define militance, since all it was militant about was identity, not economy. The minute black nationalism became the extreme left, there was no room for an actual left. That's just what it means for discrimination to become the only metric of social justice.

AJ You seem to be saying that the Americanization (through the discussion of racism) of political cultures such as the European one is mainly an index of the defeat of the left. The more these political debates get centered around the question of racism, the less traction the left—no matter what the left represents in each country—has to actually put forward some vision.

WBM Right, it's the triumph of the American way of race. But really it's the triumph of the neoliberal idea of social justice. The US wasn't the first, but it was an early and very enthusiastic adopter.

AR That's exactly what it is. There's no notion of social justice that's even thinkable that goes beyond equality of opportunity. And if that's not a victory of global capitalist hegemony, I don't know what the fuck one could be.

WBM Exactly.

DZ We've been discussing with Anton the rise of cash transfers as a social policy—the idea was that somehow the US got there first precisely because it was early in getting rid of transactional politics. Meaning that politics is no longer about backdoor deals or about categorical expansions of welfare, where a candidate will win election by making deals with specific groups like miners, truck drivers, unions. That's a politics where you have organizations to mediate your interests: organizations between you—the individual—and the political sphere. You express those interests through those organizations. And the moment this all disappears, it becomes more attractive to speak to people in the abstract, rather than in specific categories. You reform individual income distribution rather than expand welfare for socio-professional groups. It arrived in Europe later; until the '80s, at least, you still have mass-based parties, you still have strong unions. The destruction of those intermediate bodies comes later in Europe, but now they are definitely gone. They have almost no power anymore, and so politics is way more fluid in that sense. More open to identity politics, I guess.

AJ I think, by extension, that the US shows us a distant mirror of a process that's now nearing completion in Europe. But I think we underestimate just how many dimensions there are in which the Americanization of European culture, or of other political cultures, really takes. It's expressed, for example, in the cash transfer phenomenon we talked about. But the importation of that American discourse of racism is the most powerful example of how Europe is just arriving at where the US got so much earlier. As Walter said, it wasn't the first neoliberal country, but it was the country, at least in the developed world, in which neoliberalism was implemented to the fullest. And now that we're slowly getting there as well, we're bound to see the same symptoms appear. But one of the ways you've talked about it is that, with regard to the reparations discourse, it's a way of making redistributive claims without actually having to resort to organizational channels. This is a really fascinating way in which a reparations discourse allows individuals to make what are, logistically, completely implausible claims about what they will get, and about what kind of . . .

AR Right.

AJ . . . resources they should be receiving. Without channelling those claims through classical organizational channels.

WBM Yeah, but it's a way of making them without really thinking of them as redistribution. Because they're conceived as the restitution of lost property. When Jews who had their paintings stolen from them by the Nazis in the '30s go to get those paintings back, no one thinks of it as the redistribution of paintings. It's people getting back what's been taken from them. There's no appeal to the public good; it's about rectifying the private wrong. It's like the current upsurge of interest in the terrible pogrom in Tulsa, and in the destruction of what they call Black Wall Street. The special lament here is that black people who actually had money were killed and that their money was stolen—not just from the people themselves but from their descendants who, if that hadn't happened, would now themselves be part of a larger black middle and upper middle class.

AR Yeah, especially if they slept through 1929. Walter's point underscores as well that, if I were writing about *Django Unchained* now, not only would I replace *The Help* with racial capitalism, I'd also stress even more than I did that Django's quest wasn't about challenging, much less ending, slavery but about being made whole individually by the return of his wife.

WBM So the happy ending is a society just like the one we've got, except with more rich black people.

ᴀʀ In response to Walter's observation, it occurs to me that part of what prompts the turn to moralistic identitarian claims as the only standard of social justice, is the absolute powerlessness of the claimants. Because the reparations discourse, for instance—like the Juneteenth, Tulsa, all that stuff—depends on appeals to the goodwill of governing elites. And that's either, you know, Bezos's ex-wife or . . .

ᴡʙᴍ She just gave $40 million to my university.

ᴀʀ Right, so she did one good thing. Or, if you aren't asking for a hand-out from rich people, there's the purely symbolic stuff that has no cash value that can come from the governing institutions, just like everybody in Congress voted for Juneteenth. In that sense, it's like the position that the Bookerites were in when they crafted the notion of race relations at the beginning of the twentieth century. The militancy—and this would be the Du Bois wing of the Bookerite tendency at the end of the nineteenth/beginning of twentieth century—the rhetorical force, even the militant expressions, still presume—and Black Power was like this, too, frankly—still presumed a clientelist relationship with governing elites. And that speaks back also to what Anton's observation prompted me to think: that the flip side of the decay of intermediate institutions like the labor movement and others—which would press the interests of the working class, even in interest-group terms—that a condition for the atrophy of those institutions was the stiffening of the ruling class that began in the '70s. When Thatcher said there's no alternative, that was a regime that they had set out to impose. And the way the Democrats, Labour, academics, and the chattering class responded to the proclamation of crisis in the mid-'70s says, I think, everything that you need to know about what frame of governance the ruling class had long since come to operate with. And partly what fuelled, or what helped to enable, or at least to rationalize, that dominance was the contention that government had become inefficient because of democracy. What democracy meant as a practical matter under post-war capitalism in the West was its interest-group trading processes, which rationalized limited participation with the fiction of technocracy. That notion of democracy without popular participation just kind of sets us up for the end of democracy no matter what. I mean, with or without Trump. And it'll be interesting to see what happens with the conversion, more or less, of these Wall Street Keynesians to the view that you need to alleviate entrenched inequalities for the sake of keeping the system running. And even those who are willing to say the word 'stagnation' in public . . . we'll see how long that lasts and how far it goes, and how much they understand it to be just a safety valve to get Biden past 2022, and if then they'll just hope that Trump dies or that something else happens between now and 2022 and 2024.

WBM I think your point about the clientelist thing is really important. And it helps explain something I hadn't connected with it—the panic about white saviorism. Because if your basic commitment to social justice is, Why won't the white people give us our money back, you're going to be a little sensitive about just how militant you really are. Because your entire politics is a white savior politics.

AJ I think you could say something interesting about reparations insofar as they're not public goods; they're demands for private goods that you've missed out on. But there is a kind of 'social rights without the social' aspect to it, in the sense that, once you don't have the organizational heft, you'll actually have to make demands on your own behalf. Because that's essentially what reparations is; it's one big favor and then the whole thing should be settled.

WBM It goes back to a point Adolph has often made, which is that black people speaking for the community—like being a 'community organizer'—is a job. It's not, you know, an elected position or the organic emergence somehow of a leader. And the job is asking for money on behalf of someone else—the community. The question of who you actually represent and whether you actually represent anyone is sort of moot.

AJ It's like lawyers who know they can make a lot of money off people who've been screwed over by certain companies and on whose behalf they can file insurance claims.

AR Right.

AJ But really they want the person to stay silent because, in terms of representation, it's a one-way street; they can't speak for themselves, so the lawyer has to . . .

AR My flippant comment is that the clearest sign that 'community organizer' is a bullshit job title is that Obama claimed that as his 'movement' background. Less flippantly, though, whatever it could have meant to be a community organizer a half-century ago—e.g., in the '60s and '70s groups like the National Welfare Rights Organization, the National Tenants Organization, ACORN [Association of Community Organizations for Reform Now], various Civil Rights and Alinskyite groups, even unions, hired and trained what were often called community organizers, basically as agitators—the nature of the work has changed radically since then. Now community organizers are more like extension offices—not unlike committees for defense of the counterrevolution—for neoliberal class power; an important, though often overlooked, link in the dynamics of reproduction of ideological hegemony. There's a longer story about this phenomenon that can shed light on the emergence and operation of the social structures that consolidate and reproduce neoliberalism concretely in everyday life. I just mentioned to another comrade recently how odd it is that even leftists in the US who pay attention to political economy don't think about its impact within those structures and entities here that occupy the cultural space that would be occupied by an anti-capitalist left if there were one. But that's a matter for another discussion.

The long and short of it, though, is that by the Reagan administration, if not sooner, the role of the community organizer had been generally redefined as embedded in public/private networks of service provision and of minimal popular mobilization in support of elite-driven agendas. The political organization and agitation work was what I'd been doing before I left to attend grad school in 1972, and a reason I quit when I did was that the direction in which things were moving on that front was already clear. When I've said that I went to graduate school out of a sense of political defeat, that transformation was the most direct evidence of it. I saw colleagues and comrades beginning to retool themselves as functionaries in the new social management regime—service providers and technicians in an emerging public/private social service apparatus. The community organizer in increasingly demobilized communities stood in for popular mobilization, ostensibly expressing—embodying, really—an apparent authenticity in channelling the 'voices' of the community. And those authentic voices of the community were either directly or indirectly on the payroll of, or looking for contracts from, ruling class institutions.

DZ I have an analogy that I think is relevant here. I somehow stumbled into the next [Thomas] Piketty book. Interestingly he has a whole chapter about global inequality, meaning inequality between countries. And, of course, he focuses on reparations. What he's advocating, and this is now being discussed in many countries, is reparations for slavery, or for genocide. So, you know, Germany giving billions to Namibia, and so on . . .

AR Well, wait, but how about Poland and Ukraine and Belarus . . .

DZ Of course.

AR And Lithuania. Namibia? What the fuck?

DZ I don't know what they're going to say; maybe they will, maybe they won't. But the interesting part here, again, is that he has no plan whatsoever to seriously tackle the unequal division of labor and the unequal terms of trade. Something that was at the center of post-colonial leaders' plans to build a world after empires. Dependency theories[8] never really asked for 'reparations'; they asked to rebuild the whole system on an equal basis. If Namibia receives some reparations but the terms of trade don't change and technology transfers aren't promoted for industrialization, it's really just a joke.

AR Right.

WBM Again, it's to each according to the degree to which their ancestors were ripped off. The whole idea of a common good, not to mention class struggle, is completely obliterated. And that's why it goes back to what Anton was saying before.

AJ It's worth pointing out as well the contrast with Marx's original vision. The whole point about the proletariat for Marx is that it's the dispossessed class; it's a class that doesn't own any property and therefore has to sell its labor power to survive. But Marx's political solution is not to grant that class property, but to abolish property altogether.

WBM Absolutely.

AJ And we're now stuck in the logic where everyone sees dispossession and everyone's owed a lot. It's not just the proletariat that's dispossessed now; there's loads of nations, and races, and classes as well.

AR So, yeah we can't imagine. Oh, sorry . . .

AJ Can't imagine a world in which the point is to move beyond property altogether, right?

AR Yeah, absolutely. On this point about reparations as a global question, I was just reminded of the bright, shining moment at the altar of the alter-globalization movement: the [1999] WTO demos in Seattle. In the run up to the protests the finance minister, I think it was, of one of the South Asian countries—I think it was probably Bangladesh . . . I can't recall whether he was an MIT PhD or a Chicago PhD. But he wrote an op-ed that argued forcefully against the movement against child labor, which he denounced as racist because it was an attempt to take away opportunities from these families who desperately needed the labor of their children to keep the family going. And what struck me about it wasn't just the ridiculous sophistry of his argument, nor even my own America-centric objection that you need to raise the wage floor. What struck me most of all about it was how many alter-globalization-style American leftists were completely stopped in their tracks and immobilized by this argument. And I thought, Oh my God, what the fuck have we come to here? Presumably if he had been the white manager of Cannon Mills in Kannapolis, North Carolina—if there was still a mill there, say, in 1928—then you could have seen it for what it was. But somehow because he's brown and is from a Third World country, or an LDC [least developed country] as they were mainly calling them then, it's something we really have to take seriously.

DZ Something striking to me when you read about the contemporary poverty discourse is how narrow it is, even for understanding questions in the Global South after the end of colonialism. People like Kwame Nkrumah, Julius Nyerere, or Jawaharlal Nehru were less concerned about poverty than they were about industrialization. Nyerere famously argued in the '70s that "the poor nations cannot overcome their poverty without industrialization". For them it was clear from the start that development was not simply about poverty alleviation but more generally about political and economic independence.

AR Right, yeah.

DZ Poverty is kind of a side point to industrialization. The point is that you want to catch up with the others, and to be able to be part of the global market. And it's also about imperialism, because for them imperialism exists precisely because of the uneven development between North and South. "An industrially backward country", Nehru argued in his history of India, "will continually upset the world equilibrium and encourage the aggressive tendencies of more developed countries. Even if it retains its political independence, this will be nominal only, and economic control will tend to pass to others".

AR That's right.

DZ ... to invade, or they can find other ways to keep you locked into a certain level of subdevelopment and then sell you their products. The whole framework is about contesting imperialism and industrialization. And then you have this poverty turn also in the Third World, where the only problem is people's lack of money and human capital, and where, if you give them enough human capital, you can turn a little peasant into an entrepreneur of the self.

[Crosstalk]

AR Some microfinance . . .

WBM Microloans, right.

DZ Microfinance, exactly. Or women; women are perfect entrepreneurs, so now women are the most important. And if you're a progressive, we can get rid of debt. But certainly, we do not think anymore about industrialization or about the global division of labor.

AR Right.

DZ An interesting part here is how a certain role of the state disappears. Both in the South and in the North, the whole idea of the state coercing capital into certain sites disappears.

AR That shift in how even nominally left intellectuals think about what used to be the Third World and is now the Global South is a really important one, precisely because of what you say about how the state disappears in the shift. Granted, from the '50s into the '70s import substitution was mainly a strategy in Latin America, not so much elsewhere, but the struggles there over ISI [Import Substitution Industrialization], and other struggles over development elsewhere, shone the light on class contradictions in those countries. And that came up through the dependency debates and all the rest of that stuff, and of course it turned out that the national bourgeois classes were bourgeois classes before they were national. In that construct, 'bourgeoisie' is the noun and 'national' is the adjective. So it turned out they had no real interest in ISI either. Some of the economists did. The bourgeoisies didn't have any particular interest in development, and you can see the source of the problem as class contradictions within Chile or Ecuador or India. But once the problem gets redefined as a diminished state, or as inadequate state capacity, or as an abstract relationship between the North and the South which then gets cast in more and more moralistic terms, then you can't figure your way out of inequality, even gross inequality, other than by some neoliberal gimmicks like microcredit.

DZ Or you end up in some Bono concert.

AR Oh, right, right, right. Exactly.

DZ You can do both. You can throw some bombs and you can raise a bit of US aid, and that's fine.

AR Yeah, totally. And now that the US seems to have perfected the technique of 'lawfare', as they're now calling it in Latin America, you don't have to send any troops. You don't have to do anything; just send a constitutional lawyer.

WALTER BENN MICHAELS & ADOLPH REED, JR.

Conclusion:
The Trouble With Disparity

If the COVID-19 pandemic and the killing of George Floyd are supposed to have made visible inequalities that no one had seen, the death
rates both from the virus and at the hands of the police have been met
with analyses that repeat what everyone has always said—first, in the
diagnosis of what's produced those inequalities and, second, in the rec-
ommendation for eliminating them. The problem (thought to be so ingrained in American life that it's sometimes called America's original
sin) is racism; the solution is anti-racism. And the confidence in both the
diagnosis and the cure is so high that it's produced action everywhere
from BLM protesting in the streets to the Mississippi legislature voting
to take down its flag to corporate boardrooms pledging literally billions
of dollars—all with the admirable goal of ending white supremacy.

All this takes place, of course, against the backdrop of an economy that—for white people as well as for black—has become more and
more unequal over the last half century. The Gini index (a measure of
inequality in which 0 means we all have the same while 1 means one
person has everything) has gone from .397 in 1967 to .485 today. (By
contrast, the worst current score in Europe is basically what ours was a
half century ago.) And most of the people—at least on the left—who worry about racial disparity no doubt believe that inequality between classes
is a problem too. Indeed, they may well believe that attacking racism is

also a step in the direction of attacking the gap between the top decile of American wealth and everybody else.

But they are mistaken. In fact, not only will a focus on the effort to eliminate racial disparities *not* take us in the direction of a more equal society, it isn't even the best way of eliminating racial disparities themselves. If the objective is to eliminate black poverty rather than simply to benefit the upper classes, we believe the diagnosis of racism is wrong, and the cure of anti-racism won't work. Racism is real and anti-racism is both admirable and necessary, but extant racism isn't what principally produces our inequality and anti-racism won't eliminate it. And because racism is not the principal source of inequality today, anti-racism functions more as a misdirection that justifies inequality than a strategy for eliminating it.

What makes racism look like the problem? The very real racial disparities visible in American life. And what makes anti-racism look like the solution? Two plausible but false beliefs: that racial disparities can in fact be eliminated by anti-racism and that, if they could be, their elimination would make the US a more equal society. The racial wealth gap, because it is so striking and commonly invoked, is a very good, not to say perfect, illustration of how, in our view, both the problem and solution are wrongly conceived.

It is well known by now that whites have more net wealth than blacks at every income level, and the overall racial difference in wealth is massive. Why can't anti-racism solve this problem? Because, as Robert Manduca has shown, the fact that blacks were overrepresented among the poor at the beginning of a period in which "low income workers of all races" have been hurt by the changes in American economic life has meant that they have "borne the brunt" of those changes.[1] The lack of progress in overcoming the white/black wealth gap has been a function of the increase in the rich/poor wealth gap.

In fact, if you look at how white and black wealth are distributed in the US, you see right away that the very idea of racial wealth is an empty one. The top ten per cent of white people have seventy-five per cent of white wealth; the top twenty per cent have virtually all of it. And the same is true for black wealth. The top ten per cent of black households hold seventy-five per cent of black wealth.

That means, as Matt Bruenig of the People's Policy Project recently noted, "the overall racial wealth disparity is being driven almost entirely by the disparity between the wealthiest 10 per cent of white people and the wealthiest 10 per cent of black people."[2] While Bruenig is clear that a discernible wealth gap exists across class levels, he explored the impact of eliminating the gap between the bottom 90 per cent of each group and found that after doing so 77.5 per cent of the overall gap would remain. He then examined the effect of eliminating the wealth gap between the bottom fifty per cent—the median point—of each population and found that doing so would eliminate only three per cent of the racial gap. So, ninety-seven per cent of the racial wealth gap exists among the wealthiest half of each population. And, more tellingly, more than three-fourths of it is concentrated in the top ten per cent of each. If you say to those white people in the bottom fifty per cent (people who have basically no wealth at all) that the basic inequality in the US is between black and white, they know you are wrong. More tellingly, if you say the same thing to the black people in the bottom fifty per cent (people who have even less than no wealth at all), they also know you are wrong. It's not all the white people who have the money; it's the top ten per cent of (mainly) whites, and some blacks and some Asians. The wealth gap among all but the wealthiest blacks and whites is dwarfed by the class gap, the difference between the wealthiest and everyone else across the board.

As a diagnosis, identifying disparities is taxonomic and rhetorical, not etiological. Insisting that we understand those inequalities as evidence of racism is a demand about how we should classify and feel about them, not an effort to examine their specific causes. While the wealth gap reflects the effects of racism, both past and present, it does not explain how exactly the gaps are produced, up and down the income and wealth distribution. For example, between 1968 and 2016 black Americans made significant advances into occupations and job categories to which they'd previously been denied access. Consistent with that expanded opportunity, in the paper we mentioned above, Manduca found that during that period black/white disparities in income rank—where median group income falls in the national income distribution, measured in centiles—narrowed by nearly a third. That was nowhere near parity but a definite improvement. (Black median income rose from the twenty-fifth centile to the thirty-fifth.) However, during the same period the overall black/white income gap was virtually unchanged. The reason was the extreme concentration of income at the top during that period. In fact, black median income at the twenty-fifth centile in 1968 equaled fifty-five per cent of the national mean, but in 2016 income at the thirty-fifth centile equaled only forty-eight per cent of the national income average. It's not racism that was responsible for that relative decline; it's neoliberal capitalism.

Even as a program for addressing racial disparities, anti-racism is not much of a remedy for inequality. If the racial wealth gap were somehow eliminated up and down the distribution, ninety per cent of black people would still have only twenty-five per cent of total wealth, and the top ten per cent of blacks would still hold seventy-five per cent. And this is only to be expected because in a society with sharp and increasing overall inequality, eliminating racial 'gaps' in the distribution of advantages and disadvantages by definition does not affect the larger, and more fundamental, pattern of inequality.

That inadequacy becomes clearer when we consider the argumentative sleight-of-hand that drives disparity discourse. What we're actually saying every time we insist that the basic inequality is between blacks and whites is that the only inequalities we care about are those produced by some form of discrimination—that inequality itself isn't the problem, it's only the inequalities produced by racism and sexism, etc. What disparity discourse tells us is that, if you have an economy that's getting more and more unequal, that's mainly generating jobs that don't even pay a living wage, the problem we need to solve is not how to reduce that inequality and not how to make those jobs better but how to make sure that they aren't disproportionately held by black and brown people.

It's true, as political scientist Preston H. Smith II has shown, that in the form of what he calls 'racial democracy', some black people have championed the ideal of a hierarchical ladder on which blacks and other non-whites would be represented on every rung in rough proportion to their representation in the general population.[3] But the fact that some black people have desired it doesn't make racial democracy desirable. As we have noted, separately, together, and repeatedly, the implication of proportionality as the metric of social justice is that the society would be just if one per cent of the population controlled ninety per cent of the resources so long as thirteen per cent of the one per cent were black, fourteen per cent were Hispanic, half were women, etc.

Complaints about disproportionality are liberal math. And a politics centered on challenging disproportionality comes with the imprimatur of no less a Doctor of the Church of Left Neoliberalism than economist Paul Krugman, who asserted in his role as ideologist for the 2016 Hillary Clinton campaign that "horizontal" inequality, i.e., inequalities measured "between racially or culturally defined groups", is what's really important in America and dismissed Sen. Bernie Sanders's elaborate program for social-democratic redistribution as "a pipe dream".[4]

It's the fixation on disproportionality that tells us that the increasing wealth of the one per cent would be OK if only there more black, brown, and LGBTQIA+ billionaires. And the fact that anti-racism and anti-discrimination of all kinds would validate rather than undermine the stratification of wealth in American society is completely visible to those who currently possess that wealth—all the rich people eager to embark on a course of moral purification (anti-racist training) but with no interest whatsoever in a politics (social-democratic redistribution) that would alter the material conditions that make them rich.

By contrast, the strain in black politics that converged around what Smith calls the social- (rather than racial-)democratic ideal proceeded from the understanding that, because most black Americans are in the working class—and disproportionately so, partly because of the same effects of past and current racism we allude to above—black people would also benefit disproportionately from redistributive agendas that expand social wage policies and enhance the living standards and security of working people universally. The tension between those two ideals of social justice, as Smith indicates, was, and is, a tension arising from differences in perception and values rooted in different class positions.

Thus the fact that, over the last half century (as American society has reached new heights of inequality and as Democrats have done very little more than Republicans to combat it), the racial-democratic principle in black politics, and in the society in general, has displaced the social-democratic one has been a victory for the class—black and white— that has supported it. In its insistence that proportionality is the only defensible norm and metric of social justice, anti-racist politics rejects universal programs of social-democratic redistribution in favor of what is ultimately a racial trickle-down approach according to which making more black people rich and rich black people richer is a benefit to all black people.

It is instructive in this regard that the racial wealth gap has become the gold standard, as it were, of racial injustice. For one thing, the academics, NGO functionaries, media commentators and the like who stress it as a matter for public concern are themselves typically rooted in the professional-managerial strata among which it is most visible and experienced most acutely. Complaints about white co-workers whose parents provide them with down payments on $700,000 condos do not much exist in the working class. Not only is the gap mainly an upper-status affair; defining it as a crucial marker of racial inequality, as Manduca's work illustrates, naturalizes the forces that produce the larger, more consequential framework of capitalist inequality within which wealth is produced and distributed. Indeed, fixation on the wealth gap is so thoroughly marinated in neoliberal fantasies that accumulating individual wealth is the route to security, dignity and self-respect and that racism is the only impediment to realizing those fantasies, that it obscures the more proximate sources of racial inequality, as well as more direct and concrete responses to that inequality. Dionissi Aliprantis and Daniel Carroll, in a report for the Federal Reserve Bank of Cleveland[5], found that the most important source of the persisting racial wealth gap is the income gap. They indicate, based on a sophisticated model of wealth accumulation that adjusts for different patterns of saving across the life cycle, that, if current trends persist, it would take 259 years for black mean wealth to equal ninety per cent of the white mean. Adjusting the model to assume that black/white income equality had been attained in 1962, they find that median black family wealth would have reached ninety per cent of white family wealth by 2007.

Policies of social-democratic redistribution that reduce the effective income differentials between top and bottom, combined with serious anti-discrimination measures and increased public investment that restores and expands the public sector where black and brown workers are disproportionately employed, it turns out, would do more to reduce even the racial wealth gap than genuine pipe-dream proposals like reparations or other Rube Goldberg-like asset-building strategies. Resistance to such an approach throws into relief the extent to which anti-racism as a politics is an artifact and engine of neoliberalism. It does a better job legitimizing market-based principles of social justice than increasing racial equality. And a key component of that work of legitimation is deflection of social-democratic alternatives.

We can see how this works in a recent report from the National Women's Law Center, which, in the context of the current health crisis, found not only that "Black women are disproportionately represented in front-line jobs providing essential public services" but also that the black women doing these jobs "are typically paid just 89 cents for every dollar typically paid to white, non-Hispanic men in the same roles"[6]. For example, the median hourly wage for white, non-Hispanic personal care aides, home health aides and nursing assistants (at the very front of the front lines) is $14.42; the median hourly wage for black women doing the same job is $12.84. When the authors of the survey say that "This difference in wages results in an annual loss that can be devastating for Black women and their families that were already struggling to make ends meet before the public health crisis", they are right. And this is precisely the kind of injustice that the battle against disparity is meant to address.

But it is also precisely the kind of injustice that reveals the class character of that battle. The white men are making $14.42! Disparity tells us that the problem to solve is the $1.58 an hour difference between the black women and the white men. Reality tells us that the extra $1.58 won't rescue those women from precarity. The men are also being paid starvation wages! In fact, everyone receiving an hourly wage of less than $20 is in a precarious economic position. And the problem here is not just that this report makes no reference to the need to raise the wages of all the workers in front-line occupational categories. Every time we cast

the objectionable inequality in terms of disparity we make the fundamental injustice—the difference between what front-line workers make
and what their bosses and the shareholders in the corporations their
bosses work for make—either invisible, or worse. Because if your idea
of social justice is making wages for underpaid black women equal to
those of slightly less underpaid white men, you either can't see the class
structure or you have accepted the class structure.

The extent to which even nominal leftists ignore this reality is an
expression of the extent of neoliberalism's ideological victory over the
last four decades. Indeed, if we remember Margaret Thatcher's dictum,
"economics are the method: the object is to change the soul"[7], the weap-
onizing of anti-racism to deploy liberal morality as the solution to capitalism's injustices makes it clear it's the soul of the left she had in mind.
Thus, for example, the reception of Raj Chetty and his co-authors' widely discussed 2018 study of intergenerational economic mobility[8] made
it clear that their most shocking finding was the degree to which rich
black people are less likely than their white counterparts to pass their
status on to their children, especially their male children. As if the difficulty rich people might experience in passing on their expropriated
wealth is made into a left issue by the fact that the rich people in question are black.[9] Of course, the study's authors aren't necessarily responsible for how news media represent its significance, but they are totally
responsible for the fact that their work largely disconnects economic mobility—and racial disparities—from political economy, in both diagnosis
and proposed remedies. For them "the critical question to understand
black-white income differences in the long run is: do black children have
lower incomes than white children conditional on parental income, and
if so, how can we reduce these intergenerational gaps?" Their idea of the
basic problem really isn't that unfair advantage is being passed from
generation to generation but that it's being passed more effectively between white people than between blacks.

And their solutions, which center on the putative effects of factors
like family and neighborhood, are primarily focused on the souls of both
black and white folk. As historian Touré Reed has argued, their "three
specific remedies: 'mentoring programs for black boys, efforts to reduce

racial bias among whites, or efforts to facilitate social interaction across racial groups within a given area'" are "centered largely on cultural tutelage" and "interracial understanding". [10] And, as Reed also points out, they downplay the effects of any actual redistribution—"including 'cash transfer programs', and, curiously, 'minimum wage increases'"—on the grounds they will only "improve economics for a single generation" [11]. (It's as if Workers of the World Unite has turned into don't give the man a fish, teach him . . .)

Both the study itself and the public splash it generated underscore the extent to which contemporary anti-racism presumes the Thatcherite ideological victory. Chetty and his co-authors treat the neoliberal economic order as given, unassailable nature. They don't take account of the policy interventions since the 1960s—on the one side, expansion of anti-discrimination enforcement and opening of occupational structures; on the other, public sector and social wage retrenchment, decline in unionization, and four decades of regressive income and wealth transfer—that have substantially affected black economic mobility. Nor do they consider whether the relative recency of that increased upward mobility might have consequential intergenerational effects, especially in an overall context of wage stagnation and regressive transfer. That's why they can imagine redistributive policy only in the form of weak tea interventions like increasing the minimum—not living—wage, which they immediately dismiss as inadequate. Their stress on intergenerational mobility within that narrow context buttresses the view that racial inequity should be the inequality central to our concern. And their reduction of the universe of possible intervention echoes Thatcher's other notorious dictum: "you know, there's no such thing as society. There are individual men and women and there are families." [12] And she would have been fine with Chetty et al.'s additional reification of individuals and families as neighborhoods—"It is our duty to look after ourselves and then, also, to look after our neighbours."

The overall trajectory of their account—from the study's initial formulation of the problem through its conclusions and recommendations—is that fixing the disparities requires fixing people. That construct has been a standard deflection from the broader and deeper mechanisms driving inequality proceeding from the English Poor Laws through Chicago economists' propagation of 'human capital' ideology in the 1950s and anthropologist Oscar Lewis's invention of the culture of poverty (rechristened in the 1980s and 1990s as the urban under-class) until it was formalized as policy through the victory of the cultur-alist, rather than redistributive, vision that defined the War on Poverty. That's pretty much how it has to be if political-economic structures and, specifically, capitalist class relations are defined out of the picture. The emptiness of the authors' recommendations for addressing the supposed mobility gap mirrors the emptiness of anti-racism as a political agenda, even when it comes to actually fixing disparity.

What we've been talking about so far are different ways of under-standing economic inequality, and our point has been that the very commitment to framing the inequality between rich and poor as the disparity between black and white is—if you want a more equal society—mistaken. But money isn't everything. What about those disparities that may have a class component but where it looks like race or racism plays a significant role and an autonomous role? Examining the limitations and insidious features of how disparity discourse operates in the two other areas in which it is now most prominent—COVID-19 and police killings of civilians—will demonstrate just how class-skewed and coun-terproductive it is.

We've all heard a lot about racial disparities in deaths from the coro-navirus—from the standard observation that 'black and brown' com-munities have been hardest hit to Sanjay Gupta (CNN Chief Medical Correspondent) including in a list of biological factors that heighten risk of severe effects from the virus "being a person of color—Black, Latinx or Native American" [13]. There's a sense in which both these observations are true, but there's a much more powerful sense in which they're false and in which the way that they're false, first, reproduces some of the most pernicious myths about race (the main one being that such a thing exists) and, second, deploys race and racism in a way that misrepresents the problem and thus misdescribes the solution.

Are persons of color at higher risk? [14] Most readers probably already know many of the key risk factors with respect to COVID-19: according to the Centers for Disease Control [15], among them are asthma; chronic kidney disease being treated with dialysis; hemoglobin (a protein that transports oxygen in the blood) disorders; chronic lung disease; diabetes; immunocompromised status; liver disease; serious heart conditions; severe obesity; age of sixty-five or older; residence in nursing homes or long-term care facilities. All but the last two categories are specific medical conditions that can affect anyone in the general population. Those conditions have been shown to increase risk of serious harm from infection either clinically, by examination of specific effects the virus can have on people with those conditions, or statistically, by showing that people with those conditions are significantly more likely than the general population to succumb to the worst effects of the virus, or both.

The last two categories in particular are tied also to specific social circumstances, mainly advanced point in the life cycle, which is associated with diminished abilities to fight off disease. But other social circumstances are involved with them, as well as with many of the other conditions. For instance, nursing homes and long-term care facilities not only are likely to house people with conditions that make them especially vulnerable; they typically depend on care-giving workers who are underpaid and exploited and are themselves likely to be at greater risk of infection, and hence of transmitting the infection, than the general population. As we all know, these 'essential workers' may be celebrated as 'heroes', but in a for-profit healthcare system, where operators of such facilities, increasingly private equity and other investment firms, are likely to cut corners to maintain their bottom lines, the heroes are not just badly paid, their health is a secondary concern[16].

Healthcare workers, and essential workers in general, are disproportionately likely to get sick, and they are disproportionately black. More generally, we know that in the United States, people classified as black and Hispanic are disproportionately likely to be poor and economically marginal, to have inadequate access to healthcare, to work jobs that are hazardous, debilitating, and, in the case of COVID-19, likely to expose them to infection, and to live in relatively congested circumstances and in areas with elevated exposure to environmental toxins—all conditions that undermine basic health. In that sense, race is associated with risk because it is an umbrella category that encompasses relatively high proportions of people who live within the social circumstances that increase risk. It's a kind of shorthand, a 'proxy measure'. Proxy measures are what researchers use to try to get at the effects of a variable when they don't have direct information on the variable itself. They use other variables that appear to move along with the one they're interested in but for which they don't have direct data to try to *infer* the significance of the category they're interested in accounting for. Researchers commonly acknowledge using *race* as a proxy for *class*.

But why do we need a proxy for class? Why not just use class? Because, more often than not, we can't. Although Vicente Navarro's remark (to the 2003 graduating class of the Johns Hopkins Medical School), "The United States is one of the very few countries that do not include class in its national health and vital statistics", no doubt overstated the case, his observation that the US prefers to collect "health and vital statistics by race and gender"[17] is on target. Comparing EU and US approaches to eliminating disparities in health, Elizabeth Docteur and Robert A. Berenson note the EU focus on "inequalities between the most advantaged and disadvantaged sections of the population", that is, "populations with lower education, a lower occupational class, or lower income". "By contrast", they go on to say, the US data they analyze presents "health disparities associated with race and ethnicity as the primary focus of its drive to increase health equity".[18] So, scholars who want to examine class effects of COVID-19, for example, must rely on proxy measures—for example, ZIP codes, education levels, or race—to try to get at the question indirectly. Thus, whatever the role played by race in actually producing the vulnerability of any individual to the virus, the role played by race in explaining that vulnerability is foregrounded: the headline is black and brown communities bear the brunt of COVID-19, not working-class people bear the brunt of COVID-19.

Even when this substitution names essentially the same people, it's a problem, in several ways.

First, it works to convert race from a proxy for other factors into a substitute for those other factors. Public health scholar R. Dawn Comstock and her co-authors in a 2004 study in the *American Journal of*

Epidemiology surveyed 1,198 articles in that journal and in the *American Journal of Public Health* published between 1996 and 1999 and found that nearly eighty-six per cent mentioned race but that in most, just over fifty-seven per cent, "the purpose for using race or ethnicity as variables was not described"[19] and "only rarely were policy recommendations made on the basis of findings associated with race or ethnicity."[20] That is, researchers often use race as a category for interpreting data simply because it's already there in the way the data are collected and aggregated. Doing so seems appropriate because it is consistent with the common sense folk knowledge that 'race' matters somehow and doing so thus perpetuates the idea that race matters somehow.

Second, the idea that race itself matters perpetuates the false idea that there is such a thing as race. But, biologically speaking, there isn't. It's not surprising that researchers once put a great deal of time and effort into looking for biological markers of the differences between races. What is surprising is that, long after the search for such markers has failed and there is consensus that the reason we haven't found them is because they don't exist, we continue to organize our thinking around them—as if there were something about the biology of black bodies as a function of their blackness that made them more susceptible to COVID-19. Too many medical practitioners, including doctors, assume that blacks, for example, have distinctive biological characteristics from whites. One recent study[21] found that fifty per cent of medical students or residents endorsed at least one false belief concerning racial differences in biology between blacks and whites. A companion study found that nearly three-fourths of a sample of people without medical training endorsed at least one of those false beliefs. It is worth underscoring in this regard that there is greater genetic diversity between two species of chimpanzees, our closest primate relatives, living in the same small region of Central Africa[22] than there is within our entire species all over the globe.

There is a long and sordid history[23] of the often tragic harms that folk beliefs about racial differences in biology have caused to people in this country and around the world.[24] In the current environment, it's too easy for people to assume that racial disparities stem from differences in racial biology. And, because racialist thinking is such a cloudy mush of fantasies, the folk belief doesn't have to attribute the differences to biology. Folk beliefs about 'culture' do the same work of planting confusion and misinformation. 'Culture' in this context is typically only a polite way of saying race and one that doesn't require any claims about biology, although it's often used interchangeably to invoke essential difference. In its own way, a folk view of race as culture can be just as harmful as the biological view because it easily gives rise to victim-blaming arguments according to which people's vulnerable health conditions are their own fault due to their diets and to stereotypical destructive habits attributed to them. That in turn gives rise to arguments that 'they' need to exercise greater personal responsibility and that 'we' shouldn't be expected to pay the costs of taking care of them. We've seen much of that sentiment during the COVID-19 crisis as well.

Third, what we focus on can make it more difficult to see other, maybe equally or more important patterns. Because public health data are not collected with income as a category for analysis, we can't determine definitively whether rich people, of whatever race, have been on the average as vulnerable to the worst effects of COVID-19 as poor people of whatever race or whether rich seniors are as vulnerable as poor ones. That would be important information to have if we want to understand more clearly who in our overall population is at greater or lesser risk. We do, however, have clues. A recent study by Les Leopold and the Labor Institute examined a series of factors associated with higher death rates in New York City.

Neighborhoods with approximately one-third more African Americans than the average NYC neighborhood have nine more deaths per 100,000, making the average death rate jump from 201 per 100,000 to 210. If the percent of crowded housing increased by about a third, the death rate also increased by about nine per 100,000. Being born in Latin America, a category that includes many undocumented workers, was associated with twice the risk of dying from COVID-19 than that faced by African Americans and those who lived in crowded housing. This is likely because it is far more difficult for undocumented workers, even essential ones, to gain access to medical and financial assistance.

Being old, of course, is a major risk factor no matter your ethnicity, place of origin, or income.

But income alone, a key indicator of class, was the most influential characteristic. Lower-income neighborhoods saw an addition of nearly 28 deaths per 100,000, increasing the average death rate by more than 10 percent, from 201 deaths per 100,000 to 229.[25]

The death rate in census tracts with median annual income below $25,000 was 221.8 per 100,000 population while for the census tracts with median annual income above $240,000 the death rate was 85.7 per 100,000. You were more than two-and-a-half times more likely to die from COVID-19 if you lived in a poor neighborhood than if you lived in a rich one. And "income alone" was "the most influential characteristic".[26]

So, fourth, not only does the use of race as a proxy for class produce a misunderstanding of the problem (racism), it also produces a misunderstanding of the solution (anti-racism). The correct understanding of the problem is that it's not black and brown workers who are at risk, it's low-wage workers, especially those who have to go to work during the pandemic. And this would be true even if all the low-wage workers were in fact black and brown. Why? Because even if it's racism that has caused so many badly paid workers to be black and brown, it's not racism that causes them to be so badly paid. Krogers and Amazon and McDonald's don't pay their workers so little because so many of them are people of color. They pay them so little because that's how they make a profit. If you made the workers proportionately white and Asian, they'd still be underpaid and they'd still be getting sick.

Again, this is not to deny the effects of racism and not to deny racial disparity. Racism helps explain why so many low-wage workers are black and brown. But it doesn't explain their low wages. And all the anti-racism in the world wouldn't make the slightest contribution to raising those wages. So even if using race as a proxy for class were accurate in the sense that it named the exact same set of people, it would be profoundly misleading. Race can't be a proxy for class because race tells you the problem is discrimination against the workers while class tells you the problem is getting the maximum value out of their labor. Or, turn it around: the analytic of class tells you the problem is how we treat front-line workers; the analytic of race tells you the problem is that too many black and brown people have to be front-line workers. That's why the most ruthlessly profit-driven corporations can learn to love the most radical demands for eliminating black/white disparities. To make Jeff Bezos and his stockholders as rich as they are, Amazon needs to underpay its workers. It doesn't need to care the slightest bit what color they are.

What saves many people from COVID-19 is not that they are white or Asian but that they are rich. And this is even more vividly true of the third person of the disparitarian trinity, police killings. It may be easier for a camel to pass through the eye of a needle than for a rich person to get himself murdered by the police; but, as with COVID deaths, these deaths are only categorized by race, sex, and age, so we can't be sure. In

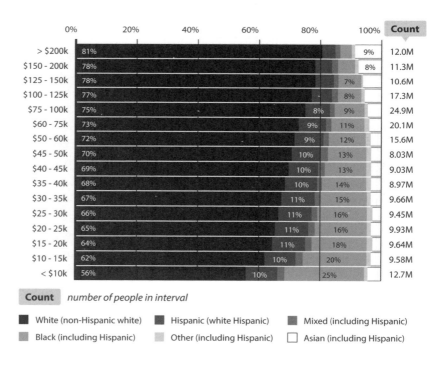

Figure 1. US household income distribution by race

any event, no one would think to protest that poor people are disproportionately killed by the police, since controlling poor people is basically
what policing is. It's the disproportionate killing of poor black men that's
the problem.

Part of this can be explained by the fact that, as we've already noted,
black men are overrepresented among the poor. Indeed, if we were to
imagine that the victims in police shootings came from the bottom three
intervals in Fig. 1, then we might conclude that, at least in part, disproportionately being killed by the police tracks disproportionate poverty.
The significance of social class here would just be a part of what researchers have shown to be its (increasing) significance with respect to
the justice system more generally, where, as Adaner Usmani has said,
incarceration has not been "defined by rising racial disparities" but by
rising class disparities, and where, in fact, while rates of incarceration
have "dramatically" increased for poor black Americans, they actually
decreased for "college-educated African Americans"[27]. A version of this
same dynamic has in fact played out in health care, where, as Frederick
J. Zimmerman and Nathaniel W. Anderson say, between 1993 and 2017
the "black-white gap showed significant improvement" but "income disparities worsened".[28]

Still, racism surely plays a significant role. For 2019, Mapping Police Violence records thirty police killings of unarmed black people and
fifty-three killings of unarmed white people.[29] And, if not for racism,
some of that disproportionality would disappear. It would, for example,
be significantly diminished if the police just killed one less black person and one more white person a month. But does anyone believe this
would count as a solution, that it's only the deaths we can blame on
racism that matter? Everyone knows George Floyd's name; neither of us
knows the names of any of the unarmed white people killed by the police this year. No one should—and we don't—deny that the disproportion
is significantly an effect of racism. But no one should—and we don't—
think that the problem of police violence is caused by racism or can
be solved by anti-racism. And yet the whole point of #BlackLivesMatter
(the reason it's called BlackLivesMatter and not WorkersLivesMatter or
PoorPeoplesLivesMatter, much less the dreaded AllLivesMatter) is to

center race and racism—to take the injustice that neoliberal capitalism needs and turn it into an injustice that neoliberal capitalism can eagerly and sincerely deplore.

In other words, every time racial disparity is invoked as the lens through which to see American inequality, the overwhelming role played by the increased inequality in the American class system is made invisible. And this is, of course, true on the right as well as the left—think of all the conservative commentators defending the police by invoking the specter of black-on-black murder. And then think of the widespread agreement among criminologists that the Gini coefficient 'predicts murder rates better than any other variable'. Conservatives who try to blame black crime on race and liberals who try to blame it on racism are both missing the point. If you want to distinguish between the left and the right, the relevant question is not what they think about race; it's what they think when race is taken out of the equation.

From this standpoint, what we're seeing today is not how the COVID-19 crisis has helped to reveal the structural inequalities of American life but how it has intensified the process of concealing them. Think of how hard Fig. 1 works to teach us to see and be shocked by the disproportionate number of whites and Asians on the top and blacks and Latinos on the bottom rather than by the difference between the top and the bottom—to shock us with disparity rather than inequality.

And no response today is less convincing than, why can't we be shocked by both? For one thing, we aren't. Even though (and here's where the graph does a little counter-hegemonic work) poor white households are a majority, the gap between rich and poor only gets traction today if it can be redescribed as the gap between white and black. There are no headlines trumpeting the discovery that poor people have worse health care than rich people, much less announcing that they are more often killed by the police. You might as well announce that poor people have less money than rich people. In fact, the commitment to addressing disparities has become so central that even when it's clear that addressing the problems of poor people rather than black people would be more effective in solving the problems of black people, the move toward universality is rejected as a refusal to 'center' black people.

In other words, centering black people has become a way of ignoring poor people—even poor black people! After all, every step in the direction of universal redistribution advances, however minimally, equality between rich and poor *and* works toward correcting racial disparities. No step in the direction of reducing disparities advances equality between rich and poor and, without universal redistribution, even the steps we do take toward reducing disparities are minimally effective. What does it mean, then, to make disparity the focus of our political agenda?

What we're trying to do here is show that seeing inequality as disparity is seeing it through a neoliberal lens. (It's worth recalling in this context that Margaret Thatcher, when asked what she considered her greatest achievement, replied "Tony Blair and New Labour. We forced our opponents to change their minds." [30]) Of course, many people committed to BlackLivesMatter may understand themselves as committed also to social measures that go beyond rectifying the disproportionality problem. But, if they are, that commitment in no way follows from identification of disparity as the most important metric of inequality. And, as we have argued, that commitment, no matter how earnestly felt, is not borne out by the substance of anti-racist political practice. For the record, this means that those who assert a 'both/and-ist' posture—from the most self-satisfied, moralizing youthful enthusiasts to the most decrepit troglodytes steeped in their nostalgic Trotskyite fantasies—to denounce advocates of political-economic analysis and working-class politics as 'class reductionists' are trying to delude either themselves or the rest of us, or both, regarding the extent to which they've capitulated to neoliberal vision.

Finally, although some anti-racists—and certainly many liberals— express indifference toward or disdain for poor and working-class whites, it is practically impossible, as generations of black proponents of social democracy understood clearly, to imagine a serious strategy for winning the kinds of reforms that would actually improve black and brown working people's conditions without winning them for all working people and without doing so through a struggle anchored to broad working-class solidarity.

And if it were possible, it would be wrong. A society where making black and white people equal means making them equally subordinate to a (mainly white but, really, what does it matter?) ruling class is not a more just society, just a differently unjust one. That's the trouble with disparity.

Notes

FOREWORD

1. Randall Lane, "Operation Wealth Speed", *Forbes*, 6 Apr. 2021 <https://www.forbes.com/sites/randalllane/2021/04/06/operation-wealth-speed-what-a-record-number-of-new-self-made-billionaires-sas-about-capitalism/?sh=6190608545fa>.

2. Randall Lane, "Forbes Fellows: Creating Opportunities Today for Tomorrow's Leaders", *Forbes*, 6 Apr. 2021 <https://www.forbes.com/sites/randalllane/2021/04/06/forbes-fellows-creating-opportunities-today-for-tomorrows-leaders/?sh=29276f1b5f19>.

3. Lane, "Operation Wealth Speed".

4. Lane, "Forbes Fellows".

5. Lane, "Operation Wealth Speed".

6. MO nieuwssite, "Interview met Walter Benn Michaels", YouTube, 8 May 2012 <https://www.youtube.com/watch?v=faLxXV1o1po>.

7. Walter Benn Michaels, *The Trouble with Diversity: How We Learned to Love Identity and Ignore Inequality* (New York: Picador, 2016; first published 2006), 204.

8. Nora Zelevansky, "The Big Business of Unconscious Bias", *New York Times*, 20 Nov. 2019 <https://www.nytimes.com/2019/11/20/style/diversity-consultants.html>.

9. Randall Lane, "Inclusive Capitalism: Entrepreneurship For All", *Forbes*, 2021 <https://www.forbes.com/sites/randalllane/2021/06/09/inclusive-capitalism/?sh=-b7193987b045>.

10. Walter Benn Michaels, "Identity Politics: A Zero Sum Game", see 156 in the present volume.

11. Touré F. Reed, "The Political Economy of Racial Inequality", *Dissent*, Summer 2021 <https://www.dissentmagazine.org/article/the-political-economy-of-racial-inequality>.

12. Adolph Reed, Jr., *Stirrings in the Jug: Black Politics in the Post-segregation Era* (Minneapolis: Minnesota University Press, 1999), 209.

13. Steven Knapp and Walter Benn Michaels, "Against Theory", *Critical Inquiry*, 8/4 (Summer, 1982), 723–42.

14. Walter Benn Michaels, *The Shape of the Signifier: 1967 to the End of History* (Princeton: Princeton University Press, 2004), 78.

15. Walter Benn Michaels, "The Ends of History", lecture given at the University of Illinois, 10 Feb. 2012.

16. Fredric Jameson, *Postmodernism, or, the Cultural Logic of Late Capitalism* (Durham, NC: Duke University Press, 1991), 187.

17. Jeffrey J. Williams, "The Political Education of Walter Benn Michaels: An Interview", *Symploke*, 22/1–2 (2014), 337–59 (344).

18. Ibid. 344.

19. Ibid. 345.

20. Walter Benn Michaels, *The Trouble with Diversity*, 188.

21. Adolph Reed, Jr., *The South: Jim Crow and Its Afterlives* (London: Verso Books, 2022), 86.

22. Twiley Barker and Jewel Prestage, "Interview with Adolph Reed, March 13, 1992", Louie B. Nunn Center for Oral History, University of Kentucky Libraries <https://kentuckyoralhistory.org/ark:/16417/xt7c862b9168>.

23. Adolph Reed, Jr., "Black Particularity Reconsidered", *Telos*, 39 (Mar. 1979), 71–93.

24. James Forman, *Locking Up Our Own* (New York: Farrar, Straus, and Giroux, 2017).

25. Adolph Reed, Jr., "Introduction", in Reed (ed.), *Race, Politics, and Culture: Critical Essays on the Radicalism of the 1960s* (New York: Greenwood Press, 1986), 9. See also Russell Jacoby, *Social Amnesia: A Critique of Conformist Psychology from Adler to Laing* (Boston: Beacon Press, 1975).

26. Ibid. 9.

27. Reed, "Black Particularity", 71.

28. Ibid.

29. Ibid.

30. Adolph L. Reed, Jr., *The Jesse Jackson Phenomenon: The Crisis of Purpose in Afro-American Politics* (New Haven: Yale University Press, 1986), 1.

31. Russell Jacoby, *Dialectic of Defeat: Contours of Western Marxism* (Cambridge: Cambridge University Press, 1981).

32. Adolph Reed, Jr., *Class Notes: Posing as Politics and Other Thoughts on the American Scene* (New York: The New Press, 2000), viii.

33. Ibid.

34. Adolph Reed, Jr., "Nothing Left: The Long, Slow Surrender of American Liberals", *Harper's Magazine*, Mar. 2014 <https://harpers.org/archive/2014/03/nothing-left-2/>.

35. William Julius Wilson, "The Black Underclass", *The Wilson Quarterly*, 8/2 (Spring 1984), 88–99.

36. Adolph Reed, Jr., "The Post-1965 Trajectory of Race, Class, and Urban Politics in the United States Reconsidered", *Labor Studies Journal*, 41/3 (July 2016), 260–91 (260).

37. Anthony Giddens, *The Third Way: The Renewal of Social Democracy* (Cambridge: Polity Press, 1998), 102.

38. Anthony Giddens and Christopher Pierson, *Conversations with Anthony Giddens: Making Sense of Modernity* (Cambridge: Polity Press, 1998), 164.

39. Walter Benn Michaels, "Why Populism is Popular", in Jacques Attali et al., *La Démocratie, enrayée?* (Brussels: Académie Royale de Belgique, Bruxelles, 2013), 212.

MARX, RACE, AND NEOLIBERALISM

1. See Adolph Reed, Jr., "Unraveling the Relation of Race and Class in American Politics", *Political Power and Social Theory*, 15 (2002), 265–74; Ellen Meiksins Wood, "Class, Race and Capitalism", *Political Power and Social Theory*, 15 (2002), 275–84; Maurice Zeitlin, "On the 'Confluence of Race and Class' in America", *Political Power and Social Theory*, 15 (2002), 285–88; Steven Gregory, "The 'Paradoxes' of Misplaced Concreteness: Thinking through the State", *Political Power and Social Theory*, 15 (2002), 289–300; and Reed, "Rejoinder", *Political Power and Social Theory*, 15 (2002), 301–15. See also my chapter, "The 'Color Line' Then and Now: *The Souls of Black Folk* and the Changing Context of Black American Politics", in Adolph Reed, Jr. and Kenneth W. Warren (eds.), *Renewing Black Intellectual History: The Ideological and Material Foundations of African American Thought* (Boulder, CO: Paradigm Publishers, 2010).

2. Edmund S. Morgan, *American Slavery, American Freedom* (New York: W. W. Norton, 1975) and Kathleen M. Brown, *Good Wives, Nasty Wenches and Anxious Patriarchs:*

Gender, Race, and Power in Colonial Virginia (Chapel Hill, NC: University of North Carolina Press, 1996). As her title indicates, Brown examines as well the interplay of race and gender in the constitution of distinctions between slave and servant, black and white.

3. Legal historian Robert J. Steinfeld in two important books examines the latter conflict. See Steinfeld, *The Invention of Free Labor: The Employment Relation in English and American Law and Culture, 1350–1870* (Chapel Hill, NC: University of North Carolina Press, 2002) and *Coercion, Contract, and Free Labor in the Nineteenth Century* (Cambridge: Cambridge University Press, 2001).

4. Hugo Münsterberg, *Psychology and Industrial Efficiency* (Boston: Houghton Mifflin, 1913), 130. Münsterberg criticized what he considered a widespread tendency among industrial firms' employment officers to use group characteristics too freely and to depend on superficial stereotypes (130–1).

5. John Bodnar, Roger Simon, and Michael P. Weber, *Lives of Their Own: Blacks, Italians, and Poles in Pittsburgh, 1900–1960* (Urbana, IL: University of Illinois Press, 1983), 240. On the history and logic of race science, see Jonathan Marks, *What It Means to Be 98% Chimpanzee: Apes, People and Their Genes* (Berkeley and Los Angeles: University of California Press, 2003), and pertinent recent histories of the eugenics movement include Edwin Black, *War Against the Weak: Eugenics and America's Campaign to Create a Master Race* (New York: Dialog Press, 2012), and Alexandra Minna Stern, *Eugenic Nation: Faults and Frontiers of Better Breeding in Modern America* (Berkeley and Los Angeles: University of California Press, 2005). For examples of race scientists' proliferation of races, see Daniel G. Brinton, *Races and Peoples: Lectures on the Science of Ethnography* (Philadelphia: David McKay, 1901), 17–50; Joseph Deniker, *The Races of Man: An Outline of Anthropology and Ethnography* (New York: Charles Scribner, 1900), 280–98; William Z. Ripley, *The Races of Europe: A Sociological Study* (London: Kegan Paul, 1900); and William P. Dillingham, *A Dictionary of Races or Peoples* (Washington, DC: GPO, 1911), 3.

6. Paul Liem and Eric Montague (eds.), "Toward a Marxist Theory of Racism: Two Essays by Harry Chang", *Review of Radical Political Economics*, 17/3 (1985), 43.

7. Ibid. 38.

8. Ibid. 39.

9. Ibid. 44.

10. For a critical examination of the 'whiteness' literature, at least as it has taken shape among historians, see "Scholarly Controversy: Whiteness and the Historians' Imagination", *International Labor and Working-Class History*, 60 (Fall 2001), 1–92, with an introduction by Judith Stein and articles by Eric Arnesen, James Barrett, David Brody,

Barbara J. Fields, Adolph Reed, Jr., Victoria C. Hattam, Eric Foner, and a response by Arnesen. See also Barbara J. Fields and Karen E. Fields, *Racecraft: The Soul of Inequality in American Life* (London: Verso, 2012).

11. Adolph Reed, Jr., and Merlin Chowkwanyun, "Race, Class, Crisis: The Discourse of Racial Disparity and its Analytical Discontents"; see 97 in the present volume. We argue as well that "left-seeming defenses that insist on the importance of race *and* class" are only attempts to deny the rhetorical force of the race line.

12. Michelle Alexander, *The New Jim Crow: Mass Incarceration in the Age of Colorblindness* (New York: New Press, 2010). For a systematic critique of the limits and counterproductive features of this approach, see James Forman, Jr., "Racial Critiques of Mass Incarceration: Beyond the New Jim Crow", *New York University Law Review*, 87 (2012), 21–69. See also Reed and Chowkwanyun, "Race, Class, Crisis" and Adolph Reed, Jr., "Three Tremés", *nonsite*, 4 July 2011, available at <http://nonsite.org/editorial/three-tremes/>.

13. Reed, "The 'Color Line' Then and Now", 261.

14. Walter Benn Michaels, *The Trouble with Diversity: How We Learned to Love Identity and Ignore Inequality* (New York: Metropolitan Books, 2007). It is telling that the reduction of concern with economic inequality to racial disparities leads to responses—for example, Sheradeen's proposed Individual Development Accounts—that seek "to create competitive individual minority agents who might stand a better fighting chance in the neoliberal rat race rather than a positive alternative vision of a society that eliminates the need to fight constantly against disruptive market whims in the first place". Reed and Chowkwanyun, "Race, Class, Crisis", 95. We note as well that "Within the racial context specifically, such proposals exude more than a whiff of racial communitarianism and collective racial self-help, along with a dollop of republican nostalgia" (95–6).

15. On evolutionary psychology, see Susan McKinnon, *Neo-Liberal Genetics: The Myths and Moral Tales of Evolutionary Psychology* (Chicago: Prickly Paradigm, 2005). On genes and politics, see Evan Charney, "Genes and Ideologies", *Perspectives on Politics*, 6/2 (June 2008), with responses from John R. Alford et al.; Rebecca J. Hannagan and Peter K. Hatemi; and a rejoinder by Charney in *Perspectives on Politics*, 6/2 (June 2008). For an illustration of state of the art in neurocriminology, see the work of University of Pennsylvania criminologist Adrian Raine at <https://crim.sas.upenn.edu/people/adrian-raine>. James J. Heckman's rather disingenuously titled essay "Promoting Social Mobility", *Boston Review*, Sept./Oct. 2012, illustrates the nexus of epigenetics and behavioral economics. See also Daniel A. Hackman and Martha J. Farah, "Socioeconomic

Status and the Developing Brain", *Trends in Cognitive Sciences*, 13/2 (Feb. 2009), 65–73. Jiannbin Lee Shiao, Thomas Bode, Amber Beyer, and Daniel Selvig, "The Genomic Challenge to the Social Construction of Race", *Sociological Theory*, 30 (June 2012), 67–88 appropriates—crucially misappropriates, actually—scholarship on the geography of human genetic variation in support of explicitly racialist arguments.

16. George W. Stocking, Jr., *Race, Culture, and Evolution: Essays in the History of Anthropology* (Chicago: University of Chicago Press, 1968), 265.

17. Adolph Reed, Jr., "The Limits of Anti-Racism"; see 49 in this volume.

18. Ibid. 51.

WHAT MATTERS

1. Kjartan Páll Sveinsson (ed.), *Who Cares about the White Working Class?* (London: Runnymede Perspectives, 2009).

THE LIMITS OF ANTI-RACISM

1. Beryl Satter, *Family Properties: Race, Real Estate, and the Exploitation of Black Urban America* (New York: Picador, 2009).

2. Robert O. Self, *American Babylon: Race and the Struggle for Postwar Oakland* (Princeton: Princeton University Press, 2005).

3. Rayford Logan (ed.), *What the Negro Wants* (Notre Dame, IN: Notre Dame University Press, 2001; first published 1944).

4. Preston H. Smith II, *Racial Democracy and the Black Metropolis: Housing Policy in Postwar Chicago* (Minneapolis: University of Minnesota Press, 2012).

FROM BLACK POWER TO BLACK ESTABLISHMENT

1. Tina L. Ligon, "'Turn this Town Out': Stokely Carmichael, Black Power, and the March Against Fear", National Archives, 7 June 2016 <https://rediscovering-black-history.blogs.archives.gov/2016/06/07/turn-this-town-out-stokely-carmichael-black-power-and-the-march-against-fear/>.

2. See Stokely Carmichael and Charles V. Hamilton, "Black Power: The Politics of Liberation in America", in Ellis Cashmore and James Jennings (eds.), *Racism: Essential Readings* (London: SAGE Publications, 2001).

3. See "The Right to Be Different", The Pluralism Project, Harvard University <https://pluralism.org/the-right-to-be-different>.

4. Kwame Ture and Charles V. Hamilton, *Black Power: The Politics of Liberation*

in America (New York: Vintage, 1992; first published 1967) <https://mygaryislike.files. wordpress.com/2016/12/black-power-kwame-ture-and-charles-hamilton.pdf>.

5. Daryl Michael Scott, *Contempt and Pity: Social Policy and the Image of the Damaged Black Psyche, 1880–1996* (Chapel Hill, NC: University of North Carolina Press, 1997).

6. Bayard Rustin, "From Protest to Politics: The Future of the Civil Rights Movement", *Commentary*, Feb. 1965 <https://www.commentarymagazine.com/articles/bayard-rustin-2/from-protest-to-politics-the-future-of-the-civil-rights-movement/>.

7. Bayard Rustin, "'Black Power' and Coalition Politics", *Commentary*, Sept. 1966 <https://www.commentarymagazine.com/articles/bayard-rustin-2/black-power-and-coalition-politics/>.

8. Jelani Cobb, "The Forgotten March on Washington", *The New Republic*, 24 Aug. 2013 <https://newrepublic.com/article/114460/march-washignton-50th-anniversary-other-march-1941>.

9. Cedric Johnson, *Revolutionaries to Race Leaders: Black Power and the Making of American Politics* (Minneapolis: University of Minnesota Press, 2007).

10. Dean E. Robinson, *Black Nationalism in American Politics and Thought* (Cambridge: Cambridge University Press, 2010).

11. Robert L. Allen, *Black Awakening in Capitalist America* (Trenton, NJ: Africa World Press, 1992).

12. Eric Levitz, "What Bernie Sanders Gets Right About Identity Politics", *New York Magazine*, 1 Dec. 2016 <https://nymag.com/intelligencer/2016/12/what-bernie-sanders-gets-right-about-identity-politics.html>.

13. Gabriel Winant, "Professional-Managerial Chasm: A Sociological Designation Turned into an Epithet and Hurled Like a Missile", *n+1*, 10 Oct. 2019 <https://nplusonemag.com/online-only/online-only/professional-managerial-chasm/>.

14. Adolph Reed, Jr., "Bookerism and the Black Elite", *The New Republic*, 18 Feb. 2020 <https://newrepublic.com/article/156419/bookerism-black-elite>.

15. Adolph Reed, Jr., "The Trouble with Uplift", *The Baffler*, 41 (Sept. 2018) <https://thebaffler.com/salvos/the-trouble-with-uplift-reed>.

BEYOND THE GREAT AWOKENING

1. St. Clair Drake and Horace R. Cayton, *Black Metropolis: A Study of Negro Life in a Northern City* (Chicago: University of Chicago Press, 2015; first published 1945).

2. Gunnar Myrdal, *An American Dilemma: The Negro Problem and Modern Democracy*

(New York: Taylor & Francis, 2017; first published 1944).

3. Rayford W. Logan (ed.), *What the Negro Wants* (Notre Dame, IN: Notre Dame University Press, 2001; first published 1944).

4. Adolph Reed, Jr., "The Trouble with Uplift", *The Baffler*, 41 (Sept. 2018) <https://thebaffler.com/salvos/the-trouble-with-uplift-reed>.

5. Vinson Cunningham, "The Argument of 'Afropessimism'", *The New Yorker*, 20 July 2020 <https://www.newyorker.com/magazine/2020/07/20/the-argument-of-afropessimism>.

6. "The 1619 Project", *New York Times Magazine*, Aug. 2019 <https://www.nytimes.com/interactive/2019/08/14/magazine/1619-america-slavery.html>.

7. Adolph Reed, Jr., "Antiracism: A Neoliberal Alternative to a Left", *Dialectical Anthropology*, 42 (22 May 2018), 105–15.

8. Adolph Reed, Jr., "The Surprising Cross-Racial Saga of Modern Wealth Inequality", *The New Republic*, 29 June 2020 <https://newrepublic.com/article/158059/racial-wealth-gap-vs-racial-income-gap-modern-economic-inequality>.

THE TROUBLE WITH DIVERSIFYING THE FACULTY

1. John H. Pryor et al., *The American Freshman: Forty Year Trends, 1966–2006* (Los Angeles: Higher Education Research Institute, 2007) <https://www.heri.ucla.edu/PDFs/pubs/TFS/Trends/Monographs/TheAmericanFreshman40YearTrends.pdf>.

2. *Chronicle of Higher Education*, "This Year's Freshmen at 4-Year Colleges: Highlights of a Survey", 21 Jan. 2010 <http://chronicle.com/article/This-Years-Freshmen-at-4-Year/63672>.

3. Camille Z. Charles, Vincent J. Roscigno, and Kimberly C. Torres, "Racial Inequality and College Attendance: The Mediating Role of Parental Investments", *Social Science Research*, 36/1 (2007), 329–52. In fact, when you net out the economics, the disadvantage in college attendance of other underrepresented groups like Native Americans and native-born Hispanics is also virtually eliminated. Furthermore, the difference between native blacks and immigrant blacks (who attend selective colleges in a much higher proportion than native blacks) also disappears when socioeconomic status is netted out (see Pamela R. Bennett and Amy Lutz, "How African American is the Net Black Advantage? Differences in College Attendance Among Immigrant Blacks, Native Blacks, and Whites", *Sociology of Education*, 82/1 (2009), 70–100).

4. Pryor et al.

5. Richard D. Kahlenberg, "Invisible Men", *Washington Monthly*, Mar. 2007, 61–3.

6. Audrey Williams June, "Professors' Pay Raises Beat Inflation; So Much for the Good News", *Chronicle of Higher Education*, 17 Apr. 2009 <https://www.chronicle.com/article/professors-pay-raises-beat-inflation-so-much-for-the-good-news/?cid2=-gen_login_refresh&cid=gen_sign_in&cid2=gen_login_refresh>.

7. Audrey Williams June, "Full-Time Instructors Shoulder the Same Burdens That Part-Timers Do", *Chronicle of Higher Education*, 18 Oct. 2009 <http://chronicle.com/article/Full-Time-Instructors -Shoulder/48841/>.

8. Modern Language Association, *Education in the Balance: A Report on the Academic Workforce in English* (New York: Modern Language Association, 2008).

9. It's also true, I'm glad to say, that at UIC we are at least a little bit worried about the situation of our adjuncts, and I am currently cochairing a committee to see what can be done about it.

10. Adolph Reed, Jr., "The Limits of Anti-Racism"; see 50 in the present volume.

11. Adolph Reed, Jr., "The 'Color Line' Then and Now: *The Souls of Black Folk* and the Changing Context of Black American Politics", in Adolph Reed, Jr. and Kenneth W. Warren (eds.), *Renewing Black Intellectual History: The Ideological and Material Foundations of African American Thought* (Boulder, CO: Paradigm Publishers, 2010), 271.

12. *Grutter v. Bollinger*, et al. US Supreme Court, No. 02-241, 23 June 2003.

13. Richard D. Kahlenberg, "Disadvantages", *The New Republic*, 3 Mar. 2010 <http://www.tnr.com/book/review/disadvantages>. More generally, although Michigan does well in admitting minority students, it does badly in admitting low-income students: "Overall, nearly 39 percent of students attending Michigan colleges and universities receive Pell Grants. Yet among University of Michigan students, only 13 percent receive Pell Grants, an indication that low-income students in the state are going elsewhere" (Charles Dervarics, "Public Colleges Do Poor Job with Minority, Low-Income Students, Study Says", *Diverse: Issues in Higher Education*, 14 Jan. 2010 <http://diverseeducation.com/article/13316/>).

14. Source: the proof brief of defendants-appellants in *Grutter v. Bollinger* (no. 01-1447) filed with the United States Court of Appeals for the Sixth Circuit on 16 May 2001. See the Cornell Law School Legal Information Institute: <https://www.law.cornell.edu/supremecourt/text/539/306>.

15. David Leonhardt, "As Wealthy Fill Top Colleges, Concerns Grow Over Fairness", *New York Times*, 22 Apr. 2004 <https://www.nytimes.com/2004/04/22/us/as-wealthy-fill-top-colleges-concerns-grow-over-fairness.html>.

16. Dan Mangan, "Boys Club Bashed: Suit Alleges Goldman Bias Against Female

Staffers", *New York Post*, 16 Sept. 2010.

17. Drew Gilpin Faust, "Baccalaureate Address to Class of 2008", 3 June 2008 <https://www.harvard.edu/president/speeches-faust/2008/2008-baccalaureate-service/>.

18. Drew Gilpin Faust, "Installation Address: Unleashing Our Most Ambitious Imaginings", 12 Oct. 2007 <https://www.harvard.edu/president/speeches-faust/2007/installation-address-unleashing-our-most-ambitious-imaginings/>.

19. "Teach for (Some of) America: Too Talented for Public Schools", *Wall Street Journal*, 29 Apr. 2009 <https://www.wsj.com/articles/SB124061253951954349>.

20. Julian Vasquez Heilig and Su Jin Jez, *Teach For America: A Review of the Evidence* (East Lansing, MI: The Great Lakes Center for Education Research and Practice, 2010).

21. Sharon Otterman, "Lauded Harlem Schools Have Their Own Problems", *New York Times*, 13 Oct. 2010 <https://www.nytimes.com/2010/10/13/education/13harlem.html>.

22. Ibid.

23. Ross Douthat, "Grading School Choice", *New York Times*, 10 Oct. 2010 <http://www.nytimes.com/2010/10/11/opinion/11douthat.html?_r=1>.

RACE, CLASS, CRISIS

1. See, for instance, Charles Bromley et al., *Paying More for the American Dream V: The Persistence and Evolution of the Dual Mortgage Market* (San Francisco: California Reinvestment Coalition, 2011); Barbara Ehrenreich and Dedrick Muhammad, "The Recession's Racial Divide", *New York Times*, 13 Sept. 2009; Kai Wright, "Mortgage Industry Bankrupts Black America", *The Nation*, 24 July 2008; Wright, "The Assault on the Black Middle Class", *The American Prospect*, 4 Aug. 2009; and the series of studies by Algernon Austin, Gregory Squires and their colleagues for the Economic Policy Institute as well as those by Amaad Rivera, Ajamu Dillahunt, Mazher Ali and their colleagues for United for a Fair Economy from 2008 to 2011.

2. Ian Shapiro, "Problems, Methods, and Theories in the Study of Politics: Or, What's Wrong with Political Science and What to Do about It", in Shapiro, *The Flight from Reality in the Human Sciences* (Princeton: Princeton University Press, 2007), 188.

3. Debbie Gruenstein Bocian, Wei Li, and Keith Ernst, *Foreclosures by Race and Ethnicity: The Demographics of a Crisis* (Durham, NC: Center for Responsible Lending, 2010); Seth Wessler et al., *Race and Recession: How Inequity Rigged the Economy and How to Change the Rules* (Oakland, CA: Applied Research Center, 2009); Institute on Race and Poverty, *Communities in Crisis: Race and Mortgage Lending in the Twin Cities* (n.p., 2009).

4. Alicia Munnell et al., "Mortgage Lending in Boston: Interpreting HMDA Data", Working Paper No. 92-7, Federal Reserve Bank of Boston, Oct. 1992, available from <http://www.bos.frb.org>.

5. For the debate that it generated, see, for example, John Goering and Ron Wienk (eds.), *Mortgage Lending, Racial Discrimination, and Federal Policy* (Washington, DC: Urban Institute Press, 1996); Stephen Ross and John Yinger (eds.), *The Color of Credit: Mortgage Discrimination, Research Methodology, and Fair-Lending Enforcement* (Cambridge, MA: MIT Press, 2002). An otherwise excellent account of both the study and the events leading up to the subprime crisis in general, Gretchen Morgenson and Joshua Rosner, *Reckless Endangerment: How Outsized Ambition, Greed, and Corruption Led to Economic Armageddon* (New York: Times Books, 2011), is unfortunately too dismissive of the study and the careful and serious methodological debates that occurred over its findings.

6. Wessler et al., *Race and Recession*, 7; Amaad Rivera et al., *State of the Dream 2009: The Silent Depression* (Boston: United for a Fair Economy, 2009), iii.

7. Wessler et al., *Race and Recession*, 47.

8. Algernon Austin, *Uneven Pain: Unemployment by Metropolitan Area and by Race*, Issue Brief No. 278, Economic Policy Institute, 8 June 2010.

9. *Communities in Crisis*, 26–34.

10. There has been an interesting critical discussion of this phenomenon in public health and epidemiological research. See R. Dawn Comstock, Edward M. Castillo and Suzanne P. Lindsay, "Four-Year Review of the Use of Race and Ethnicity in Epidemiologic and Public Health Research", *American Journal of Epidemiology*, 159 (2004), 611–9 and Camara Phyllis Jones, "Invited Commentary: 'Race', Racism and the Practice of Epidemiology", *American Journal of Epidemiology*, 154 (2001), 299–304. Also see Merlin Chowkwanyun, "The Strange Disappearance of History from Racial Health Disparities Research", *Du Bois Review: Social Science on Race*, 8 (2011), 253.

11. Douglas S. Massey and Nancy A. Denton, *American Apartheid: Segregation and the Making of the Underclass* (Cambridge, MA: Harvard University Press, 1993); Melvin L. Oliver and Thomas M. Shapiro, *Black Wealth/White Wealth: A New Perspective on Racial Inequality* (New York: Routledge, 1995).

12. Massey and Denton, *American Apartheid*, 74–8.

13. Ibid. 112.

14. Ibid. 81.

15. Michael B. Katz et al., "Immigration and the New Metropolitan Geography", *Journal of Urban Affairs*, 32/5 (2010), 523–47; Richard Alba and John Logan, "Variations

on Two Themes: Racial and Ethnic Patterns in the Attainment of Suburban Residence", *Demography*, 28/3 (1991) and "Minority Proximity to Whites in Suburbs: An Individual-Level Analysis of Segregation", *American Journal of Sociology*, 98/6 (1993).

16. Massey and Denton, *American Apartheid*, 93.

17. Ibid. 97.

18. Ibid. 107.

19. Ibid. 98.

20. Ellen Herman, *The Romance of American Psychology: Political Culture in the Age of Experts* (Berkeley and Los Angeles: University of California Press, 1996) and Leah Gordon, "The Question of Prejudice: Social Science, Education, and the Struggle to Define the 'Race Problem' in Mid-Twentieth Century America, 1935–1965", Ph.D. thesis (University of Pennsylvania, 2008).

21. Massey and Denton, *American Apartheid*, 109–10.

22. Karl Taeuber and Alma Taeuber, *Negroes in Cities* (Chicago: Aldine, 1965); Rose Helper, *Racial Policies and Practices of Real Estate Brokers* (Minneapolis: University of Minnesota Press, 1969).

23. Kenneth Jackson, *Crabgrass Frontier: The Suburbanization of the United States* (New York: Oxford University Press, 1987), chs. 11–2; Arnold Hirsch, *Making the Second Ghetto: Race and Housing in Chicago, 1940–1960* (Chicago: University of Chicago Press, 1983), ch. 4.

24. Robert O. Self, *American Babylon: Race and the Struggle for Postwar Oakland* (Princeton: Princeton University Press, 2003); Beryl Satter, *Family Properties: How the Struggle Over Race and Real Estate Transformed Chicago and Urban America* (New York: Picador, 2010); Samuel Kelton Roberts Jr., *Infectious Fear: Politics, Disease, and The Health Effects of Segregation* (Chapel Hill, NC: University of North Carolina Press, 2009), 136. It is notable that Roberts maintains this class analysis while writing about the age of Jim Crow, during which a strictly racial interpretation might be more justifiable, though hardly adequate.

25. Massey and Denton, *American Apartheid*, 10–1.

26. Ibid. 84–8.

27. Sean Reardon and Kendra Bischoff, "Income Inequality and Income Segregation", *American Journal of Sociology*, 116/4 (Jan. 2011), 1115–6.

28. Massey and Denton, *American Apartheid*, 69.

29. John Yinger, *Closed Doors, Opportunities Lost: The Continuing Costs of Housing Discrimination* (New York: Russell Sage Foundation, 1995), 120–1.

30. Ibid. 121.

31. This may partly explain why the topic has received such little attention. An important exception is Michelle Boyd's account of a Chicago neighborhood revitalization project in the late 1980s and early 1990s. See Boyd, "The Downside of Racial Uplift: The Meaning of Gentrification in an African American Neighborhood", *City and Society*, 17/2 (Dec. 2005), 265–88; Boyd, "Defensive Development: The Role of Racial Conflict in Gentrification", *Urban Affairs Review*, 43/6 (July 2008), 751–76; and Boyd, *Jim Crow Nostalgia: Reconstructing Race in Bronzeville* (Minneapolis: University of Minneapolis Press, 2008), chs. 2–5. Peter Kwong has called attention to intraracial exploitation between Chinese employers and Chinese workers in the United States. See Kwong, *The New Chinatown* (2nd edn., New York: Hill and Wang, 1996).

32. See Adolph Reed, Jr., "The Black Urban Regime: Structural Origins and Constraints", in Reed, *Stirrings in The Jug: Black Politics in the Post-Segregation Era* (Minneapolis: University of Minnesota Press, 1999), ch. 3; John Arena, "Race and Hegemony: The Neoliberal Transformation of the Black Urban Regime and Working Class Resistance", *American Behavioral Scientist*, 47/3 (Nov. 2003), 352–80.

33. Chowkwanyun has criticized a parallel quality in racial health disparities research that results from its similar reliance on large, aggregated data sets and repeated uncovering of statistical associations between race and adverse health outcomes. Constrained by methodology and type of empirical base, such research thus rarely penetrates a level deeper than these macro-level quantitative portraits to tell us what concrete policies, institutions, phenomena and actors are causing them. More generally, Robert Aronowitz identifies a similar phenomenon in post-war epidemiology and identification of quantifiable 'risk factors'. See Chowkwanyun, "Strange Disappearance"; Aronowitz, "The Social Construction of Coronary Heart Disease Risk Factors", in Aronowitz, *Making Sense of Illness: Science, Society, and Disease* (New York: Cambridge University Press, 1998).

34. See Edward Wolff, *Top Heavy: The Increasing Inequality of Wealth in America and What Can Be Done About It* (1995; 2nd edn., New York: New Press, 2002); Michael Sherraden, *Assets and the Poor: A New American Welfare Policy* (New York: M.E. Sharpe, 1991) for single-volume summations of these authors' views.

35. Oliver and Shapiro, *Black Wealth/White Wealth*, 94.

36. Ibid. 106.

37. Ibid. 91, 125.

38. Ibid. 4.

39. Ibid. 4–5.

357

40. Ibid. 5.

41. Ibid. 11–52.

42. Ibid. 51.

43. Ibid. 147–51.

44. Ibid. 156.

45. Ibid. 166.

46. Ibid. 130–3.

47. Ibid. 6–7; Thomas Shapiro, Tatjana Meschede, and Laura Sullivan, "The Racial Wealth Gap Increases Fourfold", Institute on Assets and Social Policy, May 2010. In addition to lax taxes on inheritances, Shapiro identifies persistent disparities in the labor and housing market as other culprits.

48. Robert Brenner, *The Boom and the Bubble: The US in the World Economy* (New York: Verso Books, 2002), ch. 1; Judith Stein, *Pivotal Decade: How the United States Traded Factors for Finance in the Seventies* (New Haven: Yale University Press, 2011), ch. 1; Robert Pollin, *Contours of Descent: U.S. Economic Fractures and the Landscape of Global Austerity* (2003; New York: Verso Books, 2005), chs. 2–3; Jacob Hacker, *The Great Risk Shift: The Assault on American Jobs, Families, Health Care and Retirement and How You Can Fight Back* (New York: Oxford University Press, 2006).

49. David Harvey, *A Brief History of Neoliberalism* (New York: Oxford University Press, 2006), 2.

50. Shapiro advances such a claim even more forcefully in *The Hidden Cost of Being African-American: How Wealth Perpetuates Inequality* (New York: Oxford University Press, 2004), ch. 3.

51. Kenneth W. Warren has urged a similar approach for African-American literature, arguing for constricting its definition to works produced between the beginning and end of federally sanctioned legal segregation. This stands in contrast to all encompassing definitions that include black American writing from the antebellum era to the present. See Warren, *What Was African American Literature?* (Cambridge, MA: Harvard University Press, 2011), ch. 1. For two other considerations of how race's operation has changed over time that consider the limits of strictly using race as a marker of social position, see Adolph Reed, Jr., "The 'Color Line' Then and Now: *The Souls of Black Folk* and the Changing Context of Black American Politics", in Adolph Reed, Jr. and Kenneth W. Warren (eds.), *Renewing Black Intellectual History: The Ideological and Material Foundations of African American Thought* (Boulder, CO: Paradigm, 2010) and Michael Katz, Mark Stern, and Jamie Fader, "The New African American Inequality", *Journal of*

American History, 92/1 (June 2005), 75–108.

52. A considerable body of work chronicles this restructuring and the political mobilization against it, including Steven Hahn and Jonathan Prude (eds.), *The Countryside in the Age of Capitalist Transformation* (Chapel Hill, NC: University of North Carolina Press, 1985), chs. 6–7; Hahn, *The Roots of Southern Populism: Yeoman Farmers and the Transformation of the Georgia Upcountry, 1850–1890* (New York: Oxford University Press, 1983); Jack Temple Kirby, *Rural Worlds Lost: The American South, 1920–1960* (Baton Rouge, LA: Louisiana State Press, 1987). It is worth noting that this counterfactual on the lost opportunity for land redistribution in the immediate wake of the Civil War plays a central role in much pro-reparations discourse, which also mobilizes a similar long narrative of American history by highlighting cross-generational racial disadvantage. But like the one presented in this work, it is more impressionistic outline than detailed exploration of contemporary inequality's historical roots. For one example, see Raymond Winbush (ed.), *Should America Pay?: Slavery and the Raging Debate on Reparations* (New York: HarperCollins, 2003).

53. Barbara J. Fields, "Ideology and Race in American History", in J. Morgan Kousser and James M. McPherson (eds.), *Region, Race, and Reconstruction: Essays in Honor of C. Vann Woodward* (New York: Oxford University Press, 1982), 150.

54. Adolph Reed, Jr., "Review: *The New Black Middle Class*", *Political Science Quarterly*, 103 (Spring 1988), 159–61.

55. Dalton Conley, *Being Black, Living in the Red: Race, Wealth, and Social Policy in America* (Berkeley and Los Angeles: University of California Press, 1999). Curiously, both volumes are frequently cited next to one another, even though their analytical missions are quite different. In the second edition of their book and a separate volume by Shapiro, Conley is mentioned but not engaged. See Oliver and Shapiro, *Black Wealth/White Wealth: A New Perspective on Racial Inequality* (2nd edn., New York: Routledge, 2006), 232; Shapiro, *The Hidden Cost*, 96. Conley explores the role of class dynamics in blunting the racial wealth gaps' deleterious effects. Oliver and Shapiro state that this is not a primary goal when they write that they "do not intend here to engage in a discourse about class in modern American life; the concept is important but not entirely germane to our purposes", which is to show the endurance of the racial wealth gap whatever class measure they use (70).

56. Largely due to Sherraden's *Assets and the Poor*, IDAs emerged as an attractive policy idea in the 1990s. They entitle low-income applicants who promise to save an agreed upon sum of money to matching funds from local municipalities, community

organizations, or financial institutions who partner up to participate in the program, sometimes in an amount many times more than the original principal. These transfers, in turn, come with no stipulations that they be paid back but are restricted to certain usages, such as paying for college, making a down payment for a home, or starting a small business, and they usually require recipients to attend workshops on wealth management and financial responsibility. IDAs have attracted a broad spectrum of neoliberal support, including the Democratic Leadership Council, the Aspen Institute, Bill Clinton, and George W. Bush.

57. Louis Hyman, *Debtor Nation: The History of America in Red Ink* (Princeton: Princeton University Press, 2011).

58. Oliver and Shapiro, *Black Wealth/White Wealth*, 1st edn., 193. The literature on such politics and its close ties with community development efforts remains thin, but see Nicole Marwell, *Bargaining for Brooklyn: Community Organizations in the Entrepreneurial City* (Chicago: University of Chicago Press, 2007); Karen Tani, "The House that 'Equality' Built: The Asian American Movement and the Legacy of Community Action", in Annelise Orleck and Lisa Gayle Hazirjian (eds.), *The War on Poverty and Struggles for Racial and Economic Justice: Views from the Grassroots* (Athens, GA: University of Georgia Press, 2011); Kent Germany, *New Orleans after the Promises: Poverty, Citizenship, and the Search for the Great Society* (Athens, GA: University of Georgia Press, 2007).

59. Kenneth B. Clark, *Dark Ghetto: Dilemmas of Social Power* (New York: Harper & Row, 1965).

60. On the politics of racial uplift, see Kevin Gaines, *Uplifting the Race: Black Leadership, Politics, and Culture in the Twentieth Century* (Chapel Hill, NC: University of North Carolina Press, 1996); Michele Mitchell, *Righteous Propagation: African Americans and the Politics of Racial Destiny after Reconstruction* (Chapel Hill, NC: University of North Carolina Press, 2004); Touré F. Reed, *Not Alms but Opportunity: The Urban League and the Politics of Racial Uplift, 1910–1950* (Chapel Hill, NC: University of North Carolina Press, 2008); Wilson J. Moses, *The Golden Age of Black Nationalism, 1850–1925* (Oxford: Oxford University Press, 1988); August Meier, *Negro Thought in America, 1880–1915: Racial Ideologies in the Age of Booker T. Washington* (Ann Arbor: University of Michigan Press, 1963).

61. For rare critiques against this consensus, see Larry Bennett and Adolph Reed, Jr., "The New Face of Urban Renewal: The Near North Redevelopment Initiative and the Cabrini-Green Neighborhood", in Reed (ed.), *Without Justice for All* (Boulder, CO:

Westview Press, 1999); David Imbroscio, "'(U)nited and Actuated by Some Common Impulse of Passion': Challenging the Dispersal Consensus in American Housing Policy Research", *Journal of Urban Affairs*, 30/2 (Apr. 2008), 111–30; Herbert Gans, "Concentrated Poverty: A Critical Analysis", *Challenge*, 53/3 (May-June 2010), 82–96.

62. Michelle Alexander, *The New Jim Crow: Mass Incarceration in the Age of Colorblindness* (New York: New Press, 2010).

63. For a class and institutional analysis of the emergence of this identity discourse and its reach (with even the labor movement increasingly forsaking the language of class in favor of it), see Adolph Reed, Jr., *The Lesson of Obamamania: There Is No Substitute for an Anti-Capitalist Politics* (London: Verso, forthcoming, 2012).

64. Thomas S. Kuhn, *The Structure of Scientific Revolutions* (Chicago: University of Chicago Press, 1962).

65. Mara Loveman, "Is 'Race' Essential?", *American Sociological Review*, 64/6 (Dec. 1999), 896.

66. Ellen Meiksins Wood, "Class, Race, and Capitalism", *Political Power and Social Theory*, 15 (2002), 276. Wood's comment is part of a symposium on the race/class controversy. See also in the same issue: Adolph Reed, Jr., "Unraveling the Relation of Race and Class in American Politics"; Maurice Zeitlin, "On the 'Confluence of Race and Class' in America"; Steven Gregory, "The 'Paradoxes' of Misplaced Concreteness"; and Reed, "Rejoinder".

67. Donald Green and Ian Shapiro, "Revisiting the Pathologies of Rational Choice", in Shapiro, *Flight from Reality*, 95 n. 146.

THE POLITICAL ECONOMY OF ANTI-RACISM

1. Willie Legette and Adolph Reed, Jr., "The Role of Race in Contemporary U.S. Politics: V.O. Key's Enduring Insight", *nonsite*, 11 Feb. 2018 <https://nonsite.org/the-role-of-race-in-contemporary-u-s-politics/>.

2. Or, at least, our relative location within the professional-managerial class, a location that, given the ongoing casualization of academic labor, puts more and more of us just a serious illness or economic downturn away from penury. There's a reason why academics are turning to unions; the damage neoliberalism has done to the benefits won by the working class since Norris-La Guardia is felt by all of us.

3. Frances Stewart, "Horizontal Inequalities: A Neglected Dimension of Development", Center for Research on Inequality, Human Security and Ethnicity, n.d. <https://assets.publishing.service.gov.uk/media/57a08cba40f0b652dd0014fa/wp1.pdf>.

4. Paul Krugman, "Hillary and the Horizontals", *New York Times*, 10 June 2016 <https://www.nytimes.com/2016/06/10/opinion/hillary-and-the-horizontals.html?partner=rss&emc=rss&_r=0>.

5. Ta-Nehisi Coates, "The Case for Reparations", *The Atlantic*, June 2014 <https://www.theatlantic.com/magazine/archive/2014/06/the-case-for-reparations/361631/>.

6. In fact, development economists committed to fighting horizontal inequality tend to rest their case mainly on what they argue is its ability to prevent (often armed) conflict, while also suggesting that—by expanding economic activity—it can make a contribution to decreasing individual inequality. The degree to which this is true remains uncertain but, in the US, inasmuch as productivity enhancement is likely to be a less important consequence of reduced discrimination than it would in developing economies, it's hard to see a significant effect. My thanks to Benjamin Feigenberg for discussing these issues with me.

7. David Roediger, "It's Not Just Class: The Fight for Racial Justice Is Inseparable from Overcoming Capitalism", *In These Times*, 2 Aug. 2017 <https://inthesetimes.com/article/marxism-class-race-labor-unions-capital>. Actually, even this isn't right. The diversity industry that regularly insists that diversity is good for business isn't masking anything. Roediger's idea that I must think there's a 'conspiracy' of capitalists committed to propagating the idea that they care about diversity when what they really care about is profits depends on him completely misunderstanding the actual point—which is that they can be genuinely committed both to anti-discrimination and to profits and that no masking is required because they correctly see the two commitments as complementary, not contradictory.

8. From Matt Bruenig, "Wealth is Extremely Unevenly Distributed in Every Racial Group", People's Policy Project, 28 Sept. 2017 <https://www.peoplespolicyproject.org/2017/09/28/wealth-is-extremely-unevenly-distributed-in-every-racial-group/>.

9. It's from Michael I. Norton and Samuel R. Sommers, "Whites See Racism as a Zero-Sum Game That They Are Now Losing", *Perspectives on Psychological Science*, 6/3 (May 2011), 215–8. What the graph shows is "White and Black respondents' perceptions of anti-White and anti-Black bias" as measured on a ten-point scale (one is none, ten a great deal). Against the view that white racism is the default position of American society just waiting to burst out in periodic explosions of rage, these numbers—particularly when conjoined with the increases in economic inequality that began in the '70s—suggest that racism (as Judith Stein argued a long time ago) has a political economy.

10. Barbara J. Fields and Karen E. Fields, *Racecraft: The Soul of Inequality in*

American Life (London: Verso, 2012), 111.

11. "According to data from the Department of Education, more than three-quarters of U.S. undergraduates attend colleges that accept at least half their applicants; just 4 percent attend schools that accept 25 percent or less, and hardly any—well under 1 percent—attend schools like Harvard and Yale that accept less than 10 percent." Ben Casselman, "Shut Up About Harvard: A Focus on Elite Schools Ignores the Issues Most College Students Face", FiveThirtyEight, 30 Mar. 2016 <https://fivethirtyeight.com/features/shut-up-about-harvard/>.

12. Scott Jaschik, "Poll: Public Opposes Affirmative Action", Inside Higher Ed, 8 July 2016 <https://www.insidehighered.com/news/2016/07/08/poll-finds-public-opposition-considering-race-and-ethnicity-college-admissions>.

13. Although since 2002, the *New York Times* says, "Access to top colleges has not changed much", what change there has been is in the wrong direction. The number of students from the bottom quintile has declined from a little over 4 per cent to about 3.5 per cent; the number of students from the top 1 per cent has increased from a little under 10 per cent to about 11.5 per cent. "Some Colleges Have More Students from the Top 1 Percent than the Bottom 60. Find Yours.", *New York Times*, published online 18 Jan. 2017 <https://www.nytimes.com/interactive/2017/01/18/upshot/some-colleges-have-more-students-from-the-top-1-percent-than-the-bottom-60.html>.

14. Deirdre Fernandes, "The Majority of Harvard's Incoming Class Is Nonwhite", *Boston Globe*, 2 Aug. 2017 <https://www.bostonglobe.com/metro/2017/08/02/harvard-incoming-class-majority-nonwhite/5yOoqrsQ4SePRRNFemuQ2M/story.html>.

15. "Economic Diversity and Student Outcomes at Harvard University, Massachusetts", *New York Times*, published online <https://www.nytimes.com/interactive/projects/college-mobility/harvard-university>.

16. "Diversity and Inclusion", Goldman Sachs <http://www.goldmansachs.com/who-we-are/diversity-and-inclusion/>. Beneath a picture of aspiring young rich people of color, there's a quote from Lloyd Blankfein: "Diversity is at the very core of our ability to serve our clients well and to maximize return for our shareholders. Diversity supports and strengthens the firm's culture, and it reinforces our reputation as the employer of choice in our industry and beyond." It's impossible to overstate the degree to which this set of commitments has become hegemonic in the educational-financial complex. Just in the couple of days after I finished this essay and before we put it up, one of our editors received a mass email from a diversity officer at his university (which shall be nameless but where the students have a median family income of $139,800) asking the question

"What if workforce diversity is more than simply the right thing to do?" and inviting him to listen to a Mellon Foundation-financed panel discussion in which "experts across the corporate, academic, and media sectors discuss how organizations can leverage identity-and-cognitive based difference to better their bottom line." (They call it "the diversity bonus".) And at the same time another of our editors forwarded an article from <http://diverseeducation.com>, singing the praises of the "Race in the Marketplace (RIM) Research Network", a group of "scholars" studying how "race, power and privilege affect marketplace policies and practices" (Tiffany Pennamon, "Race, Power, Privilege in the Marketplace Are Focus of Interdisciplinary Network's Research", *Diverse: Issues in Higher Education*, 4 Feb. 2018 <http://diverseeducation.com/article/109427/>). Of course, it's easy to disparage these efforts as liberal rather than radical anti-racism. That's what people used to say about multiculturalism twenty years ago. But just as there was no such thing then as radical multiculturalism (it was liberal all the way down), today there's no such thing as radical anti-racism. The way to radicalize RIM's goal of "inclusive, fair, and just marketplaces" is not by making sure that rich black people can buy the same things rich white people can and poor black people can buy the same things poor white people can—it's by making sure that, when it comes to health care, housing and education, no one needs to buy anything.

17. "Economic Diversity and Student Outcomes at Princeton University", *New York Times* <https://www.nytimes.com/interactive/projects/college-mobility/princeton-university>.

18. Kimberlé Crenshaw, "Mark Lilla's Comfort Zone", *The Baffler*, 14 Sept. 2017 <https://thebaffler.com/latest/mark-lillas-comfort-zone>. The piece in general is a defense of the political model of Critical Race Studies and its only allusion to economic equality is on the between-culturally-formed-groups model—hence the Critical Race Movement is praised for articulating "a redistributional conception of law teaching jobs. They viewed these positions as resources that should be shared with communities of color." But Crenshaw is right that there's not much worth defending in Lilla's book, which is a kind of rewrite of Arthur Schlesinger, Jr.'s *The Disuniting of America*—both of them criticizing racial identity only to celebrate national identity and Lilla displaying just slightly more interest in the redistribution of wealth.

19. "Sex, Race, and Ethnic Diversity of U.S. Health Occupations (2011–2015)", US Department of Health and Human Services, Health Resources and Services Administration, National Center for Health Workforce Analysis, 2017 <https://bhw.hrsa.gov/sites/default/files/bureau-health-workforce/data-research/diversity-us-health-occupations.pdf>.

AUTOBIOGRAPHY OF AN EX-WHITE MAN

1. Richard C. Lewontin, "Of Genes and Genitals", *Transition*, 1996, 178–93 (187).

BELIEVING IN UNICORNS

1. Karen E. Fields and Barbara J. Fields, *Racecraft: The Soul of Inequality in American Life* (London: Verso, 2012).

2. Adolph Reed, Jr. and Merlin Chowkwanyun, "Race, Class, Crisis: The Discourse of Racial Disparity and its Analytical Discontents"; see 94–5 in the present volume.

FROM JENNER TO DOLEZAL

1. Zeba Blay, "Why Comparing Rachel Dolezal to Caitlyn Jenner Is Detrimental to Both Trans and Racial Progress", *HuffPost*, updated 15 June 2015 <https://www.huffingtonpost.co.uk/entry/rachel-dolezal-caitlyn-jenner_n_7569160>.

2. Michelle Garcia, "Rachel Dolezal Is Nothing Like Caitlyn Jenner—And Here's Why", *Mic*, 12 June 2015 <https://www.mic.com/articles/120604/why-rachel-dolezal-is-not-caitlyn-jenner>.

3. Darnell L. Moore, "The Huge Problem with the Rachel Dolezal Scandal That Everyone Needs to Know", *Mic*, 12 June 2015 <https://www.mic.com/articles/120574/here-s-the-most-important-thing-to-take-away-from-the-rachel-dolezal-controversy>.

4. Meredith Talusan, "There Is No Comparison between Transgender People and Rachel Dolezal", *The Guardian*, 12 June 2015 <https://www.theguardian.com/commentisfree/2015/jun/12/comparison-transgender-people-rachel-dolezal>.

5. Elinor Burkett, "What Makes a Woman?", *New York Times*, 6 June 2015 <https://www.nytimes.com/2015/06/07/opinion/sunday/what-makes-a-woman.html?_r=1>.

6. Nikki Lynette, "Don't Compare NAACP's Rachel Dolezal to Caitlyn Jenner", *Red Eye*, 12 June 2015 <https://www.chicagotribune.com/redeye/redeye-naacp-rachel-dolezal-is-not-caitlyn-jenner-20150612-column.html>.

7. Hillary Crosley Coker, "When Rachel Dolezal Attended Howard, She Was Still White", *Jezebel*, 12 June 2015 <https://jezebel.com/when-rachel-dolezal-attended-howard-university-she-was-1710941472>.

8. See Walter Benn Michaels, "Race into Culture: A Critical Genealogy of Cultural Identity", *Critical Inquiry*, 18 (Summer 1992), 655–85.

9. Kenneth W. Warren, *What Was African American Literature?* (Cambridge, MA: Harvard University Press, 2011).

10. Melissa Harris-Perry, "The Epistemology of Race Talk", *The Nation* blog, 26

Sept. 2011 <https://www.thenation.com/article/archive/epistemology-race-talk/>.

11. Joan Walsh, "White Progressives' Racial Myopia: Why Their Colorblindness Fails Minorities—And the Left", *Salon*, 1 June 2015 <https://www.salon.com/2015/06/01/white_progressives_racial_myopia_why_their_colorblindness_fails_minorities_and_the_left/>.

IDENTITY POLITICS

1. US Bureau of Labor Statistics, *Employment Status of the Civilian Population by Race, Sex, and Age* (Washington, D.C., Dec. 2009).

2. Quoted in Clea Benson, "Race Gap: Still Hard at Work", *Congressional Quarterly*, 26 July 2009.

3. Matthew Yglesias, "Ideology from the Bottom Up", *Think Progress*, 1 Dec. 2009 <https://archive.thinkprogress.org/ideology-from-the-bottom-up-9a70e31a8338/>.

4. Gary Becker, "Competitive Markets and Discrimination against Minorities", Becker-Posner Blog, 7 Sept. 2008, available <https://www.becker-posner-blog.com/2008/09/competitive-markets-and-discrimination-against-minorities-becker.html>.

5. Gary Becker, "Should Gay Marriages Be Allowed?", Becker-Posner Blog, 10 Aug. 2008 <https://www.becker-posner-blog.com/2008/08/should-gay-marriages-be-allowed-becker.html>.

6. Richard D. Kahlenberg in "Reactions: Is It Time for Class-Based Affirmative Action?", *Chronicle of Higher Education*, 16 Dec. 2009, available at <http://chronicle.com/article/Reactions-Is-It-Time-for/62615>.

7. Richard Kim, "Asian-Americans for Affirmative Action", *The Nation*, 9 Jan. 2007, available at <https://www.thenation.com/article/archive/asian-americans-affirmative-action/>. I cite Richard Kim here because he was originally supposed to take part in this discussion, but, of course, the enthusiasm for rich kids of color is not his alone.

DJANGO UNCHAINED, OR, THE HELP

1. Kenneth M. Stampp, *The Peculiar Institution: Slavery in the Ante-Bellum South* (New York: Random House, 1956), 5.

2. Robert Steinfeld, *The Invention of Free Labor: The Employment Relation in English and American Law and Culture, 1350–1870* (Chapel Hill, NC: University of North Carolina Press, 2002) and *Contract, Coercion and Free Labor in the Nineteenth Century* (Cambridge: Cambridge University Press, 2001).

3. Manohla Dargis, "War Is Heaven", *Los Angeles Times*, 28 Dec. 2003, available at

<https://www.latimes.com/archives/la-xpm-2003-dec-28-ca-dargis28-story.html>.

4. Ronald Butt, "Margaret Thatcher: Interview for *Sunday Times*", *Sunday Times*, 3 May 1981.

5. A key early compendium illustrating the basic fault lines in the debate is Bernard Rosenberg and David Manning White (eds.), *Mass Culture: The Popular Arts in America* (Glencoe, IL: Free Press, 1956).

6. Erin Aubry Kaplan, "'Django' an Unsettling Experience for Many Blacks", *Los Angeles Times*, 28 Dec. 2012, available at: <https://www.latimes.com/entertainment/la-xpm-2012-dec-28-la-et-django-reax-2-20121228-story.html>.

7. Andrew O'Hehir, "Tarantino's Incoherent Three-Hour Bloodbath", *Salon*, 26 Dec. 2012, available at: <http://www.salon.com/2012/12/26/tarantinos_incoherent_three_hour_bloodbath/>.

8. Omali Yeshitela, "*Django Unchained*, Or, 'Killing White While Protecting White Power': A Review", *Black Agenda Report*, 30 Jan. 2013, available at: <http://www.black-agendareport.com/content/django-unchained-or-"killing-whitey-while-protecting-white-power"-review> is one of the few commentaries I've encountered that makes that observation, although otherwise the essay shows the limits of a racial critique of capitalism.

9. Ryan Brooke, "The Truth About 'Django Unchained'", *Daily Kos*, 10 Jan. 2013, available at: <http://www.dailykos.com/story/2013/01/10/1177813/-The-Truth-About-Django-Unchained>.

10. Michael Rudolph West, *The Education of Booker T. Washington: Black Leadership in the Age of Jim Crow* (New York and London: Columbia University Press, 2008).

11. Adolph Reed, Jr. and Merlin Chowkwanyun, "Race, Class, Crisis: The Discourse of Racial Disparity and its Analytical Discontents"; see 95 in the present volume.

12. Dr. Kwa David Whitaker, "Django Unchained Reflections" available at <http://ibw21.org/news-and-commentary/django-unchained-reflections/>. Dr. Whitaker seems to have made his own peace with neoliberalism, not least as an operator, through his Ashe Cultural Center, of a half-dozen Cleveland-area charter schools which, in addition to making their contribution to the destruction of public education, have run afoul of the Ohio Department of Education for being so poorly managed as to be judged 'unauditable'. See: Edith Starzyk, "6 Charter Schools Sponsored by Ashe Cultural Center Declared Unauditable", *Cleveland Plain Dealer*, 24 Nov. 2010; Starzyk, "Charter Schools to Lose State Funds Because of Poorly Kept Financial Records", *Cleveland Plain Dealer*, 13 Apr. 2011; and Starzyk, "Lion of Judah Charter School Leader Indicted, Accused of Illegally Spending $1.2 Million in Public Money", *Cleveland Plain Dealer*, 15 Feb. 2013.

13. Notable exceptions to the film's generally warm reception are Kelly Candaele, "The Problematic Political Messages of *Beasts of the Southern Wild*", *Los Angeles Review of Books*, 9 Aug. 2012; Armond White, "How Do You Pronounce Quvenzhan", *The Spirit*, 17 Feb. 2015, available at: <http://www.westsidespirit.com/news/how-do-you-pronounce-quvenzhan-BVNP1320130201302019999>; Vince Mancini, "The Case Against *Beasts of the Southern Wild*", *Filmdrunk*, 3 Dec. 2012, available at: <http://filmdrunk.uproxx.com/2012/12/the-cast-against-beasts-of-the-southern-wild>; and Ben Kenigsberg, "Beasts of the Southern Wild: A Republican Fantasy", *Time Out*, 6 July 2012.

14. See, for example, Leni Riefenstahl: *Vanishing Africa* (New York: Harmony Books, 1982); *Africa* (Cologne: Taschen, 2010), and *The Last of the Nuba* (London: Tom Stacey Ltd., 1973). For access to an additional layer of complication in these exoticizing accounts, I suggest juxtaposing the first two photographs that appear in the *Africa* volume.

15. Howard Gensler, "Maggie Gyllenhaal Talks Unions, Education and Motherhood", *Philadelphia Daily News*, 28 Sept. 2012. She even compared her character to Norma Rae and Erin Brockovich. (Carol Lloyd, writing on the GreatSchools, Inc. website, proclaimed the film "the *Silkwood . . .* for education reformers"; "*Won't Back Down*: A Movie Review", 10 Mar. 2014, available at <https://www.greatschools.org/gk/articles/wont-back-down-movie-review-parent-trigger-law/>) Gyllenhaal went on to aver "there are huge problems with the teachers union" and invoked that empty liberal phraseology to call for having the temerity to "look at things that are broken". I won't speculate as to where being 'left of Trotsky' might place Gyllenhaal on the political spectrum, but this patter brings to mind a conversation I had with our provost at the New School, the well-known post-colonial anthropologist Arjun Appadurai, when the adjunct faculty, who were ninety per cent of the institution's total, were organizing with the United Auto Workers for collective bargaining rights. Appadurai had been even more aggressively hostile to the unionization effort than our unindicted former war criminal president, Bob Kerrey. I sought Appadurai out at a colleague's cocktail party to remonstrate with him about his manifest hostility to the unionization effort. He very warmly and genially assured me that he loves unions and that, if the New School were a place that *really* exploited its adjuncts, like Harvard or Yale, he'd be all for the effort. But, he said, the New School is such a fragile institution that it simply couldn't afford to take the risk. I told him that he sounded like the human resources director at Whole Foods or Walmart.

16. Howard Gensler, "Director Daniel Barnz Defends *Won't Back Down*", *Philadelphia Daily News*, 28 Sept. 2012. Barnz upped the ante by addressing criticism that Christian fascist billionaire Philip Anschutz bankrolled the film. For Barnz, "What's really

going on here is a refreshing reach across the ideological divide. This is a conservative, Republican evangelical Christian who hired the Jewish liberal Democrat—that's me—to helm this movie. . . . This is someone who said: 'This is a problem in our country. I have the resources to help a wide exploration of this that could reach a lot of people and I'm going to go out and do it.' And he let us go out and do it and he empowered us. He empowered me and he empowered this very liberal cast and producers to do that." Karen Butler, "Gyllenhaal, Barnz: 'Won't Back Down' Doesn't Bash Teachers' Union", UPI News Service, 28 Sept. 2012, available at: <http://www.upi.com/Entertainment_News/Movies/2012/09/28/Gyllenhaal-Barnz-Wont-Back-Down-doesnt-bash-teachers-union/UPI-26961348868531/>. Can Barnz be that stupid and gullible? Or does he just imagine the rest of us are?

17. Kathryn Bigelow, "Kathryn Bigelow Addresses 'Zero Dark Thirty' Torture Criticism", *Los Angeles Times*, 15 Jan. 2013, available at: <https://www.latimes.com/entertainment/movies/la-xpm-2013-jan-15-la-et-mn-0116-bigelow-zero-dark-thirty-20130116-story.html>.

18. Jon Wiener, "'Django Unchained': Quentin Tarantino's Answer to Spielberg's 'Lincoln'", *The Nation*, 25 Dec. 2012, available at: <http://www.thenation.com/blog/171915/django-unchained-quentin-tarantinos-answer-spielbergs-lincoln>.

19. Jon Wiener, "The Trouble with Steven Spielberg's 'Lincoln'", *The Nation*, 26 Nov. 2012, available at: <http://www.thenation.com/blog/171461/trouble-steven-spielbergs-lincoln>.

20. Doug McAdam, *Political Process and the Development of Black Insurgency, 1930–1970* (Chicago: University of Chicago Press, 1982 and 1999). The change is especially striking because McAdam's account is driven by examination of structural processes and the dynamics of collective resource mobilization, perhaps to a fault.

21. Minister J. Kojo Livingston, "The Hard Truth—Why I Liked *Django*", *Louisiana Weekly*, 14 Jan. 2013, available at: <http://www.louisianaweekly.com/the-hard-truth-why-i-liked-django-another-minority-opinion/>.

22. Lawrence D. Bobo, "Slavery on Film: Sanitized No More", *The Root*, 9 Jan. 2013, available at <https://www.theroot.com/slavery-on-film-sanitized-no-more-1790894819>. In one breath he proclaims *Django* to be "the most cinematically and culturally important film dealing with race since Spike Lee's *Do the Right Thing*". Two paragraphs later he defends the film against those who have criticized its historical absurdities: "But the film is intended as entertainment, not as historical documentary-making. Indeed, it is explicitly pitched as a revenge fantasy, making the spaghetti

Western an almost perfect template. This is movie-making; this is cinema. It is art, not a history lesson."

23. See, for a smattering, Jamelle Bouie, "A Different Kind of Revenge Film", *The American Prospect*, 28 Oct. 2011, available at <http://prospect.org/article/different-kind-revenge-film>; Jelani Cobb, "Tarantino Unchained", *The New Yorker*, 2 Jan. 2013, available at <https://www.newyorker.com/culture/culture-desk/tarantino-unchained>; Adam Serwer, "In Defense of Django", *Mother Jones*, 7 Jan. 2013, available at <http://www.motherjones.com/mixed-media/2013/01/tarantino-django-unchained-western-racism-violence>.

24. See, for example, "The Confederacy and Firefly" at <http://firefly10108.wordpress.com/2008/09/04/the-confederacy-and-firefly/>.

25. Jeff Hart, "Why Care About Cullen Bohannon?", *Culture Blues*, 17 Nov. 2011.

26. Alexander H. Stephens, "Cornerstone Speech", 21 Mar. 1861, Savannah, Georgia, available at: <https://teachingamericanhistory.org/document/cornerstone-speech/>.

27. Patricia Storace's fine essay "Look Away, Dixie Land", *New York Review of Books*, 19 Dec. 1991, discusses Margaret Mitchell's and her family's roles in crafting and purveying that ideology. Her father was president of the Atlanta Historical Society, one of the many such societies created in the years around World War I for the express purpose of propagating the South's story. Storace also notes Mitchell's mutual admiration with Thomas Dixon—a direct link to *Birth of a Nation*—including the gushing fan letter he sent her on her novel's publication and her equally gushing, appreciative reply.

28. Adolph Reed, Jr., "Crocodile Tears & Auto-critique of the Bourgeoisie: *Rollerball* & Rebellion in Mass Culture", *Endarch*, 1 (Winter 1976).

29. It is chilling in this connection to note that H. Bruce Franklin, *Vietnam and Other American Fantasies* (Amherst, MA: University of Massachusetts Press, 2001) and Jerry Lembcke, *The Spitting Image: Myth, Memory and the Legacy of Vietnam* (New York: New York University Press, 2000) examine the extent to which representations in those films that reverse iconic images from the war, along with repeated rehearsal of urban legends like the anti-war protesters spitting on returning GIs, have shaped collective memory of the war, including even veterans' memories of their own experiences. Also see Penny Lewis, *Hardhats, Hippies and Hawks: The Antiwar Movement as Myth and Memory* (Ithaca, NY: Cornell University Press, 2013).

30. This brings to mind historian Barbara Jeanne Fields's objection to the mindset among historians and others who "think of slavery in the United States as primarily a system of race relations—as though the chief business of slavery were the production

of white supremacy rather than the production of cotton, sugar, rice and tobacco". See Fields, "Slavery, Race and Ideology in the United States of America", *New Left Review*, 1/181 (May/June 1990) reprinted in Karen E. Fields and Barbara J. Fields, *Racecraft: The Soul of Inequality in American Life* (London: Verso, 2012), 117.

31. *Racecraft*, 20-24. Also see Walter Benn Michaels's review, "Believing in Unicorns"; see 131–7 in the present volume.

32. Stephens's "Cornerstone Speech", Hammond's "Mudsill Speech", and Calhoun's "Speech on the Reception of Abolition Petitions, Delivered in the Senate, February 6, 1837" are all available in Paul Finkelman (ed.), *Debating Slavery: Proslavery Thought in the Old South: A Brief History with Documents* (Boston: Bedford/St. Martin's, 2003).

33. Reginald Horsman, *Josiah Nott of Mobile: Southerner, Physician, and Racial Theorist* (Baton Rouge, LA: Louisiana State University Press, 1987), 130 and 258, reports that Nott owned as many as sixteen slaves and in 1860 recorded assets of $40,000 in real estate, $10,000 personal property, and an annual income in excess of $10,000.

34. Samuel A. Cartwright, "Diseases and Peculiarities of the Negro Race", *De Bow's Review*, XI (July 1851), 64–9 and (Sept. 1851), 331–6. It is reprinted in Paul F. Paskoff and Daniel J. Wilson (eds.), *The Cause of the South: Selections from De Bow's Review, 1846–1867* (Baton Rouge, LA: Louisiana State University Press, 1982). On Cartwright's place among antebellum Southern apologists, see James Denny Guillory, "The Pro-Slavery Arguments of Dr. Samuel A. Cartwright", *Louisiana History*, 9 (Summer 1968), 209–27.

35. Paul Liem and Eric Montague (eds.), "Toward a Marxist Theory of Racism: Two Essays by Harry Chang", *Review of Radical Political Economics*, 17/3 (1985), 38–9. See also Adolph Reed, Jr., "Marx, Race, and Neoliberalism" (25–35 in the present volume).

36. Karl Marx and Friedrich Engels, *The German Ideology*, ed. C.J. Arthur, trans. W. Lough, C. Dutt and C.P. Magill (New York: International Publishers, 1970), 64. They elaborated: "The class which has the means of material production at its disposal, has control at the same time over the means of mental production, so that thereby, generally speaking, the ideas of those who lack the means of mental production are subject to it. The ruling ideas are nothing more than the ideal expression of the dominant material relationships, the dominant material relationships grasped as ideas". This insight is straightforward and should be clear enough to anyone not in thrall to the various academic and other discourses that have taken shape around the project of rendering capitalism invisible and obfuscating its class dynamics.

37. Michelle Alexander, *The New Jim Crow: Mass Incarceration in the Age of*

Colorblindness (New York: New Press, 2010). For a systematic critique of the limits and counterproductive features of this approach as both history and politics, see James Forman, Jr., "Racial Critiques of Mass Incarceration: Beyond the New Jim Crow", *New York University Law Review*, 87 (2012), 21–69. See also Reed and Chowkwanyun, "Race, Class, Crisis" and Adolph Reed, Jr., "Three Tremés", *nonsite*, 4 July 2011, available at <https://nonsite.org/editorial/three-tremes>.

38. See, for example, Mahmood Mamdani, "The Politics of Naming: Genocide, Civil War, Insurgency", *London Review of Books*, 8 Mar. 2007.

39. Reed, "Marx, Race, and Neoliberalism", 32.

WHO GETS OWNERSHIP OF PAIN AND VICTIMHOOD?

1. R.L. Nave, "Emmett Till Murder: The Full Text Testimony of Carolyn Bryant", *Mississippi Today*, 12 July 2018 <https://mississippitoday.org/2018/07/12/emmett-till-murder-the-full-text-testimony-of-carolyn-bryant/>.

2. See Timothy B. Tyson, *The Blood of Emmett Till* (New York: Simon and Schuster, 2017).

3. Christian Viveros-Fauné, "Painting Pumps Its Fist at the Whitney Biennial", *Artnet*, 16 Mar. 2017 <https://news.artnet.com/art-world/post-trump-painting-pumps-its-fist-at-the-whitney-biennial-894050>.

4. Zeba Blay, "When White People Profit Off Of Black Pain", *HuffPost*, 22 Mar. 2017 <https://www.huffingtonpost.co.uk/entry/when-white-people-profit-off-of-black-pain_n_58d2a435e4b0b22b0d18ee3d?ri18n=true>.

5. Alex Greenberger, "'The Painting Must Go': Hannah Black Pens Open Letter to the Whitney about Controversial Biennial Work", *ARTnews*, 21 Mar. 2017 <https://www.artnews.com/artnews/news/the-painting-must-go-hannah-black-pens-open-letter-to-the-whitney-about-controversial-biennial-work-7992/>.

6. Parker Bright, "Help Parker Reclaim His Image", GoFundMe, 16 Feb. 2018 <https://www.gofundme.com/f/parkerbrightprotest>.

7. Zeba Blay, "When White People Profit Off Of Black Pain".

8. Henry Louis Gates, Jr., "Black America and the Class Divide", *New York Times*, 1 Feb. 2016 <https://www.nytimes.com/2016/02/07/education/edlife/black-america-and-the-class-divide.html>.

9. "Racial Gaps in Household Income Persist", Pew Research Center, 22 June 2016 <https://www.pewresearch.org/social-trends/2016/06/27/1-demographic-trends-and-economic-well-being/st_2016-06-27_race-inequality-ch1-03-2/>.

10. Tyson, *The Blood of Emmett Till*, 133.

11. John Bachtell, "From Emmett Till to Harold Washington: Arlene Brigham: Foot Soldier for Equality", *People's World*, 12 Aug. 2005 <https://peoplesworld.org/article/from-emmett-till-to-harold-washington-arlene-brigham-foot-soldier-for-equality/>.

CHRIS KILLIP AND LATOYA RUBY FRAZIER

1. Sebastião Salgado, *Workers: An Archaeology of the Industrial Age* (London: Aperture, 1993).

2. Sebastião Salgado quoted in Pepe Karmel, "A Unified Vision of the World's Varied Workers", *New York Times*, 24 Feb. 1995 <www.nytimes.com/1995/02/24/arts/photography-review-a-unified-vision-of-the-world-s-varied-workers.html>.

3. Walter Fernandes and Gita Bharali, "Coal Mining in Northeastern India in the Age of Globalisation", in Kuntala Lahiri-Dutt (ed.), *Coal Nation: Histories, Ecologies and Politics of Coal in India* (Burlington, VT: Ashgate, 2014), 183–96 (184).

4. At its peak (just before and after World War I), the British coal-mining industry employed over a million workers; during the period in which Killip was photographing (1975–1987), the number shrank from 231,000 to 81,000; today, it's about 6,000. Department for Business, Energy, and Industrial Strategy, *Historical Coal Data: Coal Production, Availability, and Consumption, 1853 to 2016* (2017). Distributed by the United Kingdom Government Coal Statistics.

5. Sabina Deitrick and Christopher Briem, *Allegheny County Economic Trends* (Pittsburgh, PA: University Center for Social and Urban Research, 2005).

6. It's perhaps worth pointing out that, differently inflected, these relations matter not just for documentary photography but for art photography as well, and not just for photography but also for painting. A crucial point for us would be that such relations cannot be understood to have only a sociological or biographical interest but that, as Michael Fried has shown in a series of texts, they are fundamental to the internal structure of the work and that, as we argue here, this internal structure is fundamental to the work's politics.

7. Sebastião Salgado quoted in John Berger, *Understanding a Photograph* (London: Penguin, 2013), 173.

8. UNICEF People, "Sebastião Salgado", 2003 <www.unicef.org/people/people_sebastiao_salgado.html>, accessed 13 Dec. 2017.

9. Sebastião Salgado, *Sahel: The End of the Road* (Berkeley and Los Angeles: University of California Press, 2004).

10. Salgado's photographs, distributed by Médecins Sans Frontières, were part of a larger humanitarian campaign. The 1985 Live Aid concert to raise funds for the famine, for example, was watched on television by more than 1.5 billion people. The same year, many of the artists involved in the concert recorded the famous song "We Are the World", written by Michael Jackson and Lionel Ritchie, which became one of the best-selling singles ever.

11. As Salgado writes in his autobiography *From My Land to the Planet*: "No photo, on its own, can change poverty in the world. Nevertheless, combined with text, films and all the efforts of humanitarian and environmental organizations, my images are part of a wider movement denouncing violence, exclusion and ecological issues. These means of information contribute to raising awareness in those who see them, of the ability of all of us to change the destiny of humanity." Salgado, *From My Land to the Planet* (Rome: Contrasto, 2014).

12. Sebastião Salgado quoted in Berger, *Understanding a Photograph*, 174.

13. Parvati Nair, *A Different Light: The Photography of Sebastião Salgado* (Durham, NC: Duke University Press, 2011), 97.

14. Sebastião Salgado quoted in Berger, *Understanding a Photograph*, 174.

15. Fred Ritchin, "The Lyric Documentarian", in Sebastião Salgado, *An Uncertain Grace* (New York: Aperture, 1990), 143–51 (146).

16. Eduardo Galeano, "Salgado, 17 Times", trans. Asa Satz, in Salgado, *An Uncertain Grace*, 7–15 (11).

17. Susan Sontag, *Regarding the Pain of the Others* (New York: Picador, 2003).

18. John Berger and Sylvia Grant, "Walking Back Home", in Chris Killip, *In Flagrante* (London: Secker & Warburg, 1988), 85–93 (87).

19. There is only one explicit picture in *In Flagrante* of the bitter miners' strike of 1984–85.

20. Gerry Badger, "Dispatches from a War Zone", in Chris Killip, *In Flagrante* (New York: Books on Books, Errata Editions, 2009).

21. Chris Killip, *Arbeit/work* (Göttingen, Germany: Steidl Verlag, 2012).

22. David Schonauer, "The Sight of Despair", *American Photographer*, 1 (1990), 39–45 (39).

23. Killip, *In Flagrante*, 2009.

24. Chris Killip, *Seacoal* (Göttingen, Germany: Steidl Verlag, 2011).

25. Chris Killip quoted in Mark Haworth-Booth, "Chris Killip: Scenes from Another Country", *Aperture*, 103 (1986), 16–31 (31).

26. Adam Bell, "Chris Killip", *Brooklyn Rail*, 3 June 2016 <https://brooklynrail.org/2016/06/art_books/chris-killip>.

27. Clive Dilnot, "Chris Killip: The Last Photographer of the Working Class", *Afterimage*, May/June 2012, 15–8 (15).

28. Badger, "Dispatches from a War Zone".

29. Or, as suggested by Ian Jeffrey, "a bracket opening and closing the series". Jeffrey, "Review of In Flagrante", *Creative Camera*, May 1977, 36.

30. That is perhaps why industry itself, within the book and most of his work, is always represented as a landscape.

31. John Yau, "What Will You Do About Chris Killip's Challenge?", *Hyperallergic*, 21 Feb. 2016 <hyperallergic.com/277025/what-will-you-do-about-chris-killips-challenge>.

32. Ibid.

33. Ibid.

34. Ibid.

35. Killip, *In Flagrante*, 1988, v.

36. LaToya Ruby Frazier, *The Notion of Family* (New York: Aperture, 2016), 41.

37. Frazier, "LaToya Ruby Frazier, 2015 MacArthur Fellow", YouTube, 28 Sept. 2015 <www.youtube.com/watch?v=Rvmu5y3m9Yc>.

38. Institute of Contemporary Art Boston, "Interview with LaToya Ruby Frazier", YouTube, 22 Dec. 2015.

39. Frazier, *Notion of Family*, 90.

40. Pierre Bourdieu, *Photography: A Middle-brow Art*, trans. Shaun Whiteside (Stanford, CA: Stanford University Press, 1990), 71.

41. Ibid. 19.

42. Institute of Contemporary Art Boston, "Interview with LaToya Ruby Frazier".

43. Chris Killip quoted in Badger, "Dispatches from a War Zone".

44. Furthermore, doubling down on making the photographer the photographed subject, it's Frazier's mother who is credited with making the image, as if to insist that even the portrait of Frazier made by someone else (*Mom Making an Image of Me*) is at the same time a portrait of the photographer made by herself.

45. There's no space to discuss (much less reproduce) them here, but the entirely unposed pictures we describe above as suggesting an extraordinary intimacy between photographer and subject actually—with respect to the beholder—produce an effect not unlike that of the posed pictures. The intimacy disidentifies the viewer from the photographer—you'd have to be a member of the family to have taken the pictures—and

functions as another way of shutting the beholder out.

46. Julian Stallabrass, "Sebastião Salgado and Fine Art Photojournalism", *New Left Review*, 1/223 (May/June 1997) <newleftreview.org/I/223/julian-stallabrass-sebastiao-salgado-and-fine-art-photojournalism>.

47. Kate Soper quoted in ibid.

48. David Levi Strauss, *Between the Eyes: Essays on Photography and Politics* (London: Aperture, 2003), 49.

49. MSF (Médecins Sans Frontières), "MSF Charter and Principles", 2017 <www.msf.org/en/msf-charter-and-principles>, accessed 13 Dec. 2017.

50. Ibid.

51. From Christoph Lakner and Branko Milanovic, "Global Income Distribution: From the Fall of the Berlin Wall to the Great Recession", *World Bank Economic Review*, 30/2 (2016), 203–32.

52. "The New Political Divide", *The Economist*, 30 July 2016 <https://www.economist.com/leaders/2016/07/30/the-new-political-divide>.

INTERVIEW ONE

1. Kent Germany, *New Orleans After the Promises: Poverty, Citizenship, and the Search for the Great Society* (Athens, GA: University of Georgia Press, 2006); Robert O. Self, *American Babylon: Race and the Struggle for Postwar Oakland* (Princeton: Princeton University Press, 2005); Chris Rhomberg, *No There There: Race, Class and Political Community in Oakland* (Berkeley and Los Angeles: University of California Press, 2007).

2. AR: The Panthers trained their cadre to treat Mao's *Quotations* as a catechism rather than an analytical tool.

3. Corey Robin, *The Enigma of Clarence Thomas* (New York: Metropolitan Books, 2019).

4. Kenneth W. Warren discusses Crouch's and Murray's—and others'—efforts to read Ellison as a conservative champion in *So Black and Blue: Ralph Ellison and the Occasion of Criticism* (Chicago: University of Chicago Press, 2003).

5. See Adolph Reed, Jr., "*Django Unchained*, or, *The Help*: How 'Cultural Politics' Is Worse than No Politics at All, and Why" (157–93 in the present volume).

6. See "The Irish Laborers and the New Basin Canal", Old New Orleans <http://old-new-orleans.com/NO_Irish_Memorial.html>.

7. Michelle Alexander, *The New Jim Crow: Mass Incarceration in the Age of*

Colorblindness (New York: New Press, 2010).

8. Preston H. Smith II, *Racial Democracy and the Black Metropolis: Housing Policy in Postwar Chicago* (Minneapolis: University of Minnesota Press, 2012).

9. Adolph L. Reed, Jr., "Black Particularity Reconsidered", *Telos*, 39 (20 Mar. 1979), 71–93.

10. "The 1619 Project", *New York Times Magazine*, Aug. 2019 <https://www.nytimes.com/interactive/2019/08/14/magazine/1619-america-slavery.html>; Isabel Wilkerson, "America's Enduring Caste System", *New York Times Magazine*, 1 July 2020 <https://www.nytimes.com/2020/07/01/magazine/isabel-wilkerson-caste.html>.

11. WBM: This refers to the measures taken by Paul Volcker, the chair of the Federal Reserve System, to curb inflation in 1979, driving Federal fund interest rates to twenty per cent in 1980, which did indeed push inflation down while driving unemployment up.

12. WBM: His exact words were "Race is the modality in which class is lived."

13. Russell Jacoby, *The Last Intellectuals: American Culture in the Age of Academe* (New York: Basic Books, 1987).

14. Adolph L. Reed, Jr., *The Jesse Jackson Phenomenon: The Crisis of Purpose in Afro-American Politics* (New Haven: Yale University Press, 1986).

15. AR: *Regents of the University of California v. Bakke* upheld but narrowed the parameters of affirmative action policy by establishing pursuit of 'diversity' as a legitimate basis for taking race into account in university admissions processes.

16. Fight for Fifteen is a political movement focused on raising the federal minimum wage to $15 per hour.

INTERVIEW TWO

1. AR: Wags commonly observed that *Nightline's* founding host, Ted Koppel, bore an uncanny resemblance to a 1950s children's television show's eponymous marionette, Howdy Doody.

2. See Adolph Reed, Jr., "The 'Color Line' Then and Now: *The Souls of Black Folk* and the Changing Context of Black American Politics", in Adolph Reed, Jr. and Kenneth W. Warren (eds.), *Renewing Black Intellectual History: The Ideological and Material Foundations of African American Thought* (Boulder, CO: Paradigm Publishers, 2010), 300–2, n. 87.

3. Juneteenth was a holiday celebrated originally in Galveston, Texas, oddly, to commemorate the arrival of Federal troops to proclaim Emancipation two and a half years after Lincoln's Emancipation Proclamation had gone into effect.

4. See Julie Bosman, "Chicago Suburb Shapes Reparations for Black Residents: 'It Is the Start'", *New York Times*, 22 Mar. 2021 <https://www.nytimes.com/2021/03/22/us/reparations-evanston-illinois-housing.html>.

5. "It is difficult to get a man to understand something when his salary depends upon his not understanding it."

6. WBM: In *Running Steel, Running America* (Chapel Hill, NC: University of North Carolina Press, 1998), Stein brilliantly describes the difference between, and the consequences of choosing between, the effort to make employment discrimination illegal and the effort to "tackle the structural source of black unemployment" (69), especially in a labor market where factory jobs in general were decreasing. More generally, her attention to the political economy of racism—to what it did, to whom, and for whom—and her alertness to what would become the political and economic uses of anti-racism are wonderfully illuminating for anyone trying to understand race and racism in modes that aren't purely moral.

7. Harry Braverman, *Labor and Monopoly Capital: The Degradation of Work in the Twentieth Century* (New York: Monthly Review Press, 1974).

8. See Chapter 8 of Adolph L. Reed, Jr., *W.E.B. Du Bois and American Political Thought: Fabianism and the Color Line* (New York: Oxford University Press, 1997).

9. In *Anarchy, State, and Utopia* (New York: Basic Books, 1974) he imagines that some "past injustices might be so great" (231) that even a libertarian might argue for the desirability of state intervention in seeking to rectify them.

10. See "*Django Unchained*, or, *The Help*" (157–93 in the present volume).

11. Patricia Hill Collins, "The Social Construction of Black Feminist Thought", *Signs*, 14 (1989), 745–73.

12. AR: Both Franz Boas—see, e.g., his definitive 1932 essay "Race and Character", reprinted in the collection *Race, Language, and Culture* (New York: Macmillan Company, 1940)—and Ruth Benedict—see, e.g., her *Race: Science and Politics* (New York: Viking Press, 1945), originally a World War II pamphlet for US troops—often tended to posit race as an unproblematic category while arguing against racism, as the belief that racial differences can have invidious social consequences.

13. See, e.g., their exchange around Harris's book *Cannibals and Kings: The Origins of Cultures* (New York: Random House, 1977) in: Marshall Sahlins, "Culture as Protein and Profit", *New York Review of Books*, 23 Nov. 1978 <https://www.nybooks.com/articles/1978/11/23/culture-as-protein-and-profit/>, and Marvin Harris and Marshall Sahlins, "*Cannibals and Kings*: An Exchange", *New York Review of Books*, 28 June 1979

<https://www.nybooks.com/articles/1979/06/28/cannibals-and-kings-an-exchange/>.

14. Walter Benn Michaels, *The Shape of the Signifier* (Princeton: Princeton University Press, 2004).

15. See Walter Benn Michaels, "Who Gets Ownership of Pain and Victimhood?" (195–200 in the present volume).

16. See Adolph Reed, Jr., "Unraveling the Relation of Race and Class in American Politics" and the subsequent exchange between him and Ellen Meiksins Wood: <https://advancethestruggle.files.wordpress.com/2009/06/how_does_race_relate_to_class-2.pdf>.

INTERVIEW THREE

1. Adolph Reed, Jr., "Nothing Left: The Long, Slow Surrender of American Liberals", *Harper's Magazine*, Mar. 2014 <https://harpers.org/archive/2014/03/nothing-left-2/>.

2. Michelle Goldberg, "Adolph Reed and Electoral Nihilism", *The Nation* blog, 3 Mar. 2014 <https://www.thenation.com/article/archive/adolph-reed-and-electoral-nihilism/>.

3. Harold Meyerson, "The Left, Viewed from Space", *The American Prospect*, 3 Mar. 2014 <https://prospect.org/power/left-viewed-space/>.

4. Sawant is a Trotskyist City Councillor in Seattle; the Squad is a nickname given to four young women of color elected as insurgents to the US House of Representatives in 2018: Alexandria Ocasio-Cortez (D-NY), Ayanna Pressley (D-MA), Rashida Tlaib (D-MI), and Ilhan Omar (D-MN). Stacey Abrams is a black woman who ran unsuccessfully for Governor in Georgia, and Jaime Harrison is a black man who ran unsuccessfully for the US Senate from South Carolina.

5. Walter W Heller, *Brief Book on Economic Matters*, 20 Dec. 1962, pp. 3–4. Folder identifier JFKPOF-063a-009-p014, John F. Kennedy Presidential Library and Museum <https://www.jfklibrary.org/asset-viewer/archives/JFKPOF/063a/JFKPOF-063a-009>.

6. See 325–44 in the present volume.

7. DZ: In July 2020, *Harper's* published a letter signed by academics such as Mark Lilla, Francis Fukuyama and Cornel West, as well as writers such as Salman Rushdie and Margaret Atwood, which denounced the "forces of illiberalism" eroding "norms of open debate and toleration of differences in favor of ideological conformity". See: "A Letter on Justice and Open Debate", *Harper's*, 7 July 2020 <https://harpers.org/a-letter-on-justice-and-open-debate/>.

8. Steve Payne, "Kellogg's Delivers Memphis a Slap in the Faith", *Labor Notes*, 20

Jan. 2014 <https://labornotes.org/2014/01/kelloggs-delivers-memphis-slap-face>.

9. Stéphane Beaud and Gérard Noiriel, "Who Do You Think You Are?", *Le Monde diplomatique*, Feb. 2021 <https://mondediplo.com/2021/02/10race>.

10. WBM: The Pinkerton Detective Agency was a private police force founded by the Scotsman Allen Pinkerton in Chicago in 1850. The good news is that Pinkerton was anti-slavery and played an important role in Union intelligence during the Civil War. The bad news is that he was also radically anti-union and that his men were used over and over again against the labor movement, especially as strike-breakers. Today they're owned by the Swedish security company Securitas AB and are employed by companies like Amazon—although to what ends are a matter of dispute; see Kim Kelly, "The Pinkertons Have a Long, Dark History of Targeting Workers", *Teen Vogue*, 3 Dec. 2020 <https://www.teenvogue.com/story/who-were-the-pinkertons>. Yes, *Teen Vogue*; for a while they were actually running a column called *No Class*.

INTERVIEW FOUR

1. Mark Lilla, *The Once and Future Liberal: After Identity Politics* (New York: HarperCollins, 2017). Schlesinger's *The Disuniting of America* was published in 1991 and is criticized in Benn Michaels, *The Shape of the Signifier*.

2. See in particular: Ernesto Laclau and Chantal Mouffe, *Hegemony and Socialist Strategy: Towards a Radical Democratic Politics* (1985; 2nd edn., London: Verso, 2001).

3. Stuart Hall, "The Great Moving Right Show", *Marxism Today*, Jan. 1979, 14–20.

4. Ellen Meiksins Wood, *The Retreat from Class: A New 'True' Socialism* (London: Verso, 1986).

5. AR: Lonesome Rhodes was an itinerant entertainer elevated into a national figure as a folksy Everyman by network and advertising executives in the 1957 film *A Face in the Crowd*. The Joe Louis reference is to his sad years as a casino greeter after having lost his fortune to bad investments and conviction of tax evasion.

6. Adolph Reed, Jr., "Vote for the Lying Neoliberal Warmonger: It's Important", *Common Dreams*, 18 Aug, 2016 <https://www.commondreams.org/views/2016/08/18/vote-lying-neoliberal-warmonger-its-important>.

7. Cedric Johnson, "The Triumph of Black Lives Matter and Neoliberal Redemption", *nonsite*, 9 June 2020 <https://nonsite.org/the-triumph-of-black-lives-matter-and-neoliberal-redemption/>.

8. DZ: Essentially shaped by the Argentinian economist Raúl Prebisch, the 'dependency theory' argued that the unequal terms of trade between the North (exporting

manufactured goods) and the South (raw materials) locked the latter in a state of un-derdevelopment. Free trade under such conditions naturally widened the gap between the core and the periphery. Such theory therefore advocated an active industrial policy designed to substitute dependence on Northern metropoles with national industrialized products. Industrialization, in such a perspective, had to be planned and state-led in order to succeed.

THE TROUBLE WITH DISPARITY

1. Robert Manduca, "Income Inequality and the Persistence of Racial Economic Disparities", *Sociological Science*, 5 (Mar. 2018), 182–205 <https://sociologicalscience.com/download/vol-5/march/SocSci_v5_182to205.pdf>.

2. Matt Bruenig, "The Racial Wealth Gap Is About the Upper Classes", *Jacobin*, 5 July 2020 <https://jacobinmag.com/2020/07/racial-wealth-gap-redistribution>.

3. Preston H. Smith II, *Racial Democracy and the Black Metropolis: Housing Policy in Postwar Chicago* (Minneapolis: University of Minnesota Press, 2012) and "The Quest for Racial Democracy: Black Civic Ideology and Housing Interests in Postwar Chica-go", *Journal of Urban History*, 26 (Jan. 2000), 131–57.

4. Paul Krugman, "Hillary and the Horizontals", *New York Times*, 10 June 2016 <https://www.nytimes.com/2016/06/10/opinion/hillary-and-the-horizontals.html?partner=rss&emc=rss&_r=0>.

5. Dionissi Aliprantis and Daniel Carroll, "What Is Behind the Persistence of the Racial Wealth Gap?", Federal Reserve Bank of Cleveland, 28 Feb. 2019 <https://www.clevelandfed.org/newsroom-and-events/publications/economic-commentary/2019-eco-nomic-commentaries/ec-201903-what-is-behind-the-persistence-of-the-racial-wealth-gap.aspx>.

6. "Black women are 26.1 per cent of personal care aides, home health aides, and nursing assistants, and among those working full time, year round in these jobs, Black women are typically paid just 89 cents for every dollar typically paid to white, non-His-panic men in the same roles." Jasmine Tucker, "It's 2020 and Black Women Aren't Even Close to Equal Pay", National Women's Law Center, July 2020 <https://nwlc.org/wp-con-tent/uploads/2020/07/Black-Womens-Equal-Pay-Day-Factsheet-7.27.20-v3.pdf>. In an earlier version of this essay, we got some of our numbers mixed and produced figures that understated some of the disparities between black women and white men working front-line jobs. We regret the error and are grateful to the several readers who pointed it out. In order to avoid further confusing our readers (as we had managed to confuse

ourselves), we've simplified the example to focus on health care aides, both because of the risks they're running and because, according to the Bureau of Labor Statistics, those are the jobs with the largest expected growth over the next ten years, <https://www.bls. gov/emp/tables/occupations-most-job-growth.htm>. It's unacceptable for black women to be paid less than white men for this increasingly important job. But, and this of course is our point, it's more profoundly, structurally, unacceptable that even if that disparity is eliminated, everyone who has that job will be condemned to precarity.

7. Ronald Butt, "Margaret Thatcher: Interview for *Sunday Times*", *Sunday Times*, 3 May 1981.

8. Raj Chetty et al., "Race and Economic Opportunity in the United States: An Intergenerational Perspective", National Bureau of Economic Research, Mar. 2018, revised Dec. 2019 <https://www.nber.org/system/files/working_papers/w24441/w24441.pdf>.

9. Actually, Ken Warren's *What Was African American Literature?* (Cambridge, MA: Harvard University Press, 2012) argues that individual bourgeois ambitions (to make a lot of money, have a prestigious job, etc.) are standardly transformed into efforts to achieve social justice just by relocating them in black people. The white person's desire to be rich becomes the black person's desire to be equal. And although Warren is talking mainly about novels, it's obviously not a fiction. As we write this, Bloomberg News is reporting on worries that "Although about 10% of directors at the 200 biggest S&P 500 companies are Black . . . the percentage of Black executives joining boards in 2020 fell to 11% from 13% the year before." Jeff Green, "After Adding More Women to Boards, Companies Pivot to Race", *Bloomberg*, 19 Aug. 2020 <https://www.bloomberg.com/news/articles/2020-08-19/companies-seek-more-black-directors-after-adding-women>. Black Corporate Directors Matter! Of course, proportionate representation for women and black people on boards of directors is very much a liberal rather than a leftist issue. But equally, of course, every time you frame inequality in terms of disparity, you've committed yourself to the logic of liberalism.

10. Touré F. Reed, *Toward Freedom: The Case Against Race Reductionism* (New York: Verso, 2020), 166-67.

11. Ibid. 166.

12. "Margaret Thatcher: A Life in Quotes", *The Guardian*, 8 Apr. 2013 <https://www.theguardian.com/politics/2013/apr/08/margaret-thatcher-quotes>.

13. Sanjay Gupta and Andrea Kane, "Do Some People Have Protection against the Coronavirus?", CNN, 3 Aug. 2020 <https://edition.cnn.com/2020/08/02/health/gupta-coronavirus-t-cell-cross-reactivity-immunity-wellness/index.html>.

14. In the first place, people are more or less vulnerable as individuals, not as members of groups. In fact, there's something like a sleight-of-hand at work in calling categories sorted from large aggregate data sets 'groups'. Membership in a group in everyday usage implies some sense of cohesiveness around shared experiences or concerns. Statistical groups are numerical abstractions that researchers carve out from those aggregate data sets based on shared characteristics the researchers consider important elements of what they're trying to study. So those 'groups' are people categorized on the basis of shared characteristics that are pertinent to researchers. Those groupings can be larger or smaller, depending on researchers' interests. They can be 'nested' such that some smaller categories fit within, or under, larger ones. With regard to public health research and the notion of at-risk populations, the approach is to sort aggregate data, perhaps of the entire population, to determine what characteristics make, or seem to make, individuals more susceptible to undesirable outcomes. In the case of COVID-19, since everyone who is exposed seems to be at similar risk for contracting the virus, the critical issues are what characteristics make some individuals more likely than others to be exposed and what characteristics make those who do contract the disease more likely to suffer serious complications or death. Public health researchers and officials sort together people with those characteristics as at-risk populations, which means that, as individuals, they are more likely than the general population to experience severe complications, including death, if they contract the virus.

15. Centers for Disease Control and Prevention, "Risk of Severe Illness or Death from COVID-19", updated 10 Dec. 2020 <https://www.cdc.gov/coronavirus/2019-ncov/community/health-equity/racial-ethnic-disparities/disparities-illness.html>.

16. Matthew Goldstein, Jessica Silver-Greenberg and Robert Gebeloff, "Push for Profits Left Nursing Homes Struggling to Provide Care", *New York Times*, 7 May 2020 <https://www.nytimes.com/2020/05/07/business/coronavirus-nursing-homes.html>.

17. Vicente Navarro, "Inequalities Are Unhealthy", *Monthly Review*, 1 June 2004 <https://monthlyreview.org/2004/06/01/inequalities-are-unhealthy/>.

18. Elizabeth Docteur and Robert A. Berenson, "In Pursuit of Health Equity: Comparing U.S. and EU Approaches to Eliminating Health Disparities", Urban Institute and Robert Wood Johnson Foundation, June 2014 <https://www.urban.org/sites/default/files/publication/22731/413171-In-Pursuit-of-Health-Equity-Comparing-U-S-and-EU-Approaches-to-Eliminating-Disparities.PDF>.

19. R. Dawn Comstock, Edward M. Castillo, Suzanne P. Lindsay, "Four-Year Review of the Use of Race and Ethnicity in Epidemiologic and Public Health Research",

American Journal of Epidemiology, 159/6 (15 Mar. 2004), 611–619 (616) <https://academic.oup.com/aje/article/159/6/611/147734>.

20. Ibid. 617.

21. Kelly M. Hoffman et al., "Racial Bias in Pain Assessment and Treatment Recommendations, and False Beliefs about Biological Differences between Blacks and Whites", *PNAS*, 113/16 (19 Apr. 2016), 4296-4301 <https://www.pnas.org/content/113/16/4296>.

22. Wellcome Trust, "Nearby Chimpanzee Populations Show Much Greater Genetic Diversity than Distant Human Populations", *Science Daily*, 2 Mar. 2012 <https://www.sciencedaily.com/releases/2012/03/120302101706.htm>.

23. Linda Villarosa, "Myths about Physical Racial Differences Were Used to Justify Slavery—and Are Still Believed by Doctors Today", *New York Times*, 14 Aug. 2019 <https://www.nytimes.com/interactive/2019/08/14/magazine/racial-differences-doctors.html>.

24. We have already noted the history of medical and political mischief generated by treating race as a legitimate biological category. That mischief can derive from ostensibly benign intentions no less than from ignoble or evil ones. Jonathan Kahn, in *Race in a Bottle: The Story of BiDil and Racialized Medicine in a Post-Genomic Age* (New York: Columbia University Press, 2014), examines the alliance between Big Pharma, the Association of Black Cardiologists, and the Federal Drug Administration in the early 2000s that led to the first patent in history for a supposedly race-specific drug, a blood thinner that hadn't proven effective for general use but was approved, after dubious testing, as effective for African-American men. Of course, it wasn't. The confusion about what race is and isn't, combined with the dominance of the disparities frame, has already led to a misplaced focus on calls for racial diversity in selecting subjects for clinical trials testing possible COVID-19 vaccines. *Washington Post* science writer Carolyn Y. Johnson displays the problem clearly:

> The unprecedented scientific quest to end the pandemic with a vaccine now faces one of its most crucial tests, and nothing less than the success of the entire endeavor is at stake. A vaccine must work for everyone—young and old; Black, brown, and white. To prove that it does, many of the 30,000 volunteers for each trial must come from diverse communities. It's a scientific necessity, but also a moral imperative, as younger people of color die from coronavirus at twice the rate of White people, and Black, Hispanic and Native Americans are hospitalized at four to five times the rate of White people in the same age groups. (Carolyn Y. Johnson, "A Trial for Coronavirus Vaccine Researchers:

Making Sure Black and Hispanic Communities are Included in Studies", *Washington Post*, 26 July 2020 <https://www.washingtonpost.com/health/2020/07/26/trial-coronavirus-vaccine-researchers-making-sure-black-hispanic-communities-are-included-studies/>).

We have no quibble with the contention that researchers should select clinical trial participants from a diverse population. However, Johnson's claim presumes that racial classification can map onto biologically meaningful differences. Once again, it cannot, because race is an ideological contrivance imposed arbitrarily on a human species that certainly varies biologically, though not only not very much compared to other primate species, but in ways that have nothing to do with abstract racial taxonomy (Jared Diamond, "Race without Color", *Discover*, Nov. 1994 <http://lmcreadinglist.pbworks.com/f/Diamond%20(1994).pdf>). Regarding medical practice in particular, Darshali Vyas and co-authors recently published an article in the *New England Journal of Medicine* sounding the alarm about ways that unjustified 'race correction' in clinical algorithms can reinforce existing inequalities. They note:

> despite mounting evidence that race is not a reliable proxy for genetic difference, the belief that it is has become embedded, sometimes insidiously, within medical practice. One subtle insertion of race into medicine involves diagnostic algorithms and practice guidelines that adjust or 'correct' their outputs on the basis of a patient's race or ethnicity. Physicians use these algorithms to individualize risk assessment and guide clinical decisions. By embedding race into the basic data and decisions of health care, these algorithms propagate race-based medicine. Many of these race-adjusted algorithms guide decisions in ways that may direct more attention or resources to white patients than to members of racial and ethnic minorities. (Darshali A. Vyas, Leo G. Eisenstein, and David S. Jones, "Hidden in Plain Sight—Reconsidering the Use of Race Correction in Clinical Algorithms", *New England Journal of Medicine*, 383/9 (27 Aug. 2020), 874–82; this quotation is from 874.)

Vyas et al. report that often "algorithm developers offer no explanation of why racial or ethnic differences might exist. Others offer rationales, but when these are traced to their origins, they lead to outdated, suspect racial science or to biased data." Moreover, they observe that "racial differences found in large data sets most likely often reflect effects of racism—that is, the experience of being black in America rather than being black itself—

such as toxic stress and its physiological consequences. In such cases, race adjustment would do nothing to address the cause of the disparity. Instead, if adjustments deter clinicians from offering clinical services to certain patients, they risk baking inequity into the system" (879). In such instances, race is hardly intended as a proxy for class. Rather, it does the work that race has always done as a contrivance that makes class invisible and reads inequality into nature. And, unsurprisingly, market considerations also figure into the race corrections to the extent that cost effectiveness is an element in calculating the algorithms. Vyas et al. also report:

> A widely used clinical tool took past health care costs into consideration in predicting clinical risk. Since the health care system has spent more money, on average, on white patients than on black patients, the tool returned higher risk scores for white patients than for black patients. Those scores may well have led to more referrals for white patients to specialty services, perpetuating both spending disparities and race bias in health care. (879)

25. Les Leopold, "COVID-19's Class War", *The American Prospect*, 28 July 2020 <https://prospect.org/coronavirus/covid-19-class-war-death-rates-income/>.

26. Ibid. Barbara J. and Karen E. Fields discuss another incident that absolutely nails what's wrong-headed about this moment of 'blacks have it worse' chatter about COVID-19. In discussing this *NYT* story—Manny Fernandez, "A Study Links Trucks' Exhaust to Bronx Schoolchildren's Asthma", *New York Times*, 29 Oct. 2006 <https://www.nytimes.com/2006/10/29/nyregion/a-study-links-trucks-exhaust-to-bronx-schoolchildrens-asthma.html>—they note:

> Sometimes the fog of racecraft rolls in at the last minute, as a derailing non sequitur to an otherwise logical argument. A few years ago, the *New York Times* reported that scientists who conducted an epidemiological study of asthma among schoolchildren in South Bronx produced damning evidence about environmental pollution caused by heavy truck traffic. Their study identified the particle emissions, cited the location of major highways, and, through resourceful data collection, drew conclusions about the children's exposure, in specific neighborhoods, at different hours of the day, to "very high fine particle concentrations on a fairly regular basis." The correlations emerged: "Symptoms, like wheezing, doubled on days when pollution from truck traffic was highest." It would seem as clear as noonday that class inequality

had imposed sickness on these American schoolchildren. Yet the article's summary tails off into confused pseudo-genetics. To a list of contributors to high asthma rates that includes heavy traffic, dense population, poorly maintained housing, and lack of access to medical care, the article adds "a large population of blacks and Hispanics, two groups with high rates of asthma." Racecraft has permitted the consequence under investigation to masquerade among the causes. Susceptibility to filthy air does not depend on the census category to which the asthma sufferer belongs. (*Racecraft: The Soul of Inequality in American Life* (New York: Verso, 2014), 40–1).

27. The Editors, "Everything You Know about Mass Incarceration Is Wrong: An Interview with Adaner Usmani", *Jacobin*, 17 Mar. 2020 <https://www.jacobinmag.com/2020/03/mass-incarceration-racism-carceral-state-new-jim-crow>.

28. Frederick J. Zimmerman and Nathaniel W. Anderson, "Trends in Health Equity in the United States by Race/Ethnicity, Sex, and Income, 1993-2017", *JAMA Network Open*, 2/6 (5 June 2019) <https://www.ncbi.nlm.nih.gov/pmc/articles/PMC6604079/>; corrected *JAMA Network Open* 2/7 (24 July 2019).

29. Mapping Police Violence, "National Trends", <https://mappingpoliceviolence.org/nationaltrends>.

30. Oleg Komlik, "Thatcherism's Greatest Achievement", *Economic Sociology & Political Economy*, 19 Mar. 2018 <https://economicsociology.org/2018/03/19/thatcherisms-greatest-achievement/>.

Publication Credits

The publishers gratefully acknowledge the permissions given by the original publishers to reproduce the following articles. Every effort has been made to trace copyright holders and obtain their permissions for the use of copyright material.

Adolph Reed, Jr., "Marx, Race and Neoliberalism", *New Labor Forum*, 22/1 (2013), 49–57. © *New Labor Forum*

Walter Benn Michaels, "What Matters", *London Review of Books*, 31/16 (27 Aug. 2009). © Walter Benn Michaels

Adolph Reed, Jr., "The Limits of Anti-Racism", *Left Business Observer*, 121 (Sept. 2009). © *Left Business Observer*

Adolph Reed, Jr., "From Black Power to Black Establishment: The Curious Legacy of a Radical Slogan", *The New Republic*, 28 Apr. 2020. © Adolph Reed, Jr.

Adolph Reed, Jr., "Beyond the Great Awokening: Reassessing the Legacies of Past Black Organizing", *The New Republic*, 8 Dec. 2020. © Adolph Reed, Jr.

Walter Benn Michaels, "The Trouble with Diversifying the Faculty", *Liberal Education*, 97/2 (Winter 2011), 14–9. © The Association of American Colleges and Universities

Acknowledgements

A proper list of acknowledgments would include many more people than we can possibly list here, so we're confining ourselves to the ones without whom this book would not have existed; thanks to Jennifer Ashton, Merlin Chowkwanyun, Todd Cronan, Anton Jäger, Angus Ledingham, Charles Palermo, Daniel Shea, Anwen Tormey, Ken Warren, and Daniel Zamora.

Walter Benn Michaels is Professor of English at the University of Illinois Chicago. An influential scholar in the fields of literary theory and American literary history, Michaels is also a high-profile polemicist whose political writings have appeared in publications including *The American Prospect* and the *London Review of Books*.

Adolph Reed, Jr. is Professor Emeritus of Political Science at the University of Pennsylvania. A veteran activist and a prolific analyst of the politics of race and class, his books include *Stirrings in the Jug: Black Politics in the Post-Segregation Era*, *Class Notes: Posing as Politics and Other Thoughts on the American Scene* and *The South: Jim Crow and Its Afterlives*.

Anton Jäger is a postdoctoral researcher at KU Leuven in Belgium, working on the history of populism in the United States. Together with Daniel Zamora he is the co-author of an intellectual history of basic income.

Daniel Zamora is Professor of Sociology at the Université Libre de Bruxelles. He is the co-author of *The Last Man Takes LSD* with Mitchell Dean and of *Welfare for Markets* with Anton Jäger.